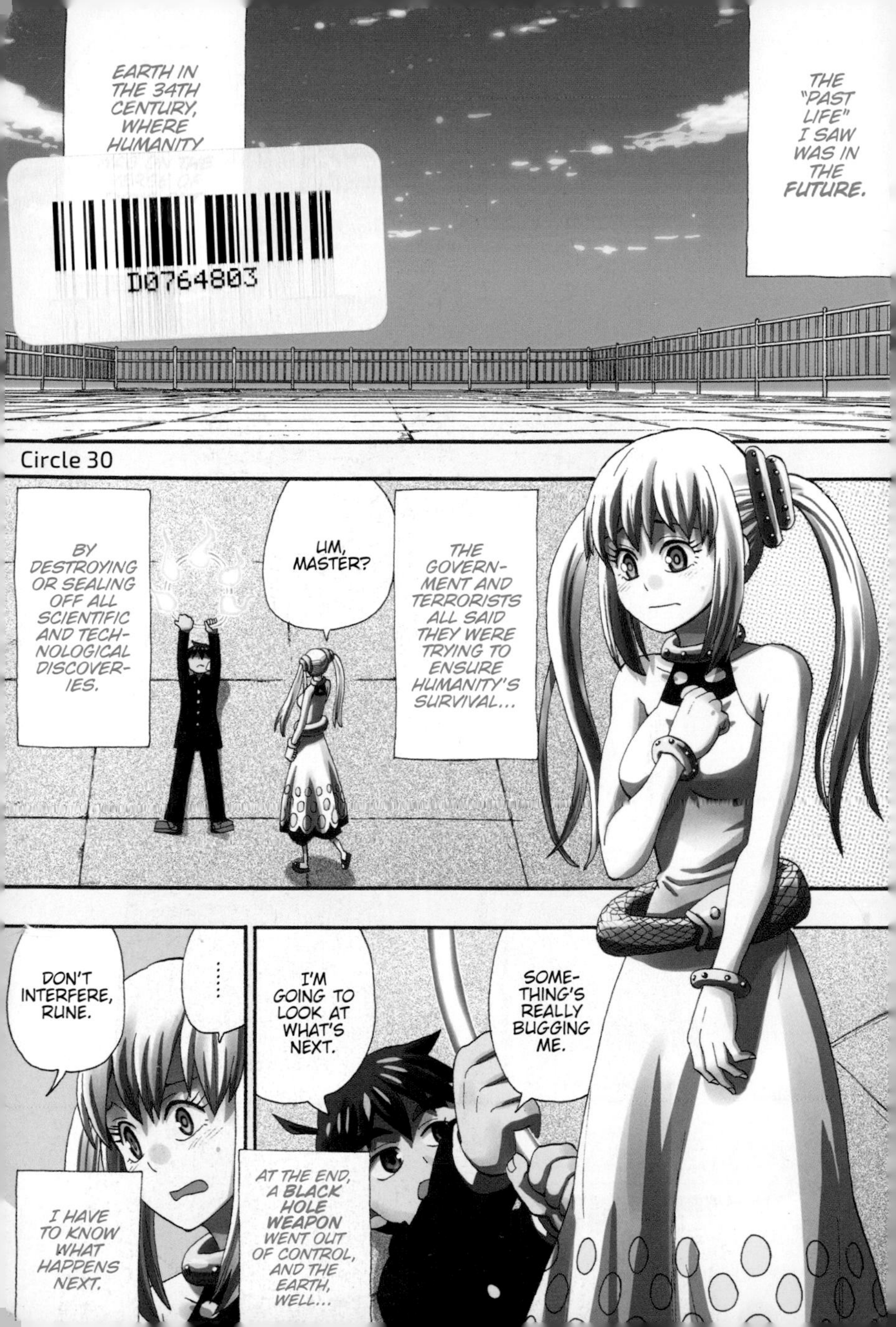
THE "PAST LIFE" I SAW WAS IN THE FUTURE.
EARTH IN THE 34TH CENTURY, WHERE HUMANITY
Circle 30
THE GOVERN-MENT AND TERRORISTS ALL SAID THEY WERE TRYING TO ENSURE HUMANITY'S SURVIVAL...
UM, MASTER?
BY DESTROYING OR SEALING OFF ALL SCIENTIFIC AND TECH-NOLOGICAL DISCOVER-IES.
SOME-THING'S REALLY BUGGING ME.
I'M GOING TO LOOK AT WHAT'S NEXT.
AT THE END, A BLACK HOLE WEAPON WENT OUT OF CONTROL, AND THE EARTH, WELL...
......
DON'T INTERFERE, RUNE.
I HAVE TO KNOW WHAT HAPPENS NEXT.

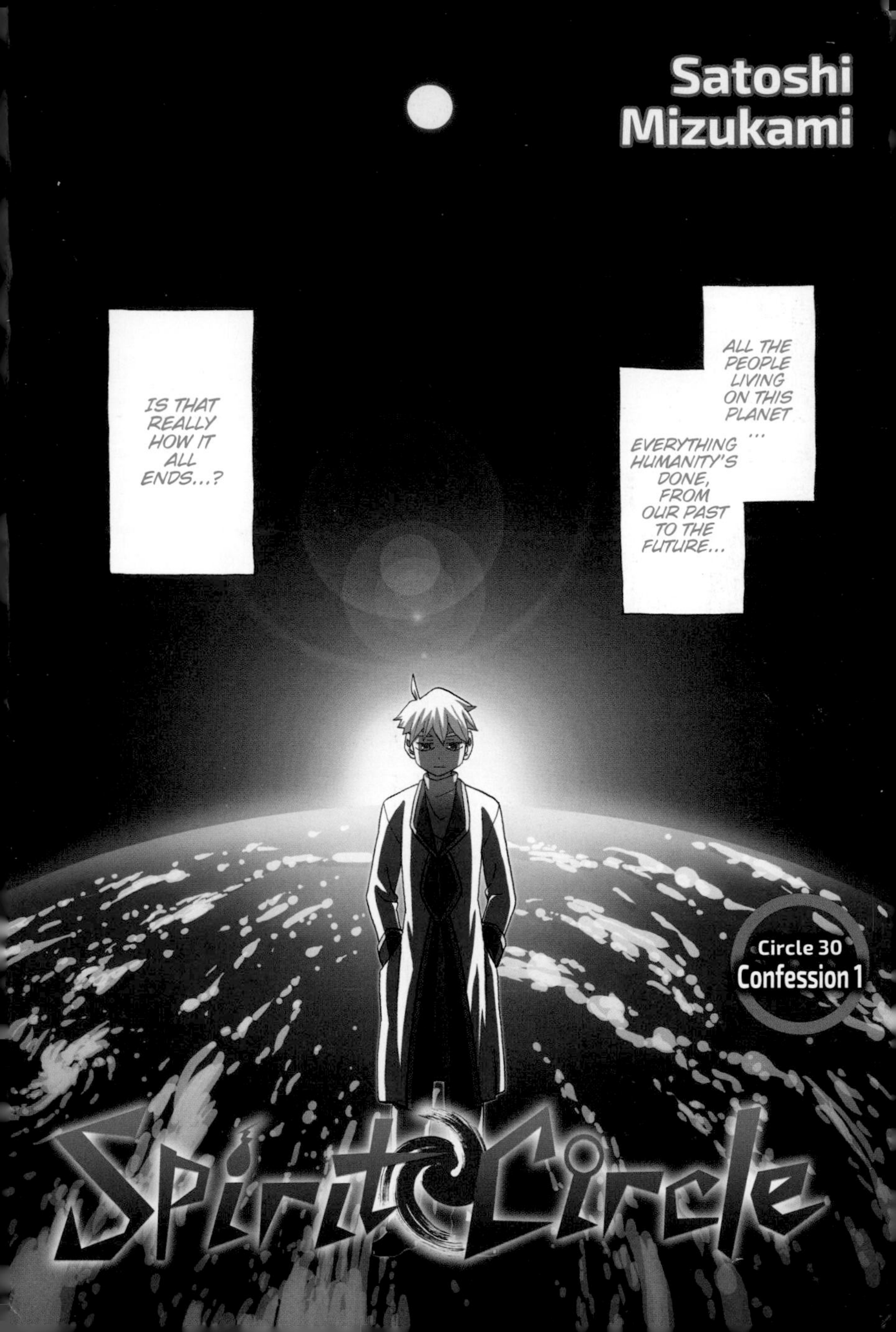
Satoshi Mizukami
ALL THE PEOPLE LIVING ON THIS PLANET...
EVERYTHING HUMANITY'S DONE, FROM OUR PAST TO THE FUTURE...
IS THAT REALLY HOW IT ALL ENDS...?
Circle 30
Confession 1
Spirit Circle

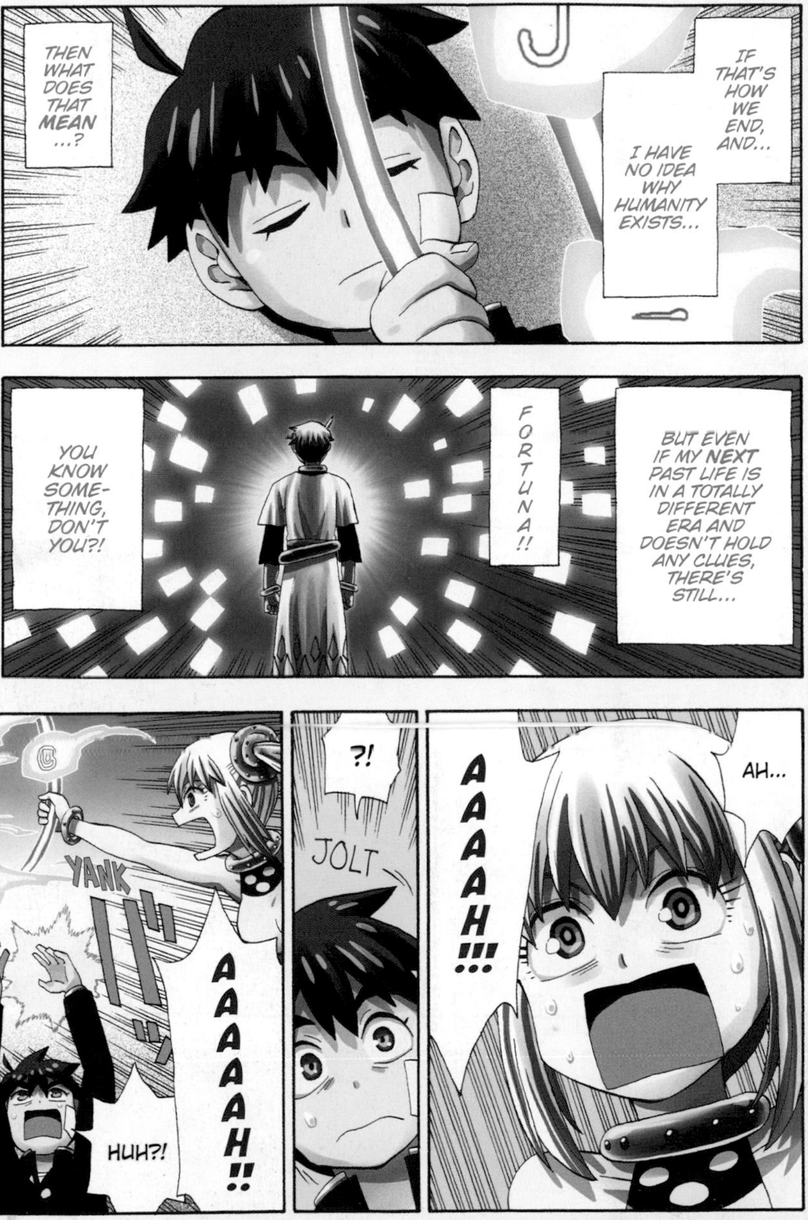
IF THAT'S HOW WE END, AND...
I HAVE NO IDEA WHY HUMANITY EXISTS...
THEN WHAT DOES THAT MEAN...?
BUT EVEN IF MY NEXT PAST LIFE IS IN A TOTALLY DIFFERENT ERA AND DOESN'T HOLD ANY CLUES, THERE'S STILL...
FORTUNA!!
YOU KNOW SOMETHING, DON'T YOU?!
AH...
AAAAAH!!!
?!
JOLT
YANK
AAAAAAH!!
HUH?!

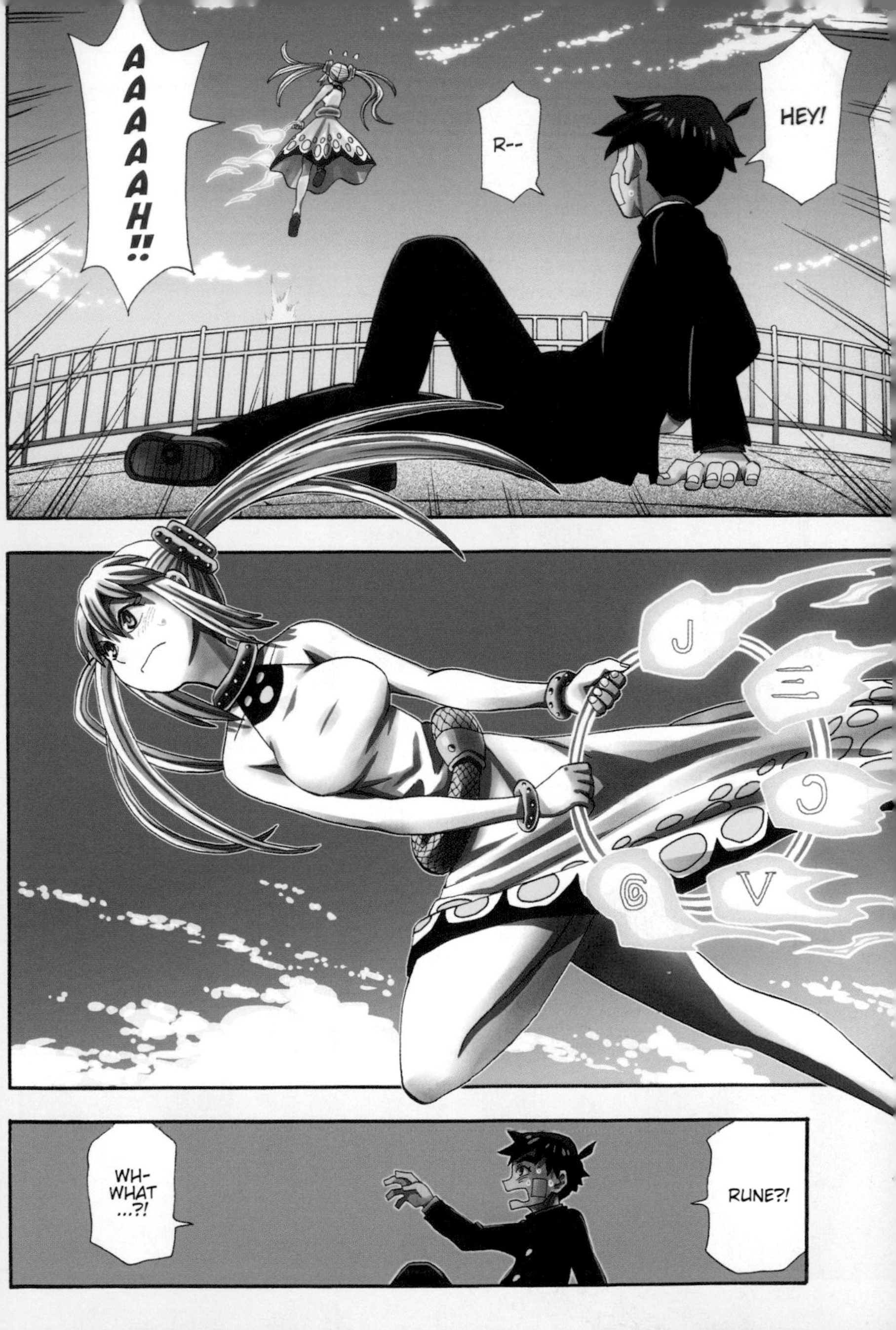
HEY!
R--
AAAAAAH!!
RUNE?!
WH-WHAT ...?!

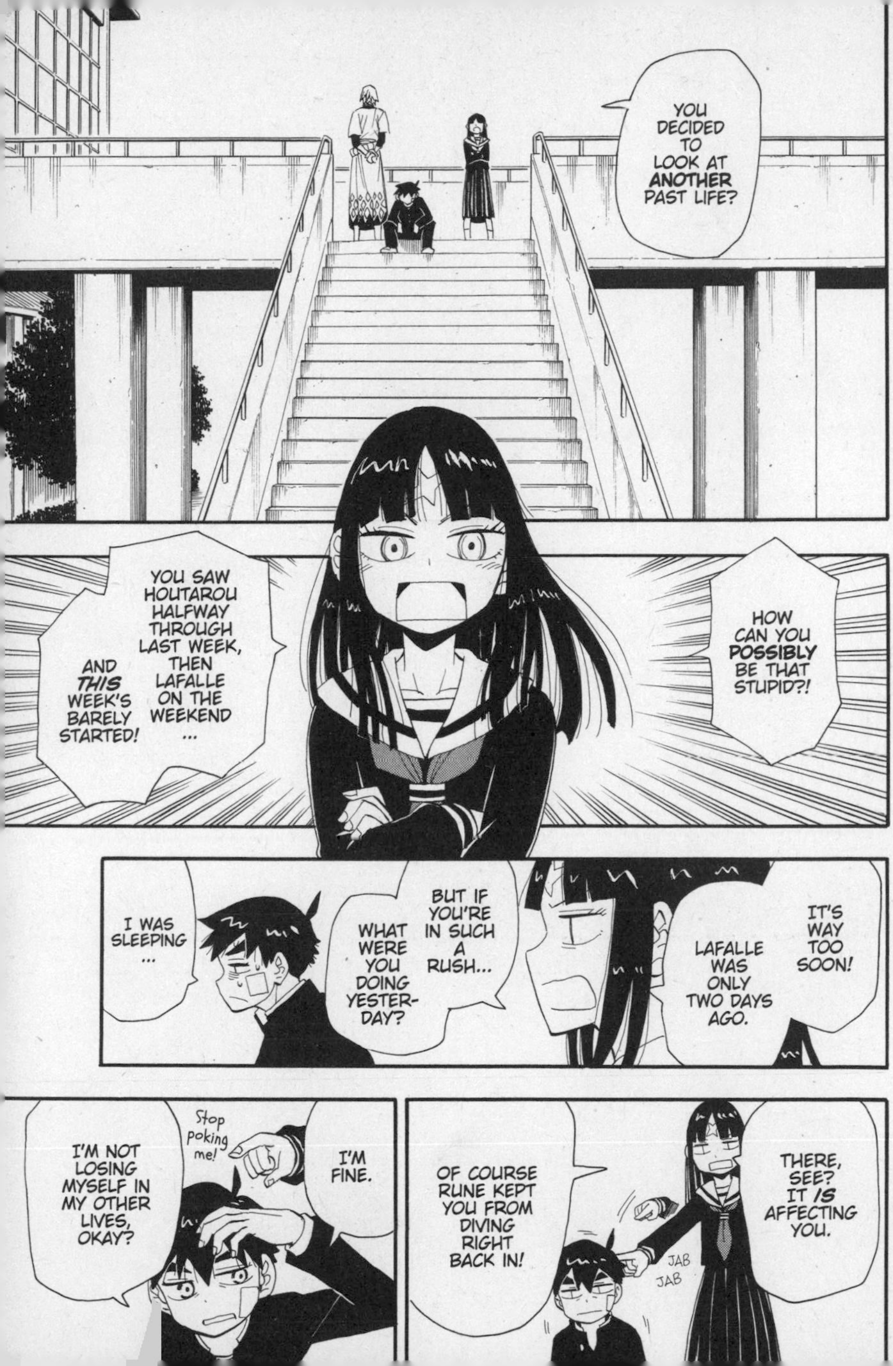
YOU DECIDED TO LOOK AT ANOTHER PAST LIFE?
HOW CAN YOU POSSIBLY BE THAT STUPID?!
YOU SAW HOUTAROU HALFWAY THROUGH LAST WEEK, THEN LAFALLE ON THE WEEKEND ...
AND THIS WEEK'S BARELY STARTED!
IT'S WAY TOO SOON!
LAFALLE WAS ONLY TWO DAYS AGO.
BUT IF YOU'RE IN SUCH A RUSH...
WHAT WERE YOU DOING YESTER-DAY?
I WAS SLEEPING ...
THERE, SEE? IT IS AFFECTING YOU.
JAB JAB
OF COURSE RUNE KEPT YOU FROM DIVING RIGHT BACK IN!
I'M FINE.
Stop poking me!
I'M NOT LOSING MYSELF IN MY OTHER LIVES, OKAY?

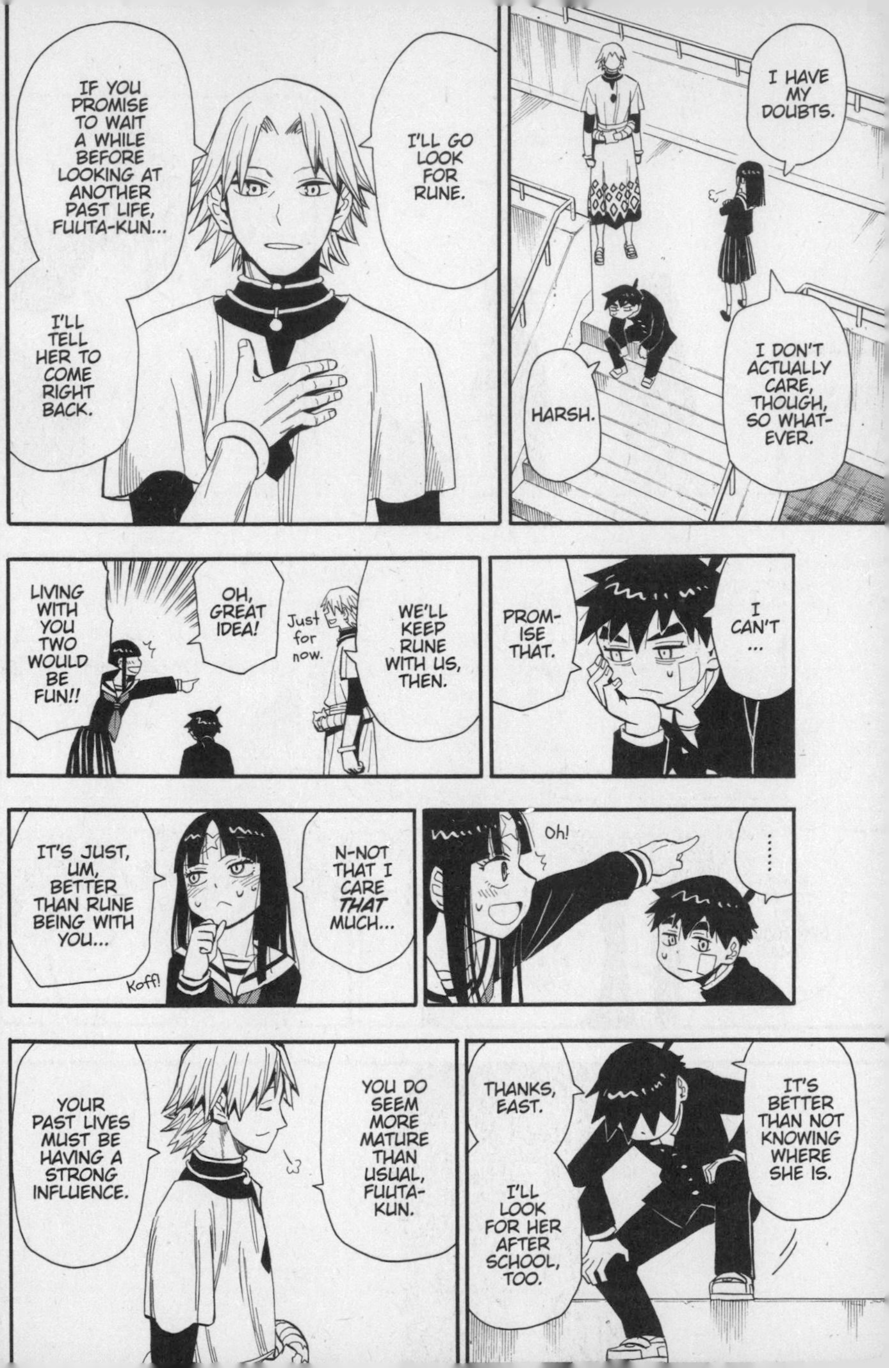
I HAVE MY DOUBTS.
I DON'T ACTUALLY CARE, THOUGH, SO WHATEVER.
HARSH.
I'LL GO LOOK FOR RUNE.
IF YOU PROMISE TO WAIT A WHILE BEFORE LOOKING AT ANOTHER PAST LIFE, FUUTA-KUN...
I'LL TELL HER TO COME RIGHT BACK.
I CAN'T ...
PROMISE THAT.
WE'LL KEEP RUNE WITH US, THEN.
Just for now.
OH, GREAT IDEA!
LIVING WITH YOU TWO WOULD BE FUN!!
......
Oh!
N-NOT THAT I CARE *THAT* MUCH...
IT'S JUST, UM, BETTER THAN RUNE BEING WITH YOU...
Koff!
IT'S BETTER THAN NOT KNOWING WHERE SHE IS.
THANKS, EAST.
I'LL LOOK FOR HER AFTER SCHOOL, TOO.
YOU DO SEEM MORE MATURE THAN USUAL, FUUTA-KUN.
YOUR PAST LIVES MUST BE HAVING A STRONG INFLUENCE.

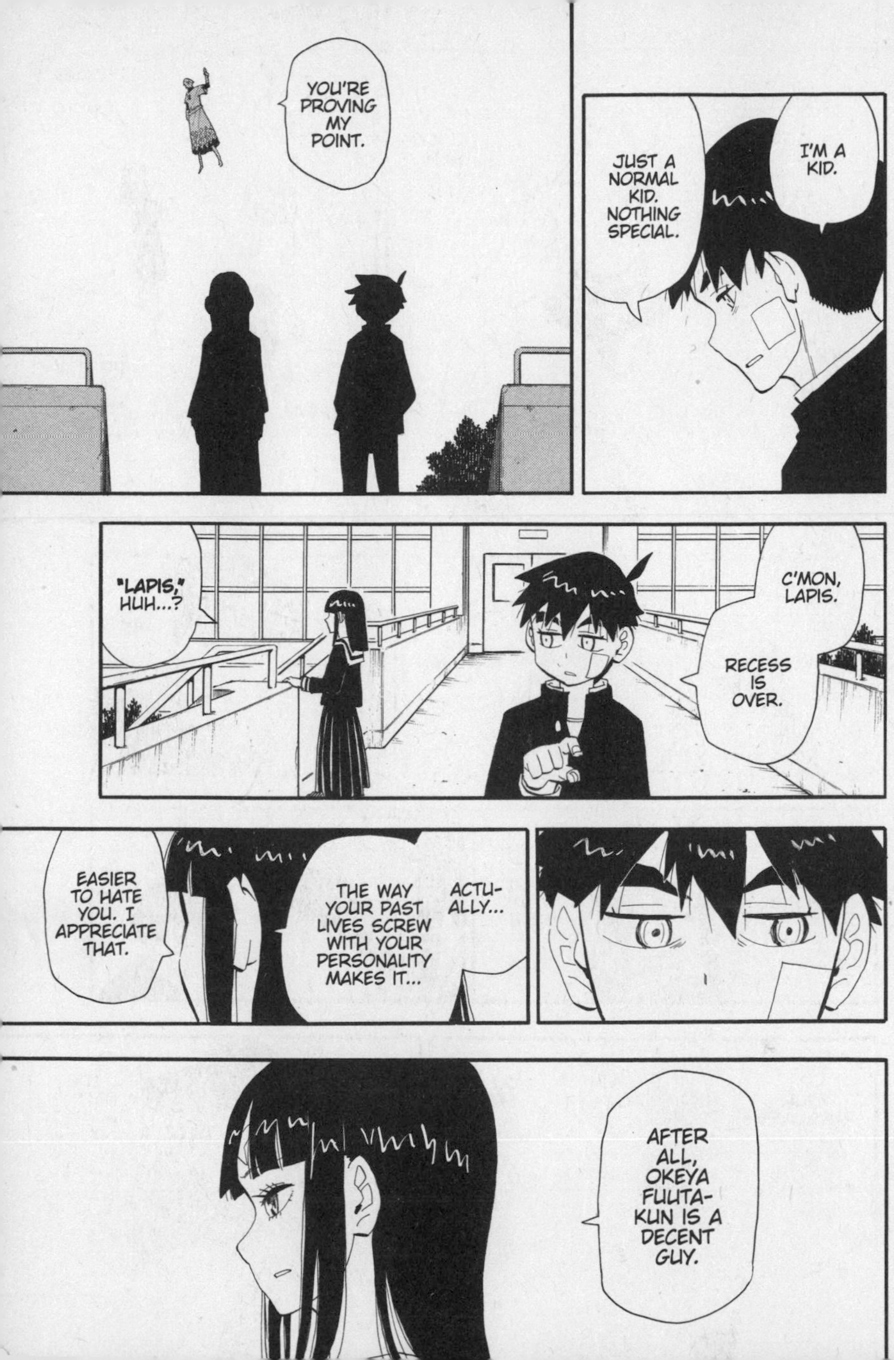
I'M A KID.
JUST A NORMAL KID. NOTHING SPECIAL.
YOU'RE PROVING MY POINT.
C'MON, LAPIS.
RECESS IS OVER.
"LAPIS," HUH...?
ACTU-ALLY...
THE WAY YOUR PAST LIVES SCREW WITH YOUR PERSONALITY MAKES IT...
EASIER TO HATE YOU. I APPRECIATE THAT.
AFTER ALL, OKEYA FUUTA-KUN IS A DECENT GUY.

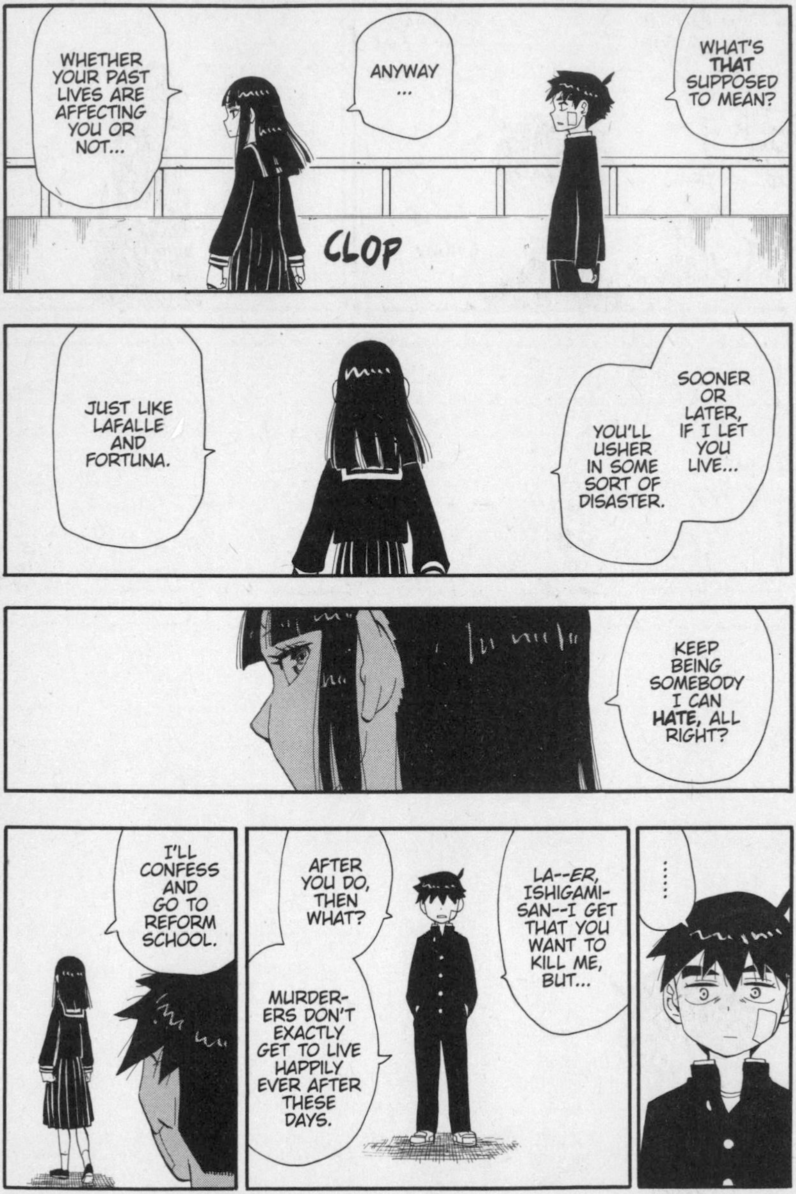
WHAT'S THAT SUPPOSED TO MEAN?
ANYWAY ...
WHETHER YOUR PAST LIVES ARE AFFECTING YOU OR NOT...
CLOP
SOONER OR LATER, IF I LET YOU LIVE...
YOU'LL USHER IN SOME SORT OF DISASTER.
JUST LIKE LAFALLE AND FORTUNA.
KEEP BEING SOMEBODY I CAN HATE, ALL RIGHT?
......
LA--ER, ISHIGAMI-SAN--I GET THAT YOU WANT TO KILL ME, BUT...
AFTER YOU DO, THEN WHAT?
MURDER-ERS DON'T EXACTLY GET TO LIVE HAPPILY EVER AFTER THESE DAYS.
I'LL CONFESS AND GO TO REFORM SCHOOL.

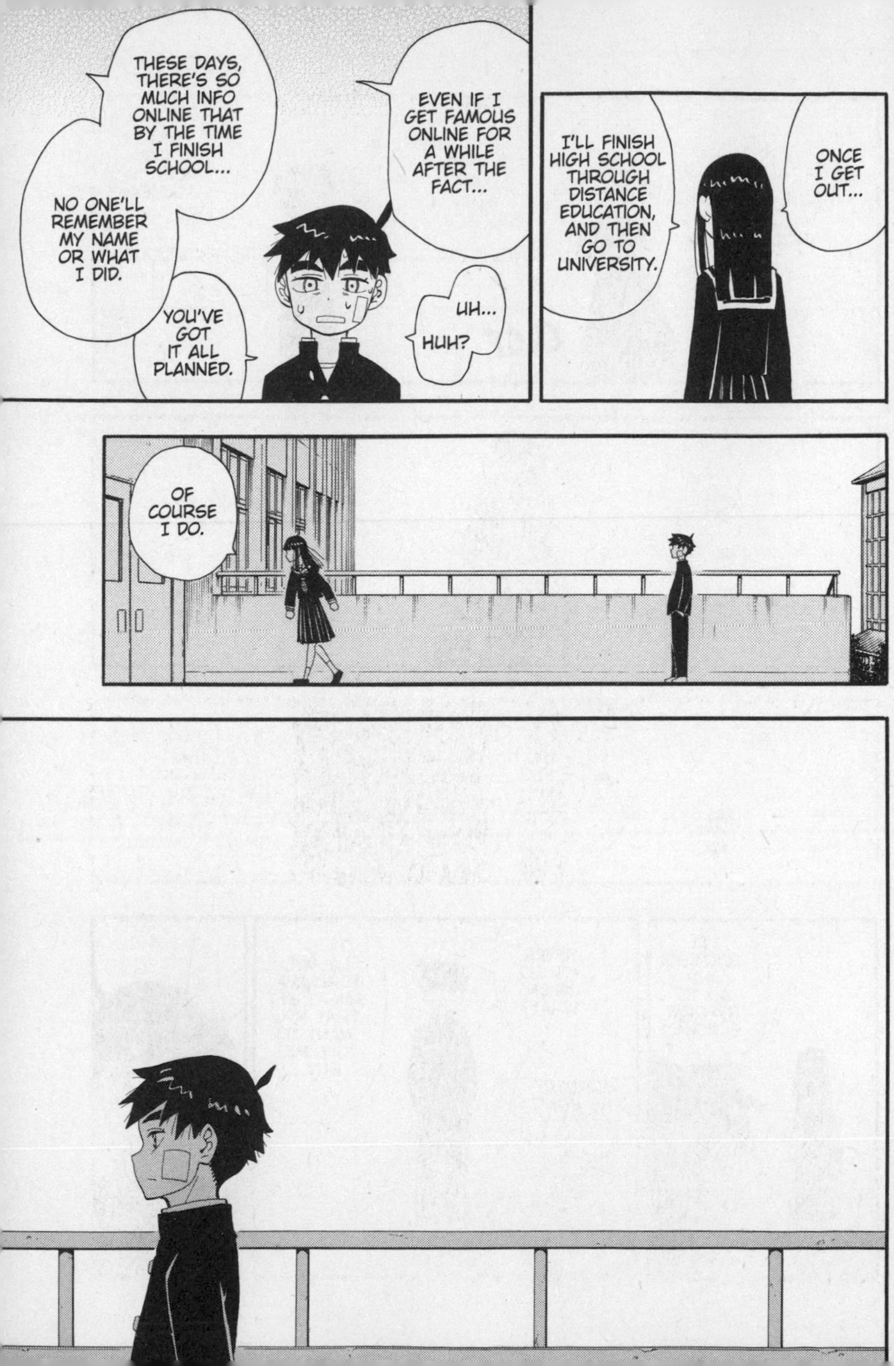
ONCE I GET OUT...
I'LL FINISH HIGH SCHOOL THROUGH DISTANCE EDUCATION, AND THEN GO TO UNIVERSITY.
EVEN IF I GET FAMOUS ONLINE FOR A WHILE AFTER THE FACT...
THESE DAYS, THERE'S SO MUCH INFO ONLINE THAT BY THE TIME I FINISH SCHOOL...
NO ONE'LL REMEMBER MY NAME OR WHAT I DID.
UH... HUH?
YOU'VE GOT IT ALL PLANNED.
OF COURSE I DO.

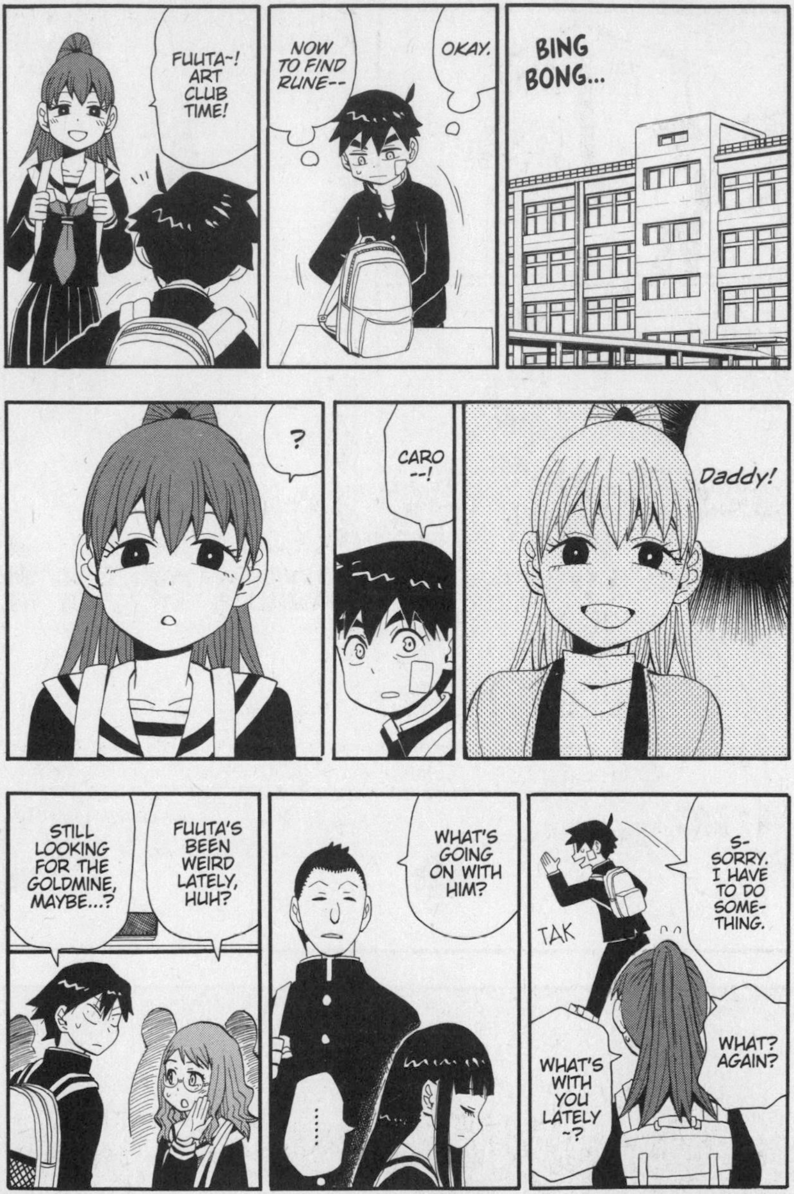
BING BONG...
OKAY.
NOW TO FIND RUNE--
FUUTA~! ART CLUB TIME!
Daddy!
CARO--!
?
S-SORRY. I HAVE TO DO SOME-THING.
TAK
WHAT? AGAIN?
WHAT'S WITH YOU LATELY~?
WHAT'S GOING ON WITH HIM?
......
FUUTA'S BEEN WEIRD LATELY, HUH?
STILL LOOKING FOR THE GOLDMINE, MAYBE...?

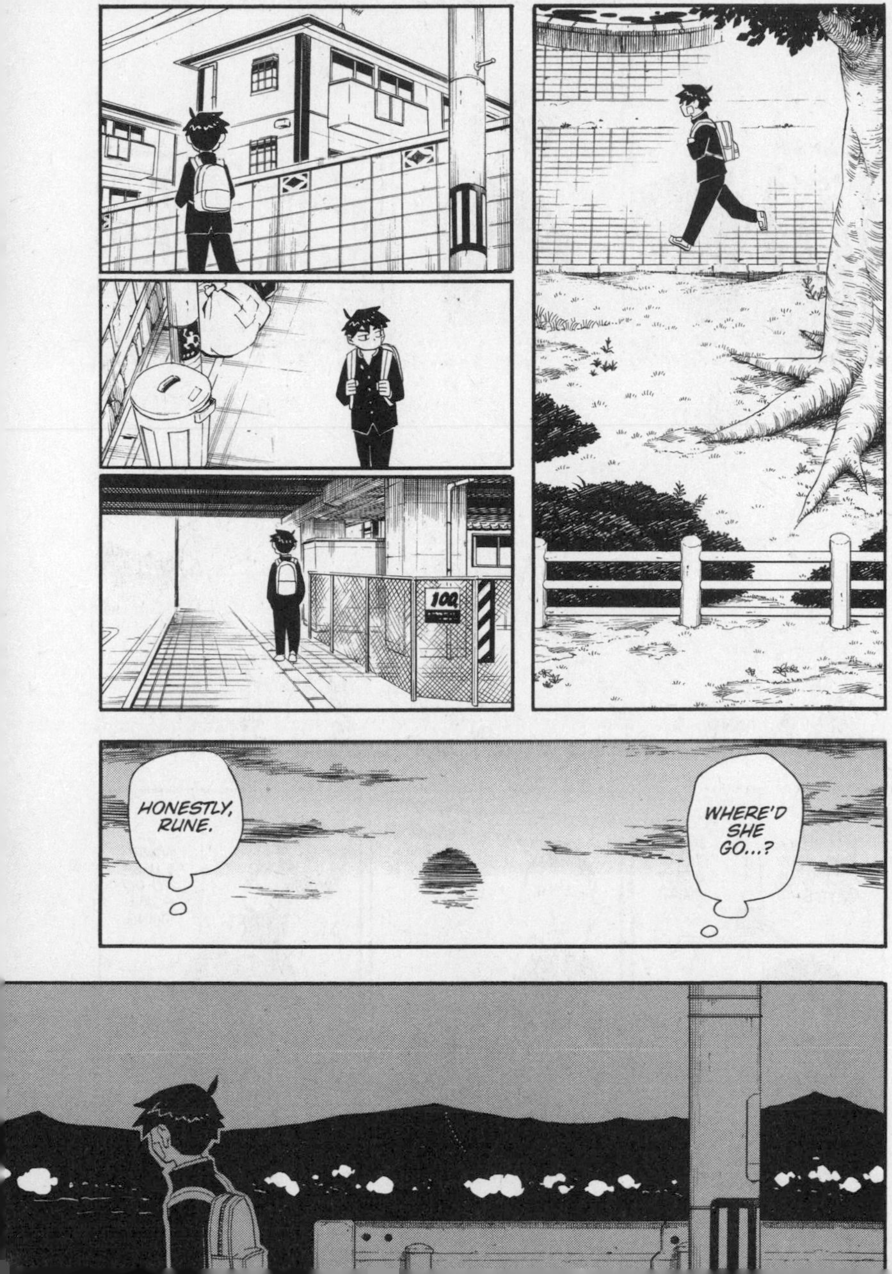
100
WHERE'D SHE GO...?
HONESTLY, RUNE.

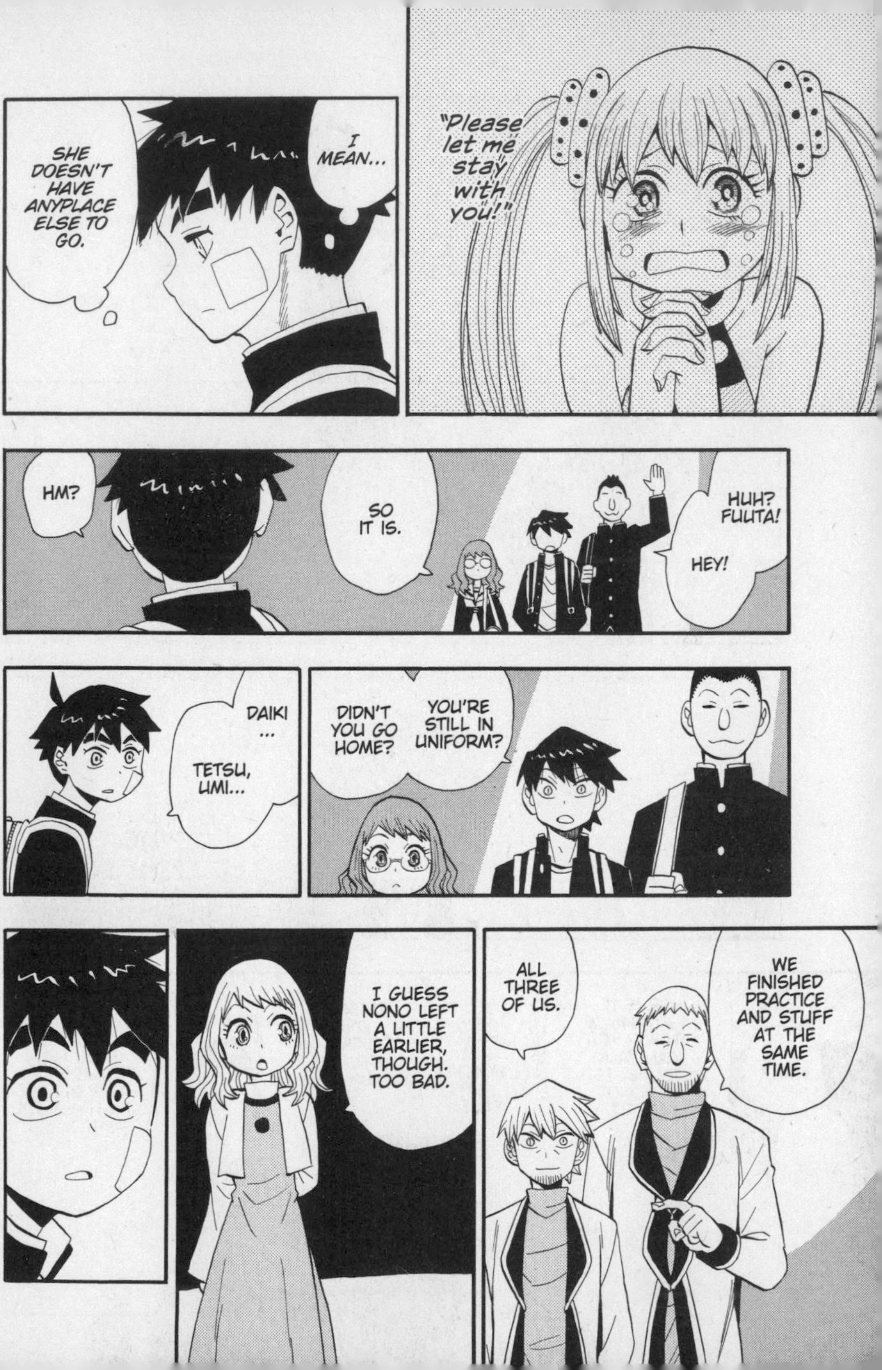
"Please let me stay with you!"
I MEAN...
SHE DOESN'T HAVE ANYPLACE ELSE TO GO.
HUH? FUUTA!
HEY!
SO IT IS.
HM?
YOU'RE STILL IN UNIFORM?
DIDN'T YOU GO HOME?
DAIKI ...
TETSU, UMI...
WE FINISHED PRACTICE AND STUFF AT THE SAME TIME.
ALL THREE OF US.
I GUESS NONO LEFT A LITTLE EARLIER, THOUGH. TOO BAD.

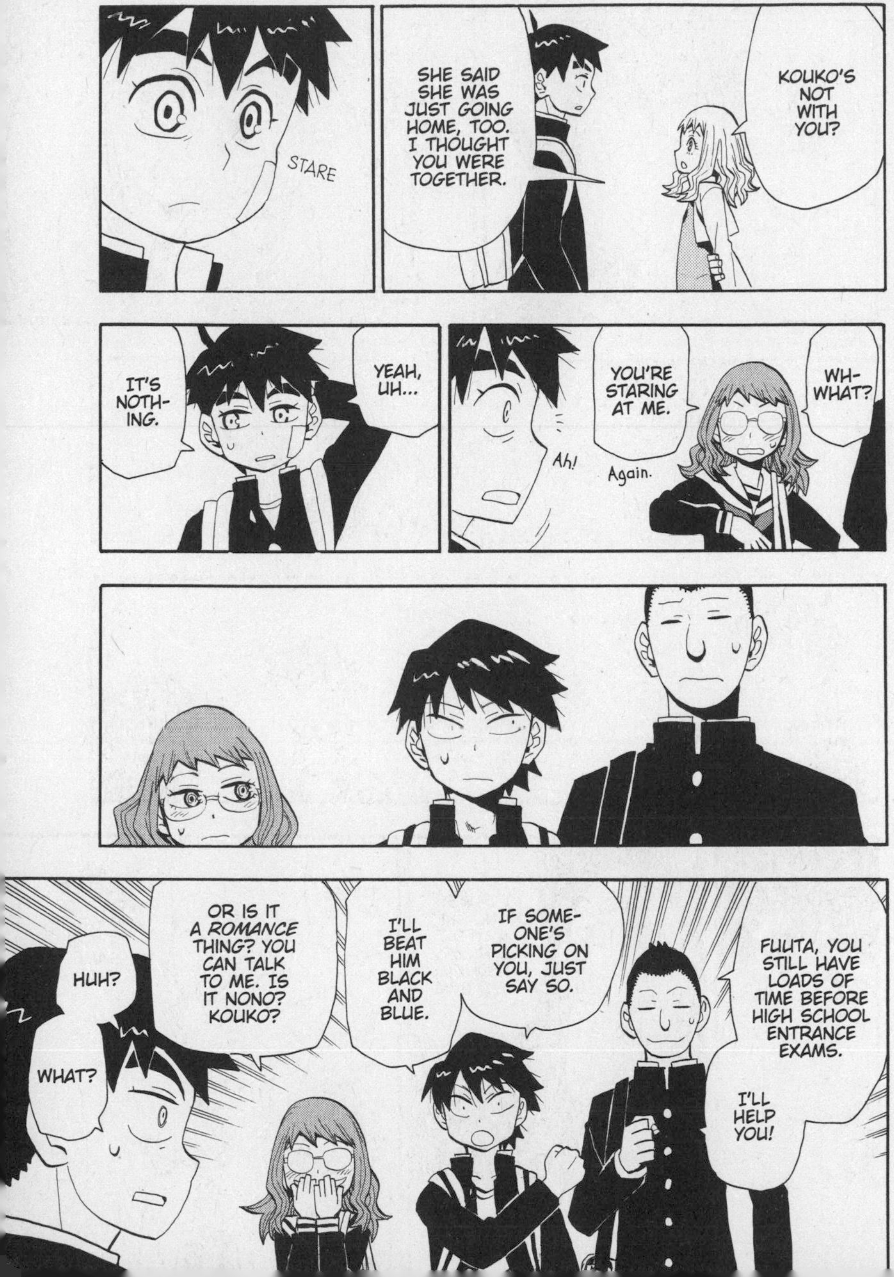
KOUKO'S NOT WITH YOU?
SHE SAID SHE WAS JUST GOING HOME, TOO. I THOUGHT YOU WERE TOGETHER.
STARE
WH-WHAT?
YOU'RE STARING AT ME.
Ah!
Again.
YEAH, UH...
IT'S NOTH-ING.
FUUTA, YOU STILL HAVE LOADS OF TIME BEFORE HIGH SCHOOL ENTRANCE EXAMS.
I'LL HELP YOU!
IF SOME-ONE'S PICKING ON YOU, JUST SAY SO.
I'LL BEAT HIM BLACK AND BLUE.
OR IS IT A *ROMANCE* THING? YOU CAN TALK TO ME. IS IT NONO? KOUKO?
HUH?
WHAT?

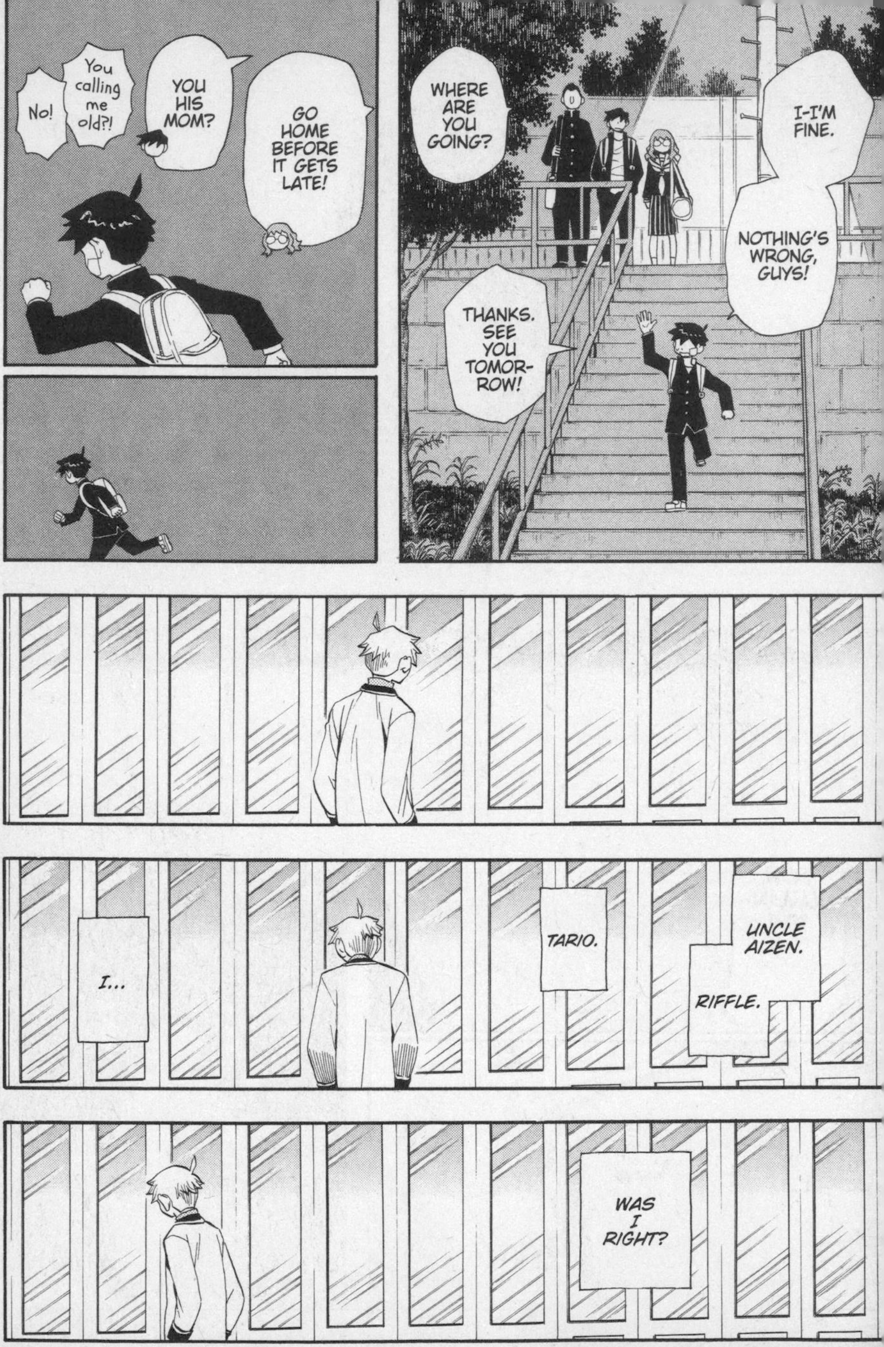
I-I'M FINE.
NOTHING'S WRONG, GUYS!
WHERE ARE YOU GOING?
THANKS. SEE YOU TOMORROW!
GO HOME BEFORE IT GETS LATE!
YOU HIS MOM?
You calling me old?!
No!
UNCLE AIZEN.
TARIO.
RIFFLE.
I...
WAS I RIGHT?

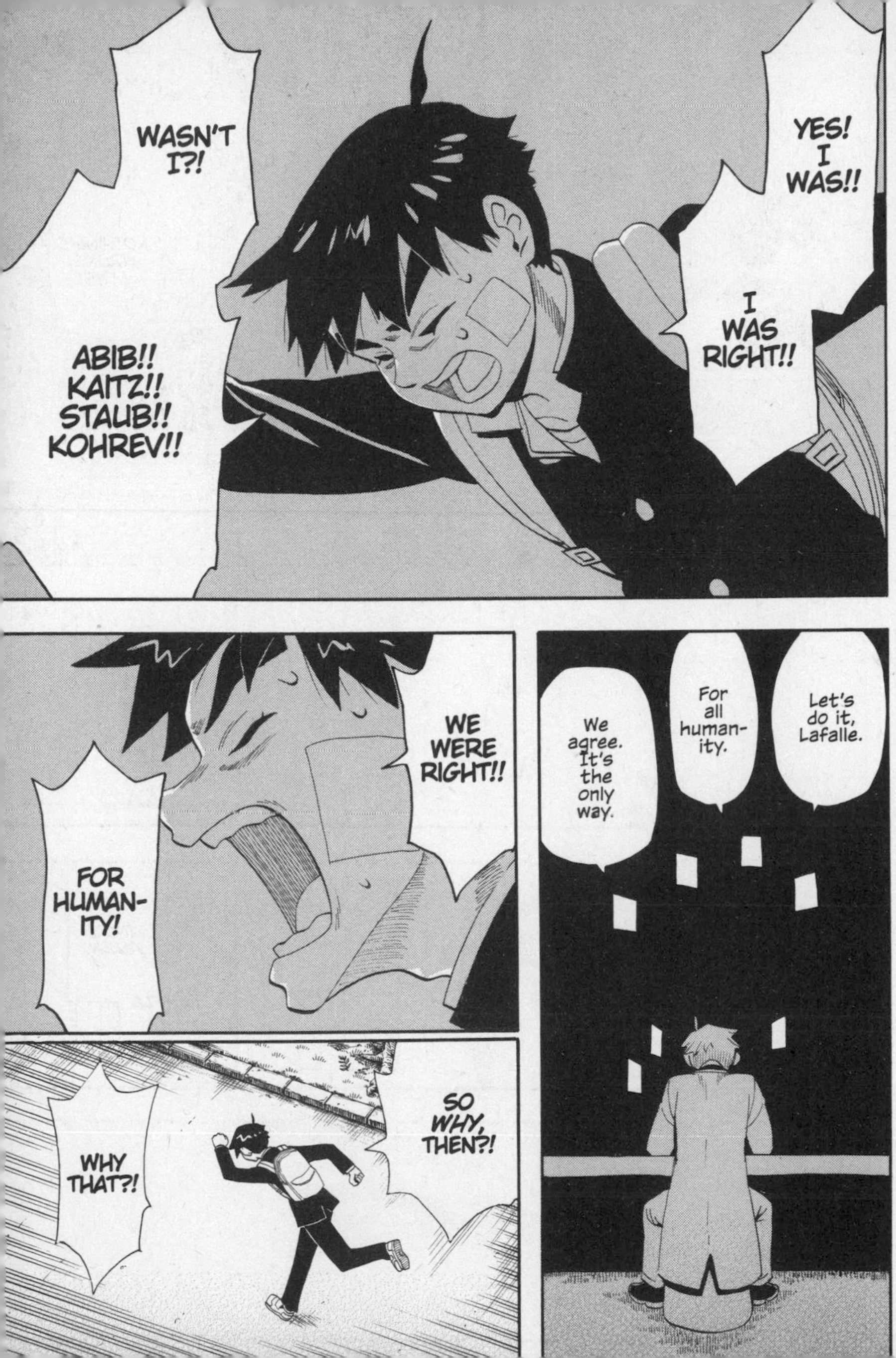
YES! I WAS!!
WASN'T I?!
I WAS RIGHT!!
ABIB!! KAITZ!! STAUB!! KOHREV!!
Let's do it, Lafalle.
For all human-ity.
We agree. It's the only way.
WE WERE RIGHT!!
FOR HUMAN-ITY!
SO *WHY*, THEN?!
WHY THAT?!

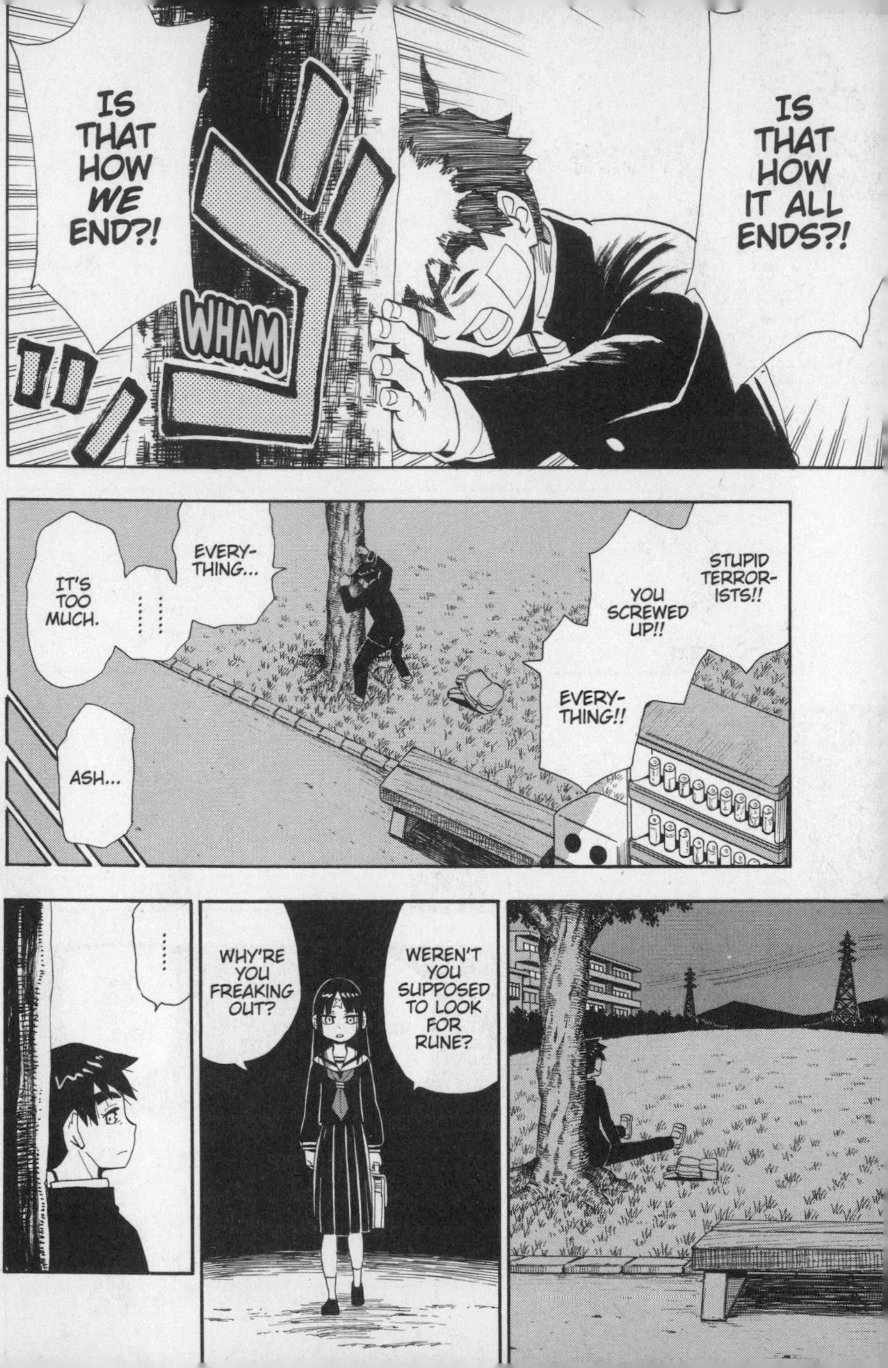
IS THAT HOW IT ALL ENDS?!
IS THAT HOW WE END?!
WHAM
STUPID TERROR-ISTS!!
YOU SCREWED UP!!
EVERY-THING!!
EVERY-THING...
......
IT'S TOO MUCH.
ASH...
WEREN'T YOU SUPPOSED TO LOOK FOR RUNE?
WHY'RE YOU FREAKING OUT?
......

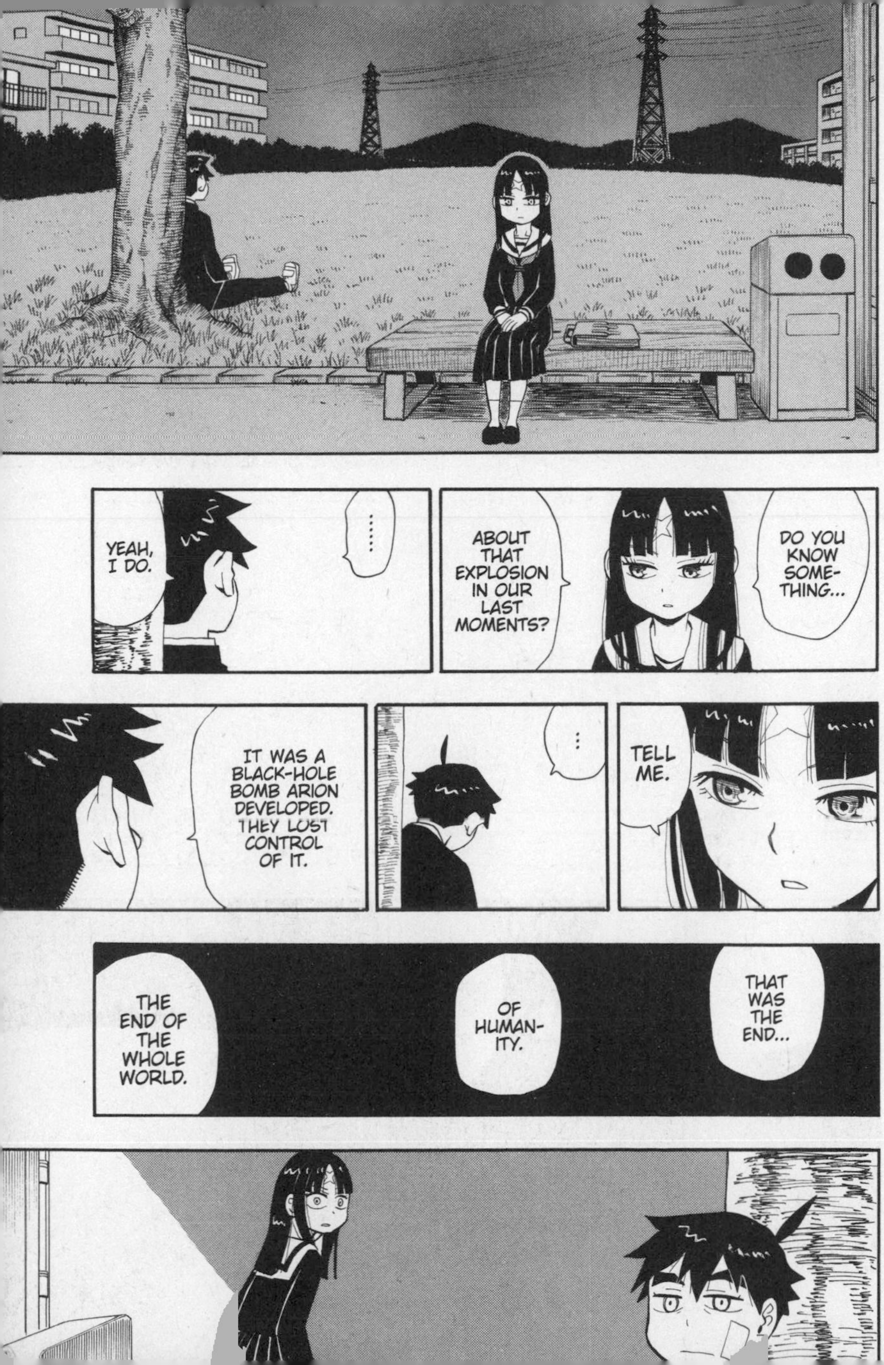
DO YOU KNOW SOME-THING...
ABOUT THAT EXPLOSION IN OUR LAST MOMENTS?
......
YEAH, I DO.
TELL ME.
...
IT WAS A BLACK-HOLE BOMB ARION DEVELOPED. THEY LOST CONTROL OF IT.
THAT WAS THE END...
OF HUMAN-ITY.
THE END OF THE WHOLE WORLD.

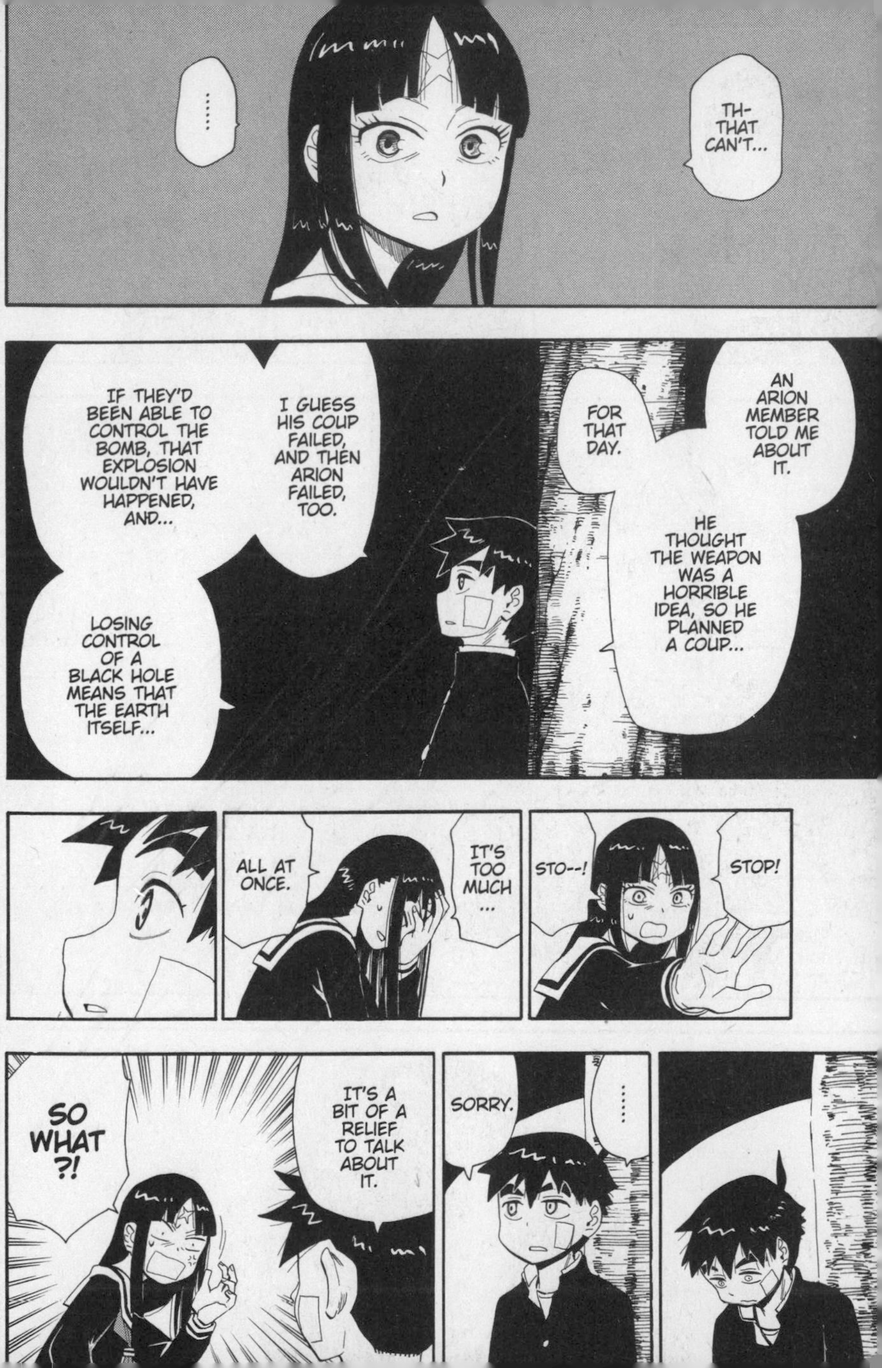
TH- THAT CAN'T...
......
AN ARION MEMBER TOLD ME ABOUT IT.
FOR THAT DAY.
HE THOUGHT THE WEAPON WAS A HORRIBLE IDEA, SO HE PLANNED A COUP...
I GUESS HIS COUP FAILED, AND THEN ARION FAILED, TOO.
IF THEY'D BEEN ABLE TO CONTROL THE BOMB, THAT EXPLOSION WOULDN'T HAVE HAPPENED, AND...
LOSING CONTROL OF A BLACK HOLE MEANS THAT THE EARTH ITSELF...
STOP!
STO--!
IT'S TOO MUCH...
ALL AT ONCE.
......
SORRY.
IT'S A BIT OF A RELIEF TO TALK ABOUT IT.
SO WHAT?!

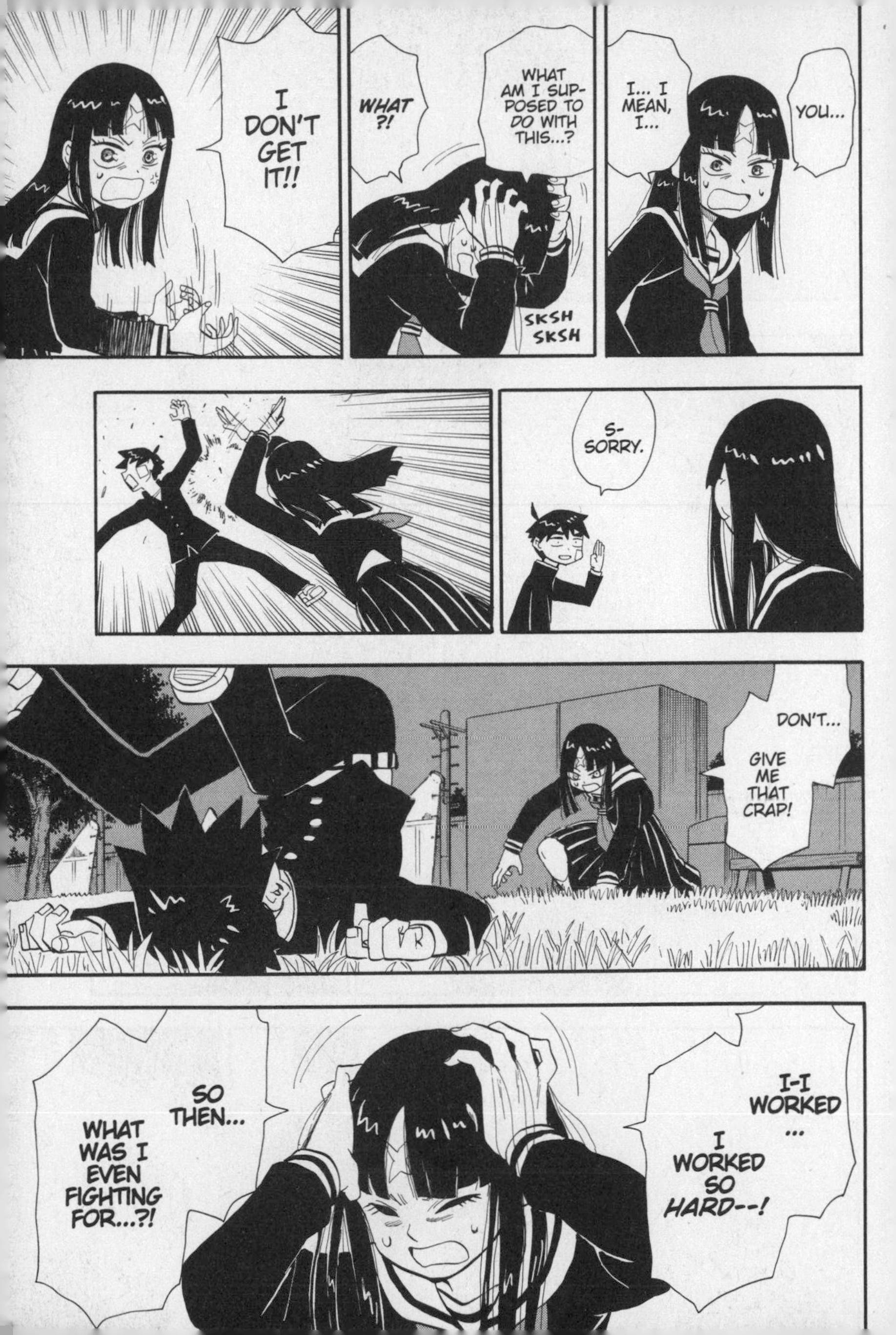

YOU...
I... I MEAN, I...
WHAT AM I SUP-POSED TO *DO* WITH THIS...?
WHAT ?!
SKSH SKSH
I DON'T GET IT!!
S-SORRY.
DON'T...
GIVE ME THAT CRAP!
I-I WORKED...
I WORKED SO *HARD--!*
SO THEN...
WHAT WAS I EVEN FIGHTING FOR...?!

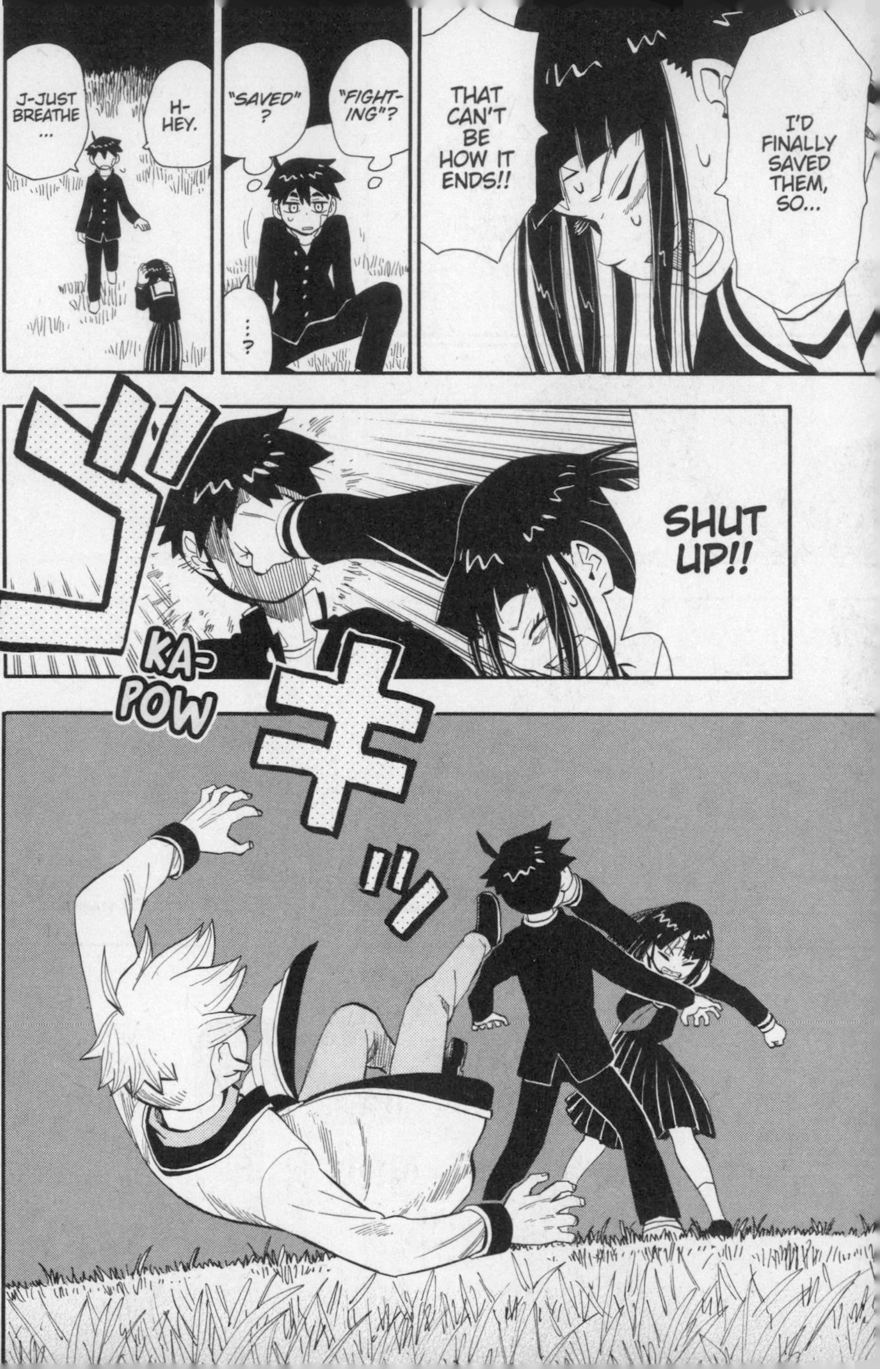
I'D FINALLY SAVED THEM, SO...
THAT CAN'T BE HOW IT ENDS!!
"FIGHTING"?
"SAVED"?
...?
H-HEY.
J-JUST BREATHE...
SHUT UP!!
KA-POW

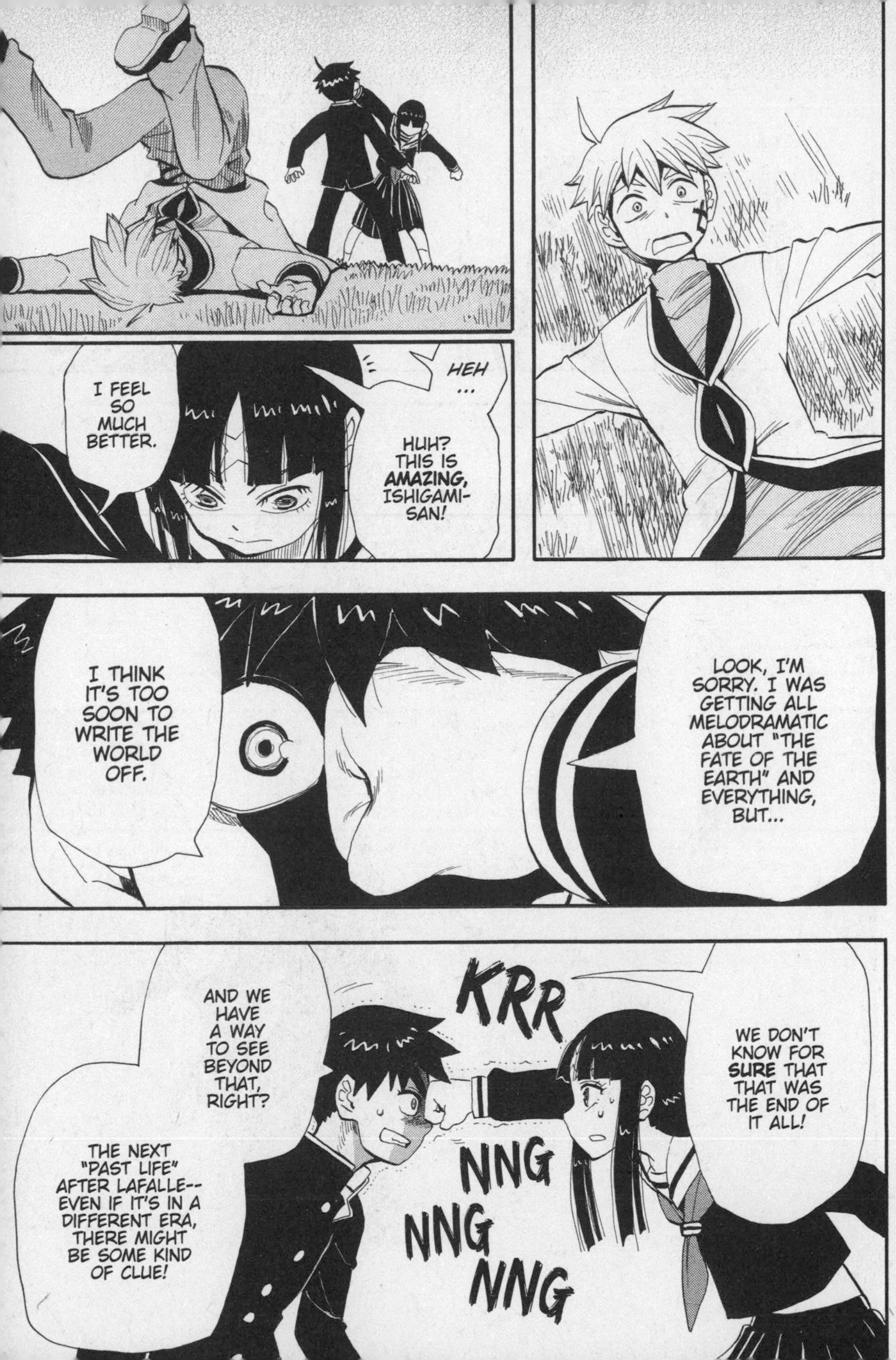
HEH...
HUH? THIS IS AMAZING, ISHIGAMI-SAN!
I FEEL SO MUCH BETTER.
LOOK, I'M SORRY. I WAS GETTING ALL MELODRAMATIC ABOUT "THE FATE OF THE EARTH" AND EVERYTHING, BUT...
I THINK IT'S TOO SOON TO WRITE THE WORLD OFF.
WE DON'T KNOW FOR SURE THAT THAT WAS THE END OF IT ALL!
KRR
NNG NNG NNG
AND WE HAVE A WAY TO SEE BEYOND THAT, RIGHT?
THE NEXT "PAST LIFE" AFTER LAFALLE-- EVEN IF IT'S IN A DIFFERENT ERA, THERE MIGHT BE SOME KIND OF CLUE!

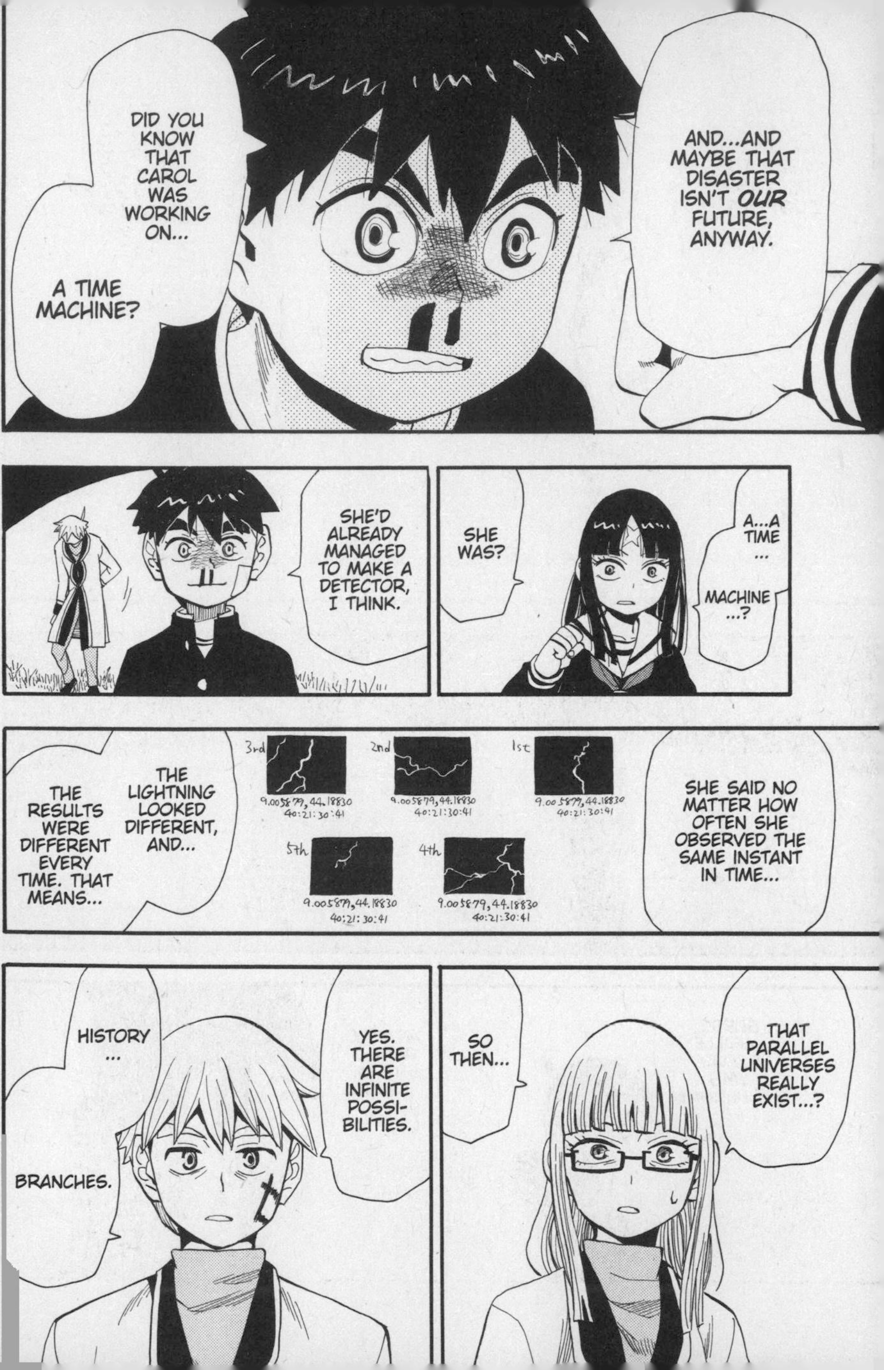
AND...AND MAYBE THAT DISASTER ISN'T *OUR* FUTURE, ANYWAY.
DID YOU KNOW THAT CAROL WAS WORKING ON...
A TIME MACHINE?
A...A TIME ...
MACHINE ...?
SHE WAS?
SHE'D ALREADY MANAGED TO MAKE A DETECTOR, I THINK.
SHE SAID NO MATTER HOW OFTEN SHE OBSERVED THE SAME INSTANT IN TIME...
1st
9.005879, 44.18830
40:21:30:41
2nd
9.005879, 44.18830
40:21:30:41
3rd
9.005879, 44.18830
40:21:30:41
4th
9.005879, 44.18830
40:21:30:41
5th
9.005879, 44.18830
40:21:30:41
THE LIGHTNING LOOKED DIFFERENT, AND...
THE RESULTS WERE DIFFERENT EVERY TIME. THAT MEANS...
THAT PARALLEL UNIVERSES REALLY EXIST...?
SO THEN...
YES. THERE ARE INFINITE POSSIBILITIES.
HISTORY ...
BRANCHES.

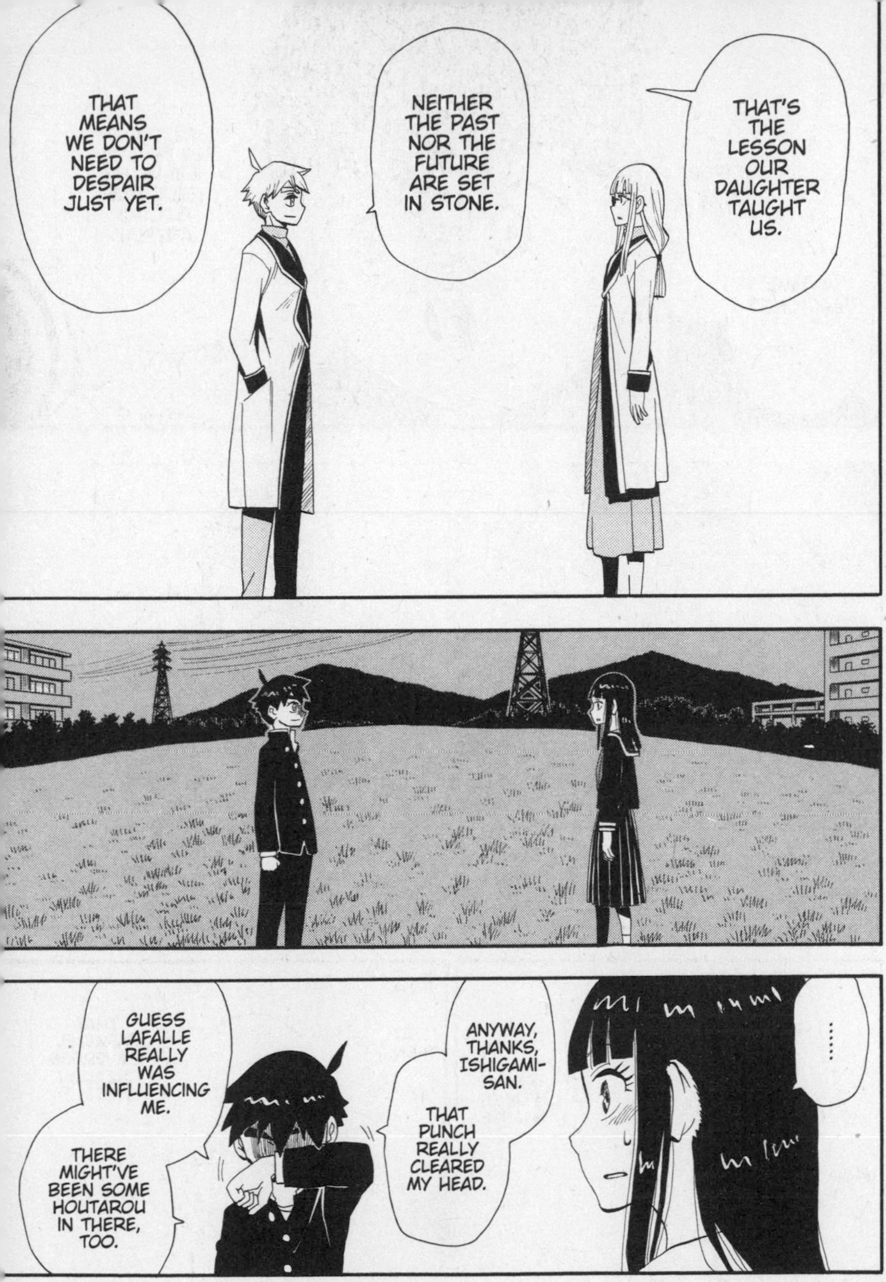
THAT'S THE LESSON OUR DAUGHTER TAUGHT US.
NEITHER THE PAST NOR THE FUTURE ARE SET IN STONE.
THAT MEANS WE DON'T NEED TO DESPAIR JUST YET.
......
ANYWAY, THANKS, ISHIGAMI-SAN.
THAT PUNCH REALLY CLEARED MY HEAD.
GUESS LAFALLE REALLY WAS INFLUENCING ME.
THERE MIGHT'VE BEEN SOME HOUTAROU IN THERE, TOO.

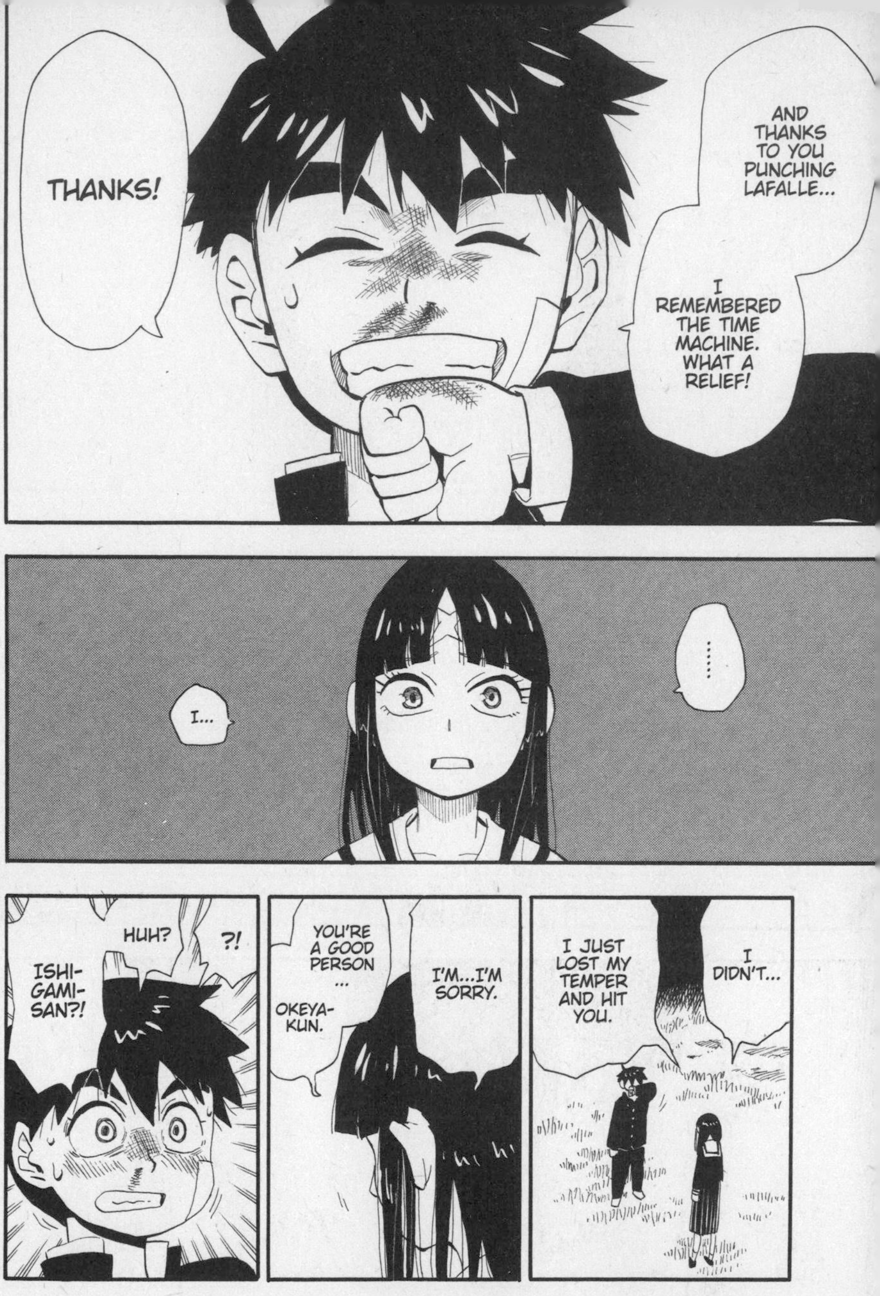
AND THANKS TO YOU PUNCHING LAFALLE...
I REMEMBERED THE TIME MACHINE. WHAT A RELIEF!
THANKS!
......
I...
I DIDN'T...
I JUST LOST MY TEMPER AND HIT YOU.
I'M...I'M SORRY.
YOU'RE A GOOD PERSON ... OKEYA-KUN.
?!
HUH?
ISHI-GAMI-SAN?!

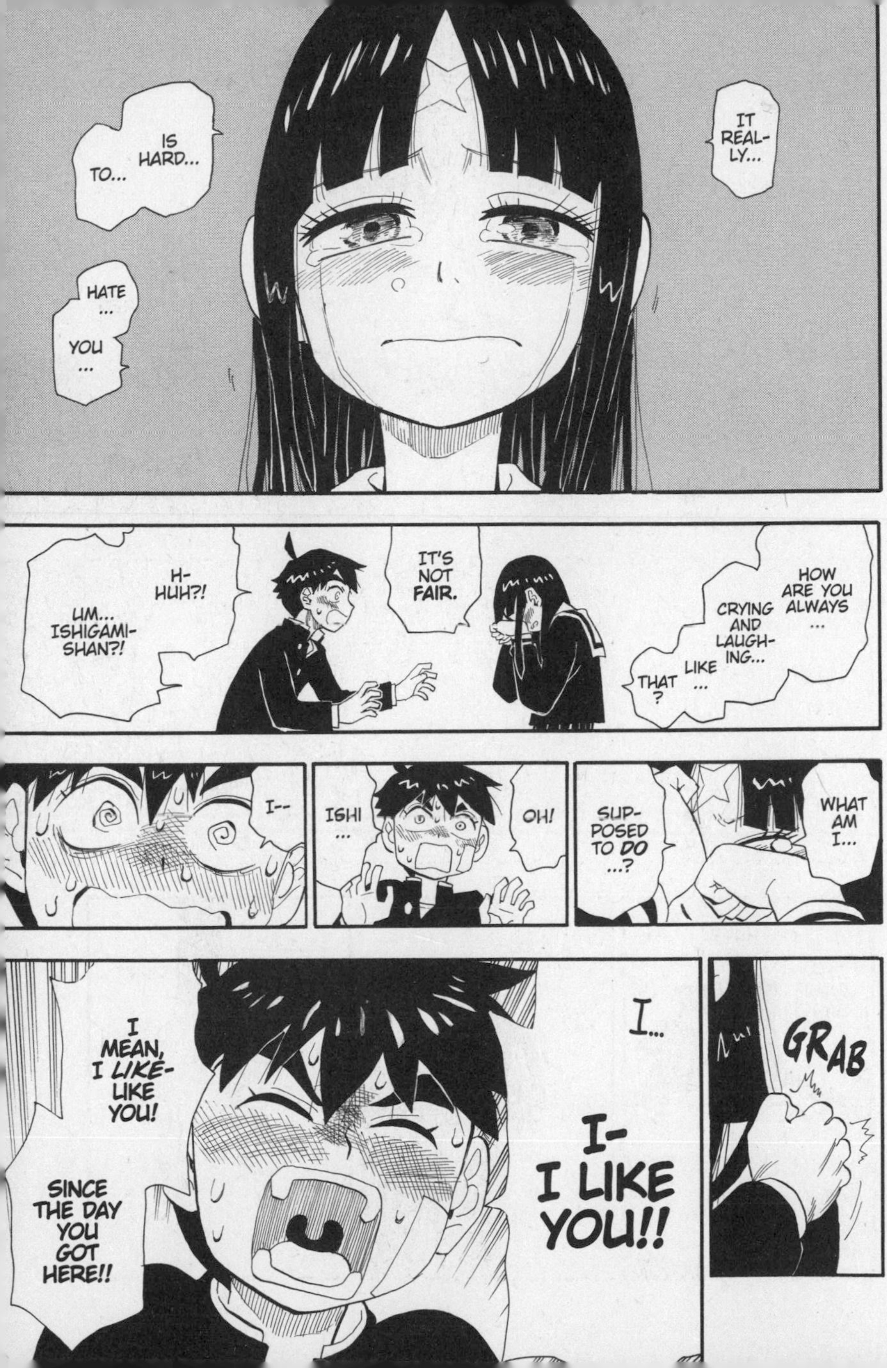
IT REAL-LY...
IS HARD... TO...
HATE ... YOU ...
HOW ARE YOU ALWAYS ... CRYING AND LAUGH-ING... LIKE ... THAT ?
IT'S NOT FAIR.
H-HUH?!
UM... ISHIGAMI-SHAN?!
WHAT AM I...
SUP-POSED TO DO ...?
OH!
ISHI ...
I--
GRAB
I...
I- I LIKE YOU!!
I MEAN, I LIKE-LIKE YOU!
SINCE THE DAY YOU GOT HERE!!

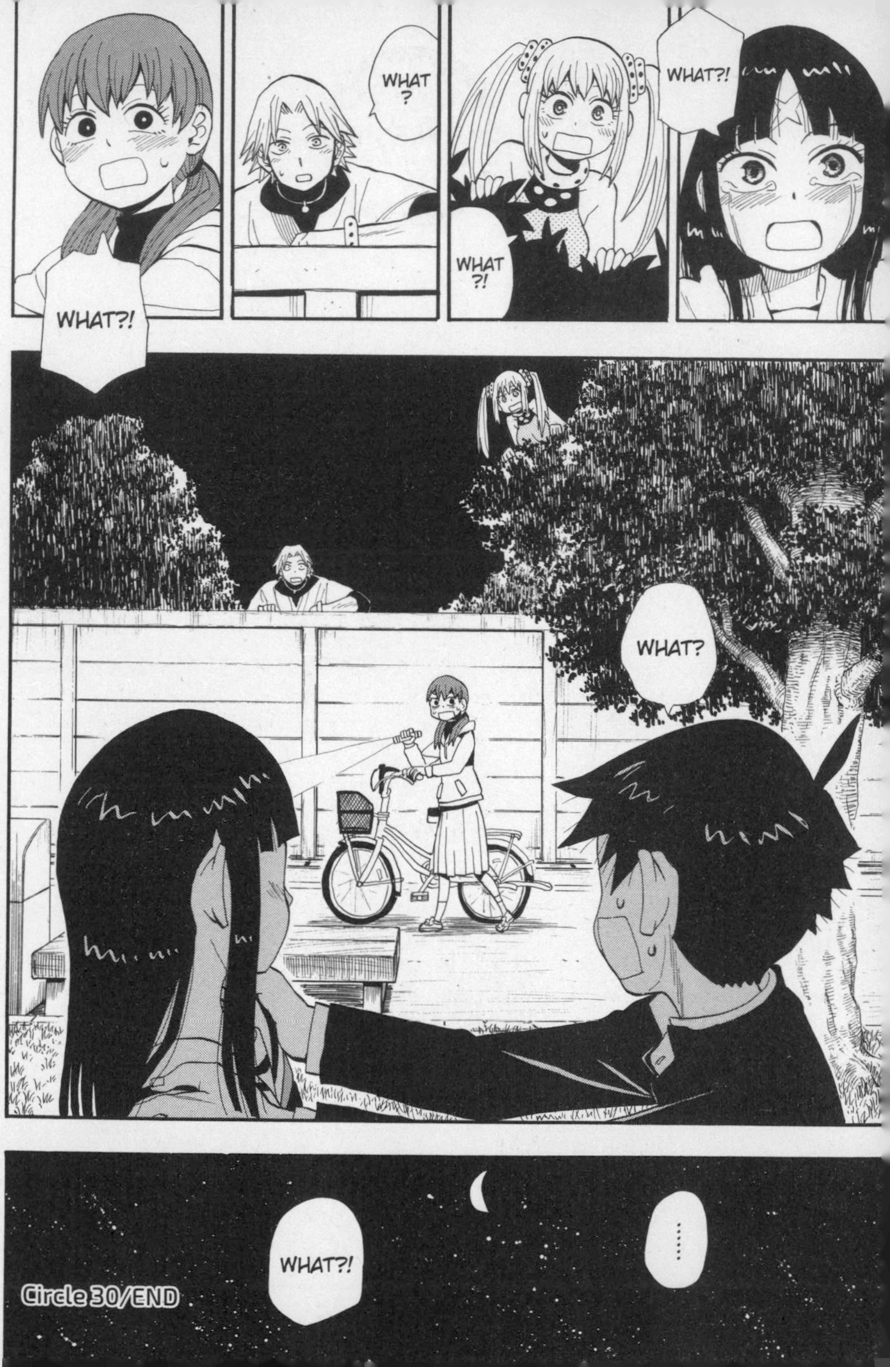
WHAT?!
WHAT ?!
WHAT ?
WHAT?!
WHAT?
......
WHAT?!
Circle 30/END

Circle 31
Confession 2

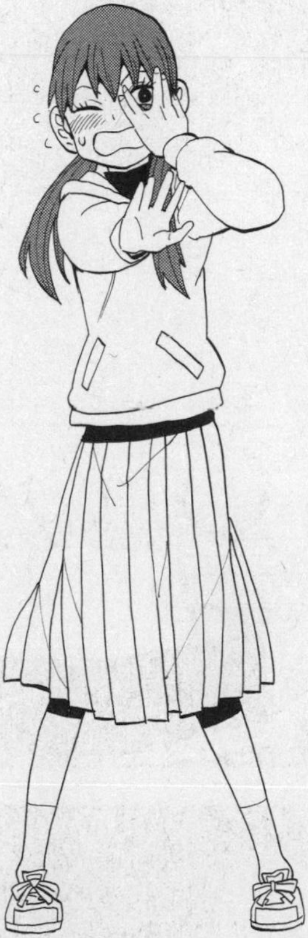

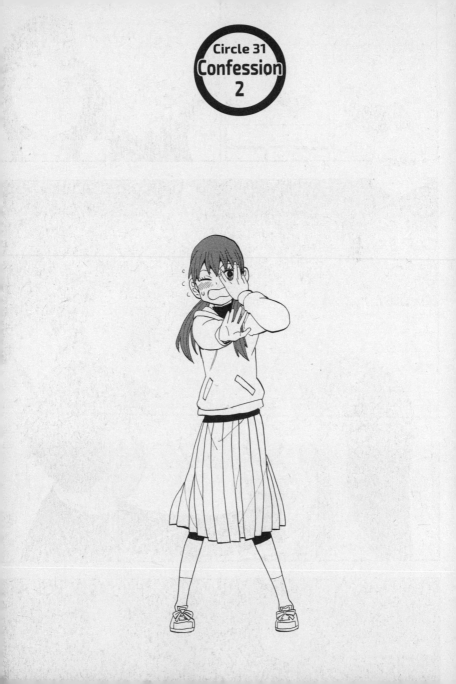

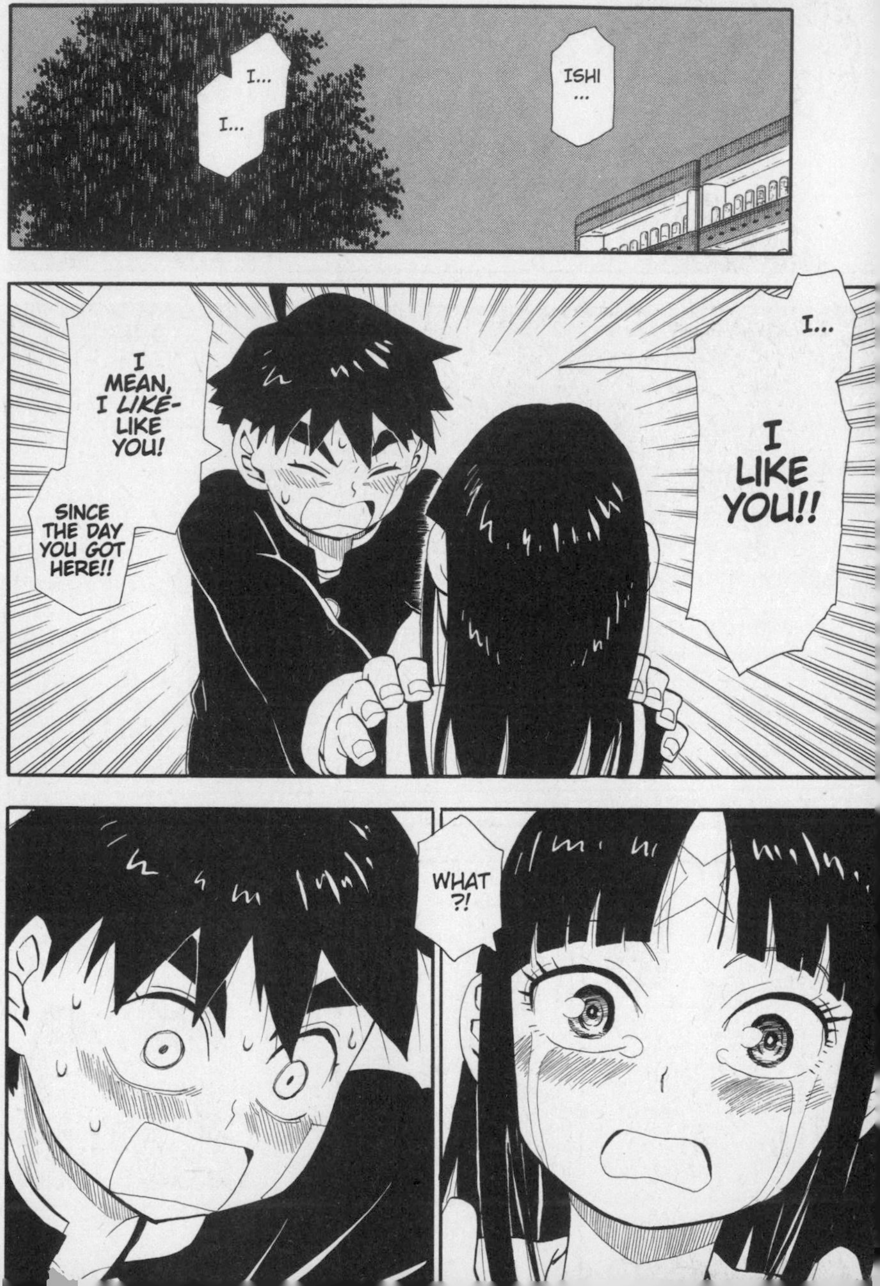
ISHI ...
I... I...
I... I LIKE YOU!!
I MEAN, I *LIKE*-LIKE YOU!
SINCE THE DAY YOU GOT HERE!!
WHAT?!

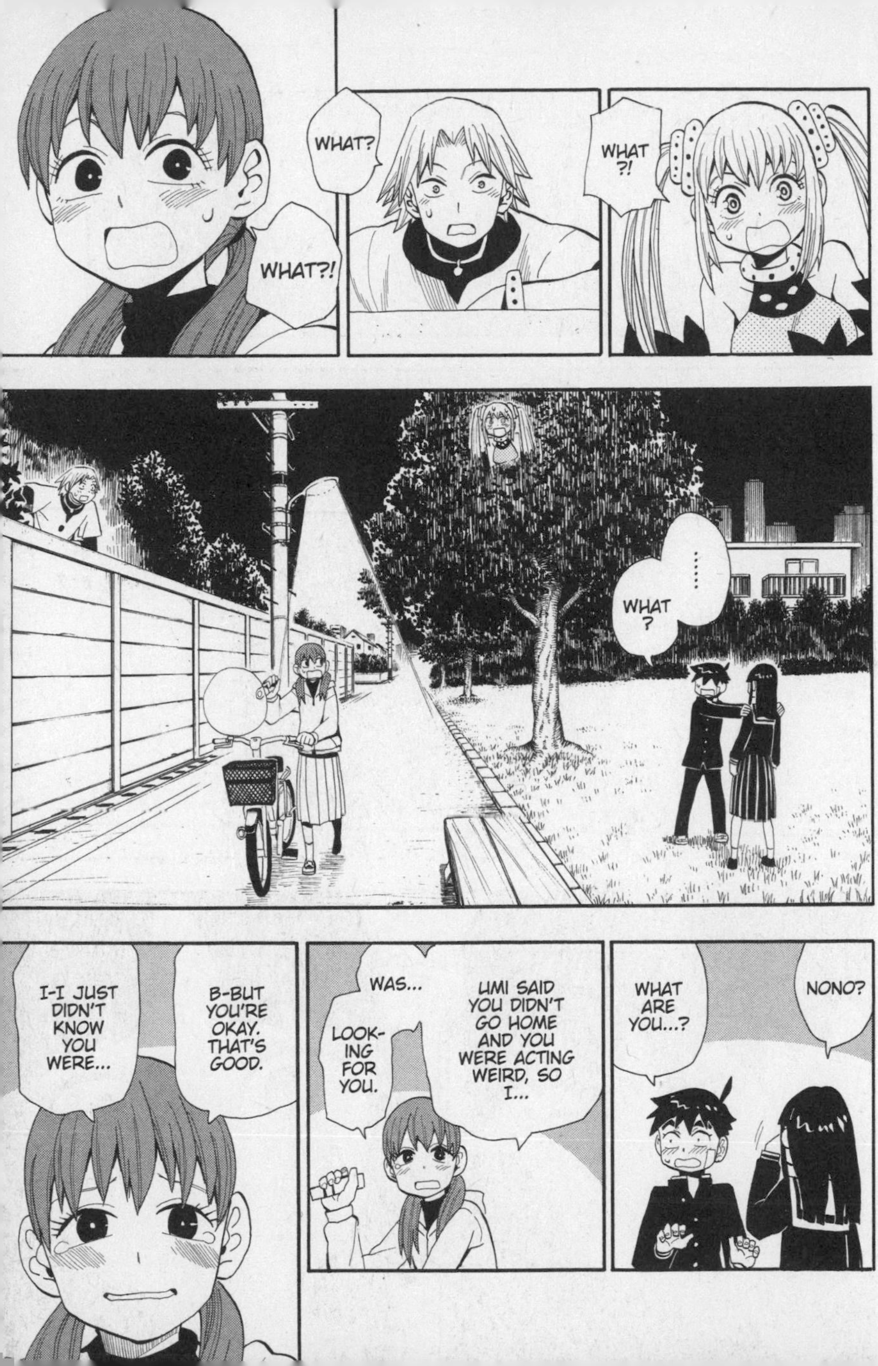
WHAT ?!
WHAT?
WHAT?!
...... WHAT ?
NONO?
WHAT ARE YOU...?
UMI SAID YOU DIDN'T GO HOME AND YOU WERE ACTING WEIRD, SO I...
WAS...
LOOKING FOR YOU.
B-BUT YOU'RE OKAY. THAT'S GOOD.
I-I JUST DIDN'T KNOW YOU WERE...

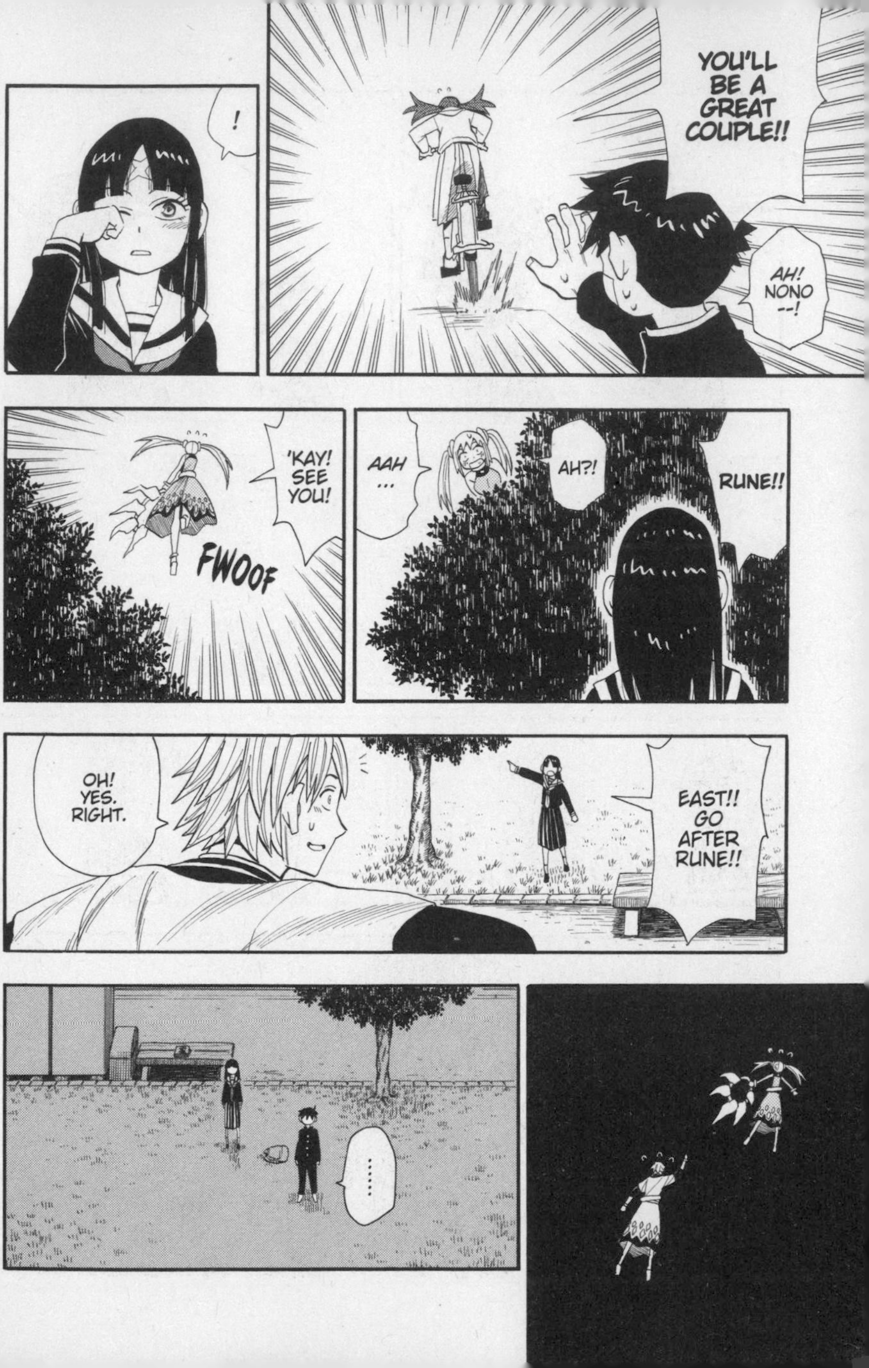
YOU'LL BE A GREAT COUPLE!!
AH! NONO --!
!
RUNE!!
AH?!
AAH ...
'KAY! SEE YOU!
FWOOF
EAST!! GO AFTER RUNE!!
OH! YES. RIGHT.
......

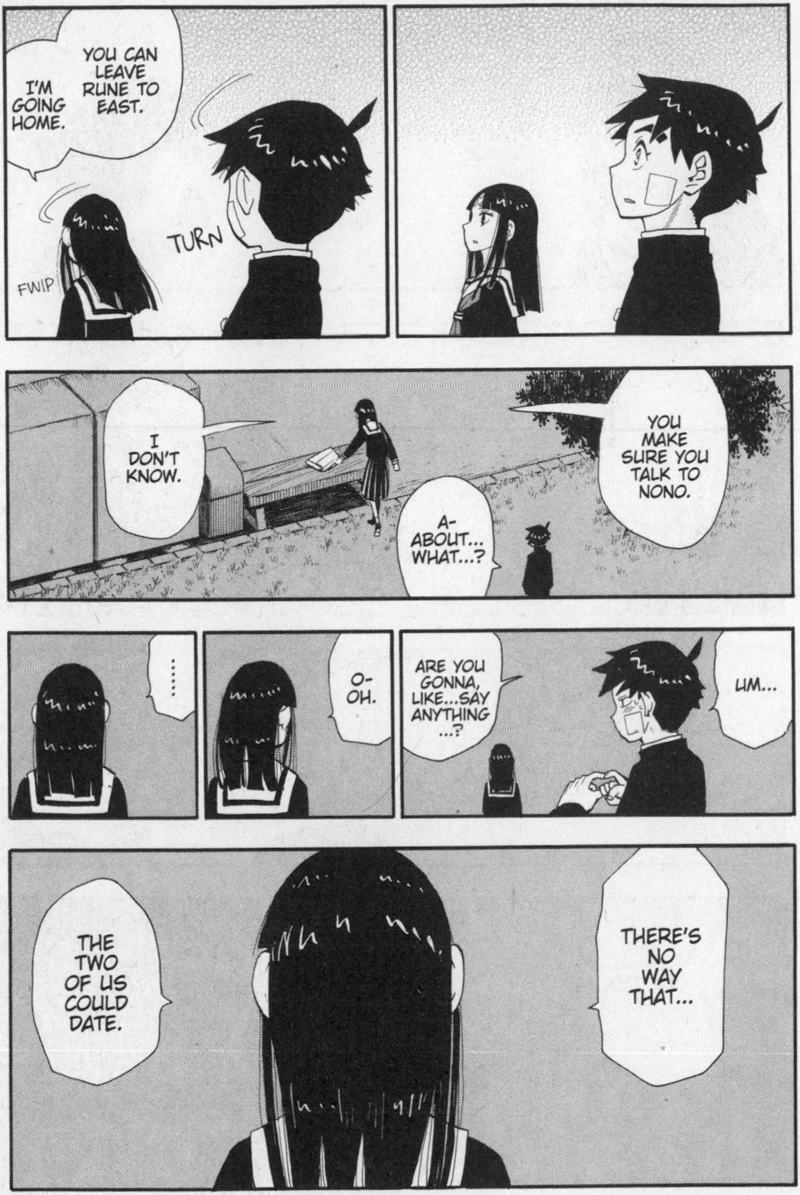
YOU CAN LEAVE RUNE TO EAST.
I'M GOING HOME.
TURN
FWIP
YOU MAKE SURE YOU TALK TO NONO.
A- ABOUT... WHAT...?
I DON'T KNOW.
UM...
ARE YOU GONNA, LIKE...SAY ANYTHING ...?
O- OH.
......
THERE'S NO WAY THAT...
THE TWO OF US COULD DATE.

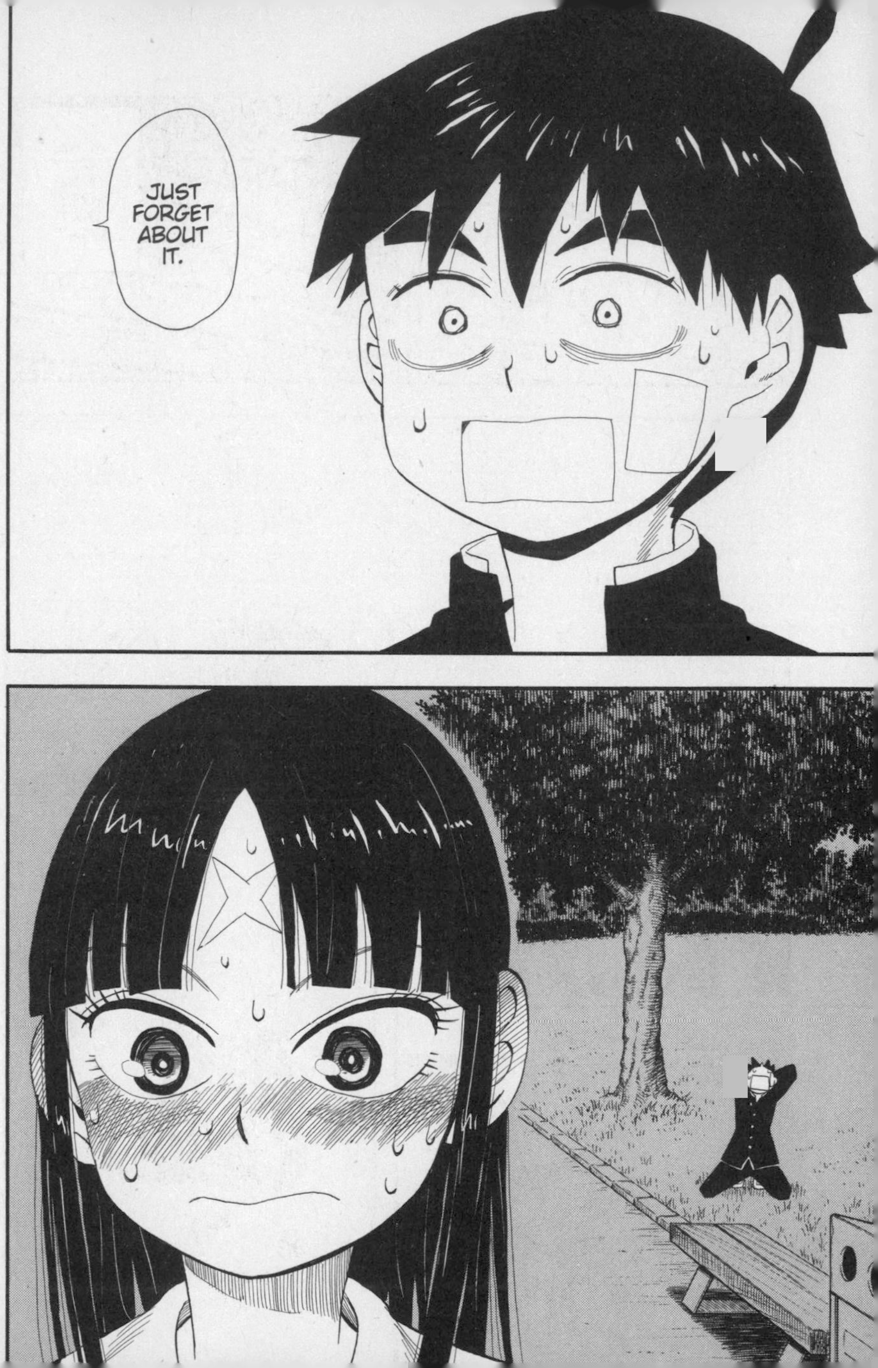
JUST FORGET ABOUT IT.

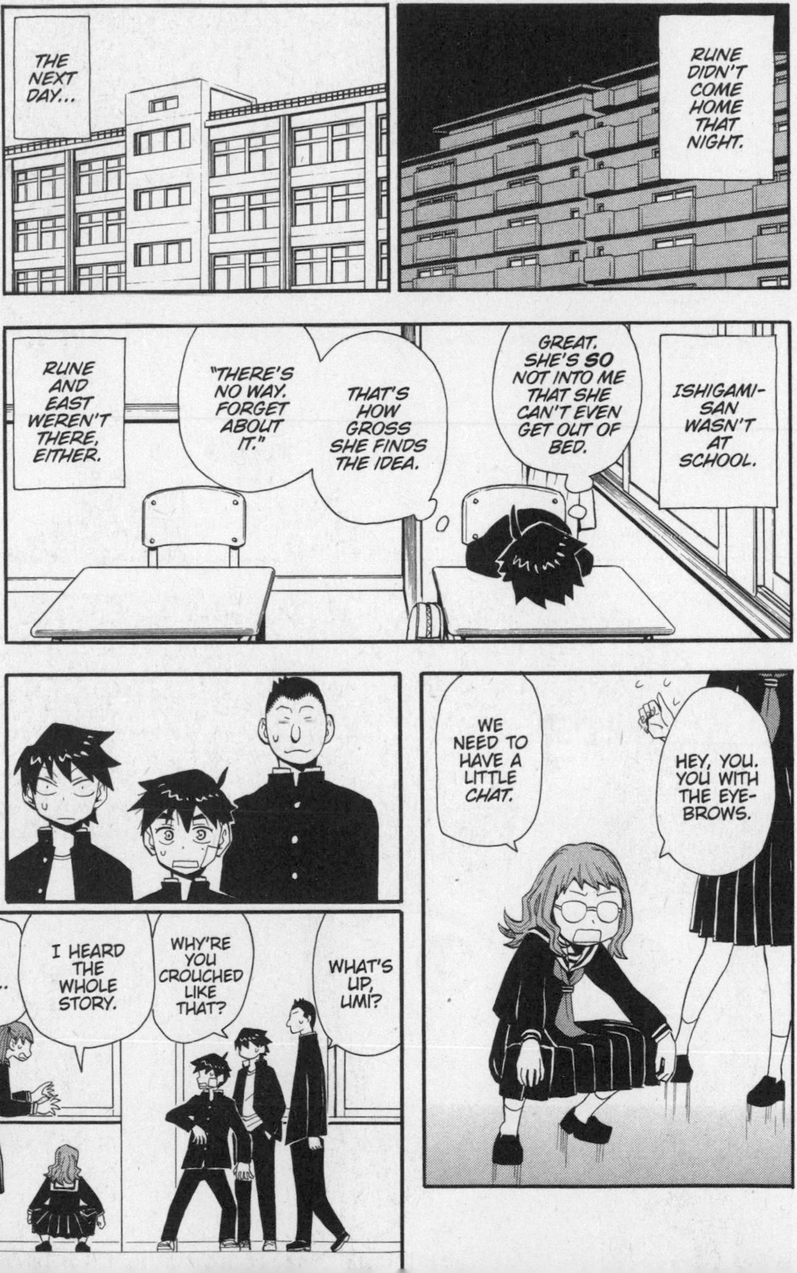
RUNE DIDN'T COME HOME THAT NIGHT.
THE NEXT DAY...
ISHIGAMI-SAN WASN'T AT SCHOOL.
GREAT. SHE'S SO NOT INTO ME THAT SHE CAN'T EVEN GET OUT OF BED.
"THERE'S NO WAY. FORGET ABOUT IT."
THAT'S HOW GROSS SHE FINDS THE IDEA.
RUNE AND EAST WEREN'T THERE, EITHER.
HEY, YOU. YOU WITH THE EYE-BROWS.
WE NEED TO HAVE A LITTLE CHAT.
WHAT'S UP, UMI?
WHY'RE YOU CROUCHED LIKE THAT?
I HEARD THE WHOLE STORY.
U-UMI...

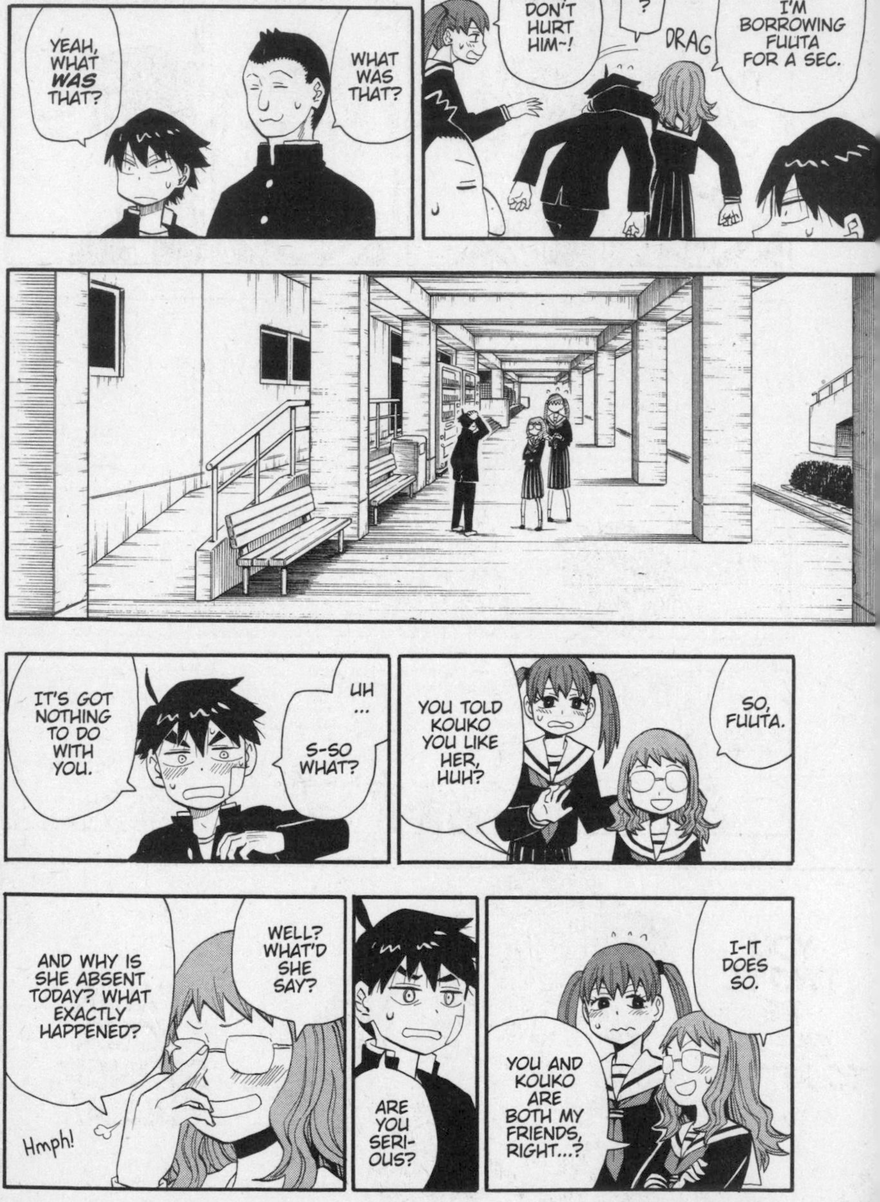
GUYS, I'M BORROWING FUUTA FOR A SEC.
DRAG
?
UMI, DON'T HURT HIM~!
WHAT WAS THAT?
YEAH, WHAT **WAS** THAT?
SO, FUUTA.
YOU TOLD KOUKO YOU LIKE HER, HUH?
UH ...
S-SO WHAT?
IT'S GOT NOTHING TO DO WITH YOU.
I-IT DOES SO.
YOU AND KOUKO ARE BOTH MY FRIENDS, RIGHT...?
ARE YOU SERI-OUS?
WELL? WHAT'D SHE SAY?
AND WHY IS SHE ABSENT TODAY? WHAT EXACTLY HAPPENED?
Hmph!

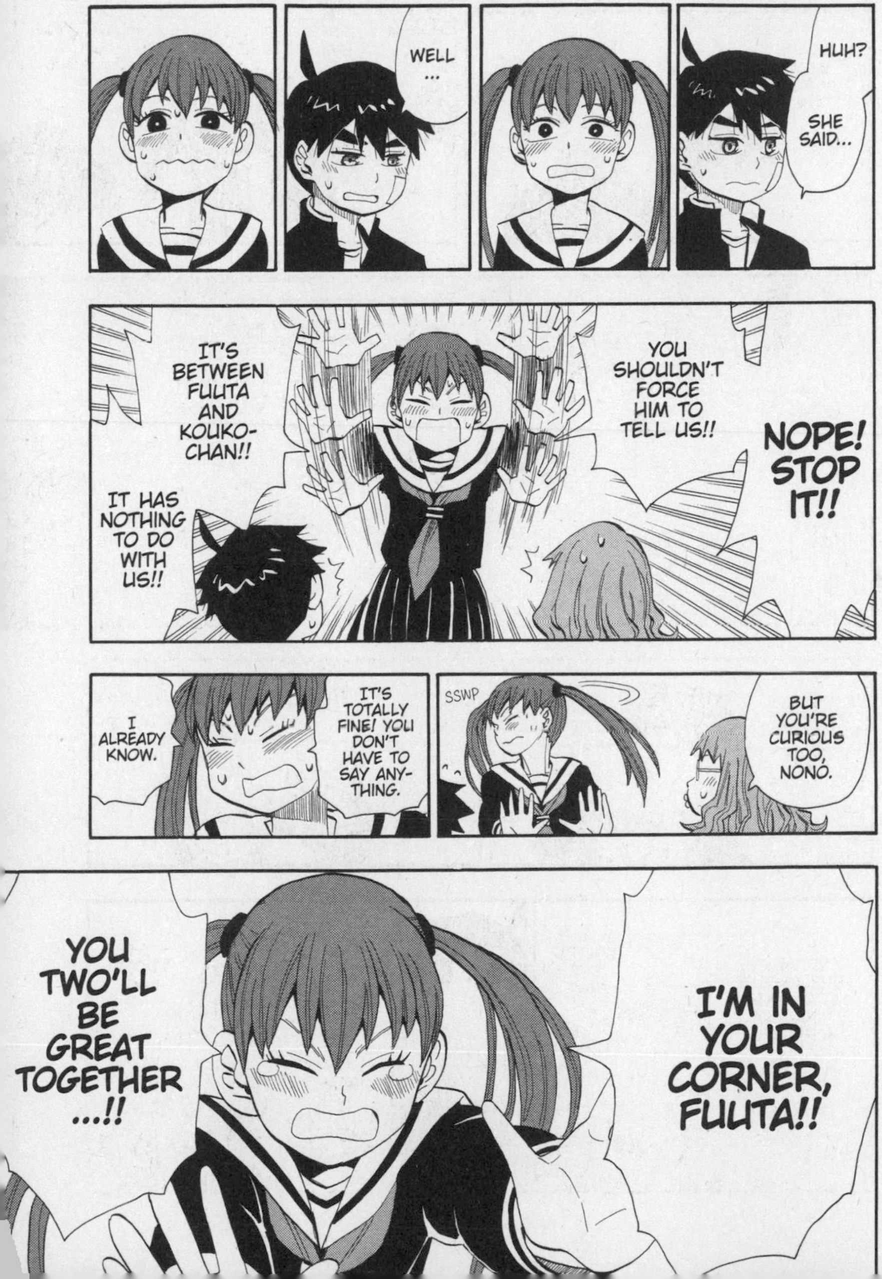
HUH?
SHE SAID...
WELL ...
NOPE! STOP IT!!
YOU SHOULDN'T FORCE HIM TO TELL US!!
IT'S BETWEEN FUUTA AND KOUKO-CHAN!!
IT HAS NOTHING TO DO WITH US!!
BUT YOU'RE CURIOUS TOO, NONO.
SSWP
IT'S TOTALLY FINE! YOU DON'T HAVE TO SAY ANY-THING.
I ALREADY KNOW.
I'M IN YOUR CORNER, FUUTA!!
YOU TWO'LL BE GREAT TOGETHER ...!!

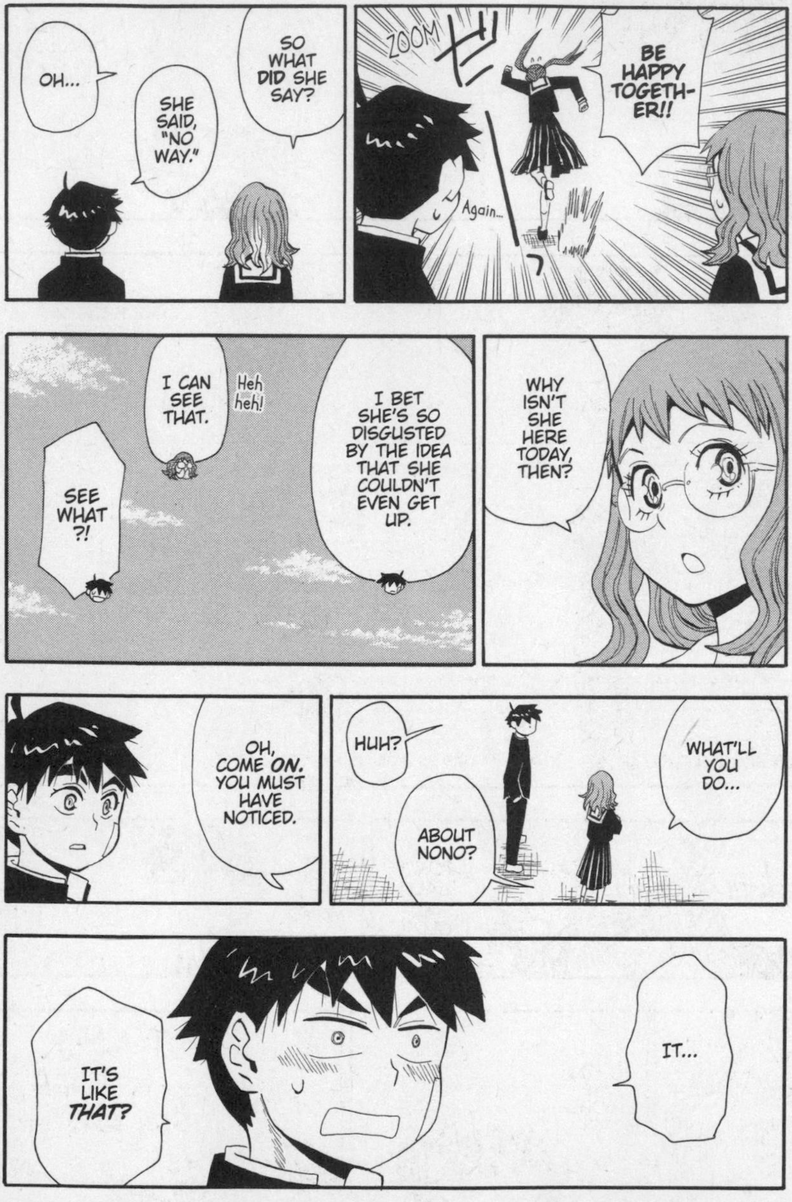
BE HAPPY TOGETH-ER!!
ZOOM
Again...
SO WHAT DID SHE SAY?
SHE SAID, "NO WAY."
OH...
WHY ISN'T SHE HERE TODAY, THEN?
I BET SHE'S SO DISGUSTED BY THE IDEA THAT SHE COULDN'T EVEN GET UP.
I CAN SEE THAT.
Heh heh!
SEE WHAT?!
WHAT'LL YOU DO...
ABOUT NONO?
HUH?
OH, COME ON. YOU MUST HAVE NOTICED.
IT...
IT'S LIKE THAT?

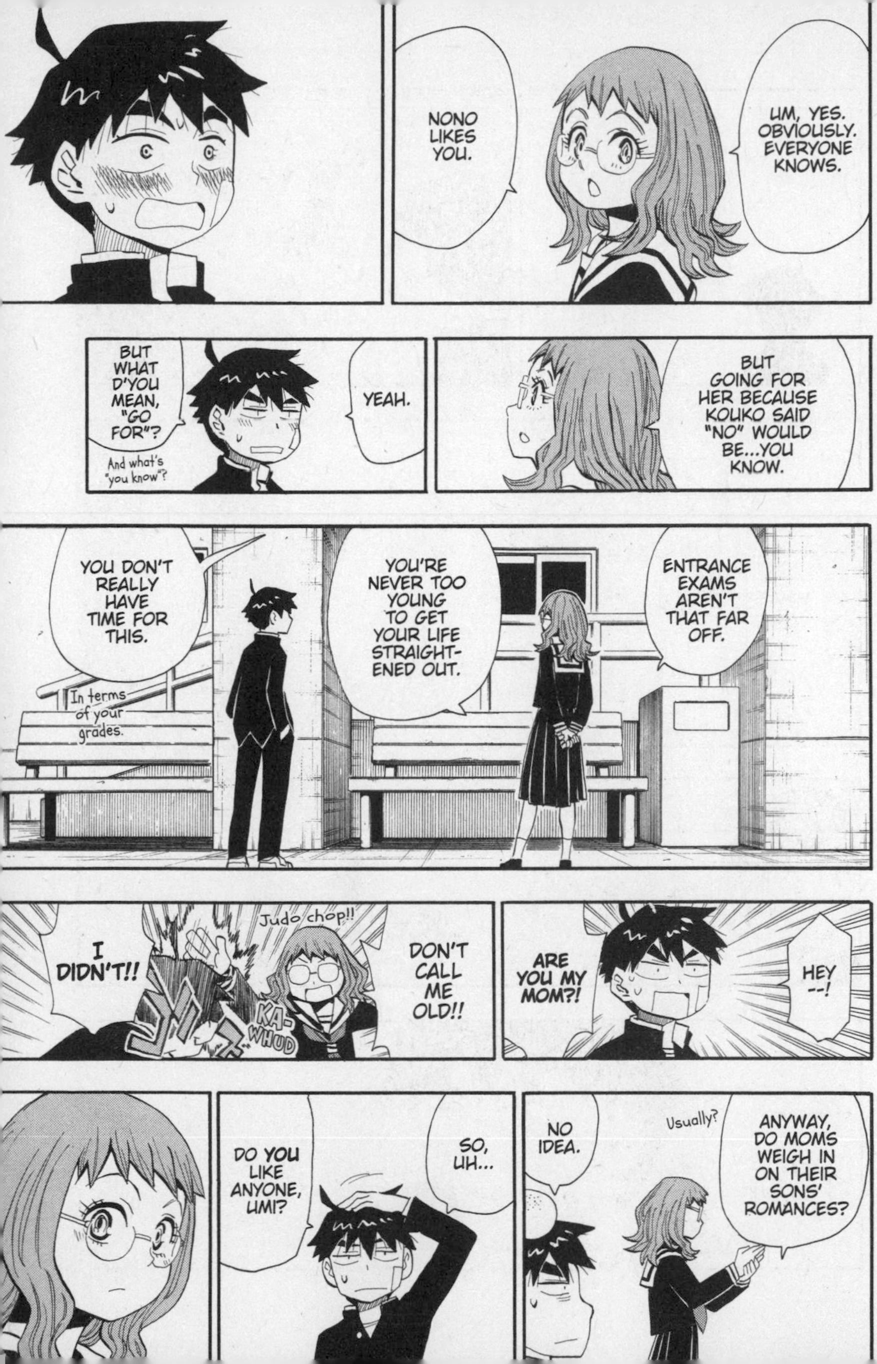

UM, YES. OBVIOUSLY. EVERYONE KNOWS.
NONO LIKES YOU.
BUT GOING FOR HER BECAUSE KOUKO SAID "NO" WOULD BE...YOU KNOW.
YEAH.
BUT WHAT D'YOU MEAN, "GO FOR"?
And what's "you know"?
ENTRANCE EXAMS AREN'T THAT FAR OFF.
YOU'RE NEVER TOO YOUNG TO GET YOUR LIFE STRAIGHT-ENED OUT.
YOU DON'T REALLY HAVE TIME FOR THIS.
In terms of your grades.
HEY--!
ARE YOU MY MOM?!
DON'T CALL ME OLD!!
Judo chop!!
KA-WHUD
I DIDN'T!!
ANYWAY, DO MOMS WEIGH IN ON THEIR SONS' ROMANCES?
Usually?
NO IDEA.
SO, UH...
DO YOU LIKE ANYONE, UMI?

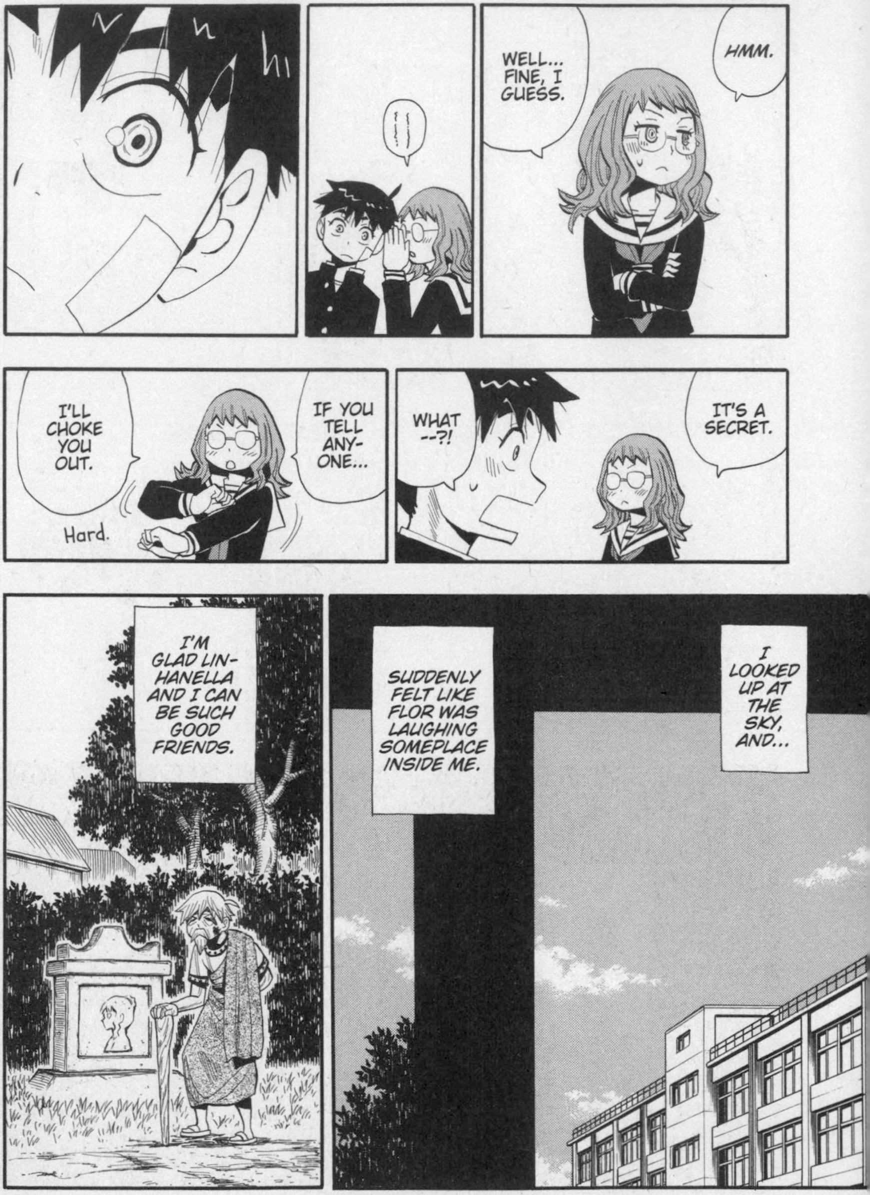
HMM.
WELL... FINE, I GUESS.
IT'S A SECRET.
WHAT --?!
IF YOU TELL ANY-ONE...
I'LL CHOKE YOU OUT.
Hard.
I LOOKED UP AT THE SKY, AND...
SUDDENLY FELT LIKE FLOR WAS LAUGHING SOMEPLACE INSIDE ME.
I'M GLAD LIN-HANELLA AND I CAN BE SUCH GOOD FRIENDS.

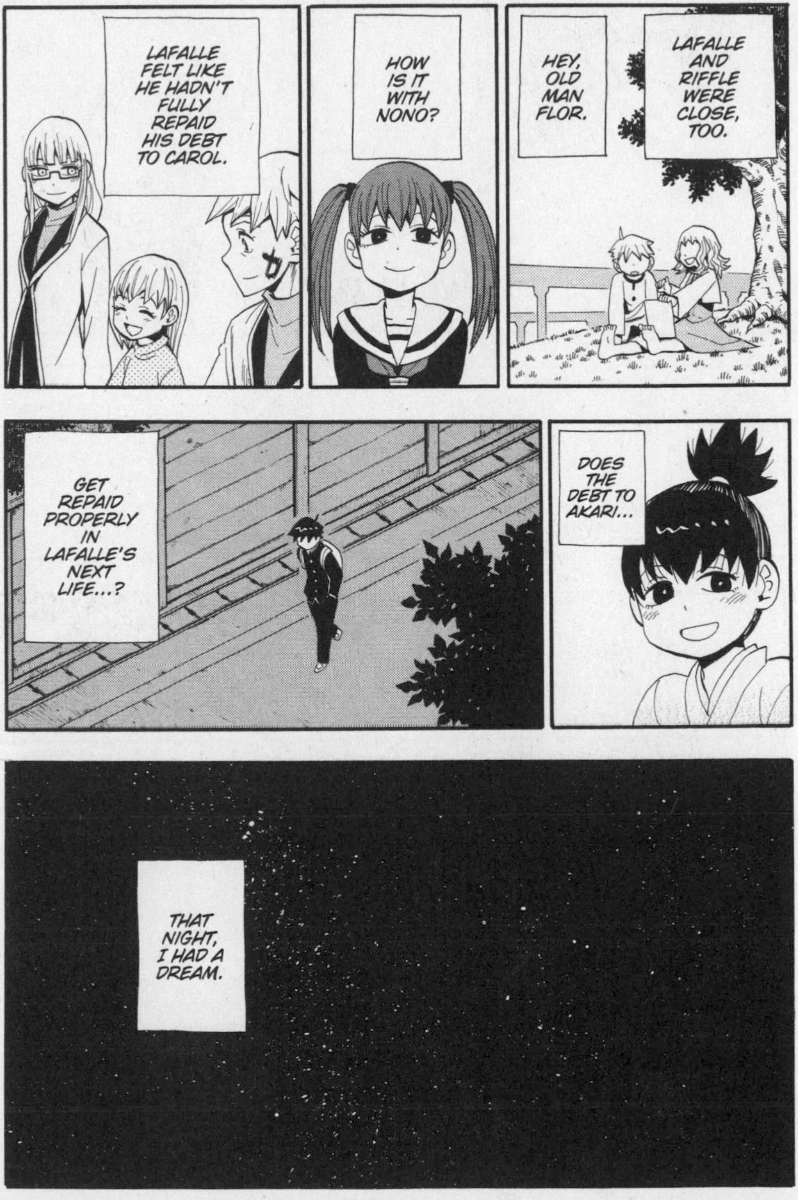
LAFALLE AND RIFFLE WERE CLOSE, TOO.
HEY, OLD MAN FLOR.
HOW IS IT WITH NONO?
LAFALLE FELT LIKE HE HADN'T FULLY REPAID HIS DEBT TO CAROL.
DOES THE DEBT TO AKARI...
GET REPAID PROPERLY IN LAFALLE'S NEXT LIFE...?
THAT NIGHT, I HAD A DREAM.

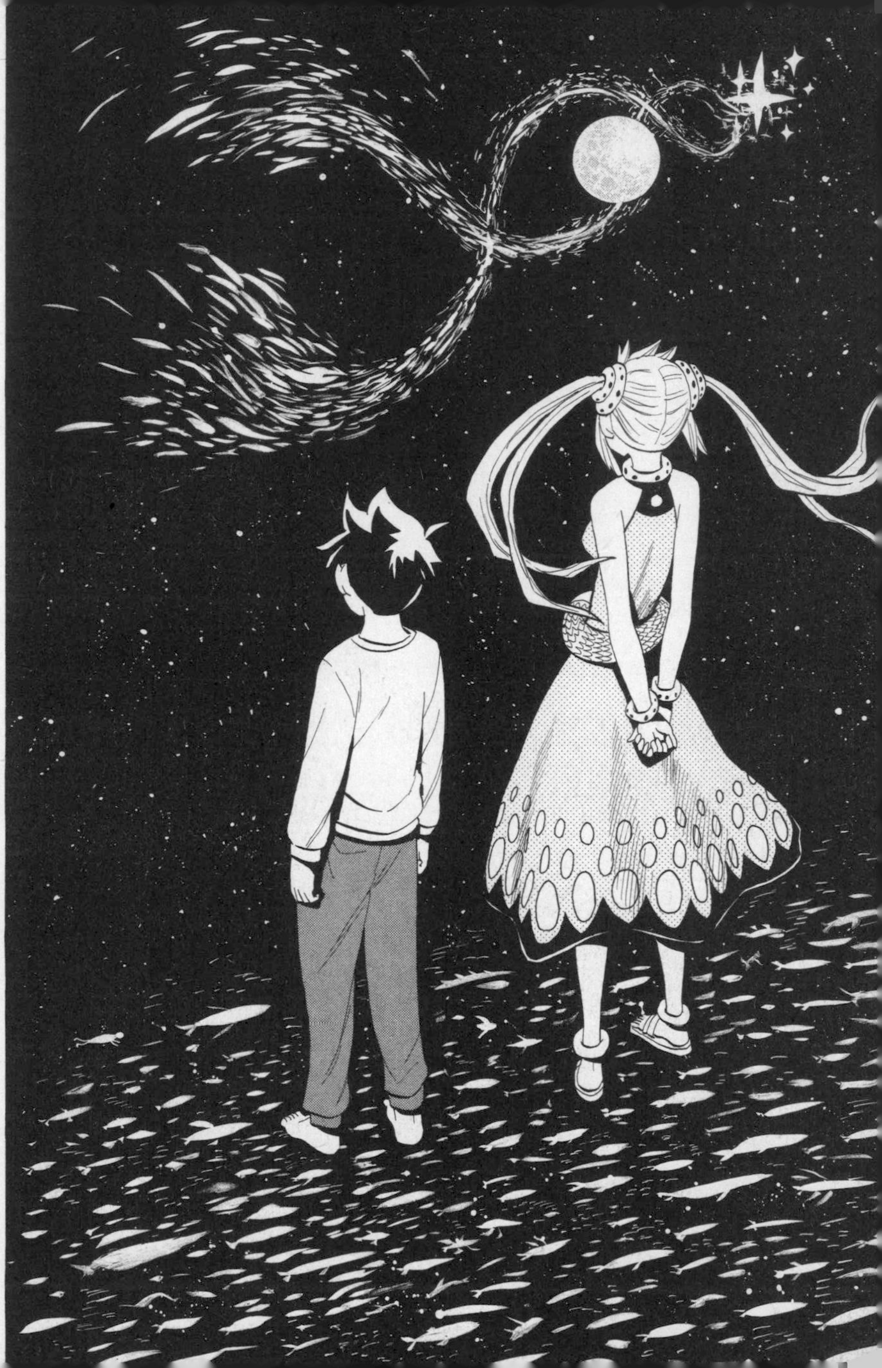

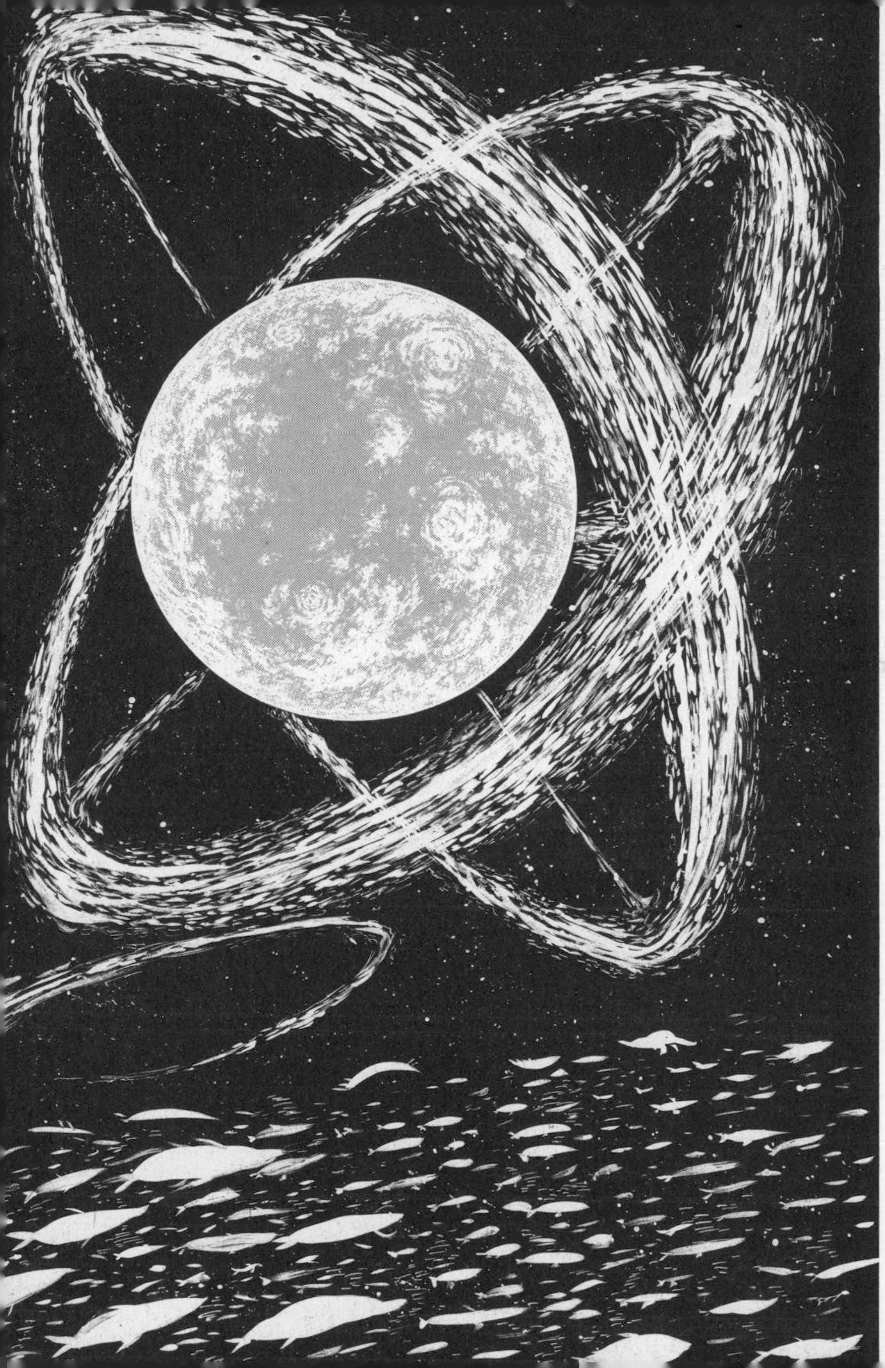

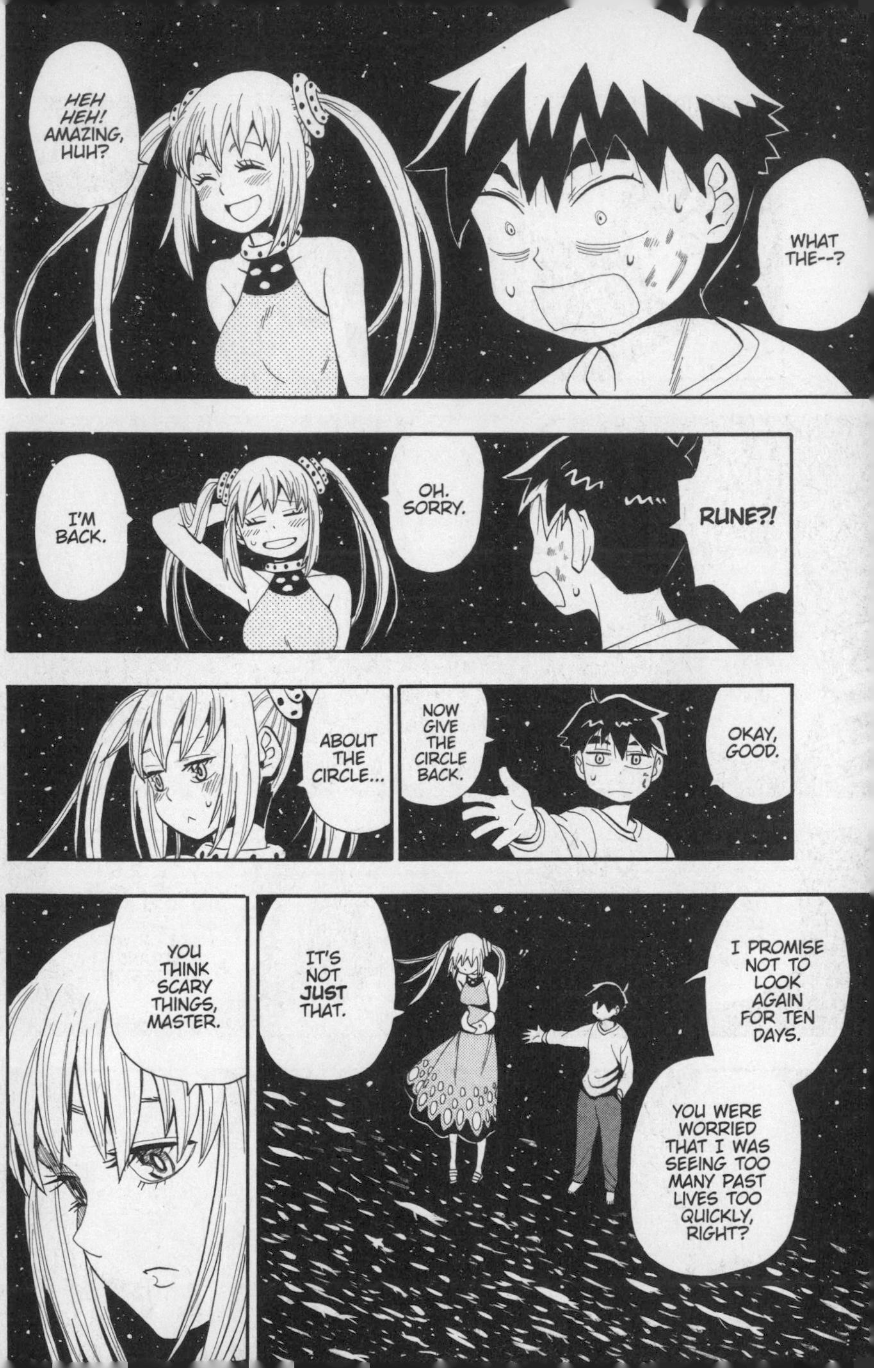
WHAT THE--?
HEH HEH! AMAZING, HUH?
RUNE?!
OH. SORRY.
I'M BACK.
OKAY, GOOD.
NOW GIVE THE CIRCLE BACK.
ABOUT THE CIRCLE...
I PROMISE NOT TO LOOK AGAIN FOR TEN DAYS.
YOU WERE WORRIED THAT I WAS SEEING TOO MANY PAST LIVES TOO QUICKLY, RIGHT?
IT'S NOT JUST THAT.
YOU THINK SCARY THINGS, MASTER.

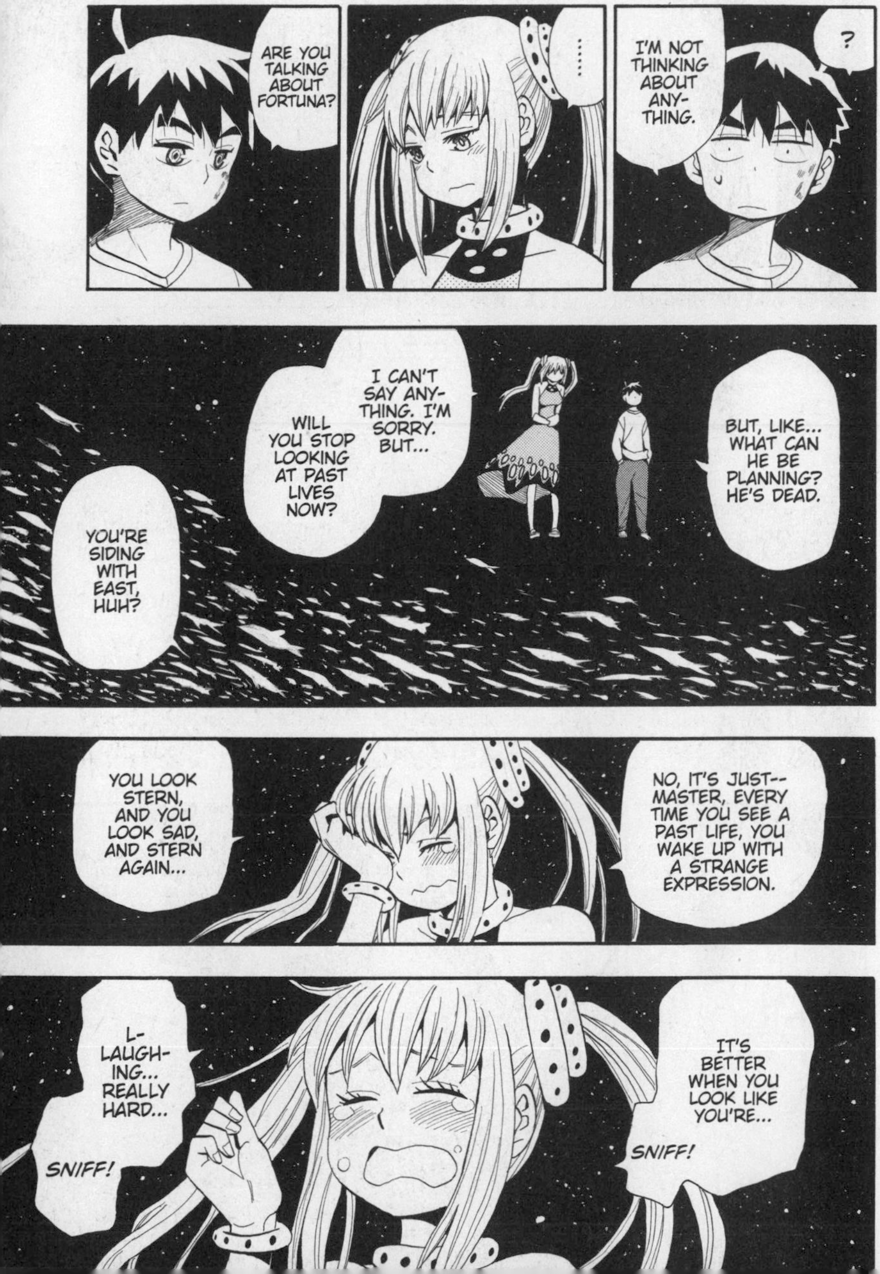
?
I'M NOT THINKING ABOUT ANYTHING.
......
ARE YOU TALKING ABOUT FORTUNA?
BUT, LIKE... WHAT CAN HE BE PLANNING? HE'S DEAD.
I CAN'T SAY ANYTHING. I'M SORRY. BUT...
WILL YOU STOP LOOKING AT PAST LIVES NOW?
YOU'RE SIDING WITH EAST, HUH?
NO, IT'S JUST-- MASTER, EVERY TIME YOU SEE A PAST LIFE, YOU WAKE UP WITH A STRANGE EXPRESSION.
YOU LOOK STERN, AND YOU LOOK SAD, AND STERN AGAIN...
IT'S BETTER WHEN YOU LOOK LIKE YOU'RE...
SNIFF!
L-LAUGHING... REALLY HARD...
SNIFF!

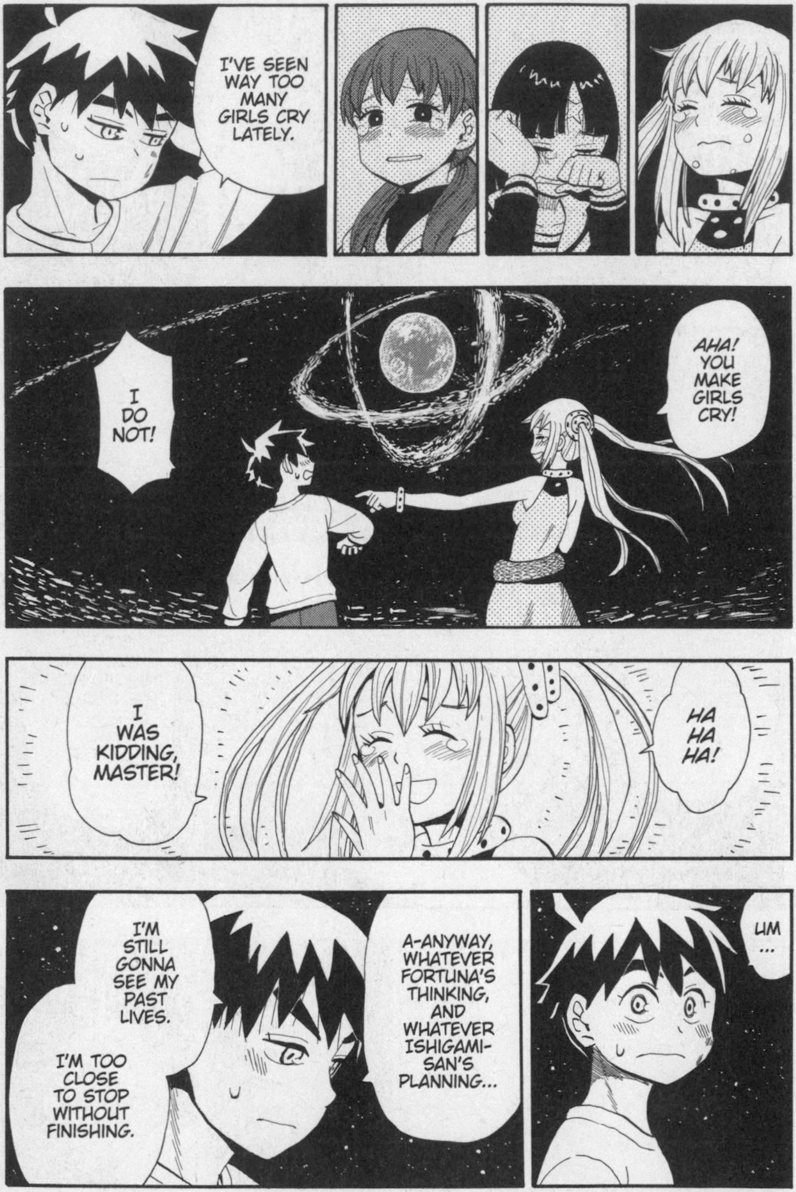
I'VE SEEN WAY TOO MANY GIRLS CRY LATELY.
AHA! YOU MAKE GIRLS CRY!
I DO NOT!
HA HA HA!
I WAS KIDDING, MASTER!
UM...
A-ANYWAY, WHATEVER FORTUNA'S THINKING, AND WHATEVER ISHIGAMI-SAN'S PLANNING...
I'M STILL GONNA SEE MY PAST LIVES.
I'M TOO CLOSE TO STOP WITHOUT FINISHING.

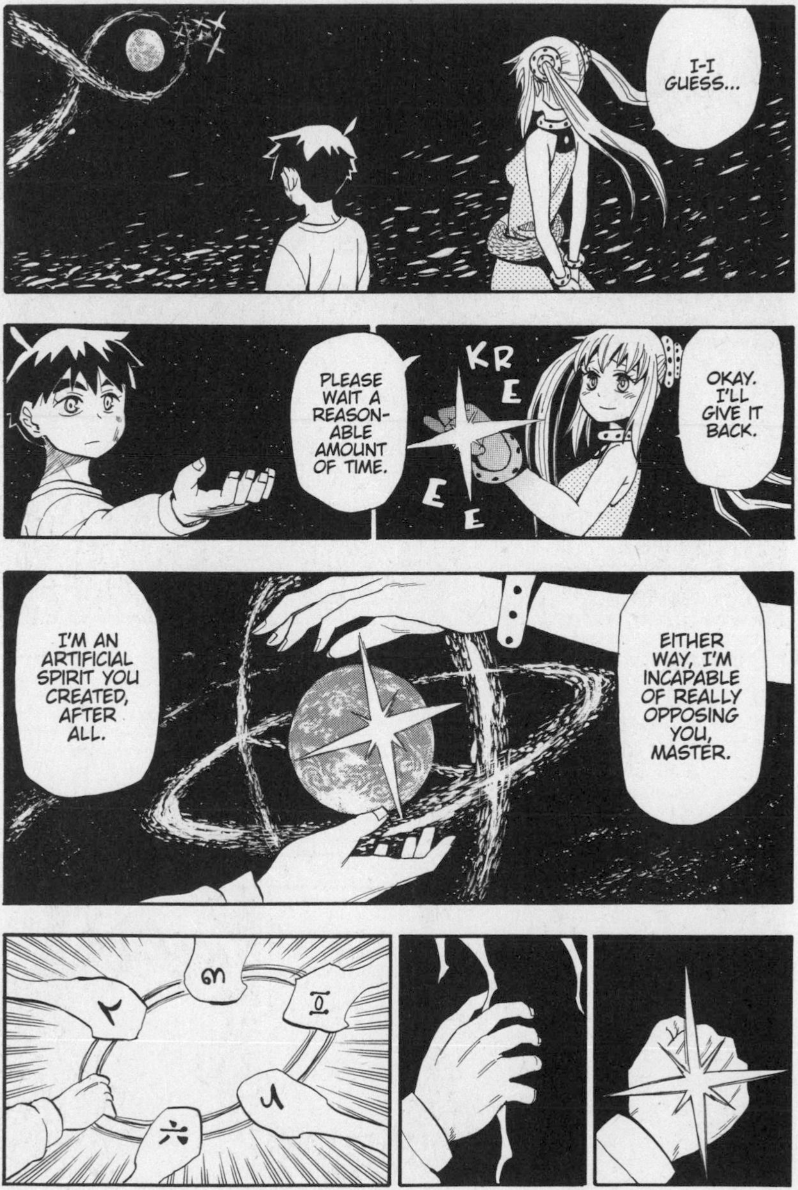
I-I GUESS...
OKAY. I'LL GIVE IT BACK.
KREEE
PLEASE WAIT A REASON-ABLE AMOUNT OF TIME.
EITHER WAY, I'M INCAPABLE OF REALLY OPPOSING YOU, MASTER.
I'M AN ARTIFICIAL SPIRIT YOU CREATED, AFTER ALL.

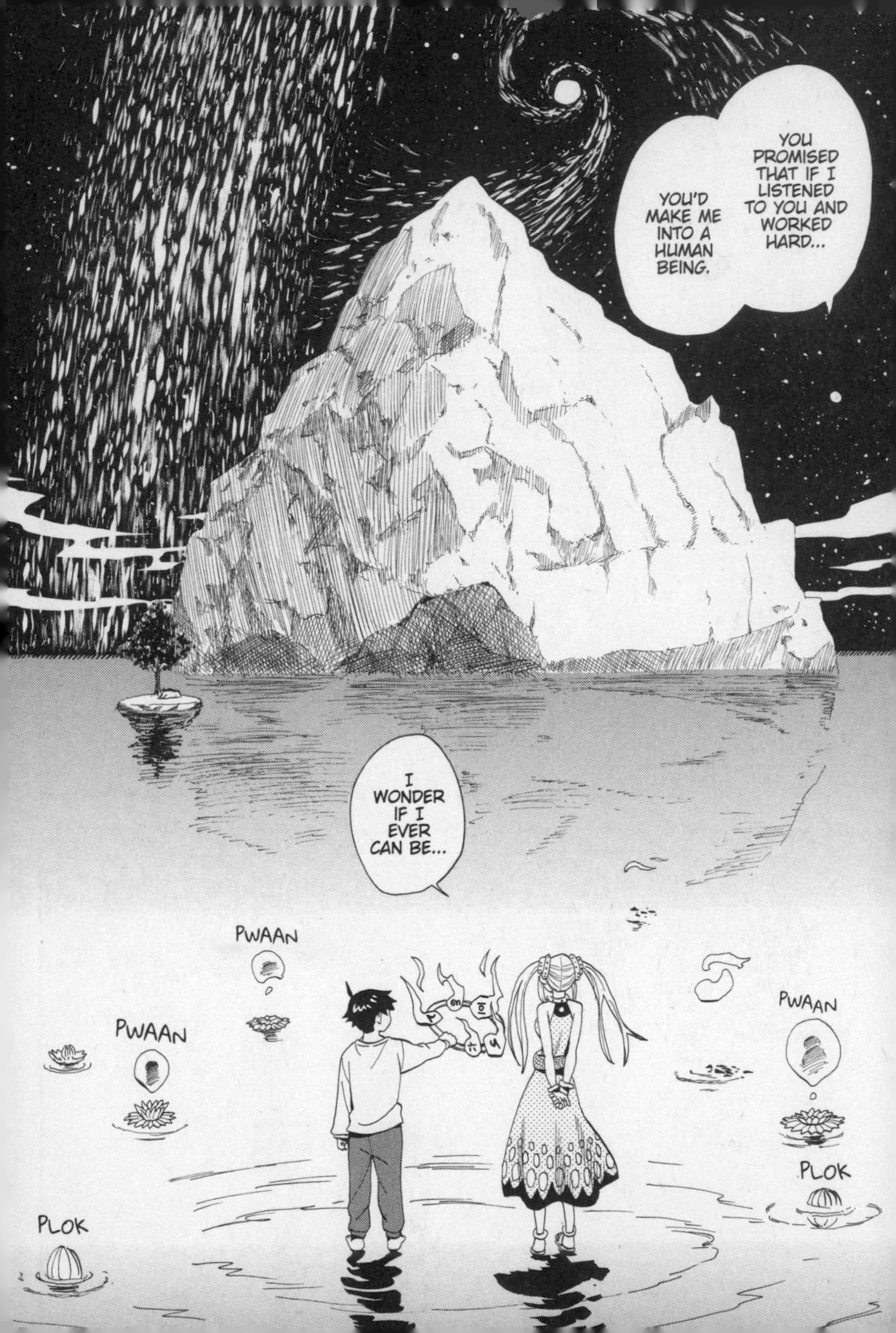
YOU PROMISED THAT IF I LISTENED TO YOU AND WORKED HARD...
YOU'D MAKE ME INTO A HUMAN BEING.
I WONDER IF I EVER CAN BE...
PWAAN
PLOK
PWAAN
PWAAN
PLOK

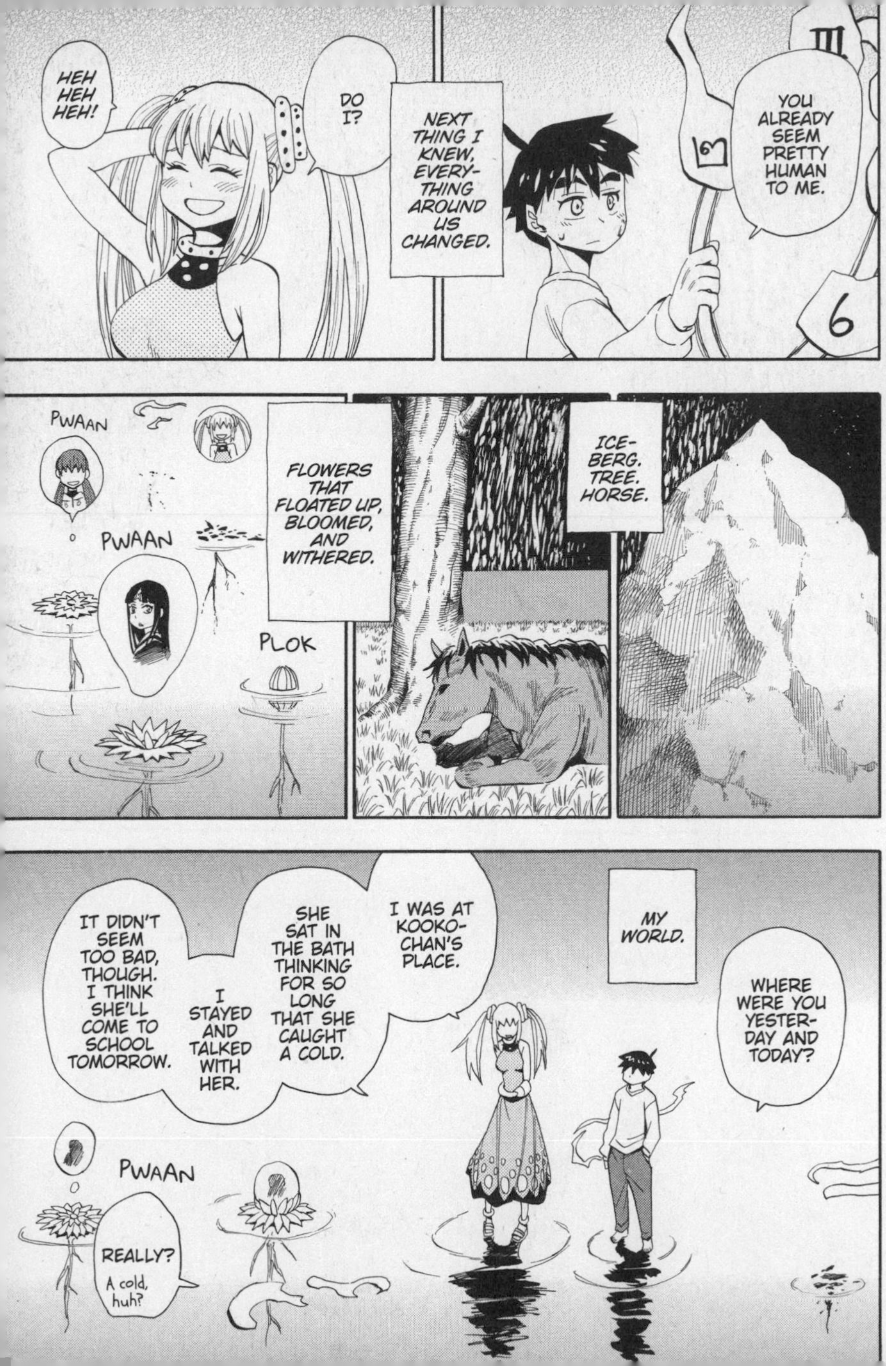
YOU ALREADY SEEM PRETTY HUMAN TO ME.
NEXT THING I KNEW, EVERYTHING AROUND US CHANGED.
DO I?
HEH HEH HEH!
ICEBERG. TREE. HORSE.
FLOWERS THAT FLOATED UP, BLOOMED, AND WITHERED.
PWAAN
PWAAN
PLOK
MY WORLD.
WHERE WERE YOU YESTERDAY AND TODAY?
I WAS AT KOOKO-CHAN'S PLACE.
SHE SAT IN THE BATH THINKING FOR SO LONG THAT SHE CAUGHT A COLD.
I STAYED AND TALKED WITH HER.
IT DIDN'T SEEM TOO BAD, THOUGH. I THINK SHE'LL COME TO SCHOOL TOMORROW.
PWAAN
REALLY?
A cold, huh?

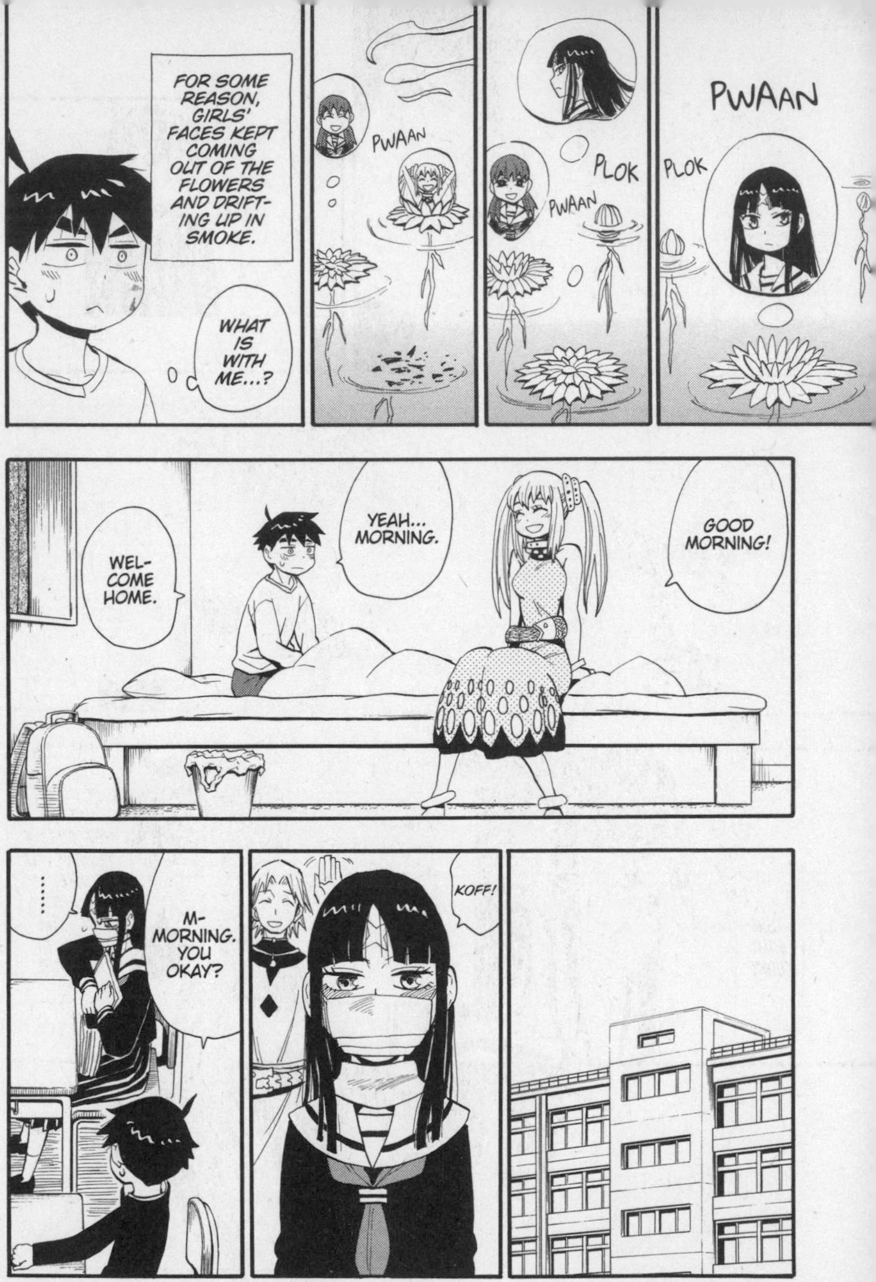
PWAAN
PLOK
PLOK
PWAAN
PWAAN
FOR SOME REASON, GIRLS' FACES KEPT COMING OUT OF THE FLOWERS AND DRIFTING UP IN SMOKE.
WHAT IS WITH ME...?
GOOD MORNING!
YEAH... MORNING.
WELCOME HOME.
KOFF!
M-MORNING. YOU OKAY?
......

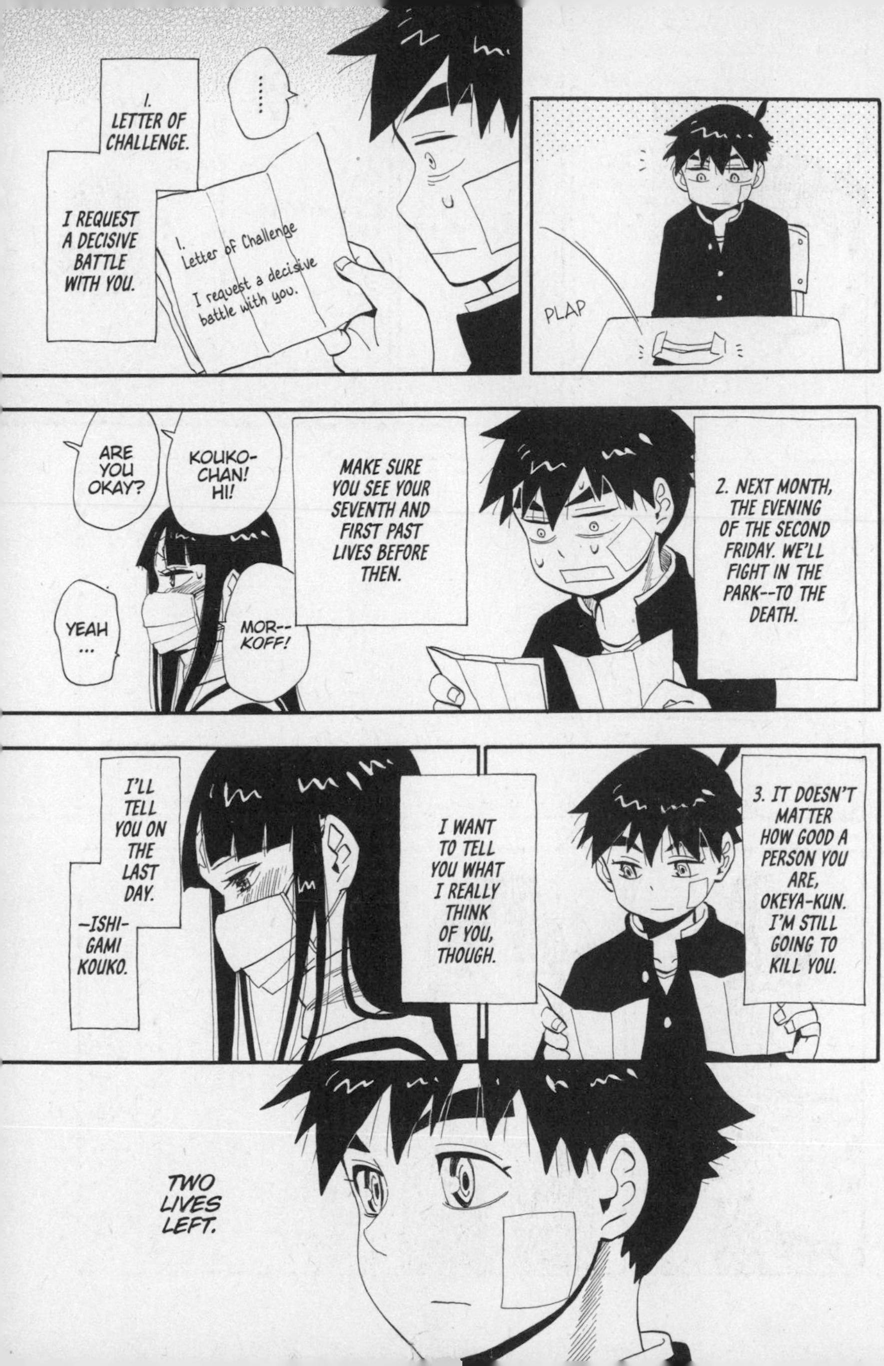
PLAP
......
1. LETTER OF CHALLENGE.
I REQUEST A DECISIVE BATTLE WITH YOU.
1. Letter of Challenge
I request a decisive battle with you.
2. NEXT MONTH, THE EVENING OF THE SECOND FRIDAY. WE'LL FIGHT IN THE PARK--TO THE DEATH.
MAKE SURE YOU SEE YOUR SEVENTH AND FIRST PAST LIVES BEFORE THEN.
KOUKO-CHAN! HI!
ARE YOU OKAY?
MOR--KOFF!
YEAH ...
3. IT DOESN'T MATTER HOW GOOD A PERSON YOU ARE, OKEYA-KUN. I'M STILL GOING TO KILL YOU.
I WANT TO TELL YOU WHAT I REALLY THINK OF YOU, THOUGH.
I'LL TELL YOU ON THE LAST DAY.
—ISHIGAMI KOUKO.
TWO LIVES LEFT.

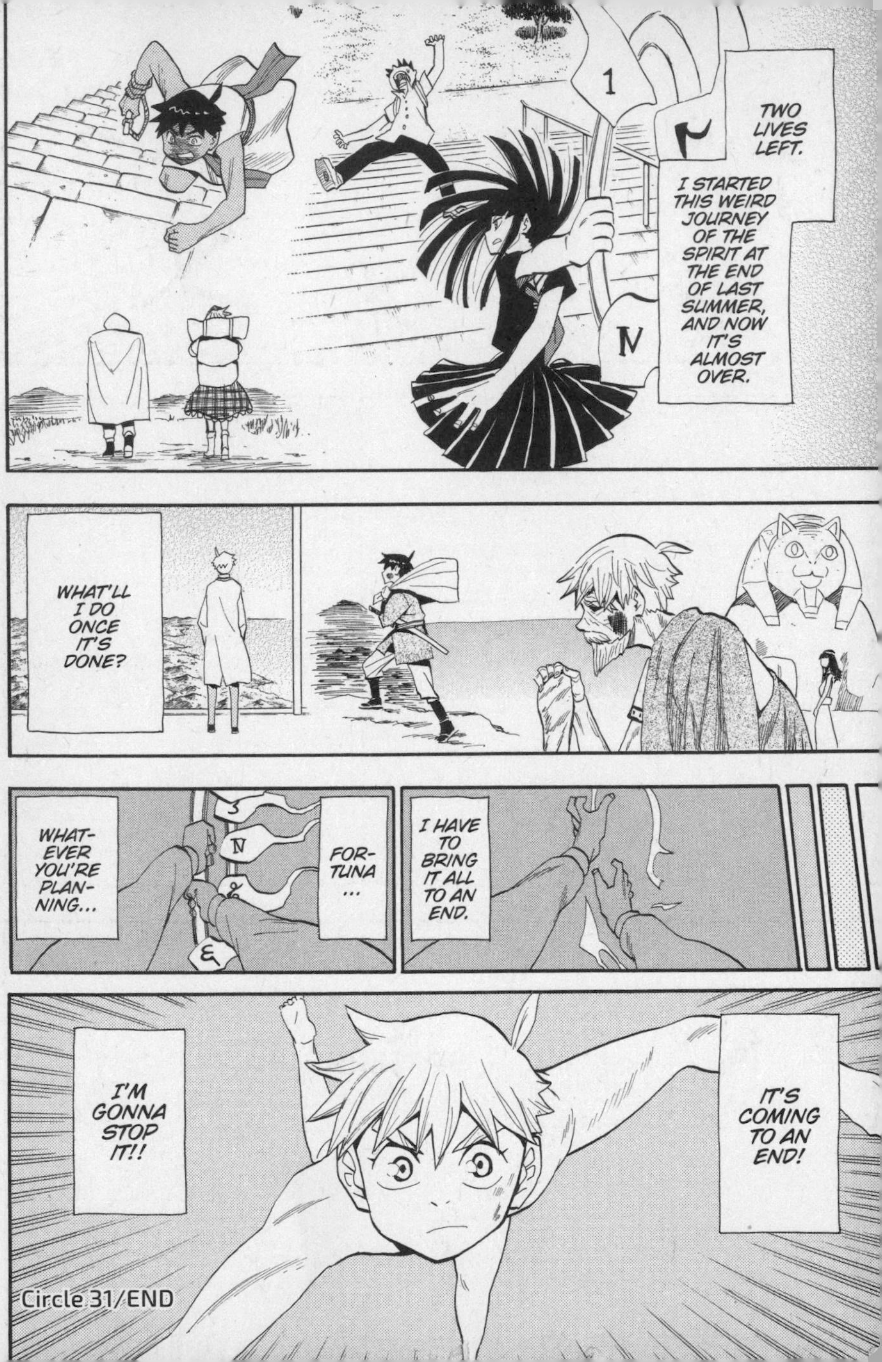
TWO LIVES LEFT.
I STARTED THIS WEIRD JOURNEY OF THE SPIRIT AT THE END OF LAST SUMMER, AND NOW IT'S ALMOST OVER.
WHAT'LL I DO ONCE IT'S DONE?
I HAVE TO BRING IT ALL TO AN END.
FOR-TUNA...
WHAT-EVER YOU'RE PLAN-NING...
IT'S COMING TO AN END!
I'M GONNA STOP IT!!
Circle 31/END

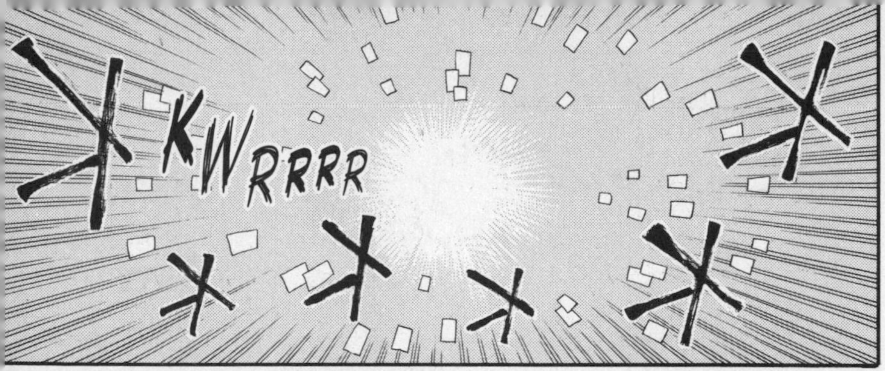
KWRRRR

Circle 32

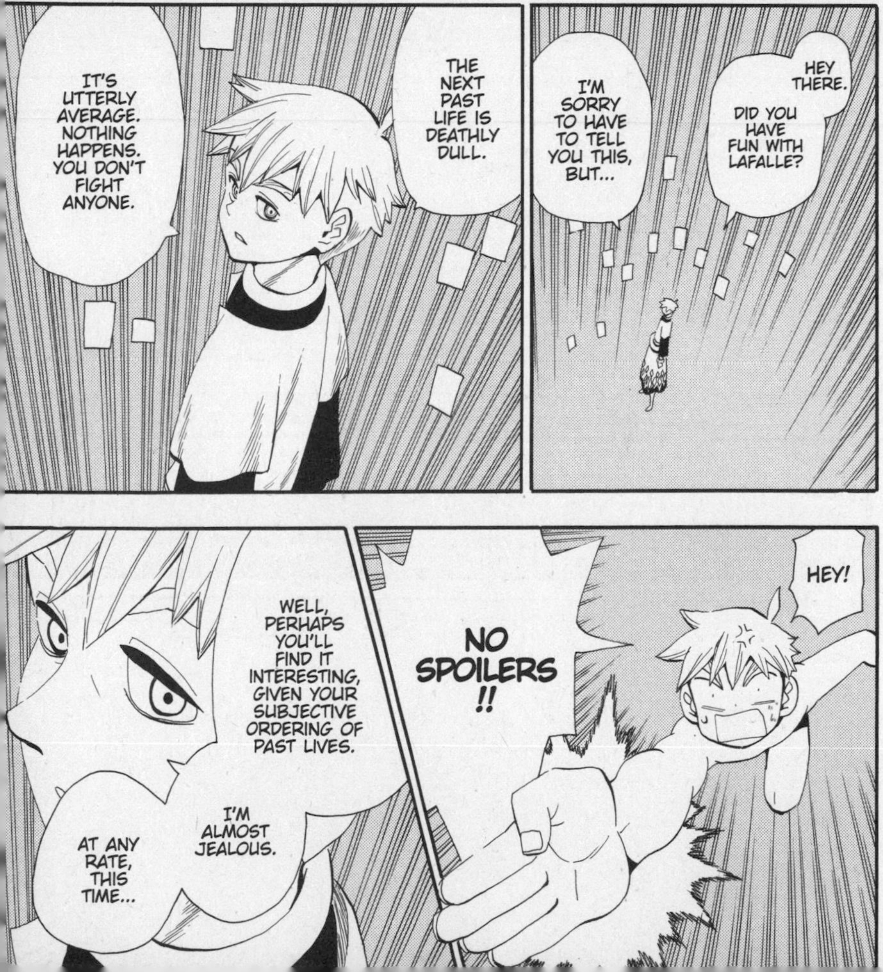
HEY THERE.
DID YOU HAVE FUN WITH LAFALLE?
I'M SORRY TO HAVE TO TELL YOU THIS, BUT...
THE NEXT PAST LIFE IS DEATHLY DULL.
IT'S UTTERLY AVERAGE. NOTHING HAPPENS. YOU DON'T FIGHT ANYONE.
HEY!
NO SPOILERS!!
WELL, PERHAPS YOU'LL FIND IT INTERESTING, GIVEN YOUR SUBJECTIVE ORDERING OF PAST LIVES.
I'M ALMOST JEALOUS.
AT ANY RATE, THIS TIME...

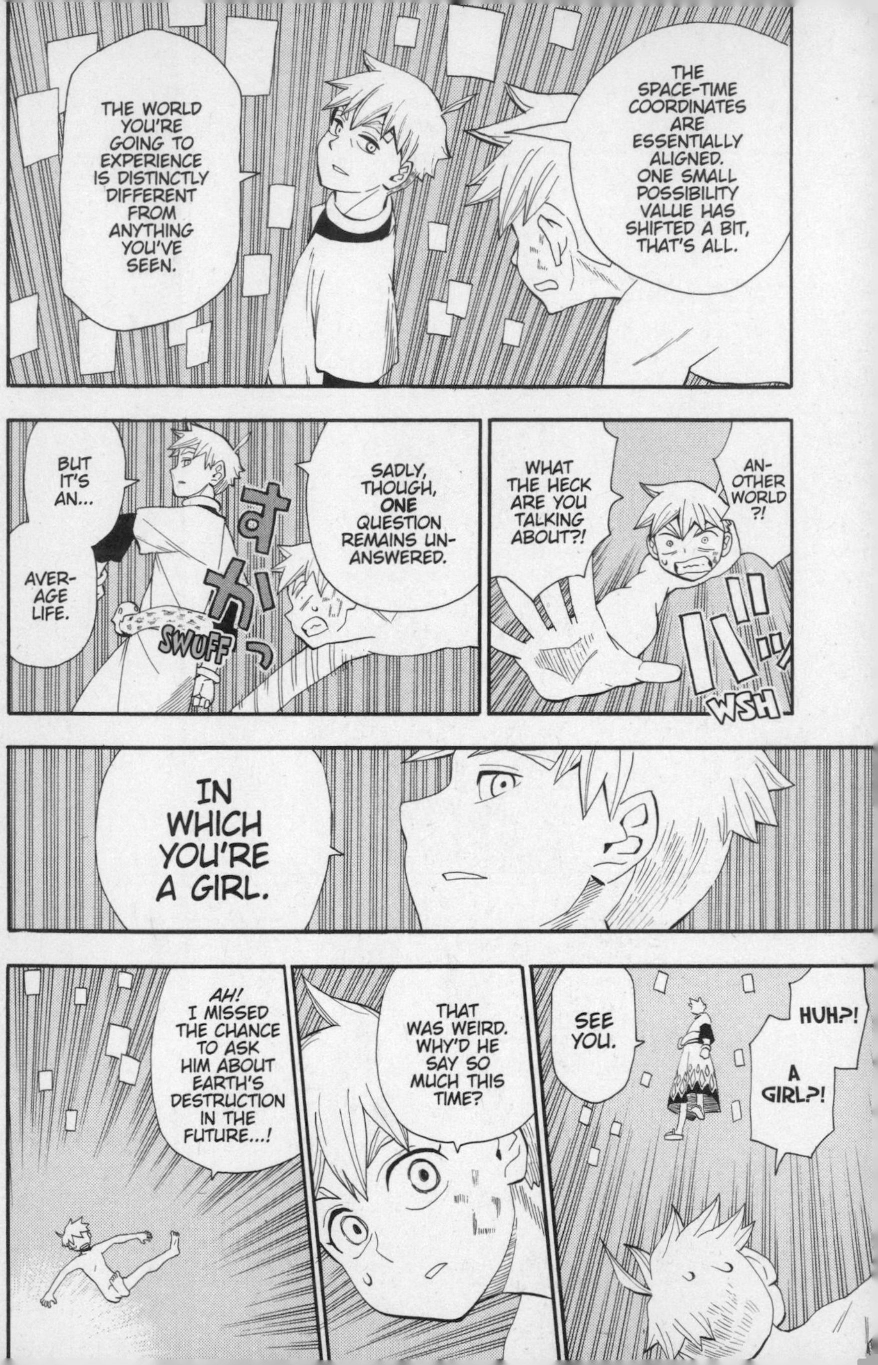
THE SPACE-TIME COORDINATES ARE ESSENTIALLY ALIGNED. ONE SMALL POSSIBILITY VALUE HAS SHIFTED A BIT, THAT'S ALL.
THE WORLD YOU'RE GOING TO EXPERIENCE IS DISTINCTLY DIFFERENT FROM ANYTHING YOU'VE SEEN.
AN-OTHER WORLD?!
WHAT THE HECK ARE YOU TALKING ABOUT?!
WSH
SADLY, THOUGH, ONE QUESTION REMAINS UN-ANSWERED.
すかっ
SWUFF
BUT IT'S AN...
AVER-AGE LIFE.
IN WHICH YOU'RE A GIRL.
HUH?!
A GIRL?!
SEE YOU.
THAT WAS WEIRD. WHY'D HE SAY SO MUCH THIS TIME?
AH! I MISSED THE CHANCE TO ASK HIM ABOUT EARTH'S DESTRUCTION IN THE FUTURE...!

Circle 32
Fuuko

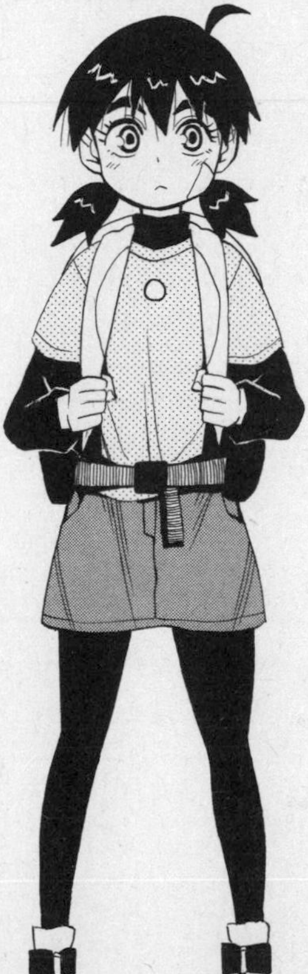

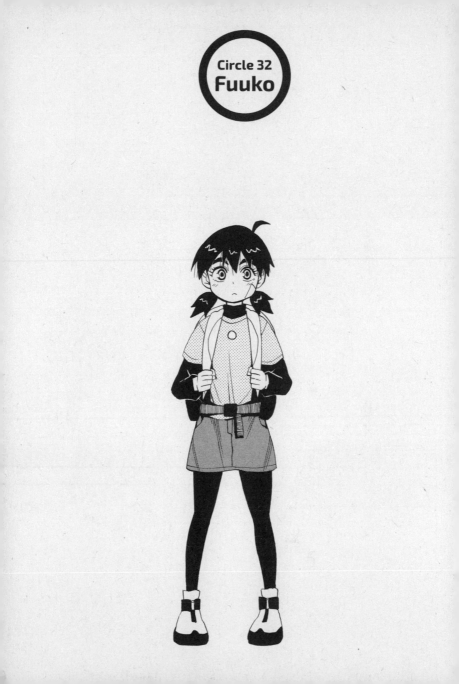

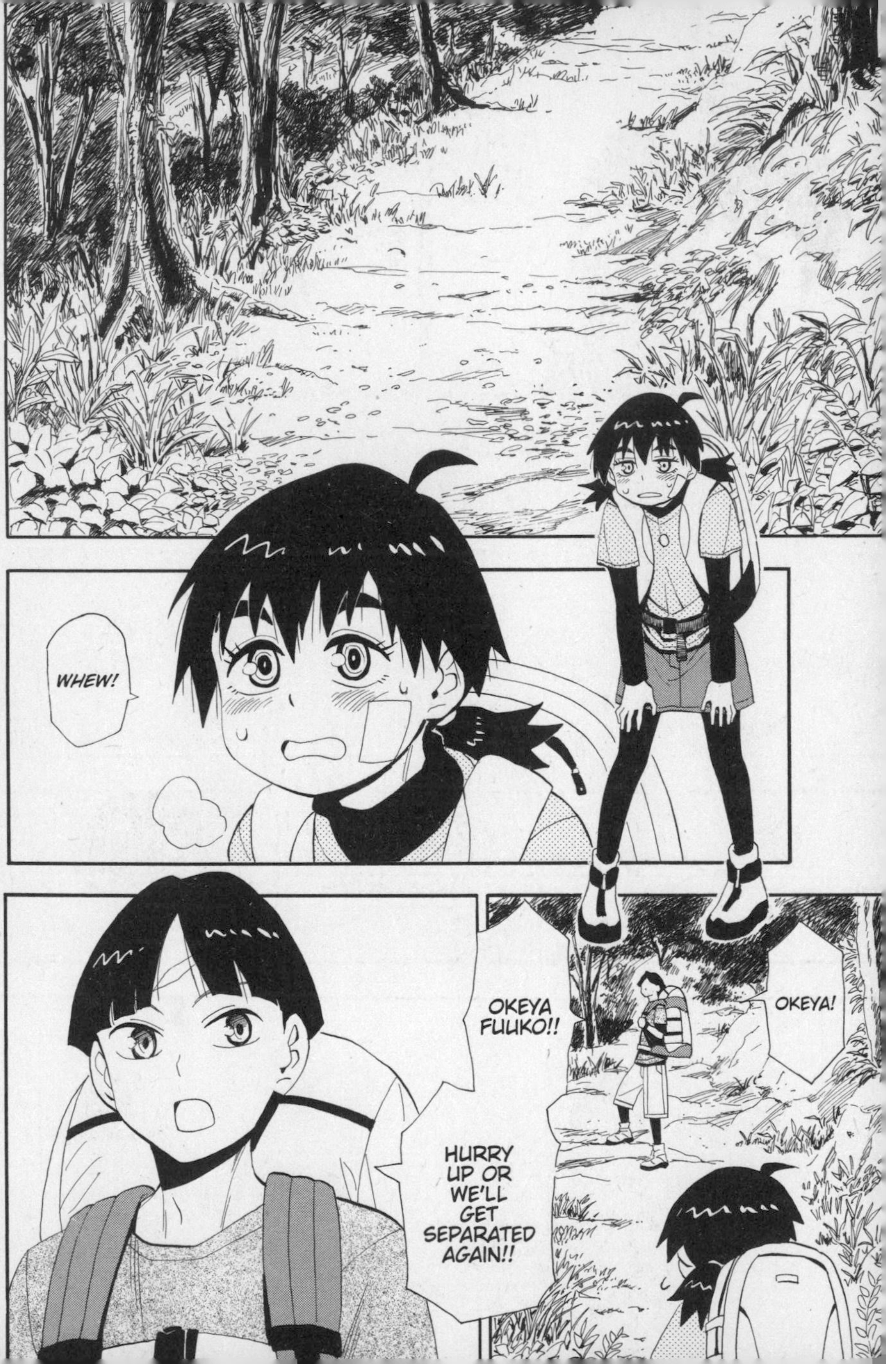
WHEW!
OKEYA!
OKEYA FUUKO!!
HURRY UP OR WE'LL GET SEPARATED AGAIN!!

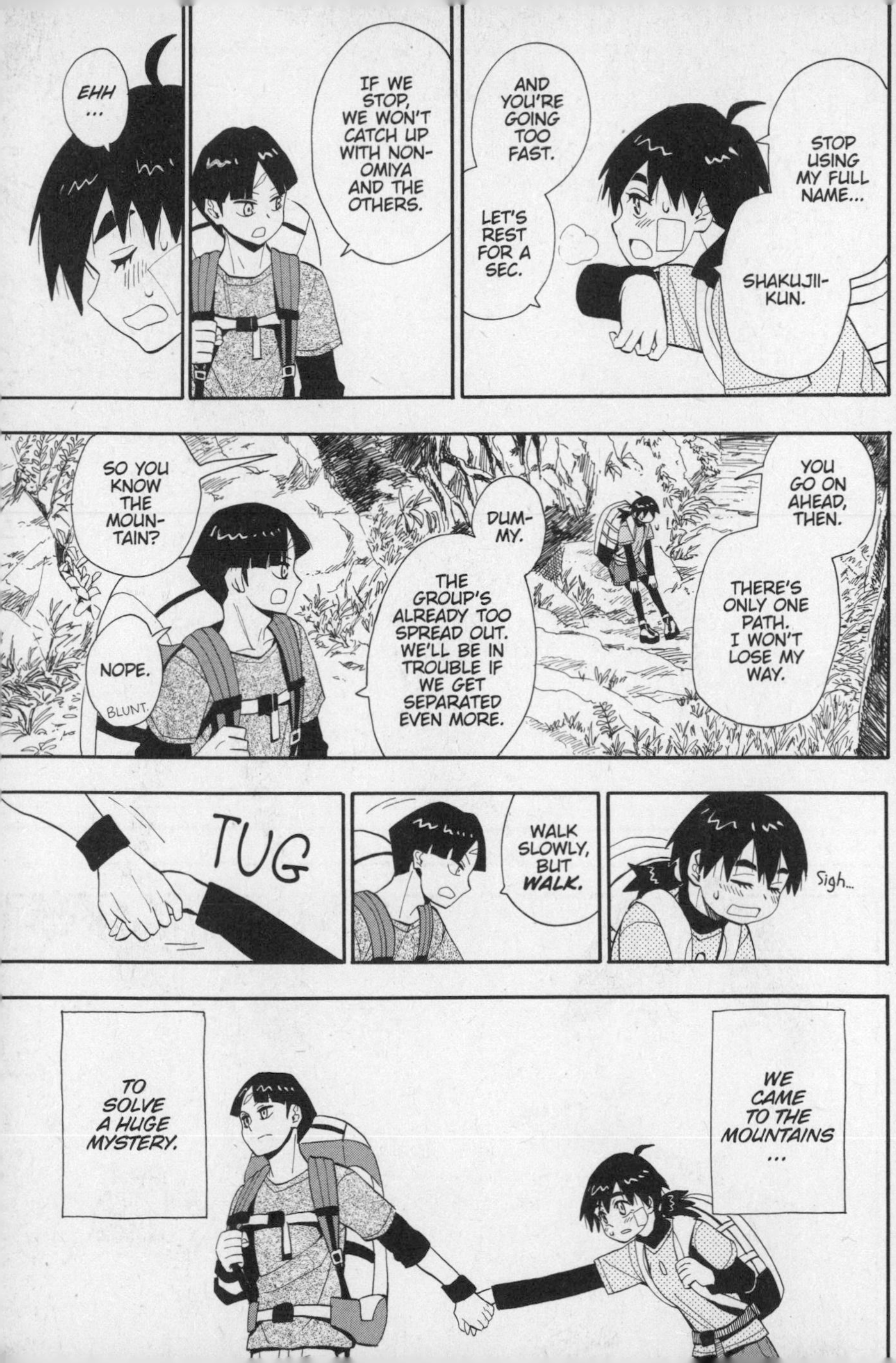
STOP USING MY FULL NAME...
SHAKUJII-KUN.
AND YOU'RE GOING TOO FAST.
LET'S REST FOR A SEC.
IF WE STOP, WE WON'T CATCH UP WITH NON-OMIYA AND THE OTHERS.
EHH ...
YOU GO ON AHEAD, THEN.
THERE'S ONLY ONE PATH. I WON'T LOSE MY WAY.
DUM-MY.
THE GROUP'S ALREADY TOO SPREAD OUT. WE'LL BE IN TROUBLE IF WE GET SEPARATED EVEN MORE.
SO YOU KNOW THE MOUNTAIN?
NOPE.
BLUNT.
Sigh...
WALK SLOWLY, BUT *WALK.*
TUG
WE CAME TO THE MOUNTAINS ...
TO SOLVE A HUGE MYSTERY.

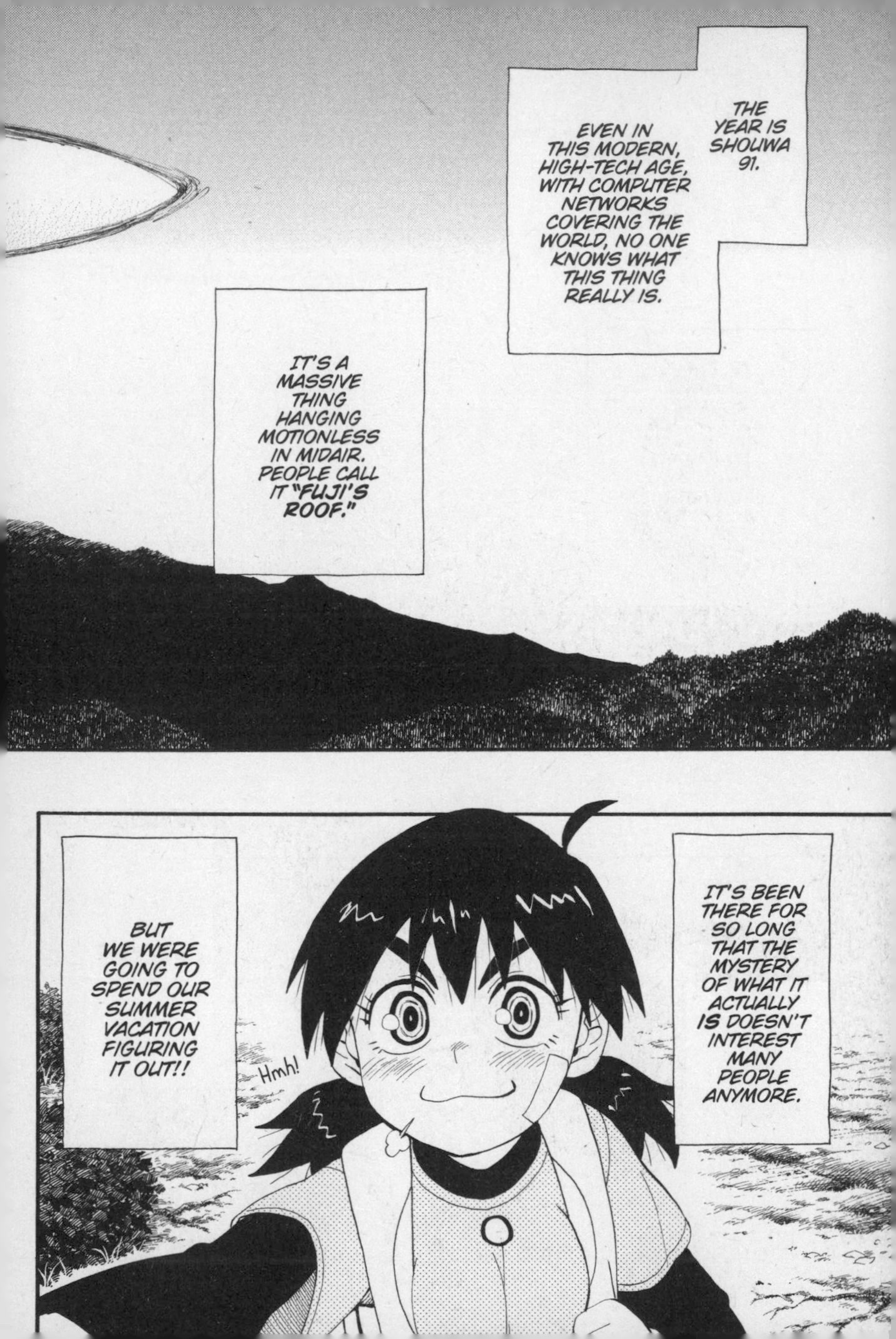
THE YEAR IS SHOUWA 91.
EVEN IN THIS MODERN, HIGH-TECH AGE, WITH COMPUTER NETWORKS COVERING THE WORLD, NO ONE KNOWS WHAT THIS THING REALLY IS.
IT'S A MASSIVE THING HANGING MOTIONLESS IN MIDAIR. PEOPLE CALL IT "FUJI'S ROOF."
IT'S BEEN THERE FOR SO LONG THAT THE MYSTERY OF WHAT IT ACTUALLY IS DOESN'T INTEREST MANY PEOPLE ANYMORE.
BUT WE WERE GOING TO SPEND OUR SUMMER VACATION FIGURING IT OUT!!
Hmh!

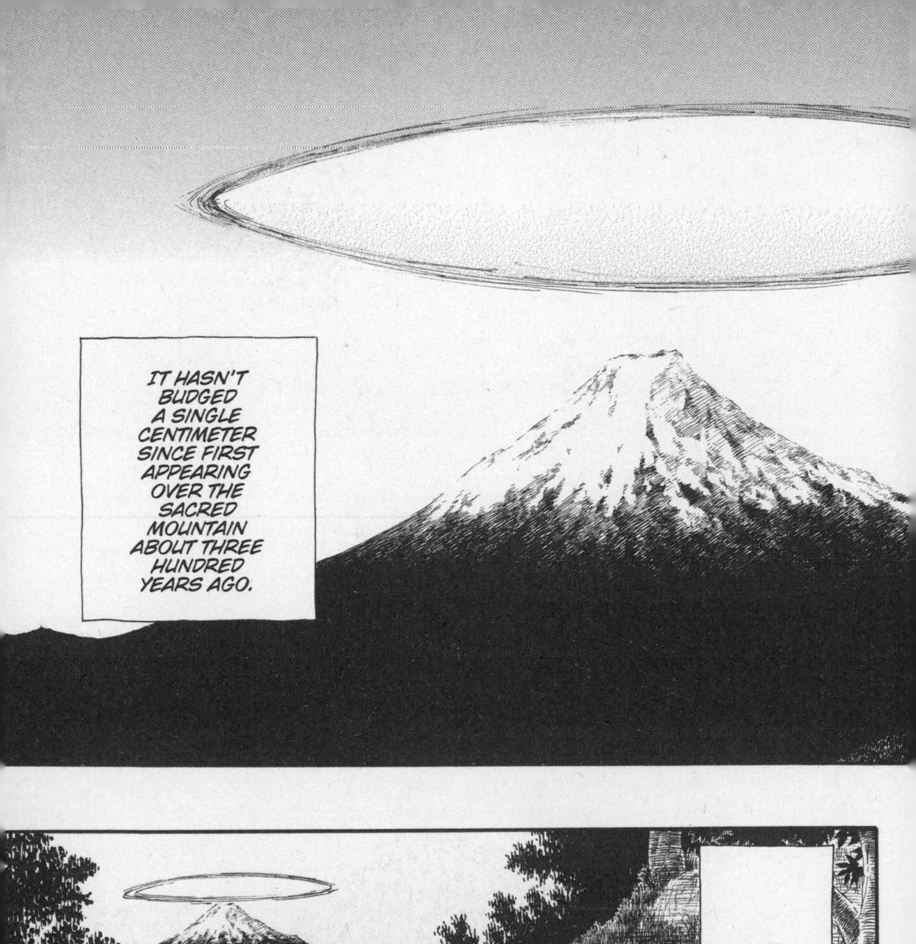
IT HASN'T BUDGED A SINGLE CENTIMETER SINCE FIRST APPEARING OVER THE SACRED MOUNTAIN ABOUT THREE HUNDRED YEARS AGO.

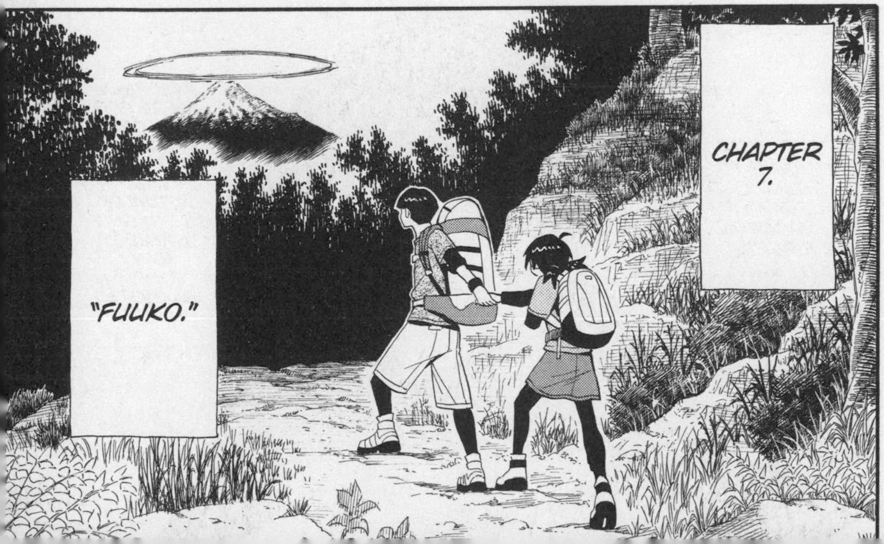
CHAPTER 7.
"FUUKO."

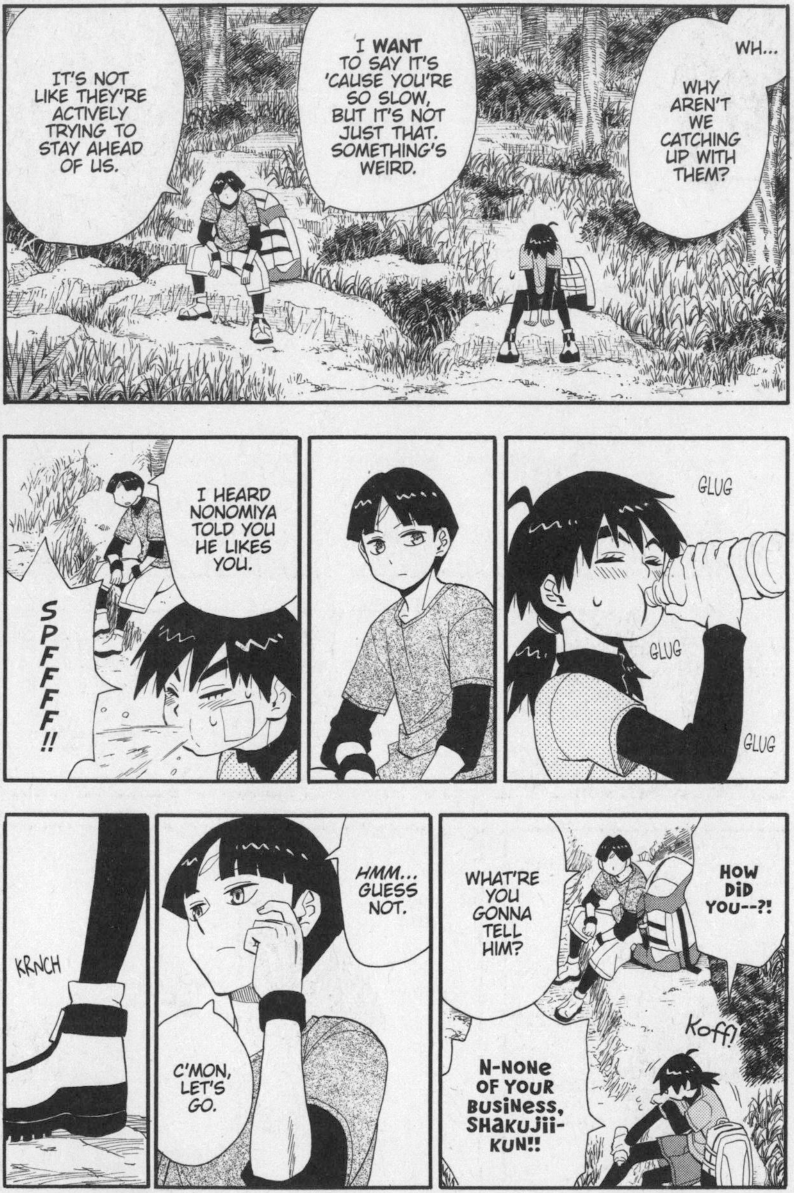
WH... WHY AREN'T WE CATCHING UP WITH THEM?
I WANT TO SAY IT'S 'CAUSE YOU'RE SO SLOW, BUT IT'S NOT JUST THAT. SOMETHING'S WEIRD.
IT'S NOT LIKE THEY'RE ACTIVELY TRYING TO STAY AHEAD OF US.
GLUG
GLUG
GLUG
I HEARD NONOMIYA TOLD YOU HE LIKES YOU.
SPFFFFF!!
HOW DID YOU--?!
WHAT'RE YOU GONNA TELL HIM?
Koff!
N-NONE OF YOUR BUSINESS, SHAKUJII-KUN!!
HMM... GUESS NOT.
C'MON, LET'S GO.
KRNCH

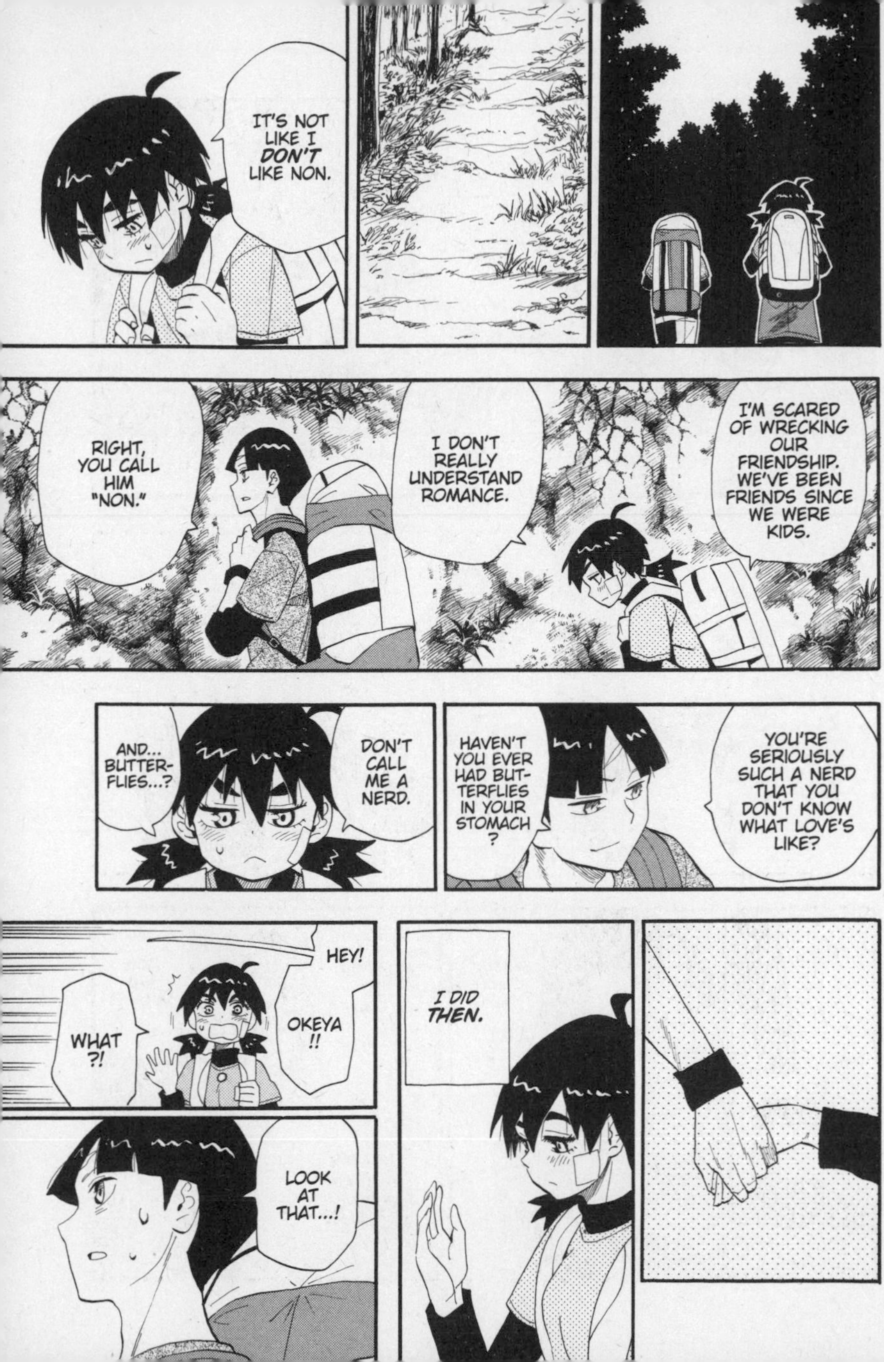
IT'S NOT LIKE I *DON'T* LIKE NON.
I'M SCARED OF WRECKING OUR FRIENDSHIP. WE'VE BEEN FRIENDS SINCE WE WERE KIDS.
I DON'T REALLY UNDERSTAND ROMANCE.
RIGHT, YOU CALL HIM "NON."
YOU'RE SERIOUSLY SUCH A NERD THAT YOU DON'T KNOW WHAT LOVE'S LIKE?
HAVEN'T YOU EVER HAD BUTTERFLIES IN YOUR STOMACH?
DON'T CALL ME A NERD.
AND... BUTTERFLIES...?
I DID ***THEN.***
HEY!
OKEYA!!
WHAT?!
LOOK AT THAT...!

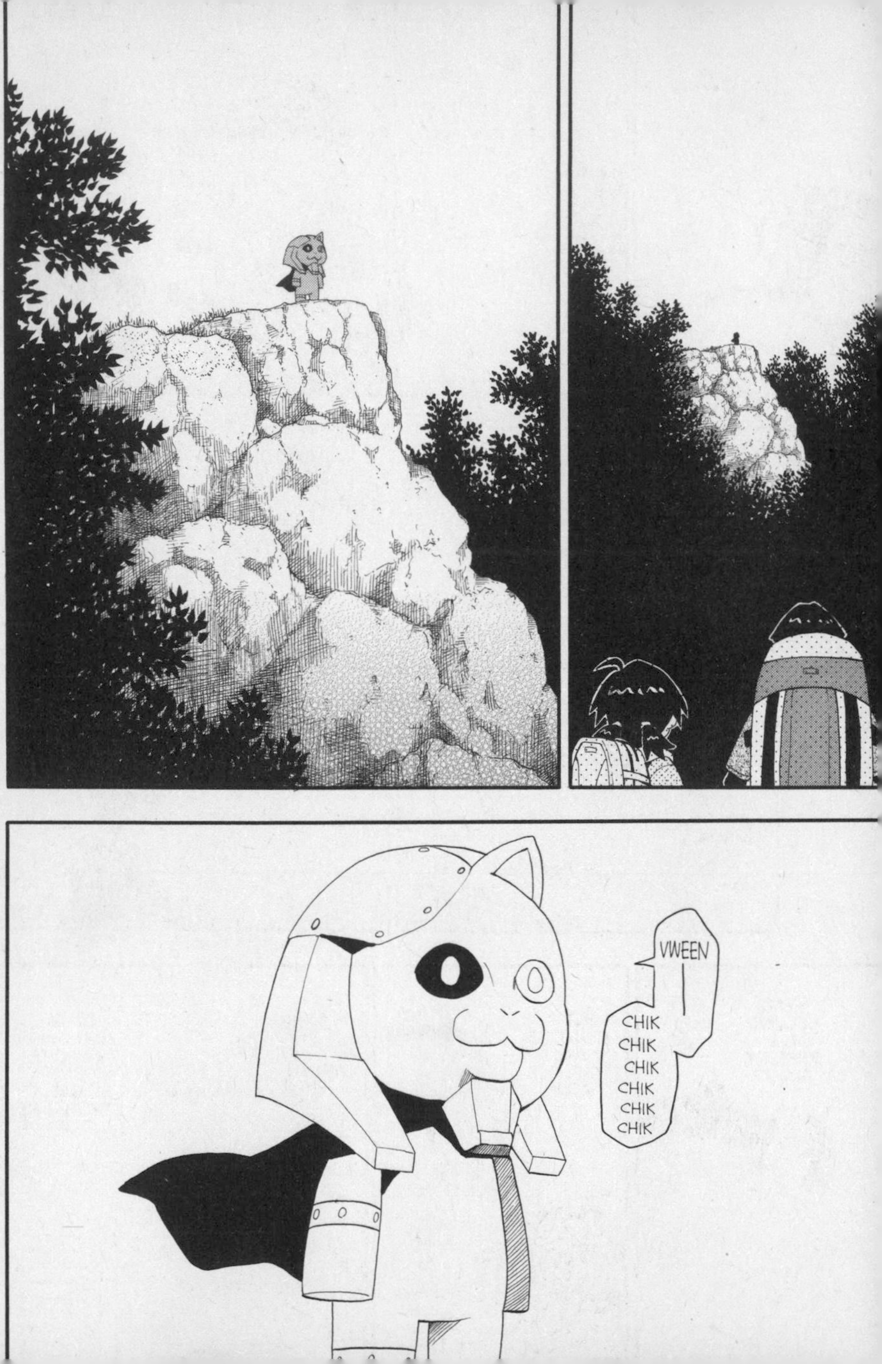
VWEEN
CHIK
CHIK
CHIK
CHIK
CHIK
CHIK

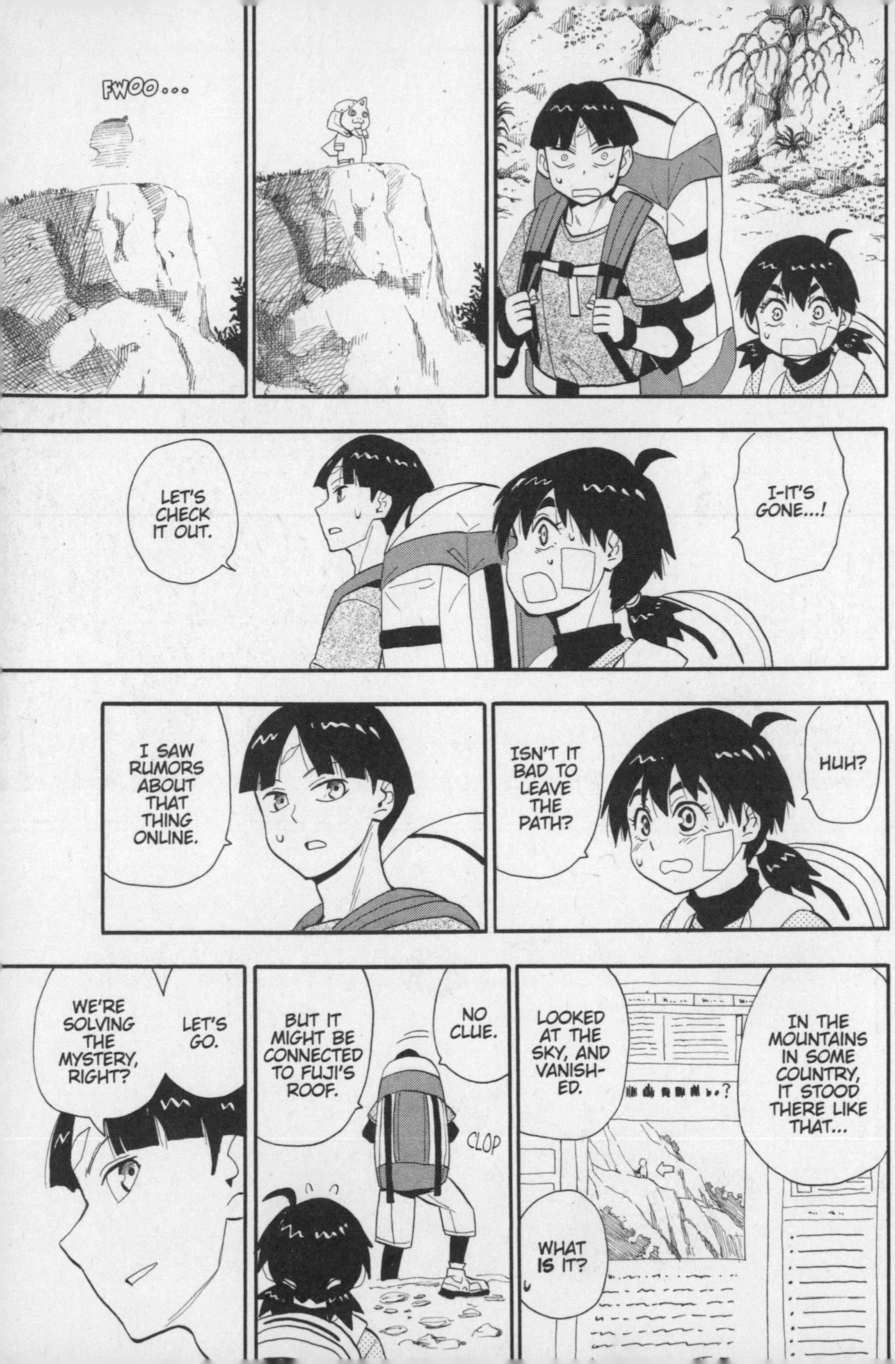
FWOO...
I-IT'S GONE...!
LET'S CHECK IT OUT.
HUH?
ISN'T IT BAD TO LEAVE THE PATH?
I SAW RUMORS ABOUT THAT THING ONLINE.
IN THE MOUNTAINS IN SOME COUNTRY, IT STOOD THERE LIKE THAT...
LOOKED AT THE SKY, AND VANISHED.
WHAT IS IT?
NO CLUE.
BUT IT MIGHT BE CONNECTED TO FUJI'S ROOF.
CLOP
LET'S GO.
WE'RE SOLVING THE MYSTERY, RIGHT?

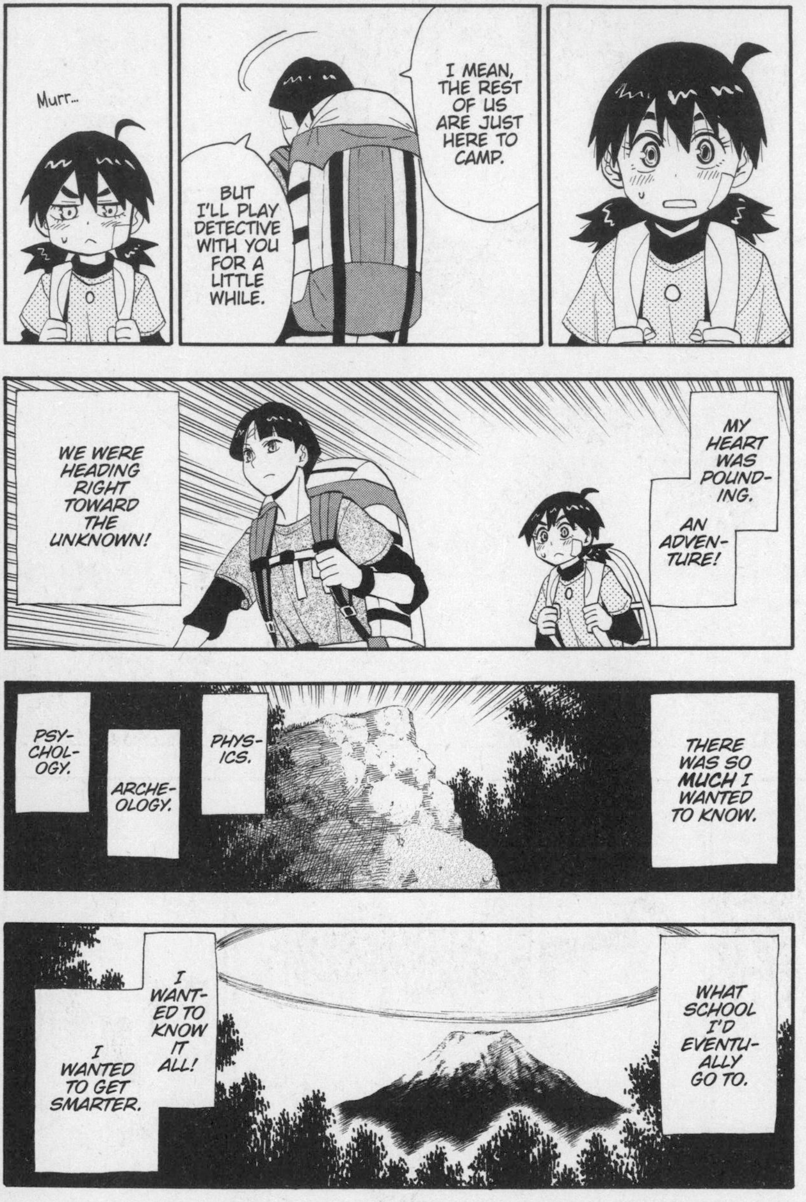
I MEAN, THE REST OF US ARE JUST HERE TO CAMP.
BUT I'LL PLAY DETECTIVE WITH YOU FOR A LITTLE WHILE.
Murr...
MY HEART WAS POUNDING.
AN ADVENTURE!
WE WERE HEADING RIGHT TOWARD THE UNKNOWN!
THERE WAS SO MUCH I WANTED TO KNOW.
PHYSICS.
ARCHEOLOGY.
PSYCHOLOGY.
WHAT SCHOOL I'D EVENTUALLY GO TO.
I WANTED TO KNOW IT ALL!
I WANTED TO GET SMARTER.

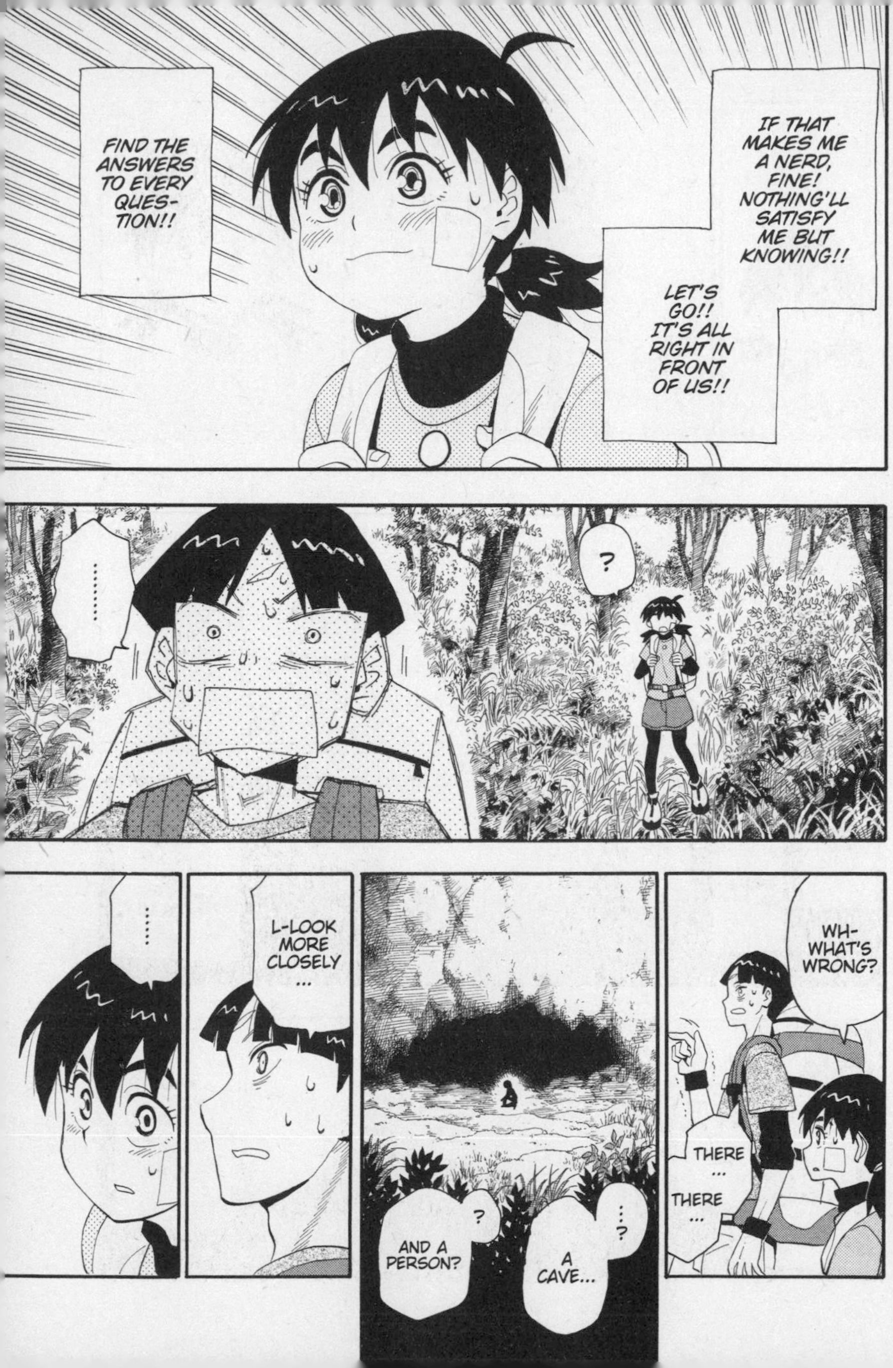
IF THAT MAKES ME A NERD, FINE! NOTHING'LL SATISFY ME BUT KNOWING!!
LET'S GO!! IT'S ALL RIGHT IN FRONT OF US!!
FIND THE ANSWERS TO EVERY QUES-TION!!
?
......
WH-WHAT'S WRONG?
THERE ... THERE ...
...?
A CAVE...
?
AND A PERSON?
L-LOOK MORE CLOSELY ...
......

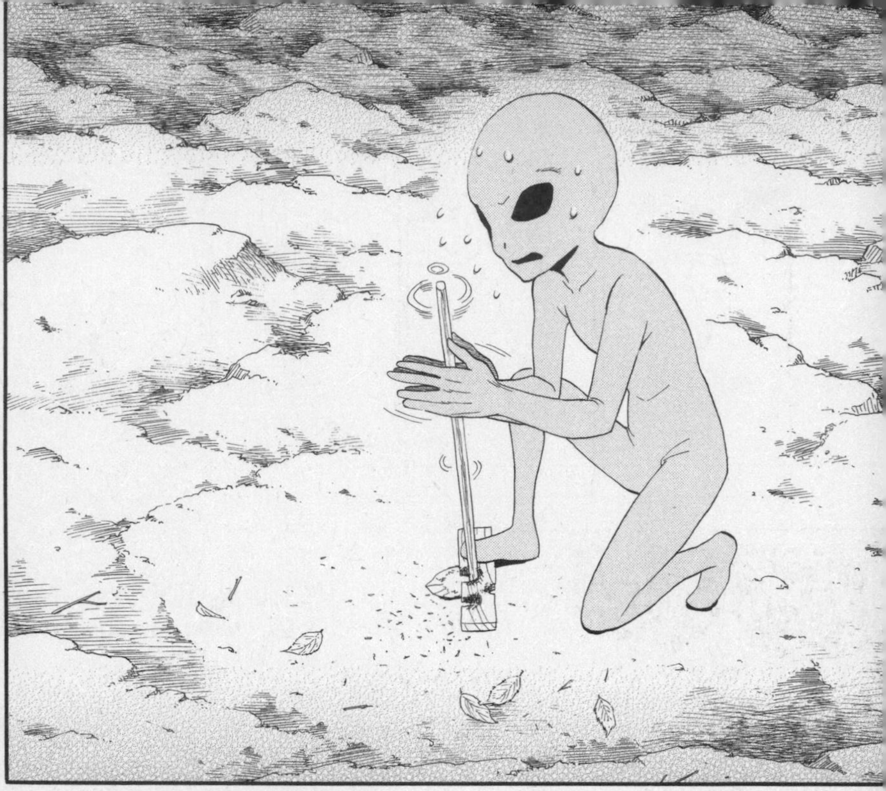
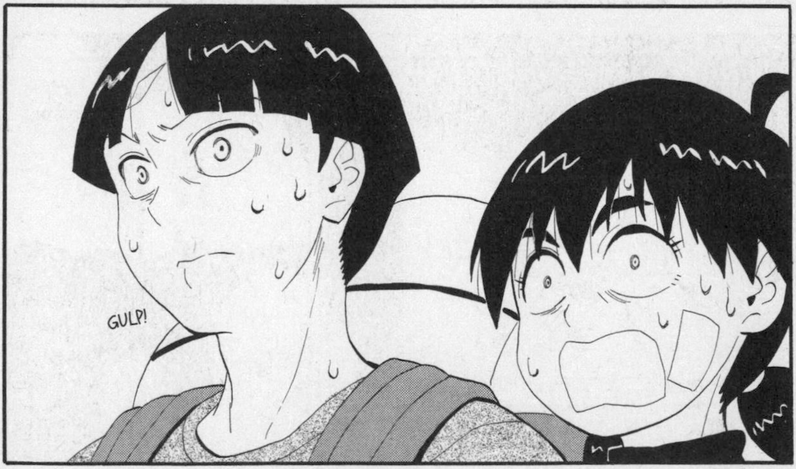
GULP!

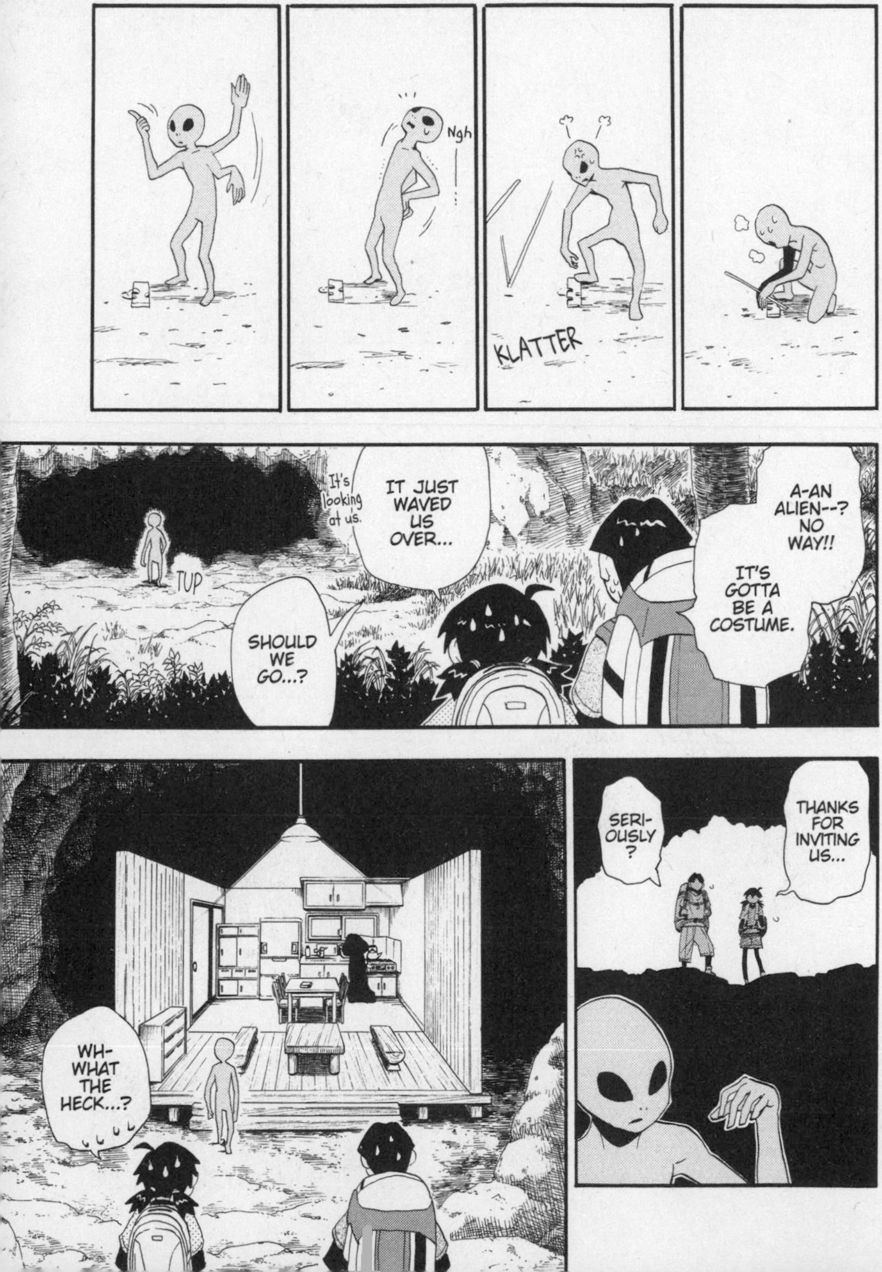
KLATTER
Ngh
A-AN ALIEN--? NO WAY!!
IT'S GOTTA BE A COSTUME.
IT JUST WAVED US OVER...
It's looking at us.
SHOULD WE GO...?
TUP
THANKS FOR INVITING US...
SERI-OUSLY?
WH-WHAT THE HECK...?

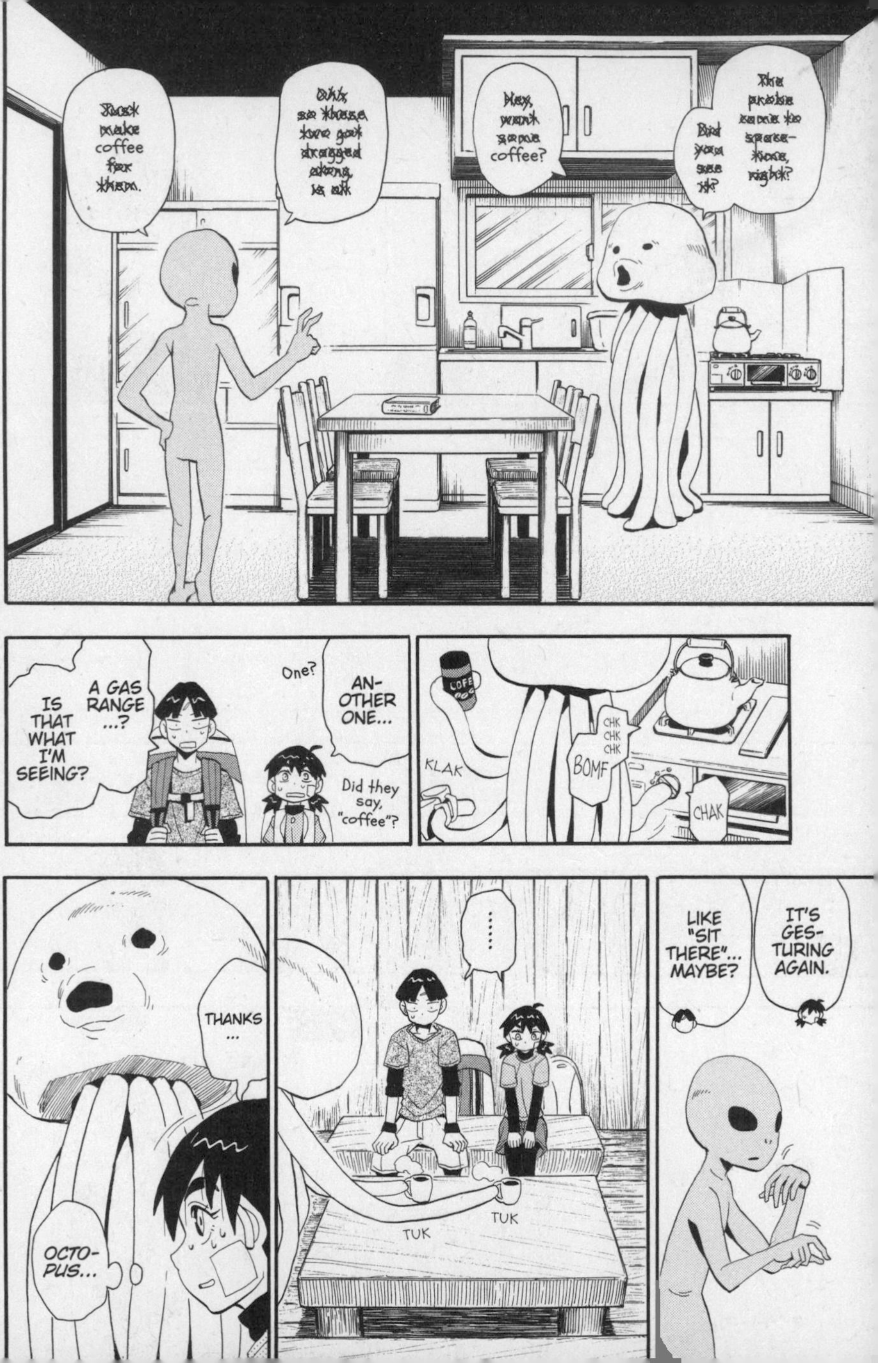
The probe came to space-time, right?
Did you see it?
Hey, want some coffee?
Oh, so these two got dragged along, is it
Just make coffee for them.
CHK CHK CHK
BOMF
KLAK
CHAK
AN-OTHER ONE...
One?
Did they say, "coffee"?
A GAS RANGE ...?
IS THAT WHAT I'M SEEING?
IT'S GES-TURING AGAIN.
LIKE "SIT THERE"... MAYBE?
......
TUK
TUK
THANKS ...
OCTO-PUS...

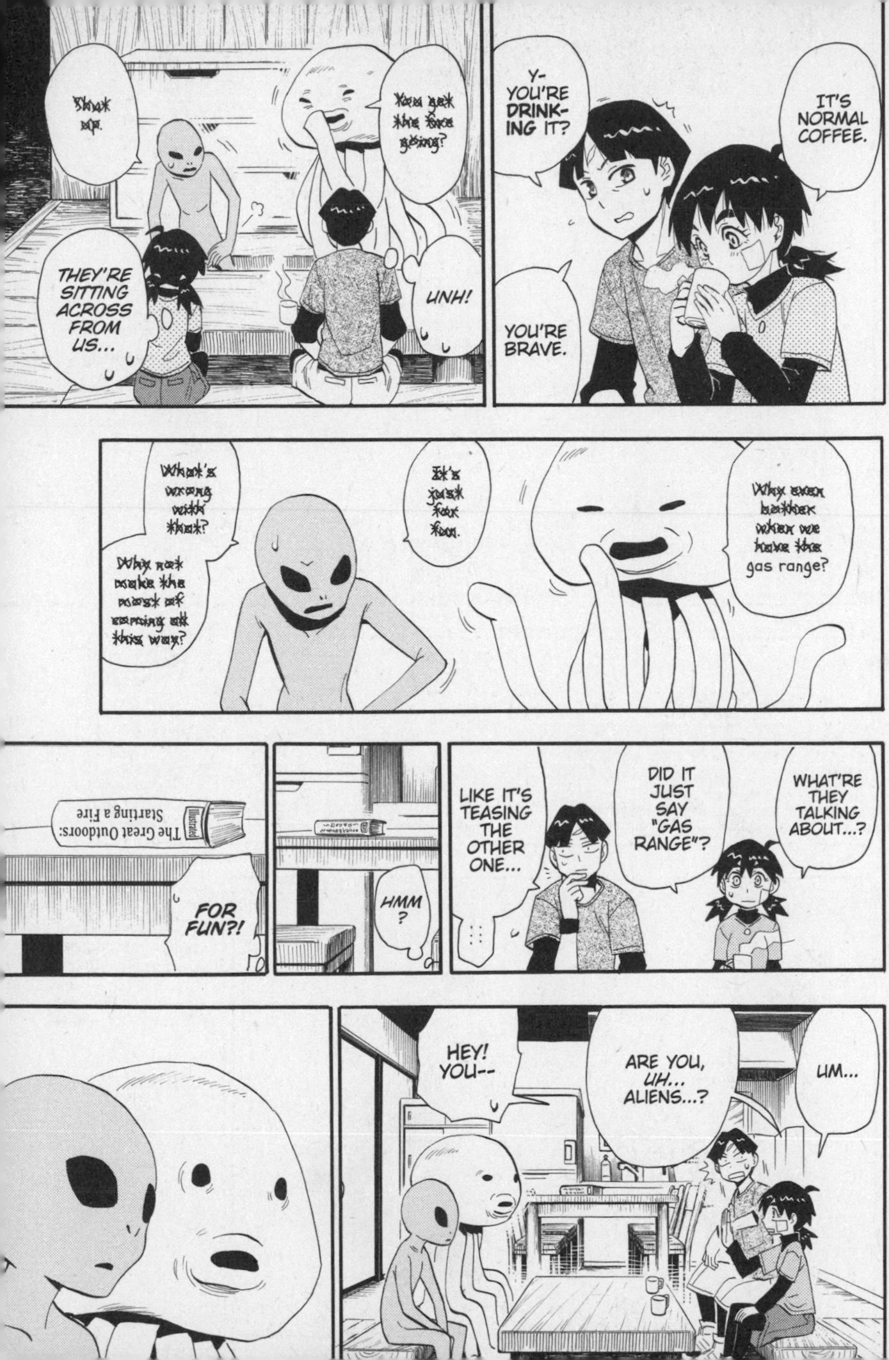
IT'S NORMAL COFFEE.
Y-YOU'RE DRINKING IT?
YOU'RE BRAVE.
You got the fire going?
UNH!
Shut up.
THEY'RE SITTING ACROSS FROM US...
Why even bother when we have the gas range?
It's just for fun.
What's wrong with that?
Why not make the most of camping out this way?
WHAT'RE THEY TALKING ABOUT...?
DID IT JUST SAY "GAS RANGE"?
LIKE IT'S TEASING THE OTHER ONE...
HMM?
Illustrated
The Great Outdoors: Starting a Fire
FOR FUN?!
UM...
ARE YOU, UH... ALIENS...?
HEY! YOU--

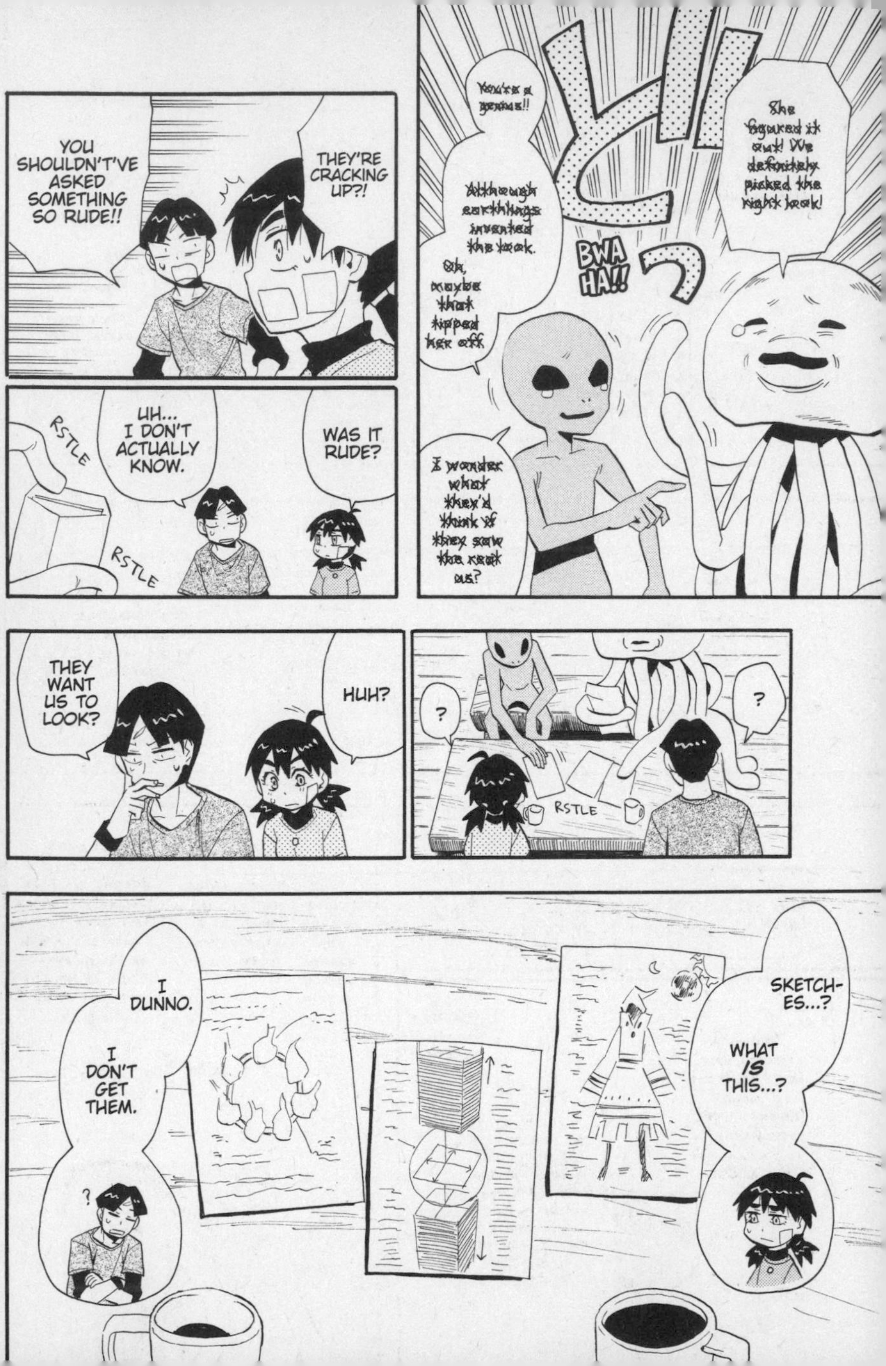

She figured it out! We definitely picked the right look!
BWA HA!!
You're a genius!!
Although earthlings invented the look.
Ok, maybe that tipped her off
I wonder what they'd think if they saw the real us?
THEY'RE CRACKING UP?!
YOU SHOULDN'T'VE ASKED SOMETHING SO RUDE!!
WAS IT RUDE?
UH... I DON'T ACTUALLY KNOW.
RSTLE
RSTLE
?
?
RSTLE
HUH?
THEY WANT US TO LOOK?
SKETCH-ES...?
WHAT *IS* THIS...?
I DUNNO.
I DON'T GET THEM.

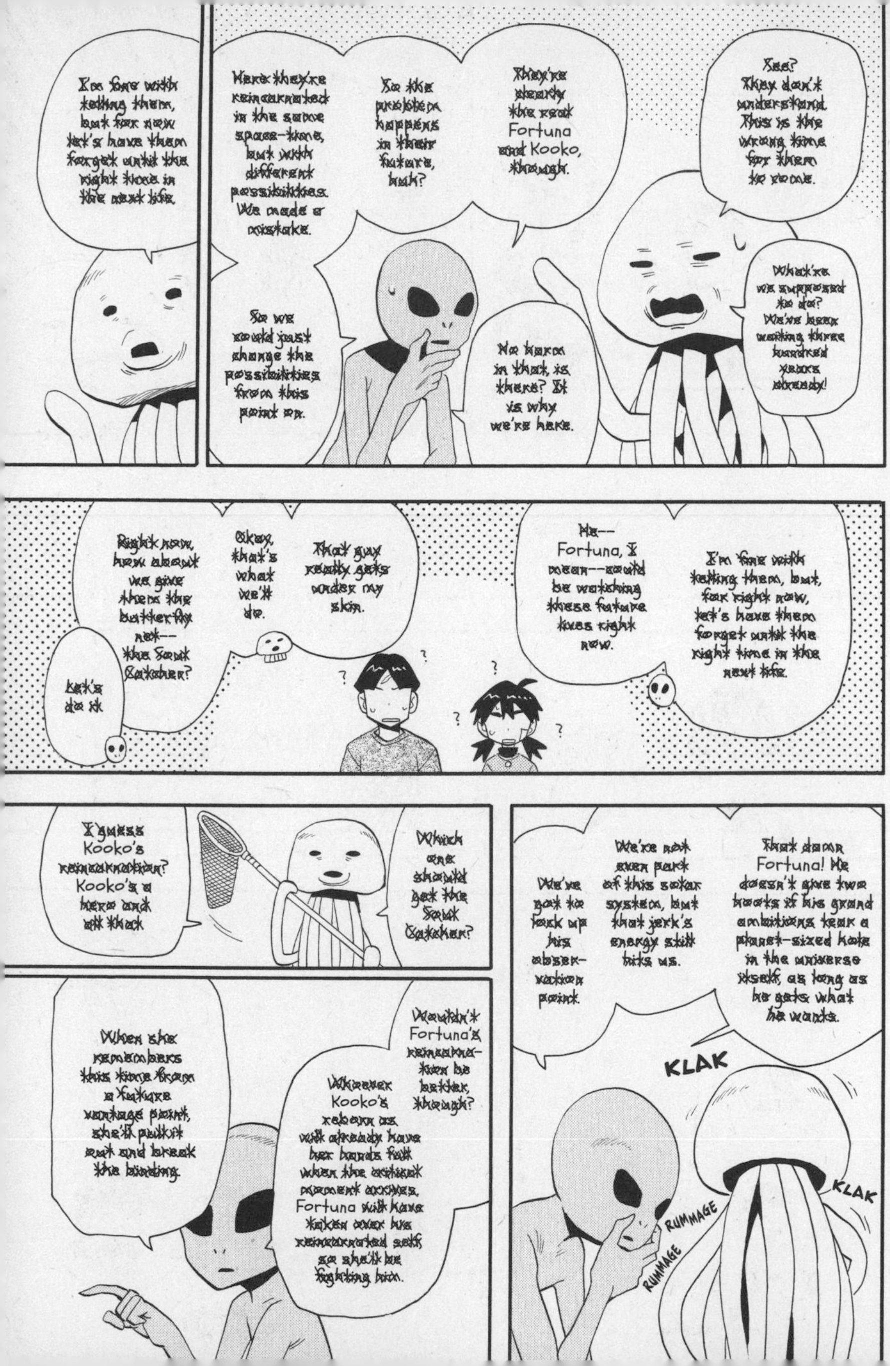
See? They don't understand. This is the wrong time for them to come.
What're we supposed to do? We've been waiting three hundred years already!
They're clearly the real Fortuna and Kooko, though.
So the problem happens in their future, huh?
Here they're reincarnated in the same space-time, but with different possibilities. We made a mistake.
No harm in that, is there? It is why we're here.
So we could just change the possibilities from this point on.
I'm fine with telling them, but for now let's have them forget until the right time in the next life.
I'm fine with telling them, but, for right now, let's have them forget until the right time in the next life.
He-- Fortuna, I mean--could be watching these future lives right now.
That guy really gets under my skin.
Okay, that's what we'll do.
Right now, how about we give them the butterfly net--the Soul Catcher?
Let's do it
That damn Fortuna! He doesn't give two hoots if his grand ambitions tear a planet-sized hole in the universe itself, as long as he gets what he wants.
We're not even part of this solar system, but that jerk's energy still hits us.
We've got to lock up his observation point.
KLAK
KLAK
RUMMAGE
RUMMAGE
Which one should get the Soul Catcher?
I guess Kooko's reincarnation? Kooko's a hero and all that
Wouldn't Fortuna's reincarnation be better, though?
Whoever Kooko's reborn as will already have her hands full when the critical moment arrives. Fortuna will have taken over his reincarnated self so she'll be fighting him.
When she remembers this time from a future vantage point, she'll pull it out and break the binding.

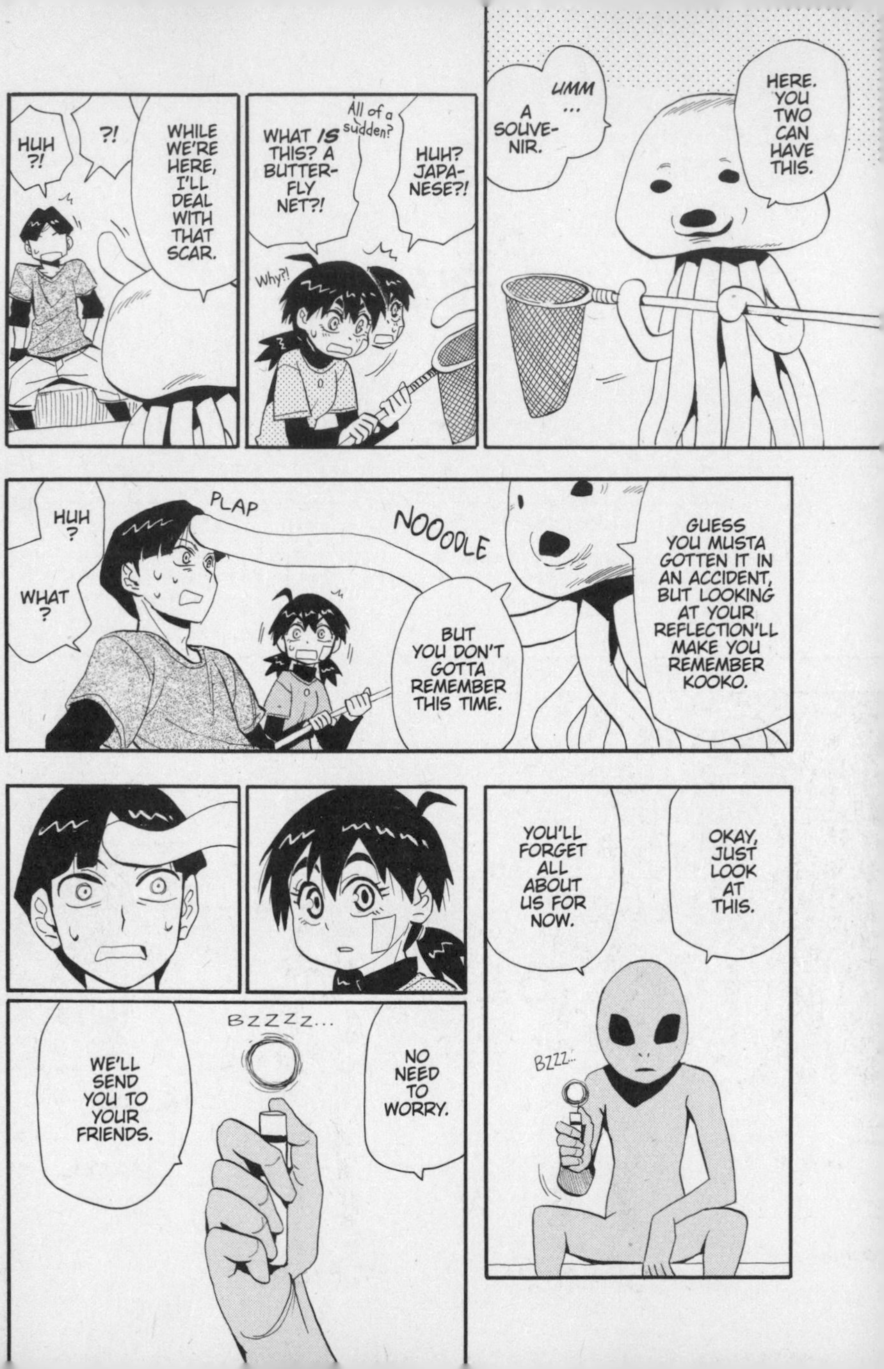
HERE. YOU TWO CAN HAVE THIS.
UMM ...
A SOUVENIR.
HUH? JAPANESE?!
All of a sudden?
WHAT IS THIS? A BUTTERFLY NET?!
Why?!
WHILE WE'RE HERE, I'LL DEAL WITH THAT SCAR.
?!
HUH?!
GUESS YOU MUSTA GOTTEN IT IN AN ACCIDENT, BUT LOOKING AT YOUR REFLECTION'LL MAKE YOU REMEMBER KOOKO.
NOOODLE
BUT YOU DON'T GOTTA REMEMBER THIS TIME.
PLAP
HUH?
WHAT?
OKAY, JUST LOOK AT THIS.
YOU'LL FORGET ALL ABOUT US FOR NOW.
BZZZ...
NO NEED TO WORRY.
BZZZZ...
WE'LL SEND YOU TO YOUR FRIENDS.

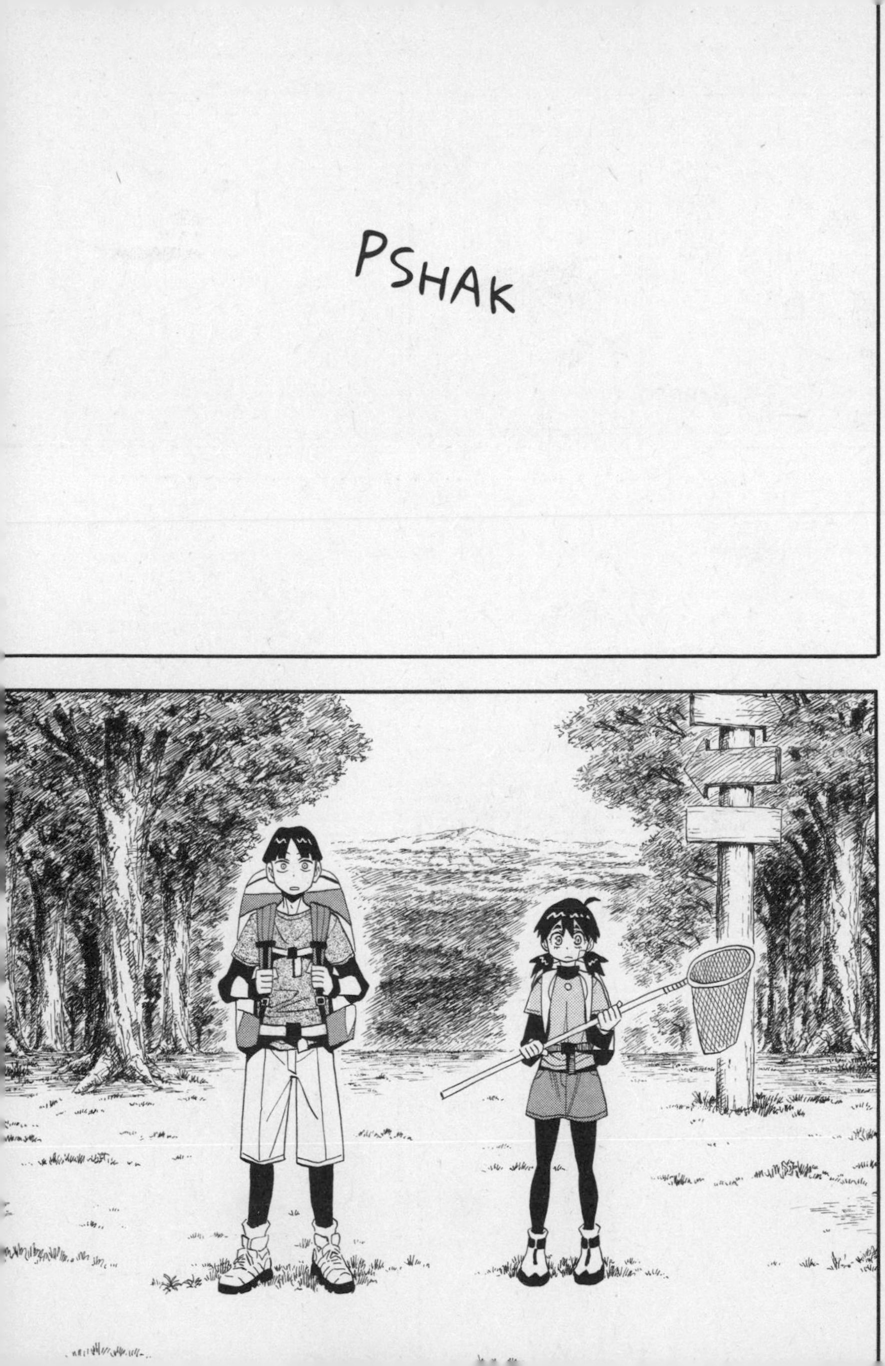
PSHAK

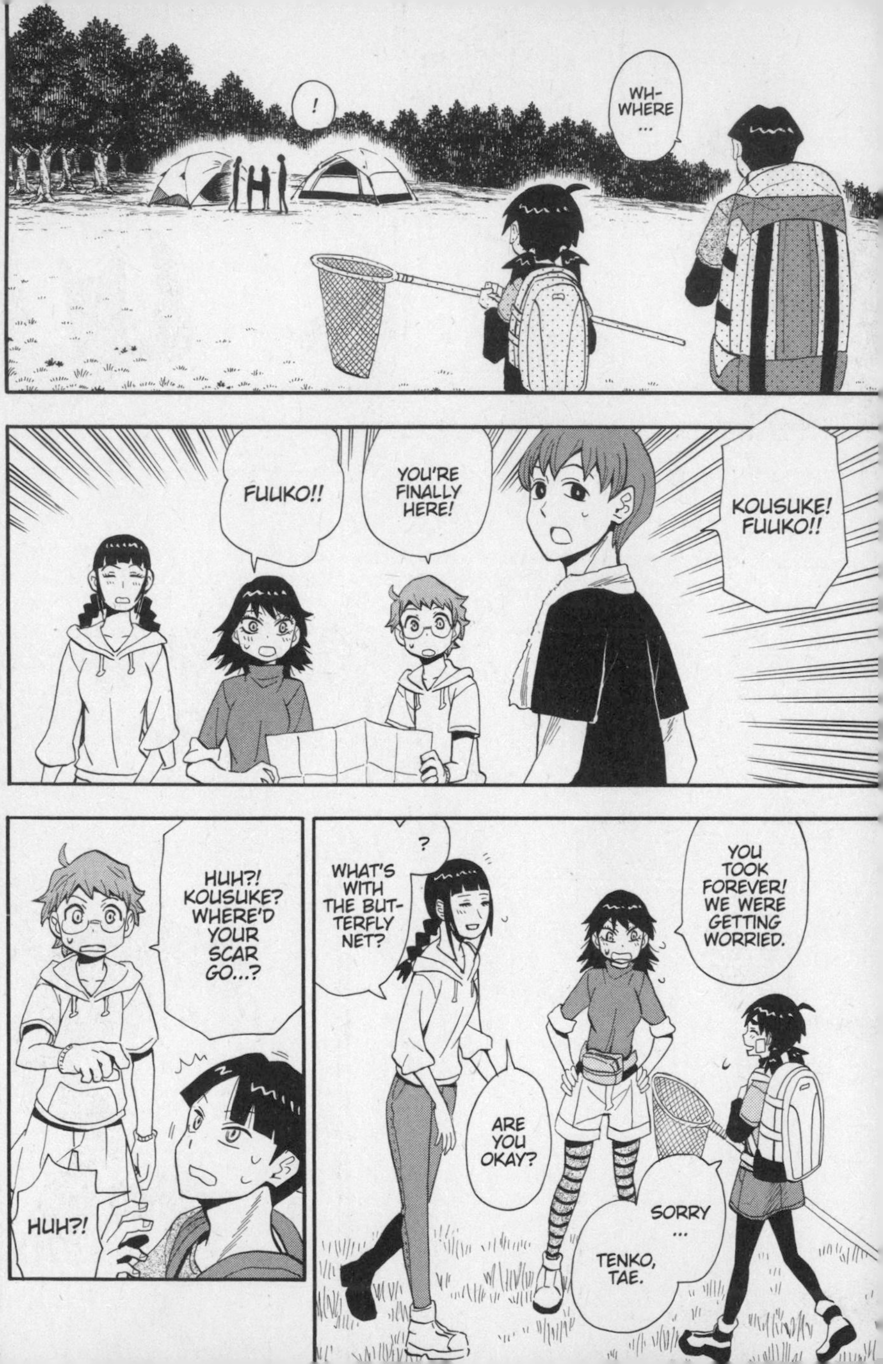
WH-WHERE ...
!
KOUSUKE! FUUKO!!
YOU'RE FINALLY HERE!
FUUKO!!
YOU TOOK FOREVER! WE WERE GETTING WORRIED.
?
WHAT'S WITH THE BUT-TERFLY NET?
ARE YOU OKAY?
SORRY ...
TENKO, TAE.
HUH?! KOUSUKE? WHERE'D YOUR SCAR GO...?
HUH?!

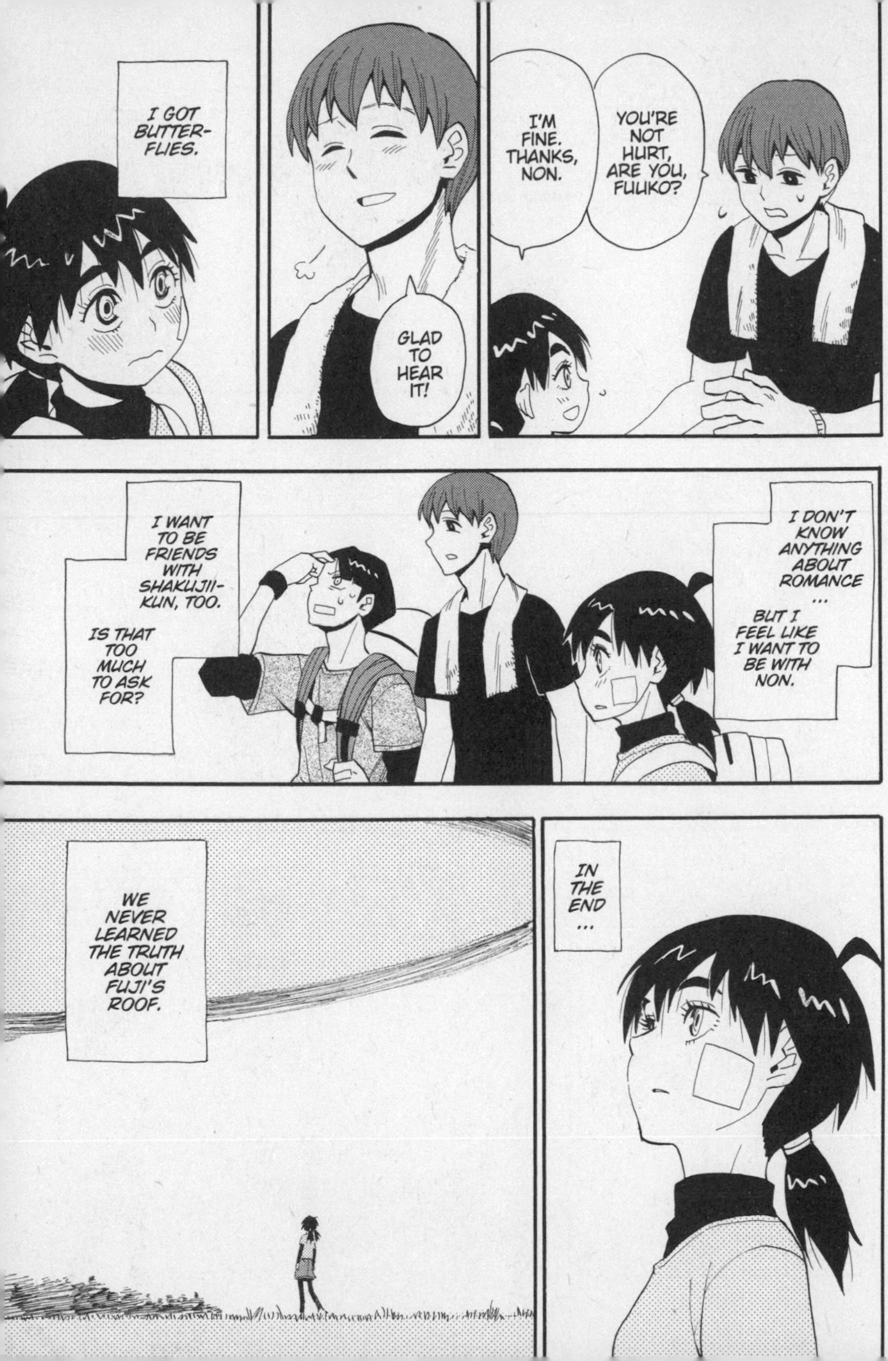
YOU'RE NOT HURT, ARE YOU, FUUKO?
I'M FINE. THANKS, NON.
GLAD TO HEAR IT!
I GOT BUTTER-FLIES.
I DON'T KNOW ANYTHING ABOUT ROMANCE...
BUT I FEEL LIKE I WANT TO BE WITH NON.
I WANT TO BE FRIENDS WITH SHAKUJII-KUN, TOO.
IS THAT TOO MUCH TO ASK FOR?
IN THE END...
WE NEVER LEARNED THE TRUTH ABOUT FUJI'S ROOF.

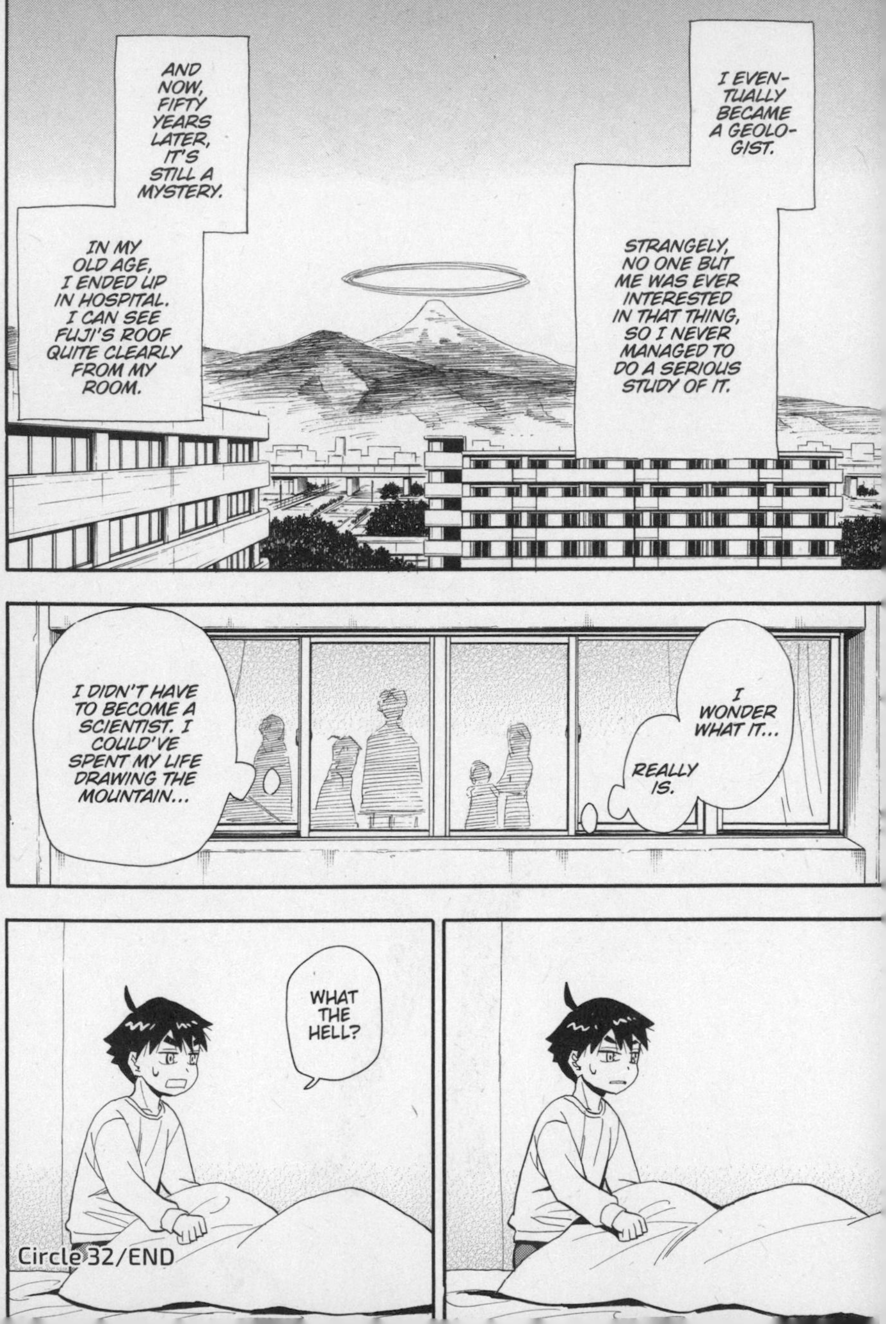
I EVEN- TUALLY BECAME A GEOLO- GIST.
STRANGELY, NO ONE BUT ME WAS EVER INTERESTED IN THAT THING, SO I NEVER MANAGED TO DO A SERIOUS STUDY OF IT.
AND NOW, FIFTY YEARS LATER, IT'S STILL A MYSTERY.
IN MY OLD AGE, I ENDED UP IN HOSPITAL. I CAN SEE FUJI'S ROOF QUITE CLEARLY FROM MY ROOM.
I WONDER WHAT IT...
REALLY IS.
I DIDN'T HAVE TO BECOME A SCIENTIST. I COULD'VE SPENT MY LIFE DRAWING THE MOUNTAIN...
WHAT THE HELL?
Circle 32/END

Circle 33
Date

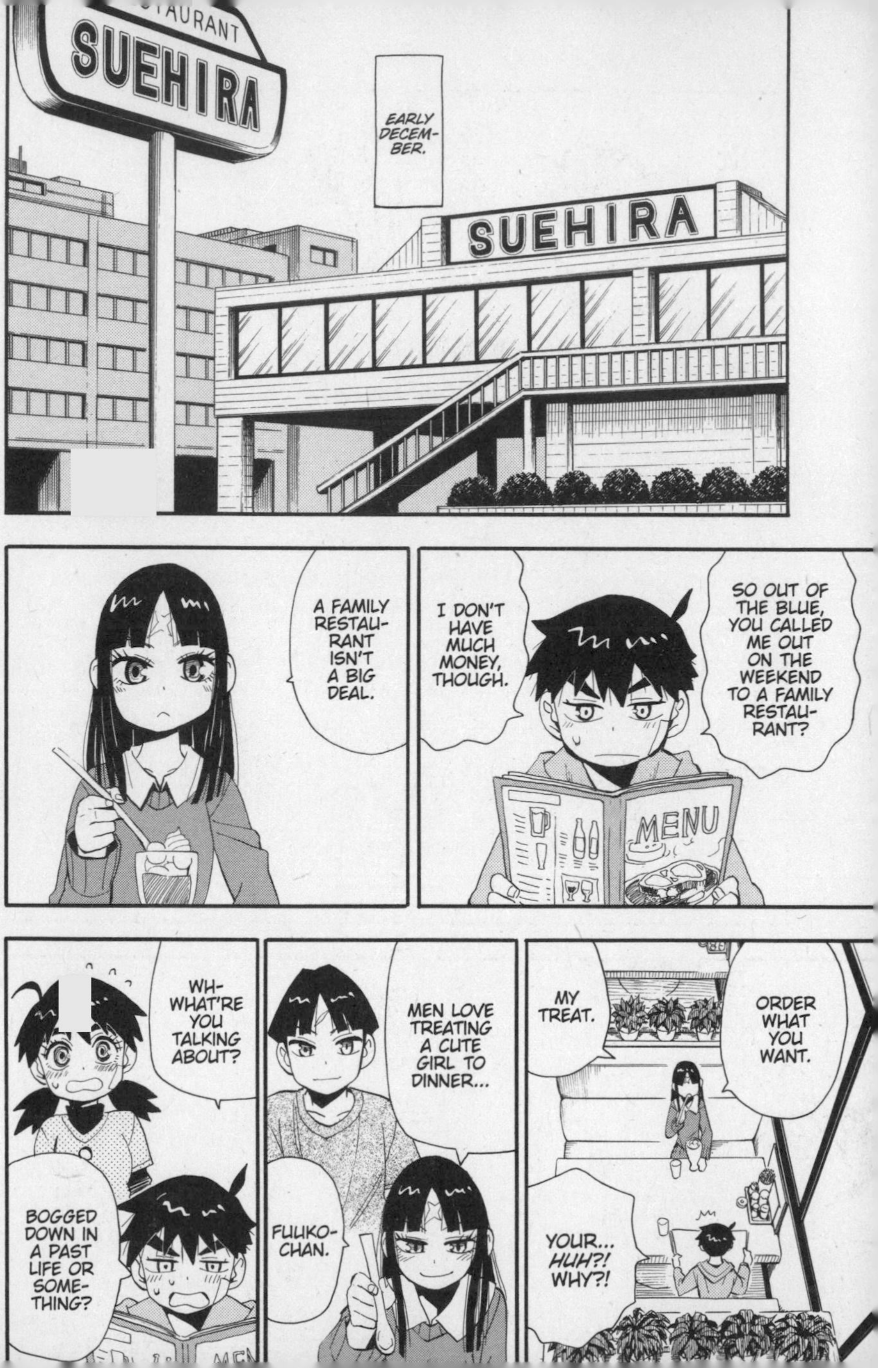
SUEHIRA
EARLY DECEM-BER.
SUEHIRA
SO OUT OF THE BLUE, YOU CALLED ME OUT ON THE WEEKEND TO A FAMILY RESTAU-RANT?
I DON'T HAVE MUCH MONEY, THOUGH.
MENU
A FAMILY RESTAU-RANT ISN'T A BIG DEAL.
ORDER WHAT YOU WANT.
MY TREAT.
YOUR... *HUH?!* WHY?!
MEN LOVE TREATING A CUTE GIRL TO DINNER...
FUUKO-CHAN.
WH-WHAT'RE YOU TALKING ABOUT?
BOGGED DOWN IN A PAST LIFE OR SOME-THING?

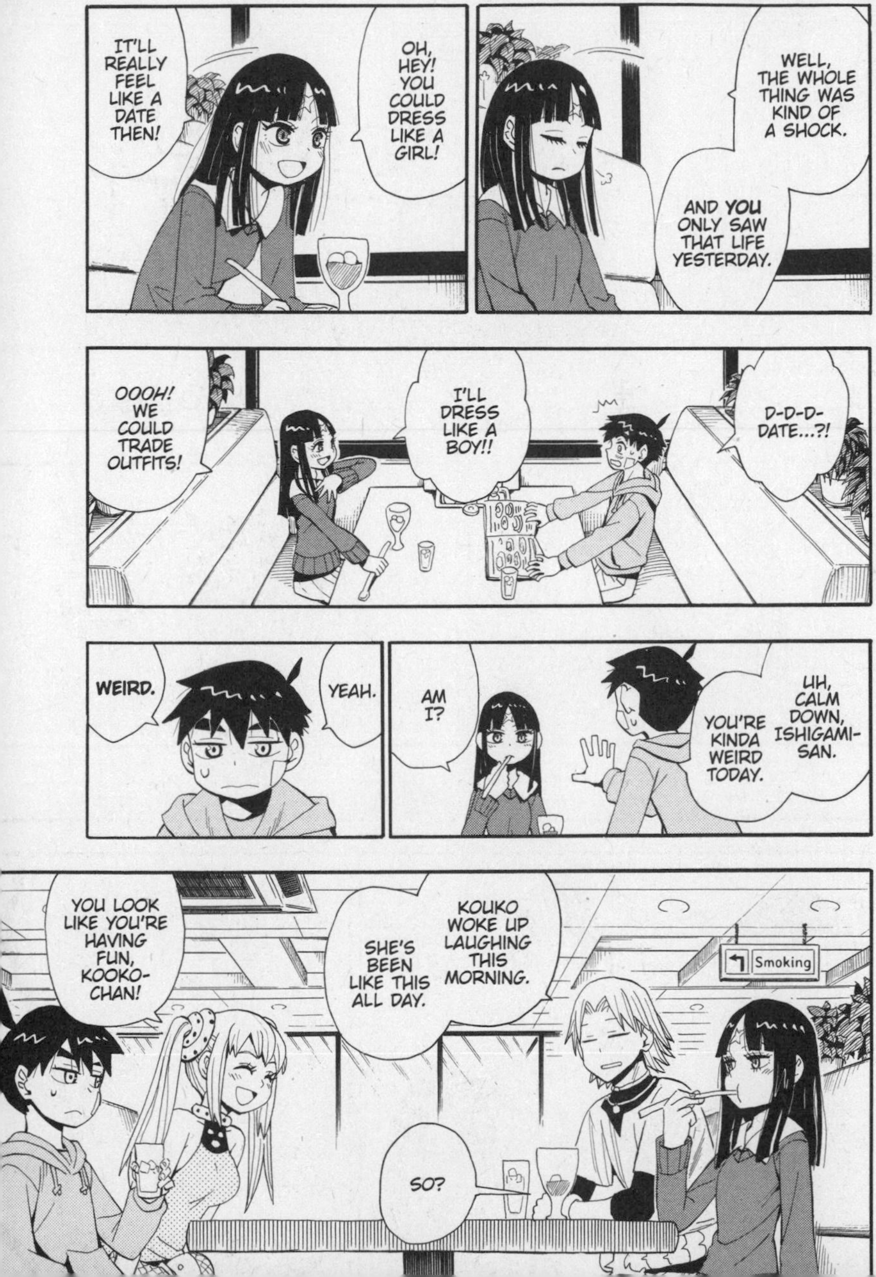
WELL, THE WHOLE THING WAS KIND OF A SHOCK.
AND YOU ONLY SAW THAT LIFE YESTERDAY.
OH, HEY! YOU COULD DRESS LIKE A GIRL!
IT'LL REALLY FEEL LIKE A DATE THEN!
D-D-D-DATE...?!
I'LL DRESS LIKE A BOY!!
OOOH! WE COULD TRADE OUTFITS!
UH, CALM DOWN, ISHIGAMI-SAN.
YOU'RE KINDA WEIRD TODAY.
AM I?
YEAH.
WEIRD.
Smoking
KOUKO WOKE UP LAUGHING THIS MORNING.
SHE'S BEEN LIKE THIS ALL DAY.
SO?
YOU LOOK LIKE YOU'RE HAVING FUN, KOOKO-CHAN!

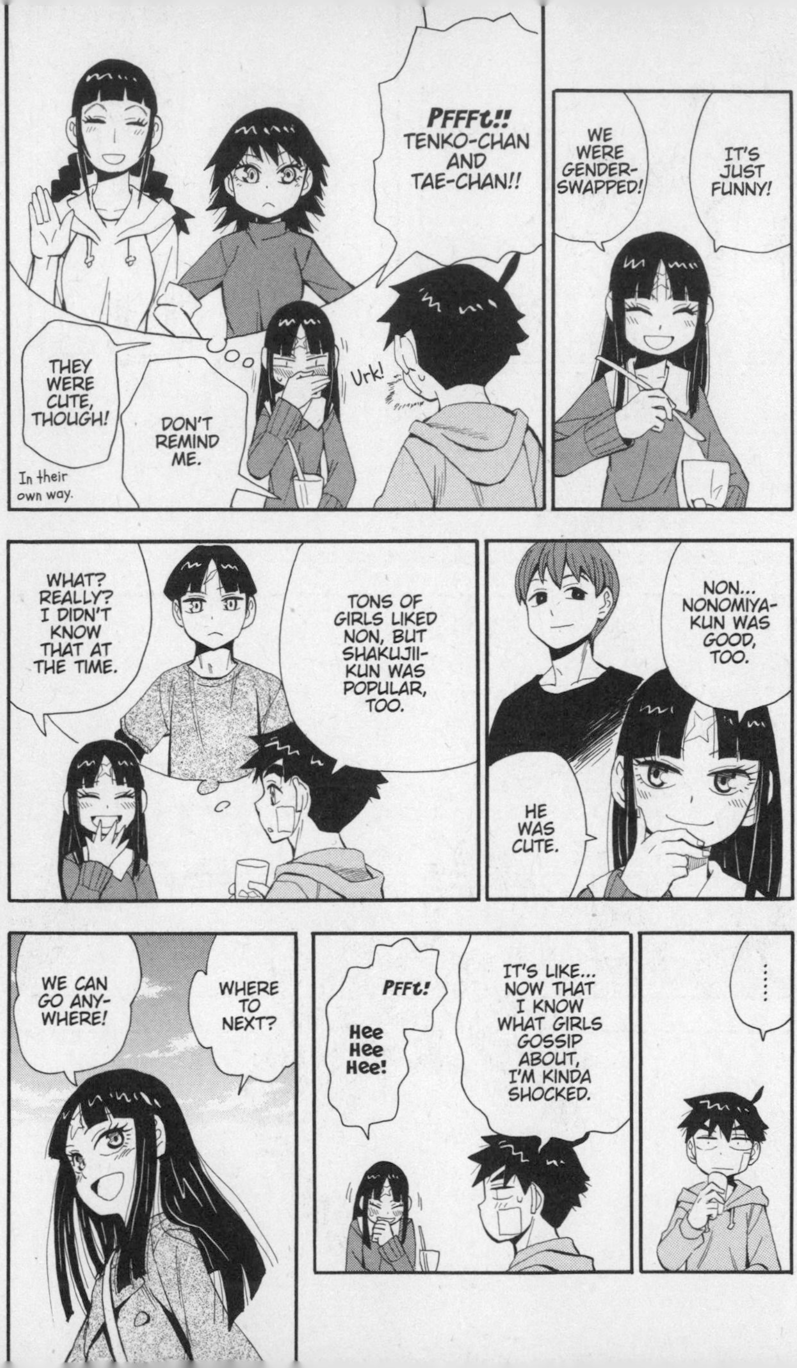
IT'S JUST FUNNY!
WE WERE GENDER-SWAPPED!
Pffft!! TENKO-CHAN AND TAE-CHAN!!
Urk!
DON'T REMIND ME.
THEY WERE CUTE, THOUGH!
In their own way.
NON... NONOMIYA-KUN WAS GOOD, TOO.
HE WAS CUTE.
TONS OF GIRLS LIKED NON, BUT SHAKUJII-KUN WAS POPULAR, TOO.
WHAT? REALLY? I DIDN'T KNOW THAT AT THE TIME.
......
IT'S LIKE... NOW THAT I KNOW WHAT GIRLS GOSSIP ABOUT, I'M KINDA SHOCKED.
Pfft!
Hee Hee Hee!
WHERE TO NEXT?
WE CAN GO ANYWHERE!

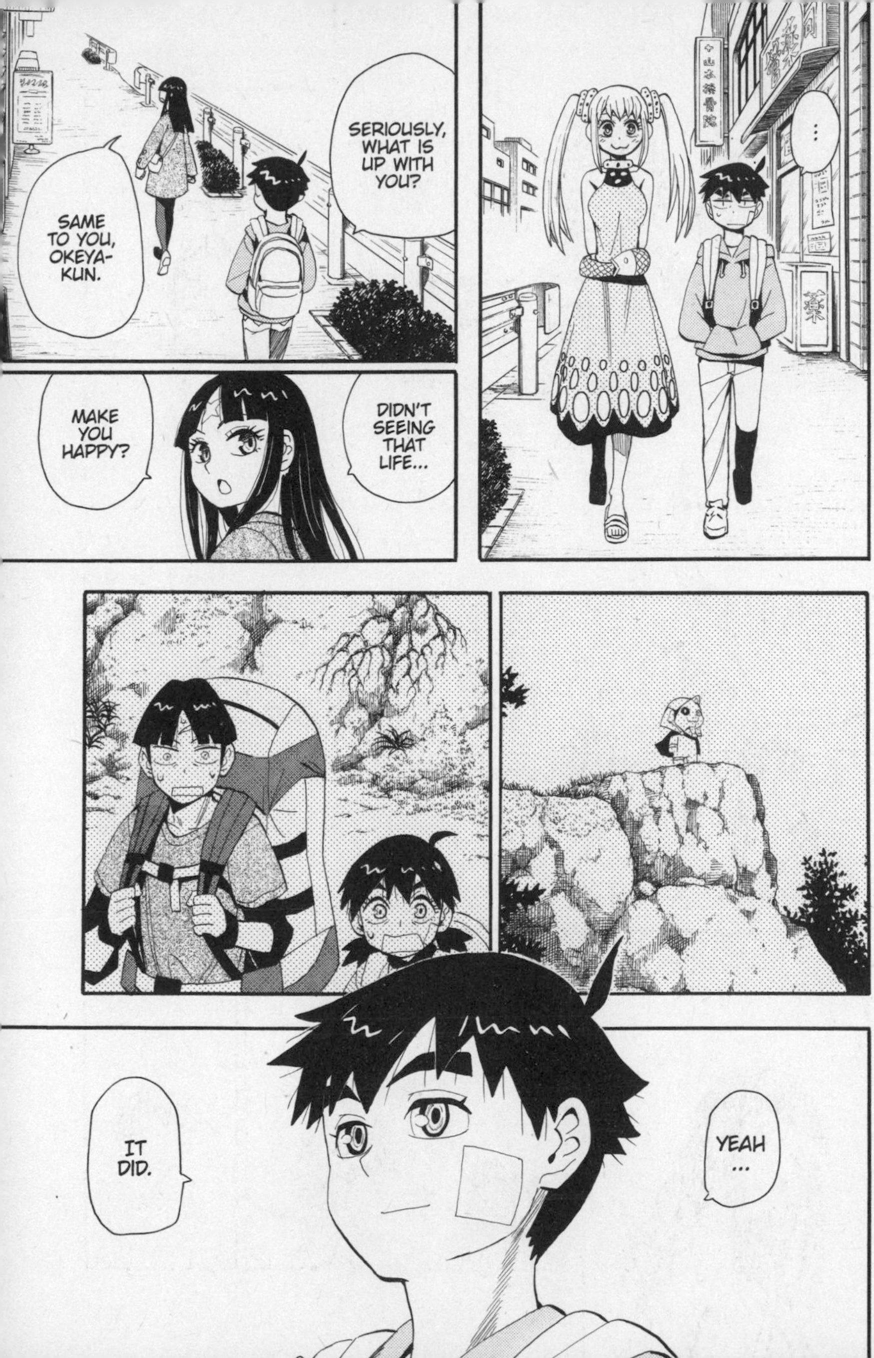
...
SERIOUSLY, WHAT IS UP WITH YOU?
SAME TO YOU, OKEYA-KUN.
DIDN'T SEEING THAT LIFE...
MAKE YOU HAPPY?
YEAH ...
IT DID.

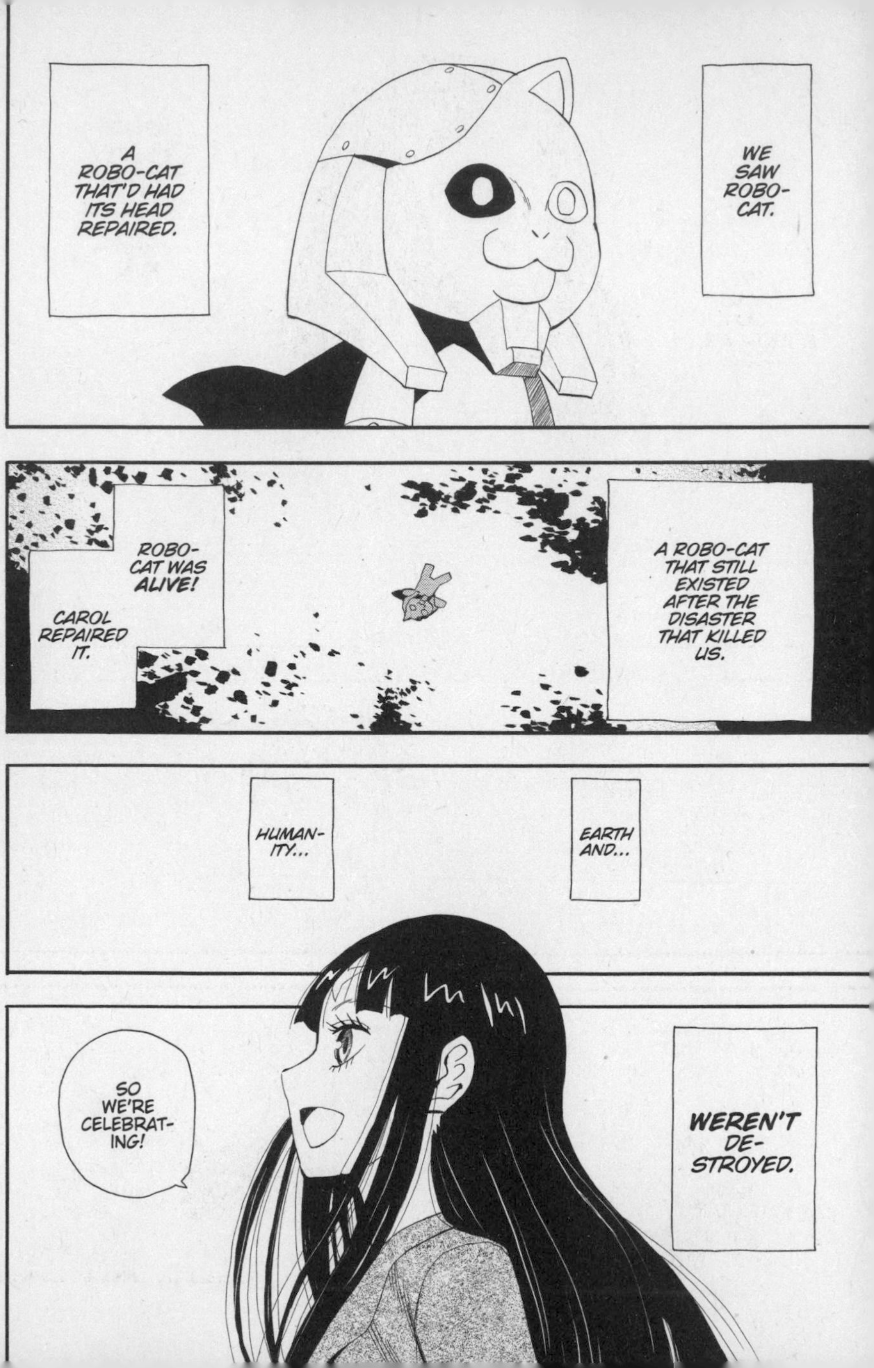
WE SAW ROBO-CAT.
A ROBO-CAT THAT'D HAD ITS HEAD REPAIRED.
A ROBO-CAT THAT STILL EXISTED AFTER THE DISASTER THAT KILLED US.
ROBO-CAT WAS ALIVE!
CAROL REPAIRED IT.
EARTH AND...
HUMANITY...
WEREN'T DESTROYED.
SO WE'RE CELEBRATING!

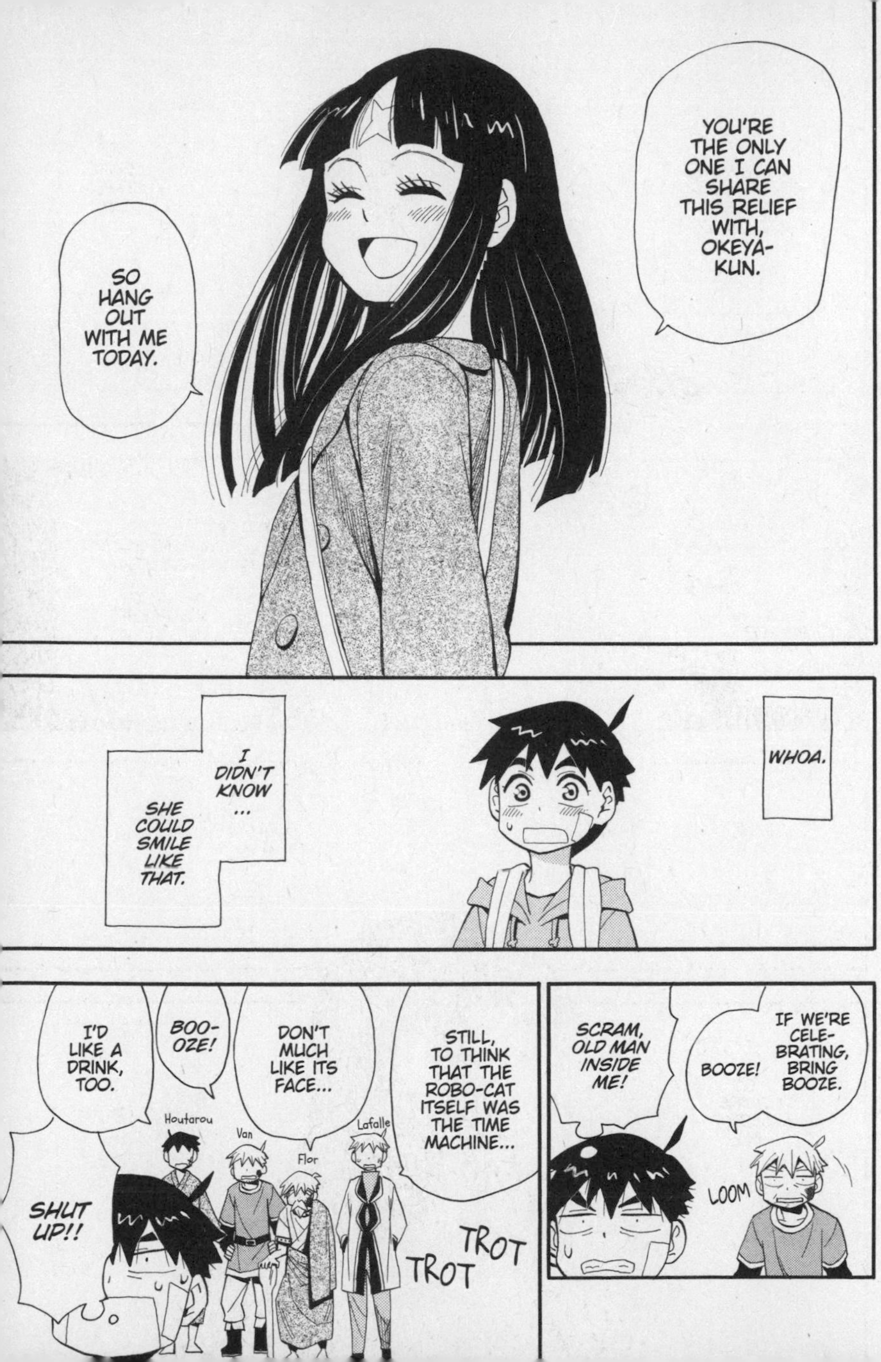
YOU'RE THE ONLY ONE I CAN SHARE THIS RELIEF WITH, OKEYA-KUN.
SO HANG OUT WITH ME TODAY.
WHOA.
I DIDN'T KNOW...
SHE COULD SMILE LIKE THAT.
IF WE'RE CELE-BRATING, BRING BOOZE.
BOOZE!
SCRAM, OLD MAN INSIDE ME!
LOOM
STILL, TO THINK THAT THE ROBO-CAT ITSELF WAS THE TIME MACHINE...
DON'T MUCH LIKE ITS FACE...
BOO-OZE!
I'D LIKE A DRINK, TOO.
Lafalle
Van
Houtarou
Flor
TROT
TROT
SHUT UP!!

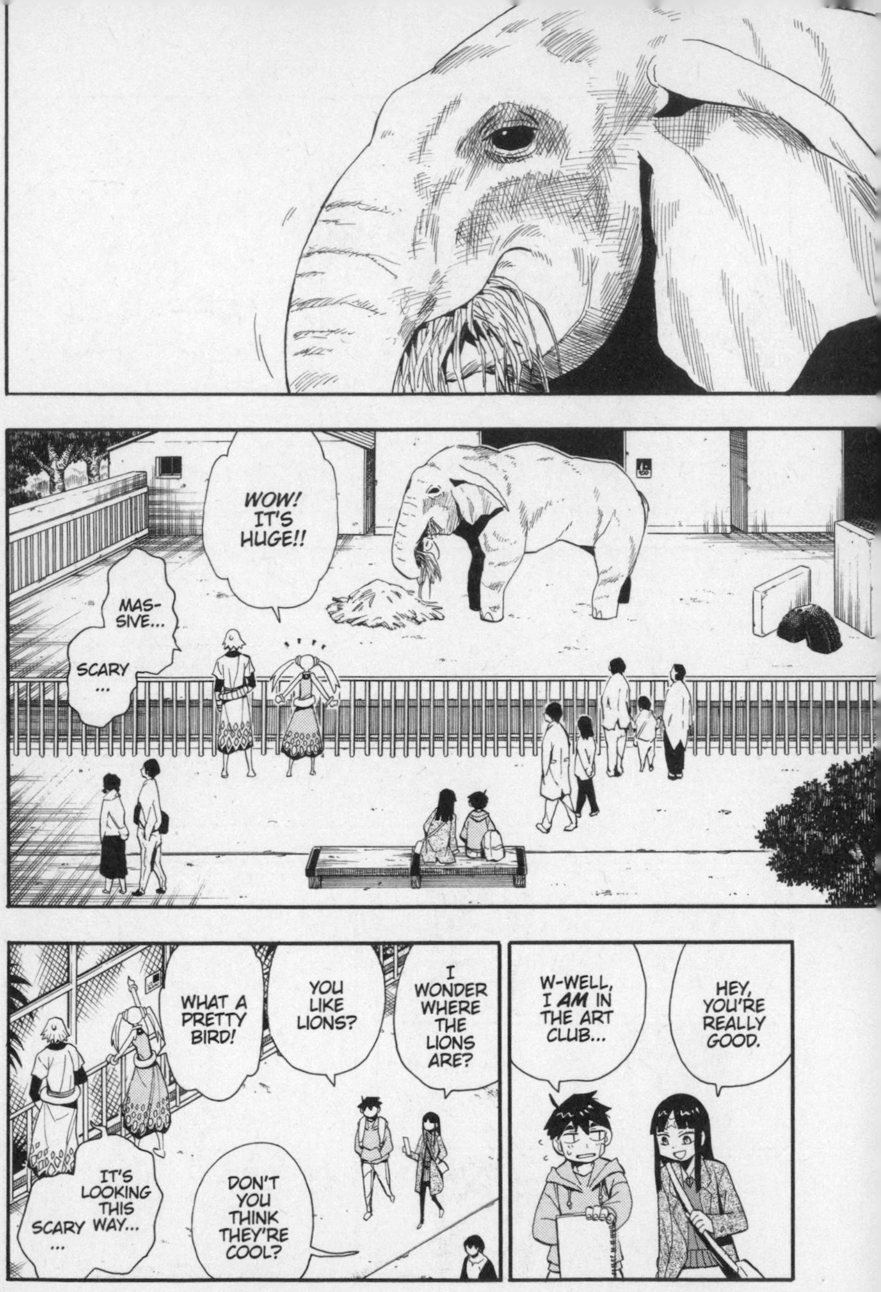
WOW! IT'S HUGE!!
MAS-SIVE...
SCARY...
HEY, YOU'RE REALLY GOOD.
W-WELL, I *AM* IN THE ART CLUB...
I WONDER WHERE THE LIONS ARE?
YOU LIKE LIONS?
WHAT A PRETTY BIRD!
DON'T YOU THINK THEY'RE COOL?
IT'S LOOKING THIS WAY...
SCARY...

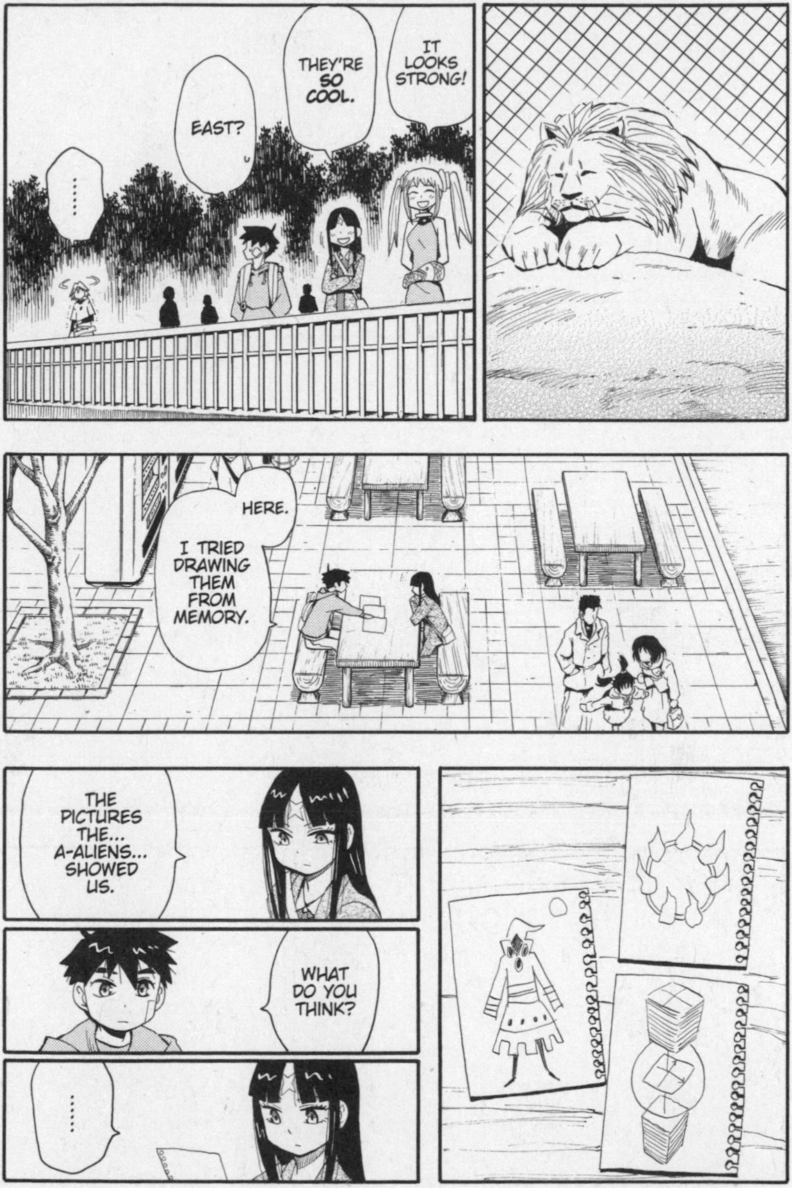
IT LOOKS STRONG!
THEY'RE SO COOL.
EAST?
......
HERE.
I TRIED DRAWING THEM FROM MEMORY.
THE PICTURES THE... A-ALIENS... SHOWED US.
WHAT DO YOU THINK?
......

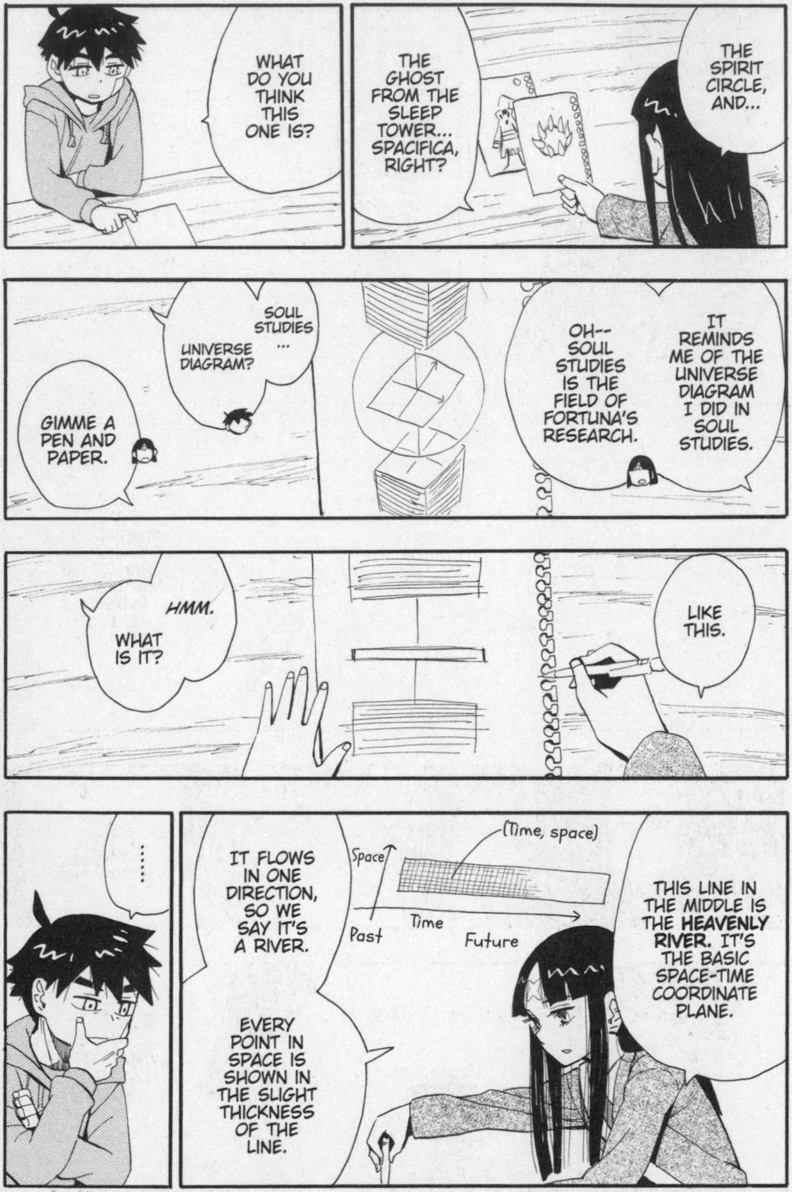
THE SPIRIT CIRCLE, AND...
THE GHOST FROM THE SLEEP TOWER... SPACIFICA, RIGHT?
WHAT DO YOU THINK THIS ONE IS?
IT REMINDS ME OF THE UNIVERSE DIAGRAM I DID IN SOUL STUDIES.
OH-- SOUL STUDIES IS THE FIELD OF FORTUNA'S RESEARCH.
SOUL STUDIES ...
UNIVERSE DIAGRAM?
GIMME A PEN AND PAPER.
LIKE THIS.
HMM.
WHAT IS IT?
THIS LINE IN THE MIDDLE IS THE **HEAVENLY RIVER.** IT'S THE BASIC SPACE-TIME COORDINATE PLANE.
(Time, space)
Space
Time
Past
Future
IT FLOWS IN ONE DIRECTION, SO WE SAY IT'S A RIVER.
EVERY POINT IN SPACE IS SHOWN IN THE SLIGHT THICKNESS OF THE LINE.
......

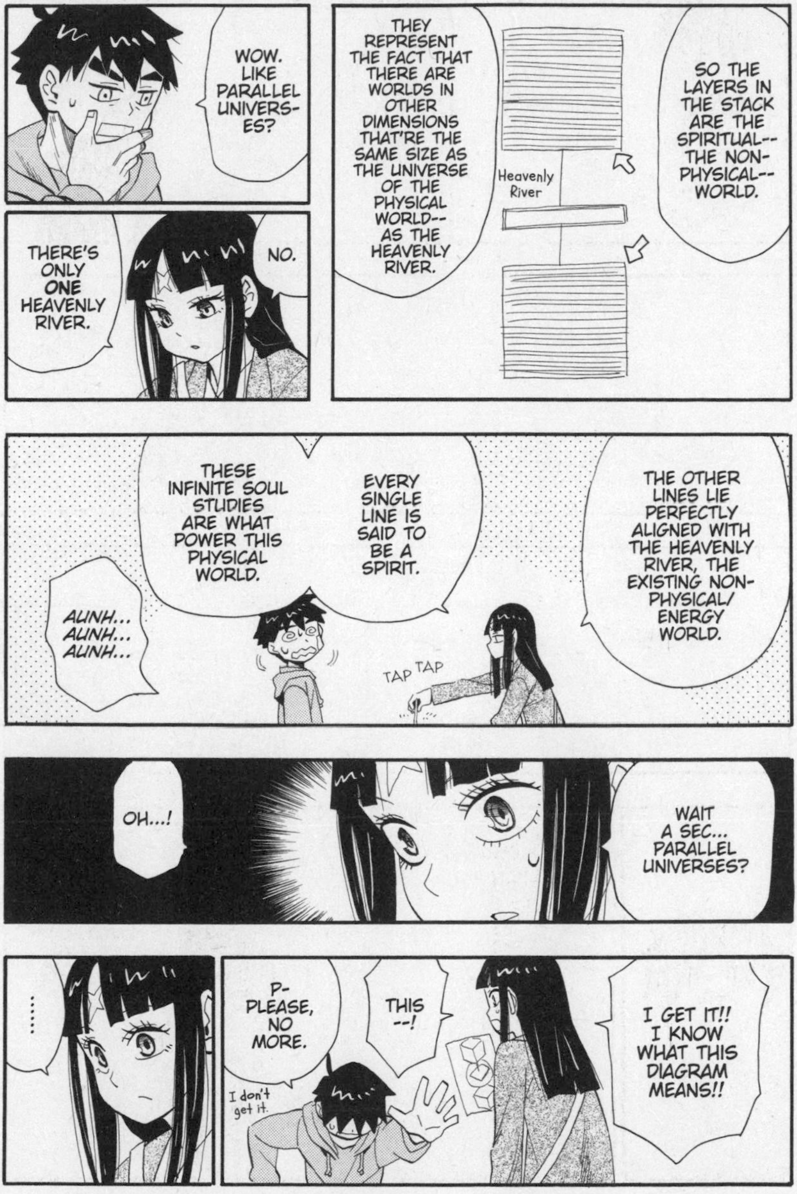
SO THE LAYERS IN THE STACK ARE THE SPIRITUAL-- THE NON-PHYSICAL-- WORLD.
THEY REPRESENT THE FACT THAT THERE ARE WORLDS IN OTHER DIMENSIONS THAT'RE THE SAME SIZE AS THE UNIVERSE OF THE PHYSICAL WORLD-- AS THE HEAVENLY RIVER.
Heavenly River
WOW. LIKE PARALLEL UNIVERS-ES?
NO.
THERE'S ONLY ONE HEAVENLY RIVER.
THE OTHER LINES LIE PERFECTLY ALIGNED WITH THE HEAVENLY RIVER, THE EXISTING NON-PHYSICAL/ ENERGY WORLD.
EVERY SINGLE LINE IS SAID TO BE A SPIRIT.
THESE INFINITE SOUL STUDIES ARE WHAT POWER THIS PHYSICAL WORLD.
TAP TAP
AUNH... AUNH... AUNH...
WAIT A SEC... PARALLEL UNIVERSES?
OH...!
I GET IT!! I KNOW WHAT THIS DIAGRAM MEANS!!
THIS --!
P- PLEASE, NO MORE.
I don't get it.
......

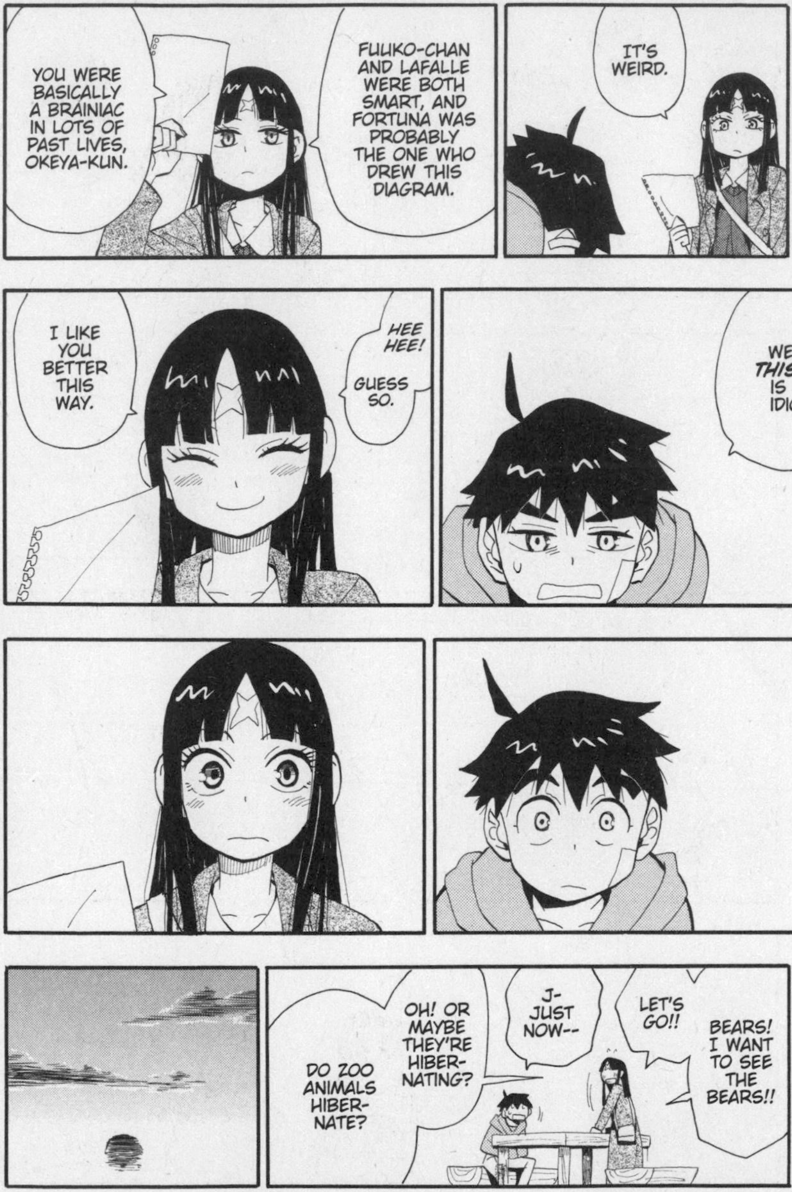
IT'S WEIRD.
FUUKO-CHAN AND LAFALLE WERE BOTH SMART, AND FORTUNA WAS PROBABLY THE ONE WHO DREW THIS DIAGRAM.
YOU WERE BASICALLY A BRAINIAC IN LOTS OF PAST LIVES, OKEYA-KUN.
WELL, *THIS* ME IS AN IDIOT.
HEE HEE!
GUESS SO.
I LIKE YOU BETTER THIS WAY.
BEARS! I WANT TO SEE THE BEARS!!
LET'S GO!!
J- JUST NOW--
OH! OR MAYBE THEY'RE HIBER- NATING?
DO ZOO ANIMALS HIBER- NATE?

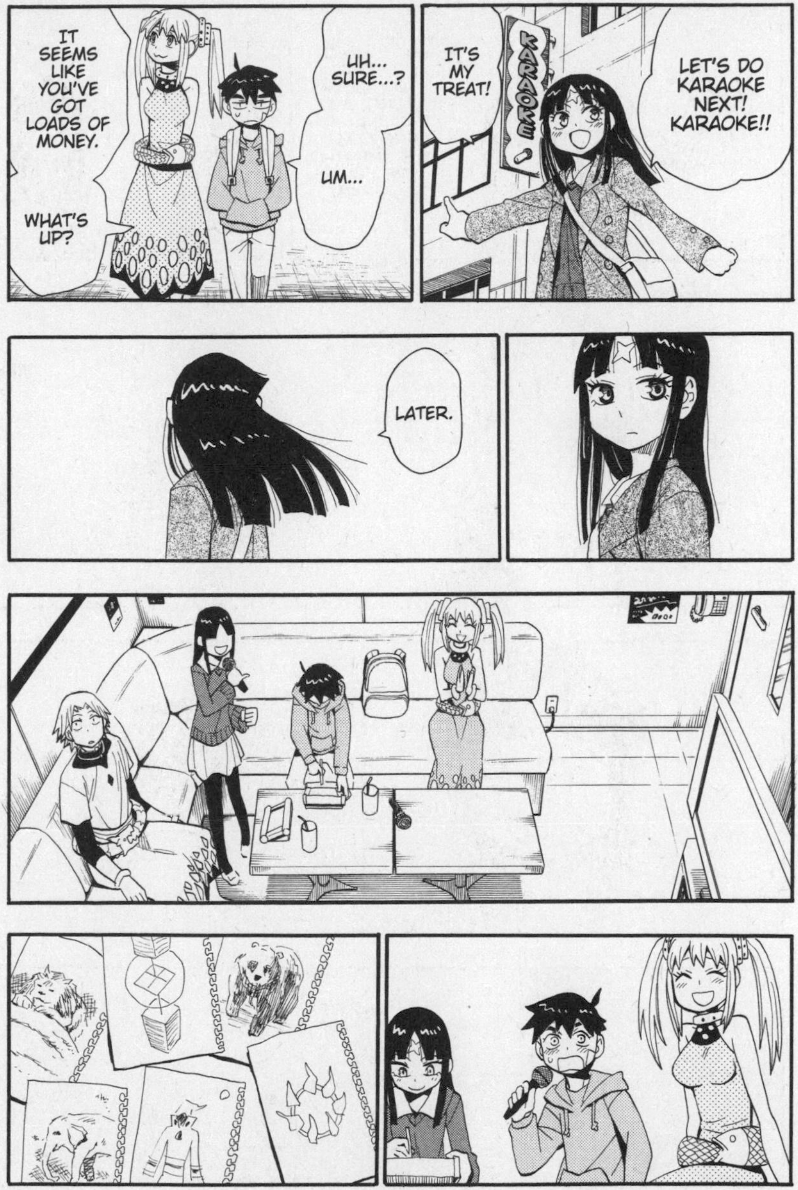
LET'S DO KARAOKE NEXT! KARAOKE!!
KARAOKE
IT'S MY TREAT!
UH... SURE...?
IT SEEMS LIKE YOU'VE GOT LOADS OF MONEY.
UM...
WHAT'S UP?
LATER.

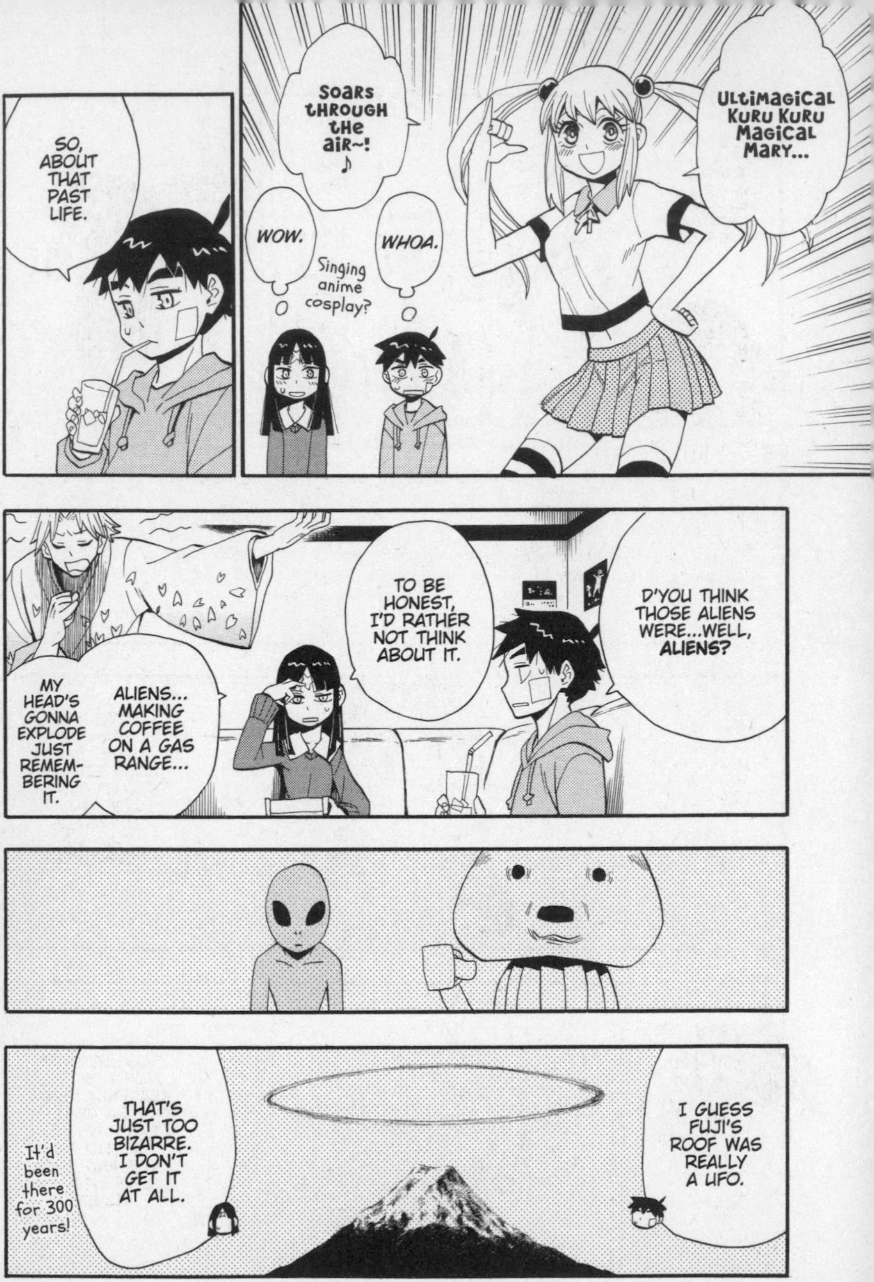
Ultimagical Kuru Kuru Magical Mary...
Soars through the air~! ♪
WHOA.
Singing anime cosplay?
WOW.
SO, ABOUT THAT PAST LIFE.
D'YOU THINK THOSE ALIENS WERE...WELL, ALIENS?
TO BE HONEST, I'D RATHER NOT THINK ABOUT IT.
ALIENS... MAKING COFFEE ON A GAS RANGE...
MY HEAD'S GONNA EXPLODE JUST REMEMBERING IT.
I GUESS FUJI'S ROOF WAS REALLY A UFO.
THAT'S JUST TOO BIZARRE. I DON'T GET IT AT ALL.
It'd been there for 300 years!

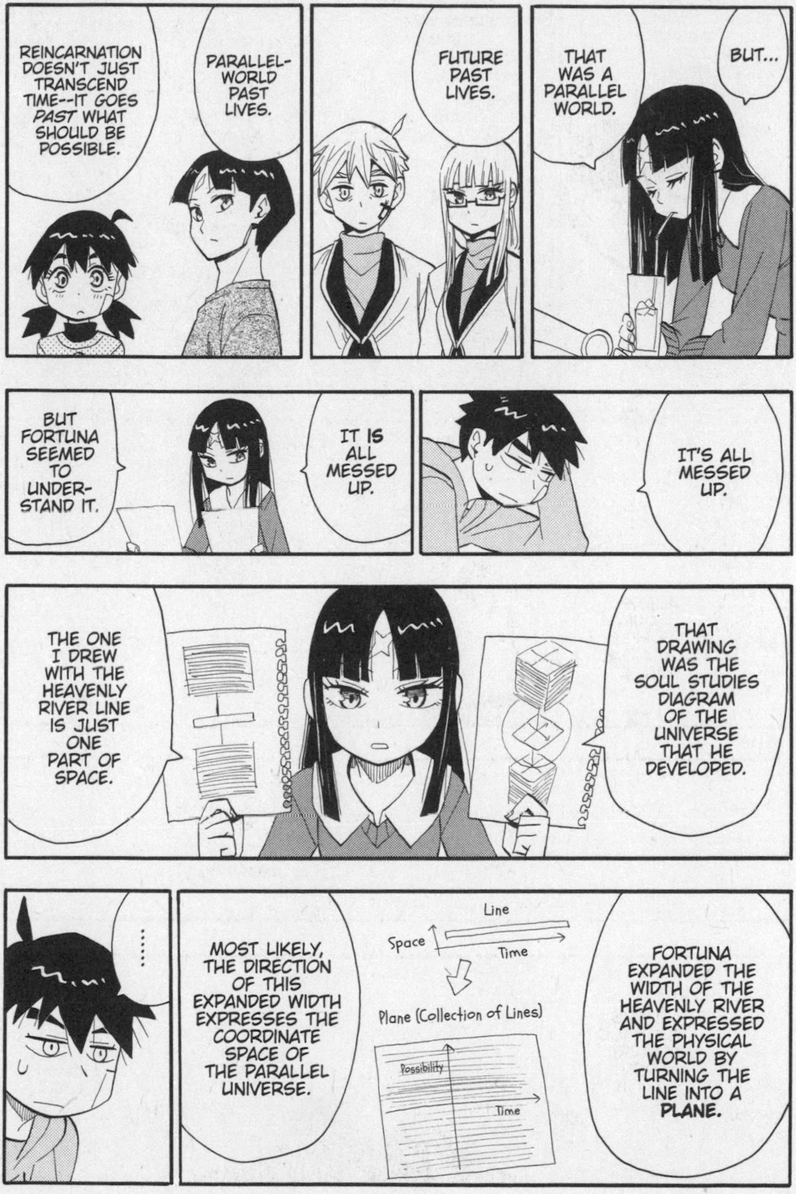
BUT...
THAT WAS A PARALLEL WORLD.
FUTURE PAST LIVES.
PARALLEL-WORLD PAST LIVES.
REINCARNATION DOESN'T JUST TRANSCEND TIME--IT GOES *PAST* WHAT SHOULD BE POSSIBLE.
IT'S ALL MESSED UP.
IT IS ALL MESSED UP.
BUT FORTUNA SEEMED TO UNDER-STAND IT.
THAT DRAWING WAS THE SOUL STUDIES DIAGRAM OF THE UNIVERSE THAT HE DEVELOPED.
THE ONE I DREW WITH THE HEAVENLY RIVER LINE IS JUST ONE PART OF SPACE.
FORTUNA EXPANDED THE WIDTH OF THE HEAVENLY RIVER AND EXPRESSED THE PHYSICAL WORLD BY TURNING THE LINE INTO A **PLANE.**
Line
Space
Time
Plane (Collection of Lines)
Possibility
Time
MOST LIKELY, THE DIRECTION OF THIS EXPANDED WIDTH EXPRESSES THE COORDINATE SPACE OF THE PARALLEL UNIVERSE.
......

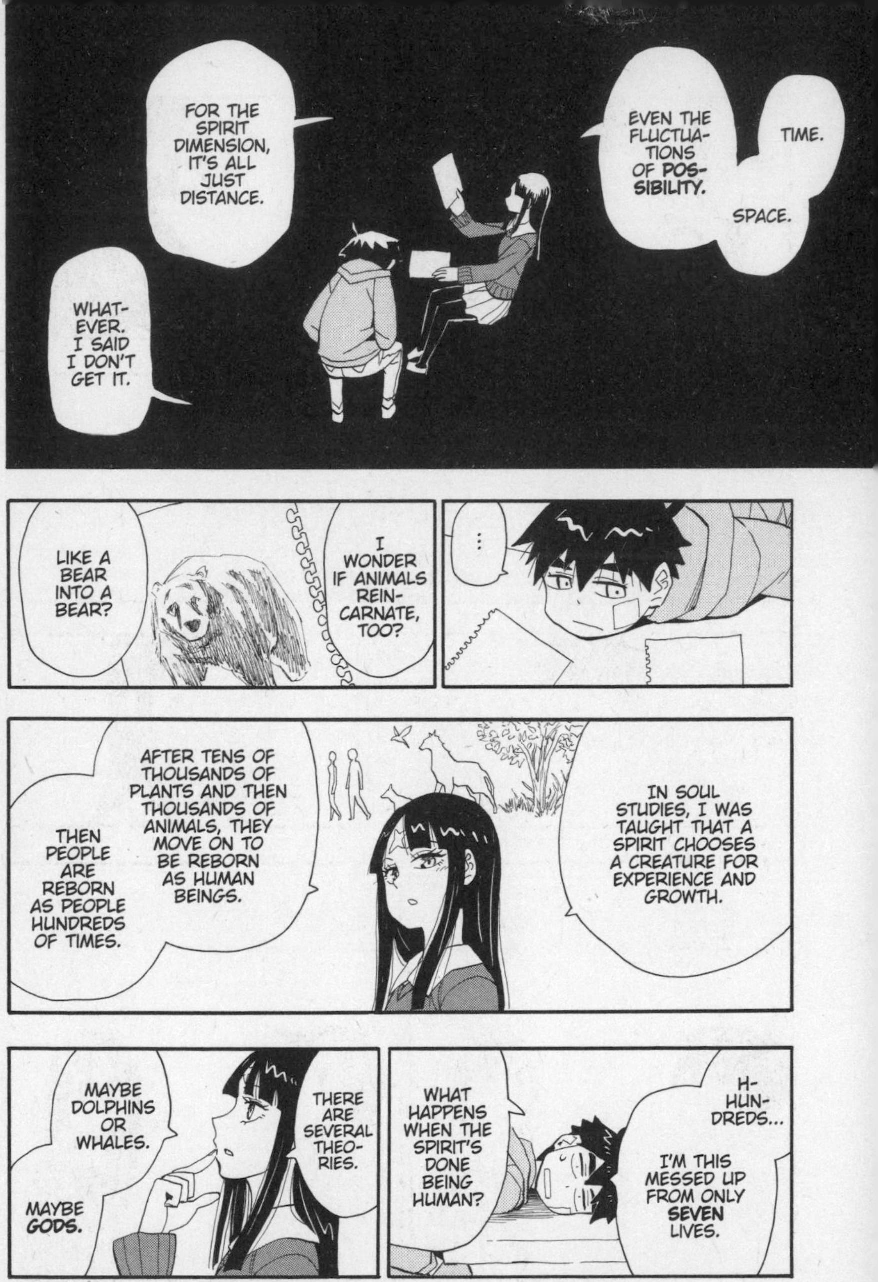
TIME.
SPACE.
EVEN THE FLUCTUATIONS OF **POSSIBILITY.**
FOR THE SPIRIT DIMENSION, IT'S ALL JUST DISTANCE.
WHATEVER. I SAID I DON'T GET IT.
...
I WONDER IF ANIMALS REINCARNATE, TOO?
LIKE A BEAR INTO A BEAR?
IN SOUL STUDIES, I WAS TAUGHT THAT A SPIRIT CHOOSES A CREATURE FOR EXPERIENCE AND GROWTH.
AFTER TENS OF THOUSANDS OF PLANTS AND THEN THOUSANDS OF ANIMALS, THEY MOVE ON TO BE REBORN AS HUMAN BEINGS.
THEN PEOPLE ARE REBORN AS PEOPLE HUNDREDS OF TIMES.
H-HUNDREDS...
I'M THIS MESSED UP FROM ONLY **SEVEN** LIVES.
WHAT HAPPENS WHEN THE SPIRIT'S DONE BEING HUMAN?
THERE ARE SEVERAL THEORIES.
MAYBE DOLPHINS OR WHALES.
MAYBE **GODS.**

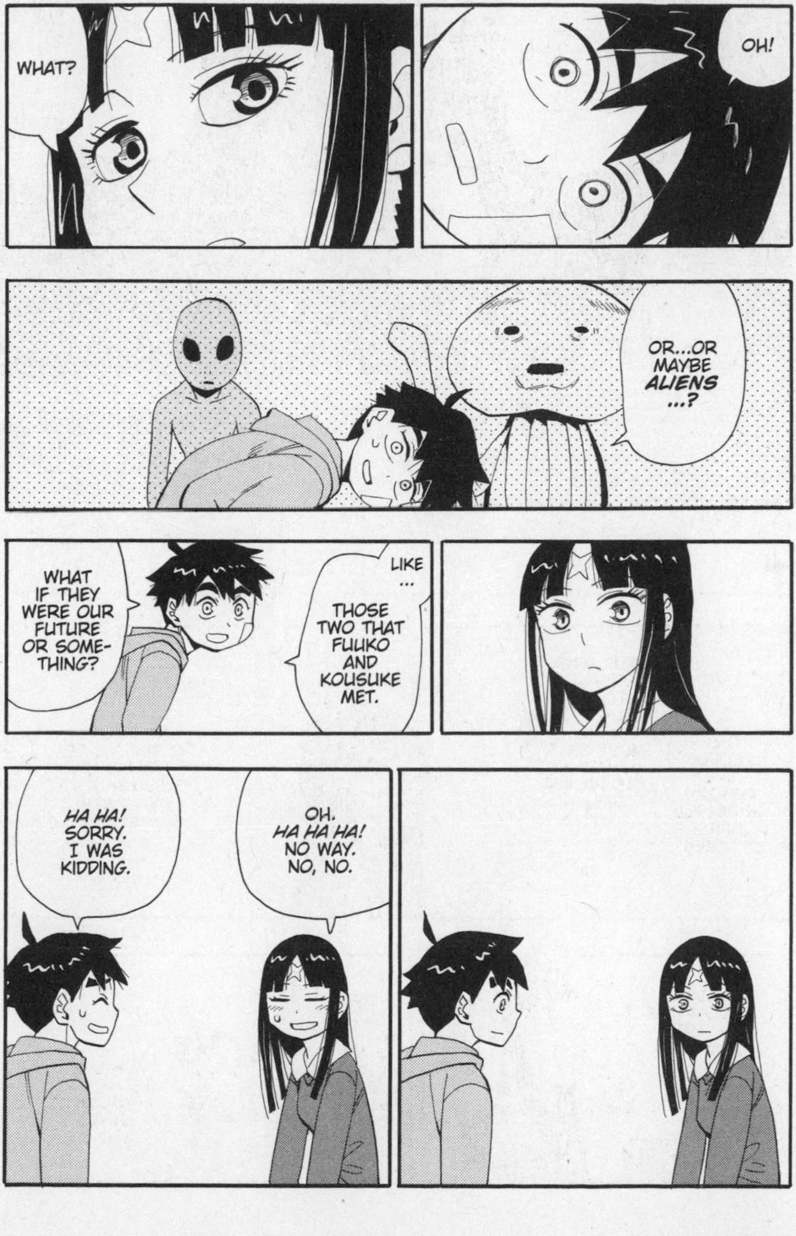
OH!
WHAT?
OR...OR MAYBE ALIENS ...?
LIKE ... THOSE TWO THAT FUUKO AND KOUSUKE MET.
WHAT IF THEY WERE OUR FUTURE OR SOME-THING?
OH. HA HA HA! NO WAY. NO, NO.
HA HA! SORRY. I WAS KIDDING.

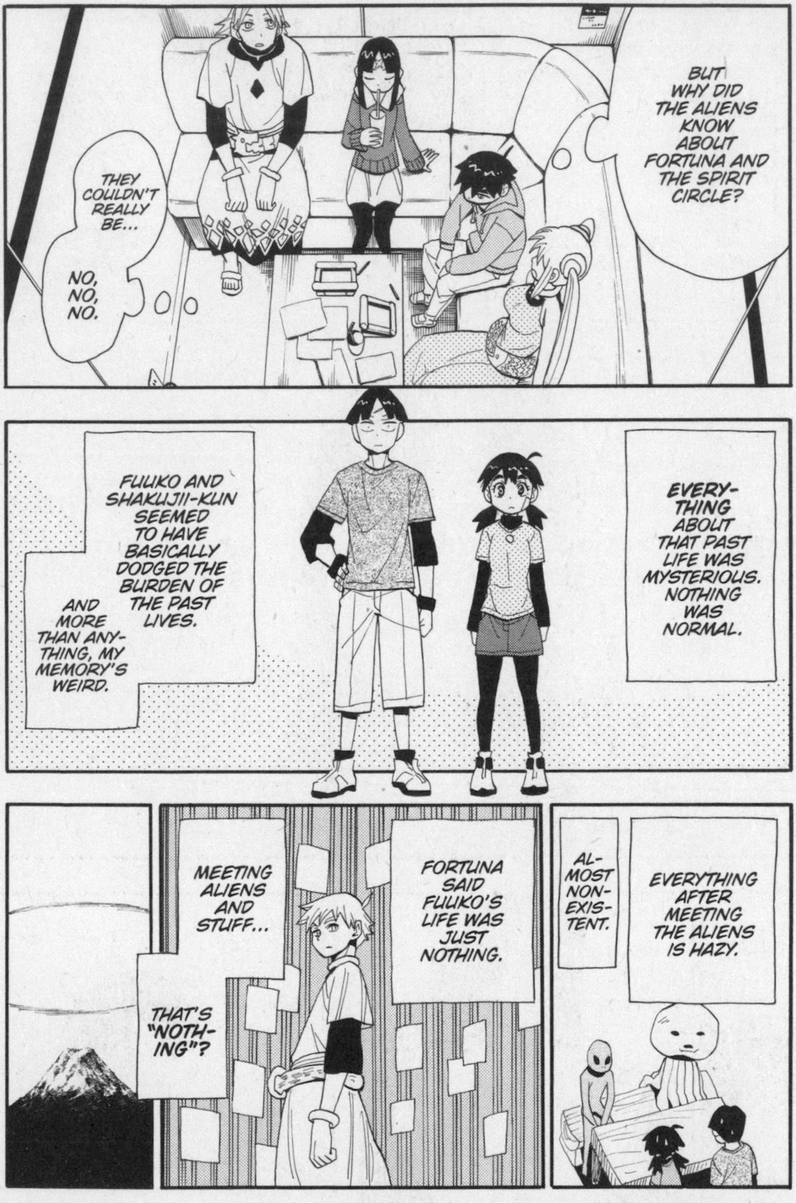
BUT WHY DID THE ALIENS KNOW ABOUT FORTUNA AND THE SPIRIT CIRCLE?
THEY COULDN'T REALLY BE...
NO, NO, NO.
EVERYTHING ABOUT THAT PAST LIFE WAS MYSTERIOUS. NOTHING WAS NORMAL.
FUUKO AND SHAKUJII-KUN SEEMED TO HAVE BASICALLY DODGED THE BURDEN OF THE PAST LIVES.
AND MORE THAN ANYTHING, MY MEMORY'S WEIRD.
EVERYTHING AFTER MEETING THE ALIENS IS HAZY.
ALMOST NON-EXISTENT.
FORTUNA SAID FUUKO'S LIFE WAS JUST NOTHING.
MEETING ALIENS AND STUFF...
THAT'S "NOTHING"?

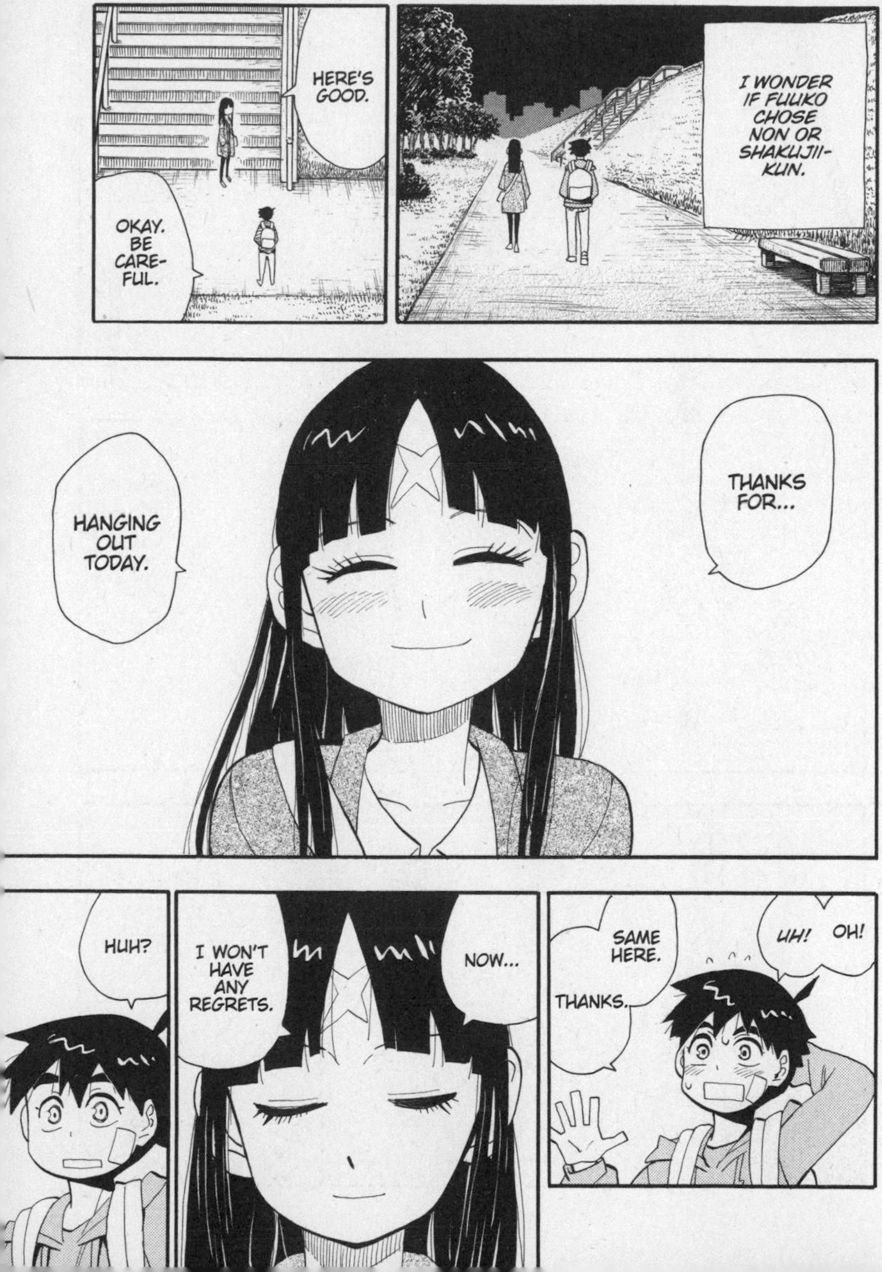
I WONDER IF FUUKO CHOSE NON OR SHAKUJII-KUN.
HERE'S GOOD.
OKAY. BE CARE-FUL.
THANKS FOR...
HANGING OUT TODAY.
UH! OH!
SAME HERE.
THANKS.
NOW...
I WON'T HAVE ANY REGRETS.
HUH?

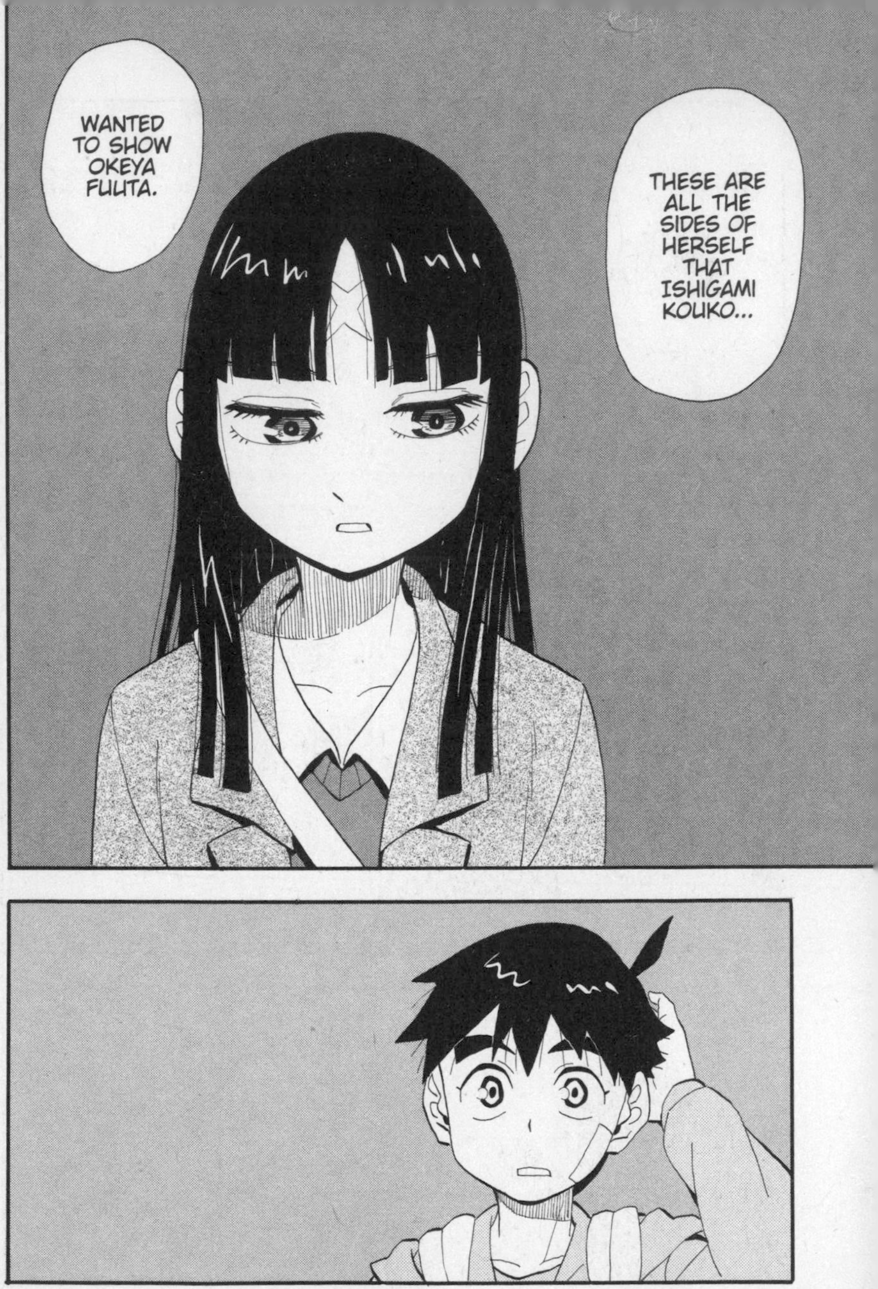
THESE ARE ALL THE SIDES OF HERSELF THAT ISHIGAMI KOUKO...
WANTED TO SHOW OKEYA FUUTA.

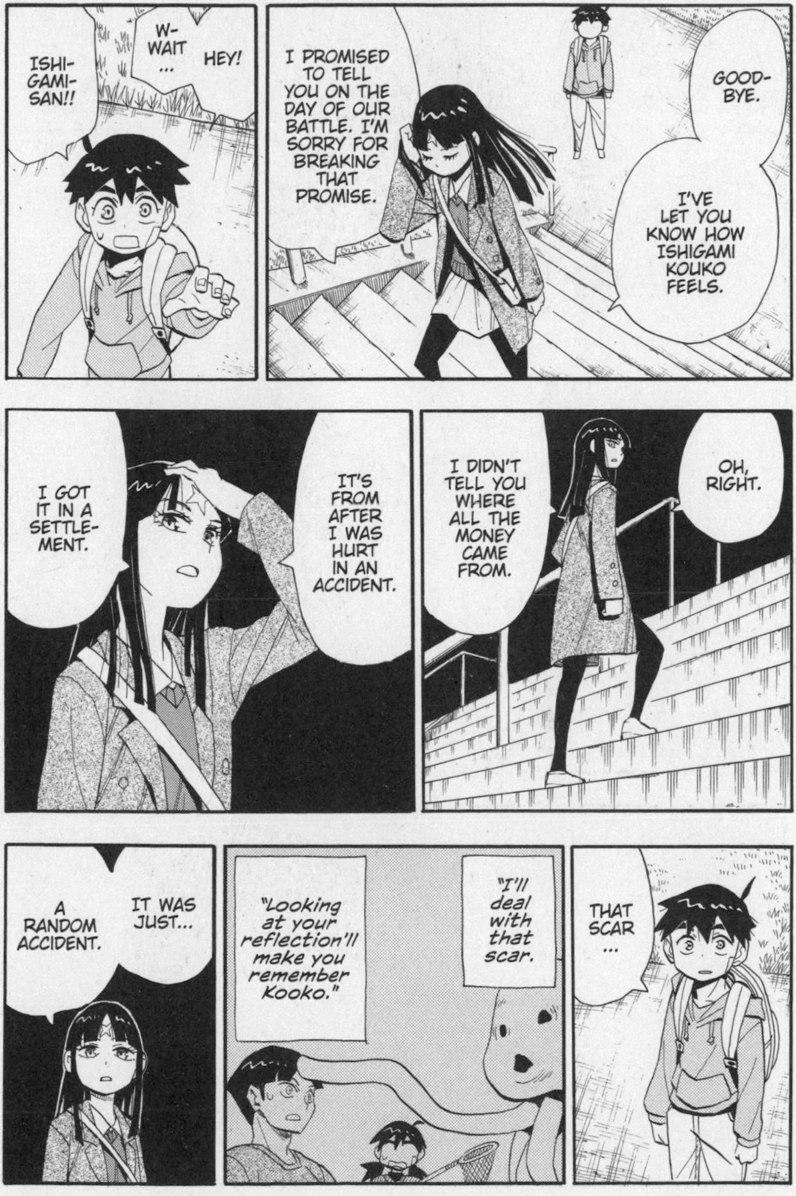
GOOD-BYE.
I'VE LET YOU KNOW HOW ISHIGAMI KOUKO FEELS.
I PROMISED TO TELL YOU ON THE DAY OF OUR BATTLE. I'M SORRY FOR BREAKING THAT PROMISE.
HEY!
W-WAIT ...
ISHI-GAMI-SAN!!
OH, RIGHT.
I DIDN'T TELL YOU WHERE ALL THE MONEY CAME FROM.
IT'S FROM AFTER I WAS HURT IN AN ACCIDENT.
I GOT IT IN A SETTLE-MENT.
THAT SCAR ...
"I'll deal with that scar.
"Looking at your reflection'll make you remember Kooko."
IT WAS JUST...
A RANDOM ACCIDENT.

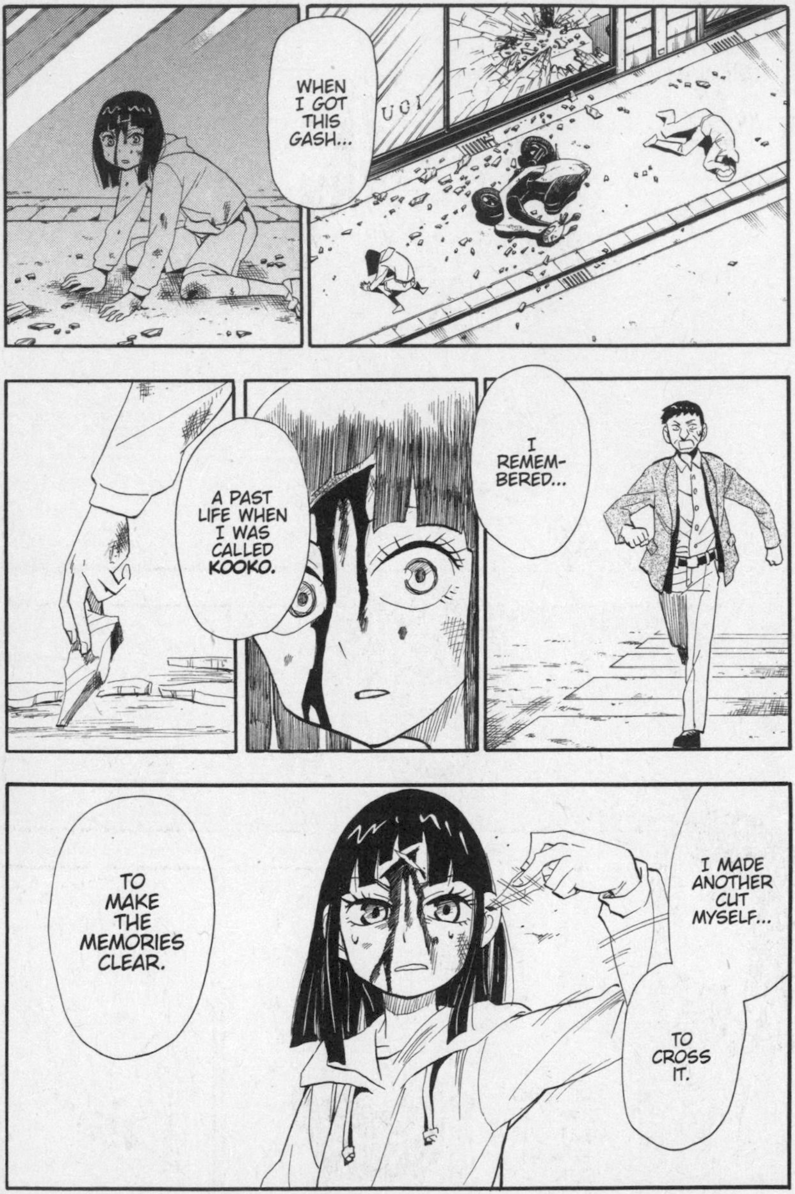
WHEN I GOT THIS GASH...
I REMEMBERED...
A PAST LIFE WHEN I WAS CALLED KOOKO.
I MADE ANOTHER CUT MYSELF...
TO CROSS IT.
TO MAKE THE MEMORIES CLEAR.

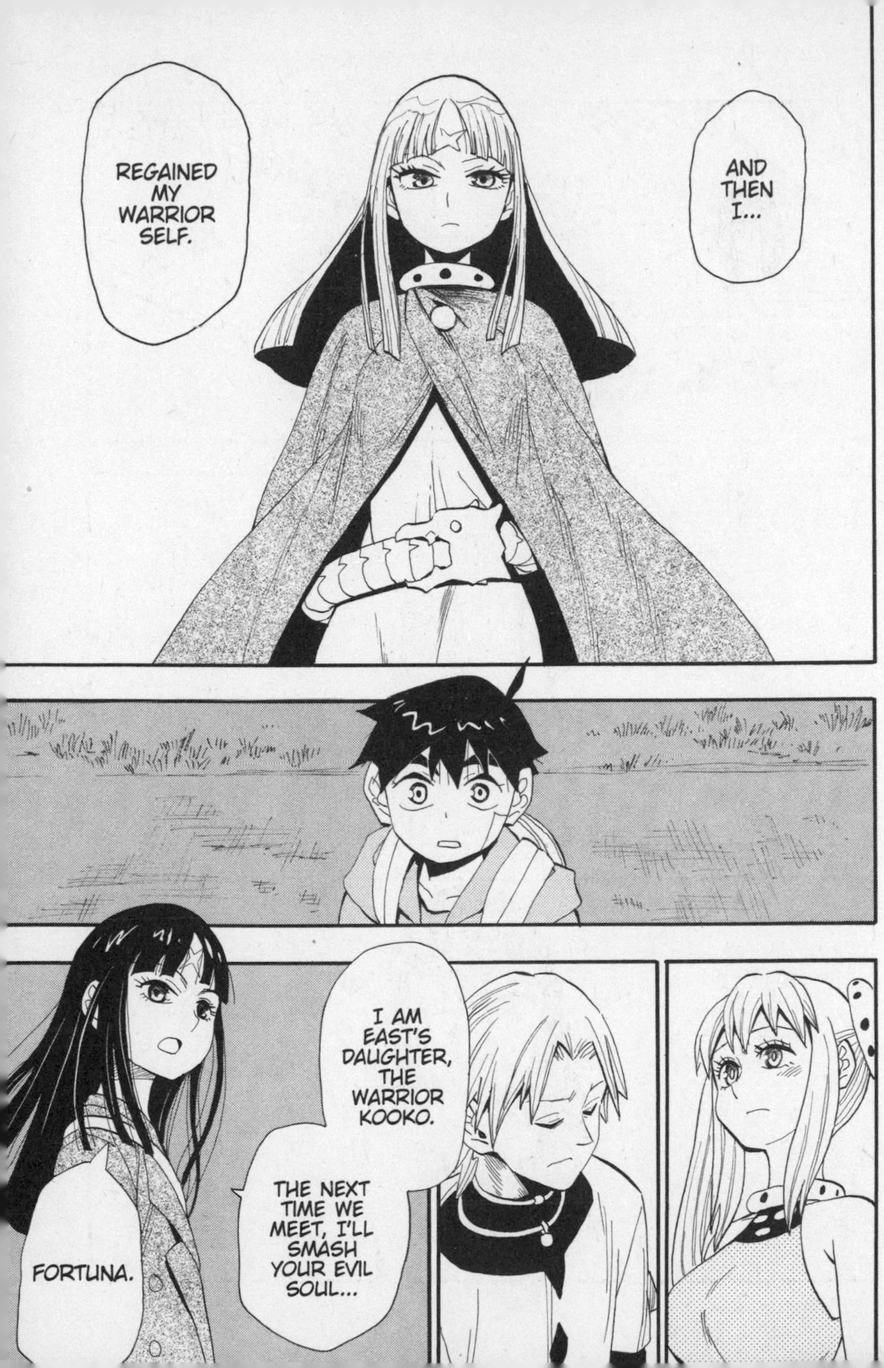
AND THEN I...
REGAINED MY WARRIOR SELF.
I AM EAST'S DAUGHTER, THE WARRIOR KOOKO.
THE NEXT TIME WE MEET, I'LL SMASH YOUR EVIL SOUL...
FORTUNA.

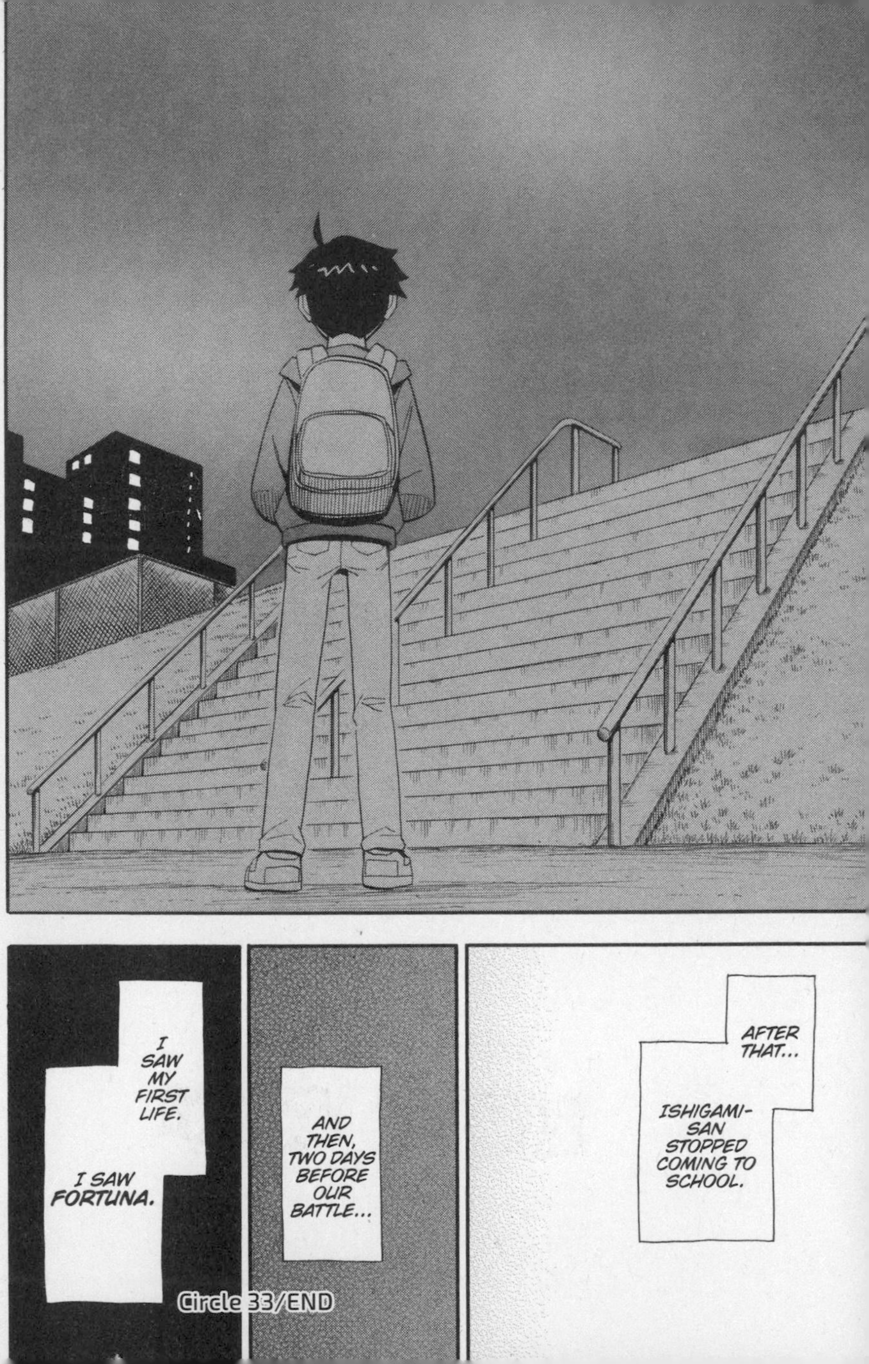
AFTER THAT...
ISHIGAMI-SAN STOPPED COMING TO SCHOOL.
AND THEN, TWO DAYS BEFORE OUR BATTLE...
I SAW MY FIRST LIFE.
I SAW FORTUNA.
Circle 33/END

Circle 34
Fortuna
1

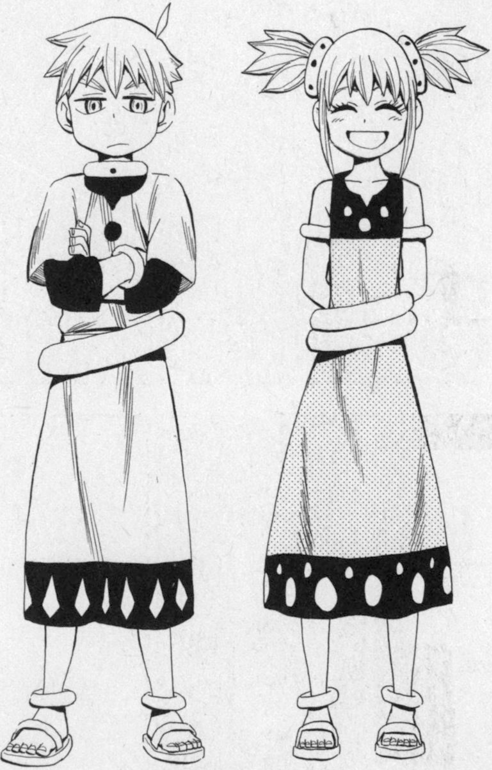

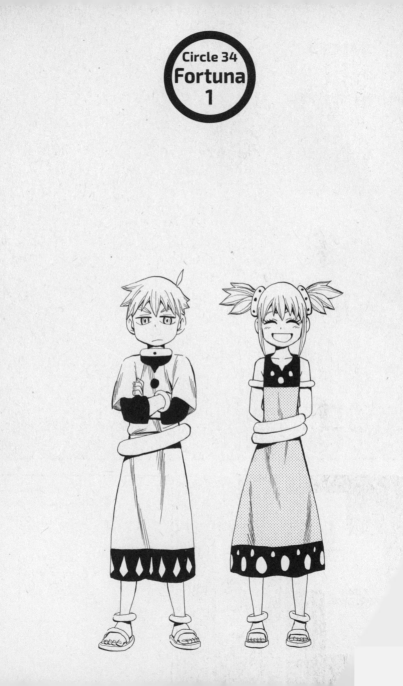

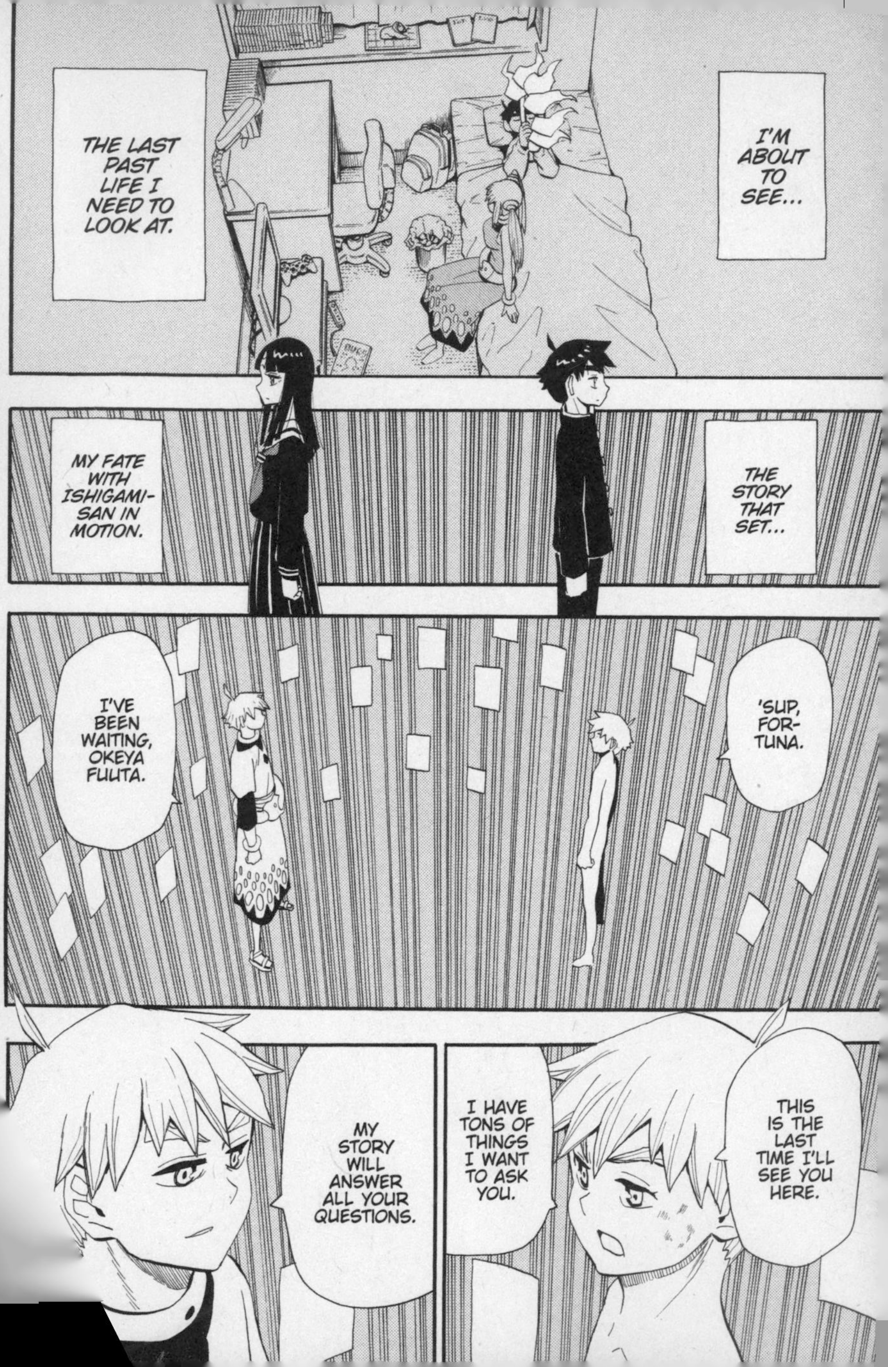
I'M ABOUT TO SEE...
THE LAST PAST LIFE I NEED TO LOOK AT.
THE STORY THAT SET...
MY FATE WITH ISHIGAMI-SAN IN MOTION.
'SUP, FOR-TUNA.
I'VE BEEN WAITING, OKEYA FUUTA.
THIS IS THE LAST TIME I'LL SEE YOU HERE.
I HAVE TONS OF THINGS I WANT TO ASK YOU.
MY STORY WILL ANSWER ALL YOUR QUESTIONS.

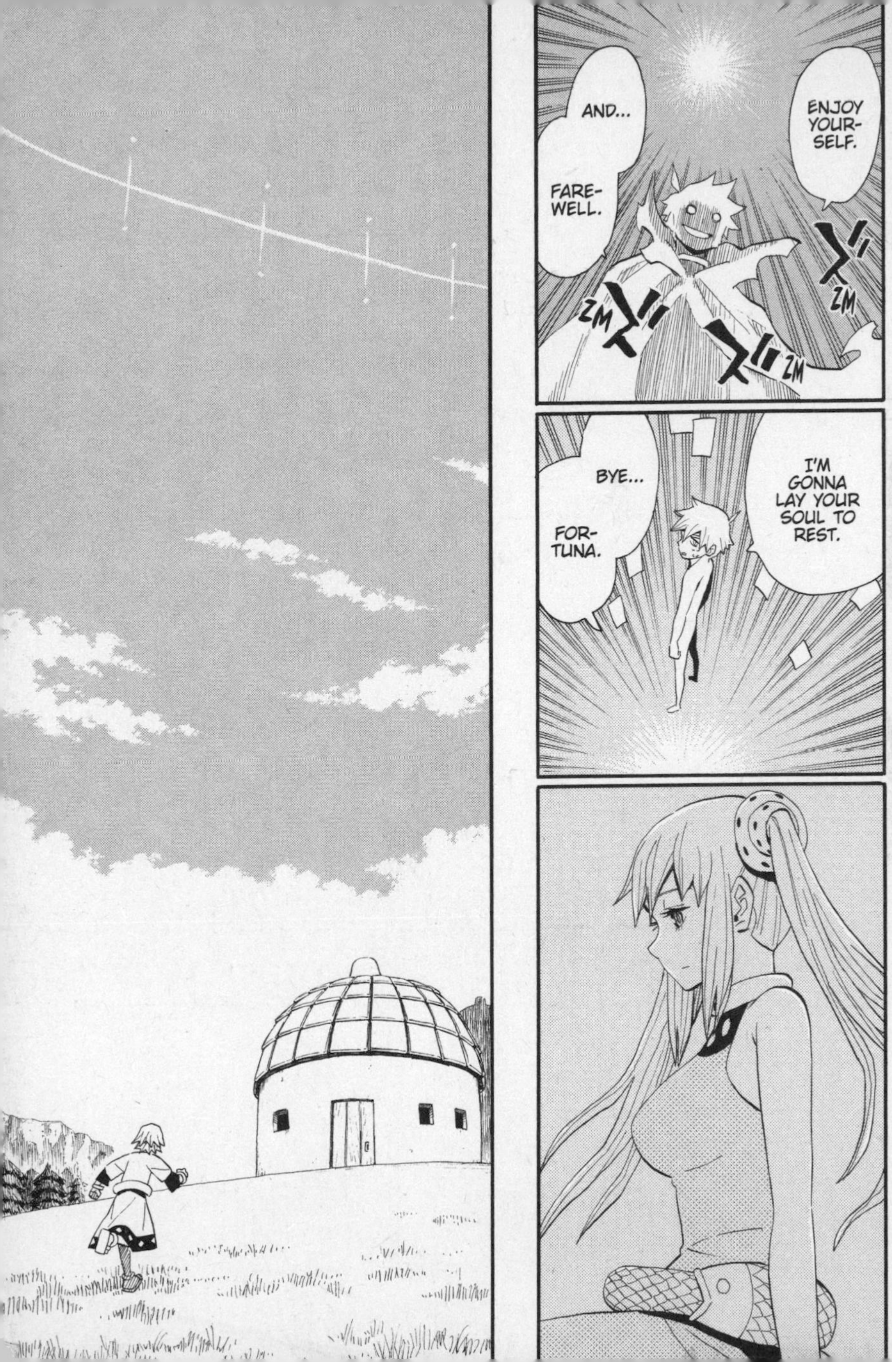
ENJOY YOUR-SELF.
ZM
AND... FARE-WELL.
ZM
ZM
I'M GONNA LAY YOUR SOUL TO REST.
BYE... FOR-TUNA.

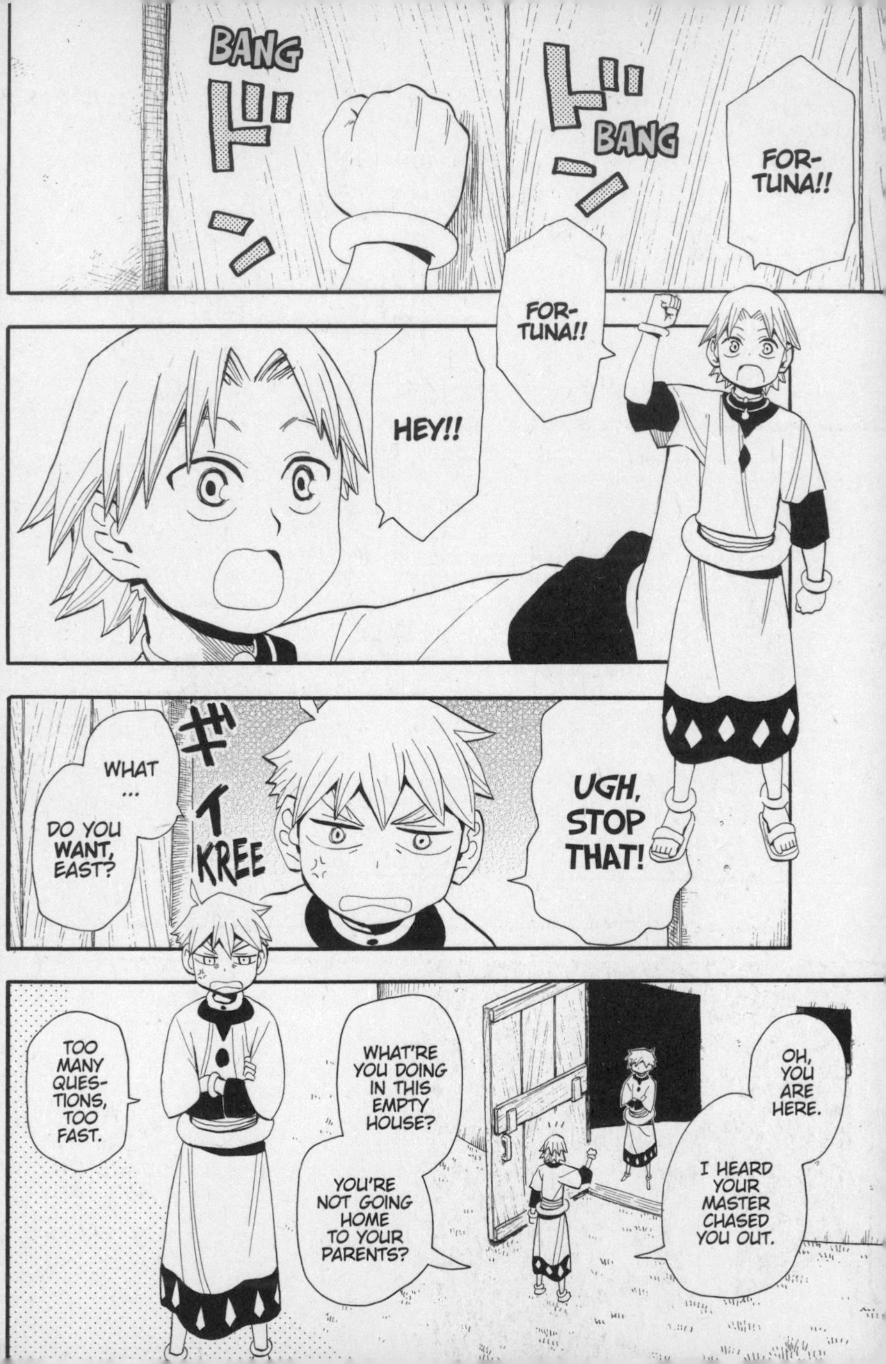
FOR-TUNA!!
BANG
BANG
FOR-TUNA!!
HEY!!
UGH, STOP THAT!
ギイ KREE
WHAT ... DO YOU WANT, EAST?
OH, YOU ARE HERE.
I HEARD YOUR MASTER CHASED YOU OUT.
WHAT'RE YOU DOING IN THIS EMPTY HOUSE?
YOU'RE NOT GOING HOME TO YOUR PARENTS?
TOO MANY QUESTIONS, TOO FAST.

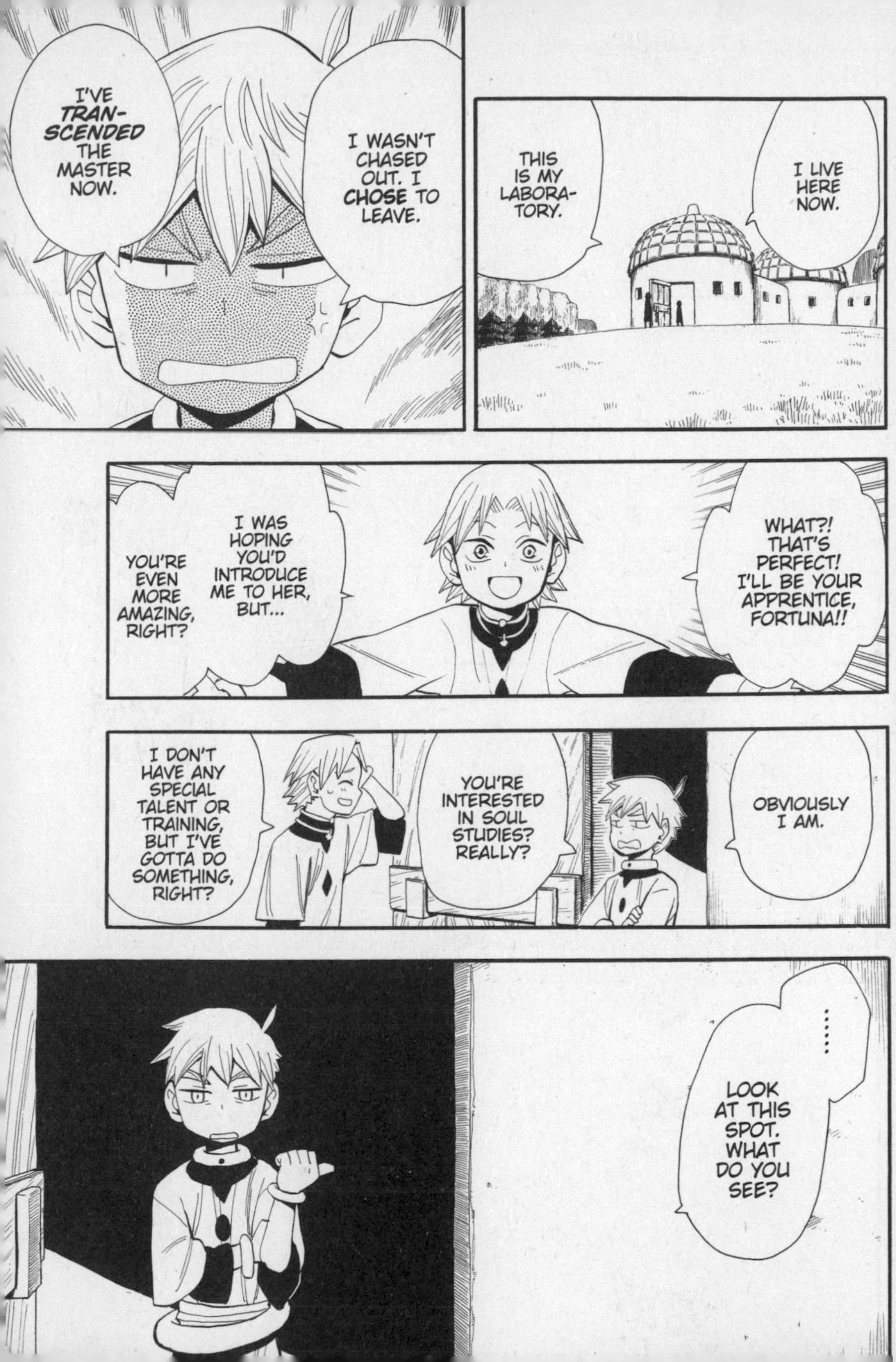
I LIVE HERE NOW.
THIS IS MY LABORATORY.
I WASN'T CHASED OUT. I **CHOSE** TO LEAVE.
I'VE ***TRANSCENDED*** THE MASTER NOW.
WHAT?! THAT'S PERFECT! I'LL BE YOUR APPRENTICE, FORTUNA!!
I WAS HOPING YOU'D INTRODUCE ME TO HER, BUT...
YOU'RE EVEN MORE AMAZING, RIGHT?
OBVIOUSLY I AM.
YOU'RE INTERESTED IN SOUL STUDIES? REALLY?
I DON'T HAVE ANY SPECIAL TALENT OR TRAINING, BUT I'VE GOTTA DO SOMETHING, RIGHT?
......
LOOK AT THIS SPOT. WHAT DO YOU SEE?

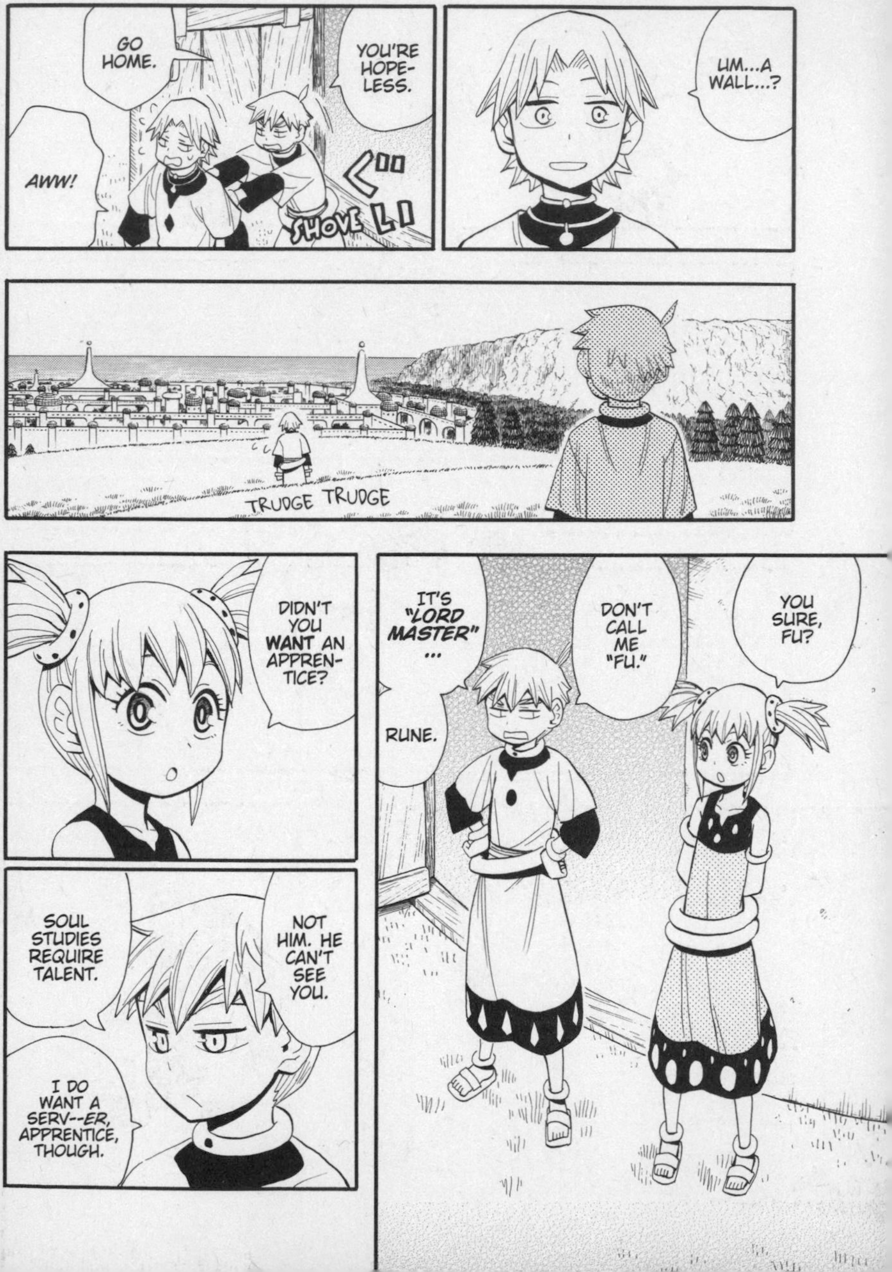
UM...A WALL...?
YOU'RE HOPE-LESS.
GO HOME.
SHOVE
AWW!
TRUDGE TRUDGE
YOU SURE, FU?
DON'T CALL ME "FU."
IT'S "LORD MASTER"...
RUNE.
DIDN'T YOU WANT AN APPREN-TICE?
NOT HIM. HE CAN'T SEE YOU.
SOUL STUDIES REQUIRE TALENT.
I DO WANT A SERV--ER, APPRENTICE, THOUGH.

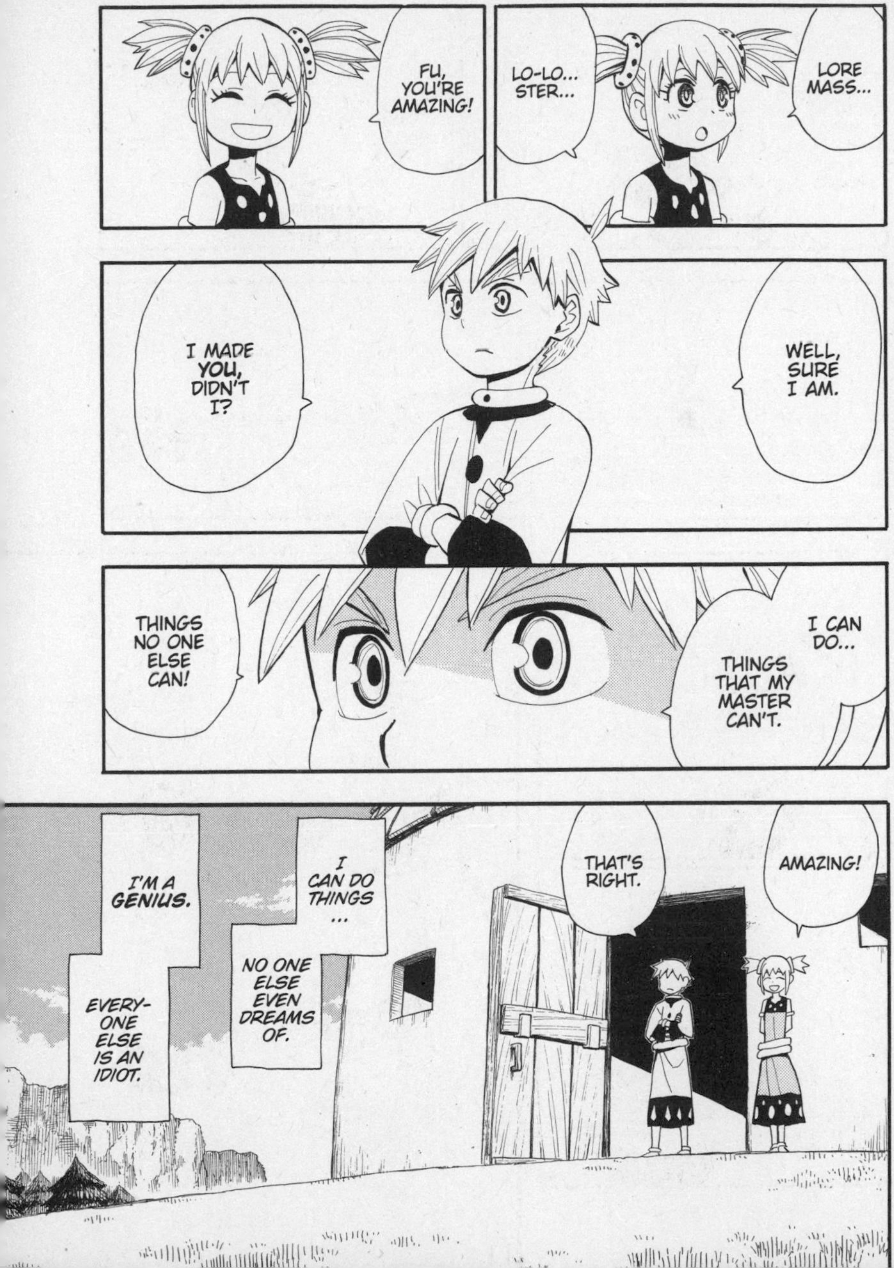
LORE MASS...
LO-LO... STER...
FU, YOU'RE AMAZING!
WELL, SURE I AM.
I MADE YOU, DIDN'T I?
I CAN DO...
THINGS THAT MY MASTER CAN'T.
THINGS NO ONE ELSE CAN!
AMAZING!
THAT'S RIGHT.
I CAN DO THINGS ...
NO ONE ELSE EVEN DREAMS OF.
I'M A GENIUS.
EVERY-ONE ELSE IS AN IDIOT.

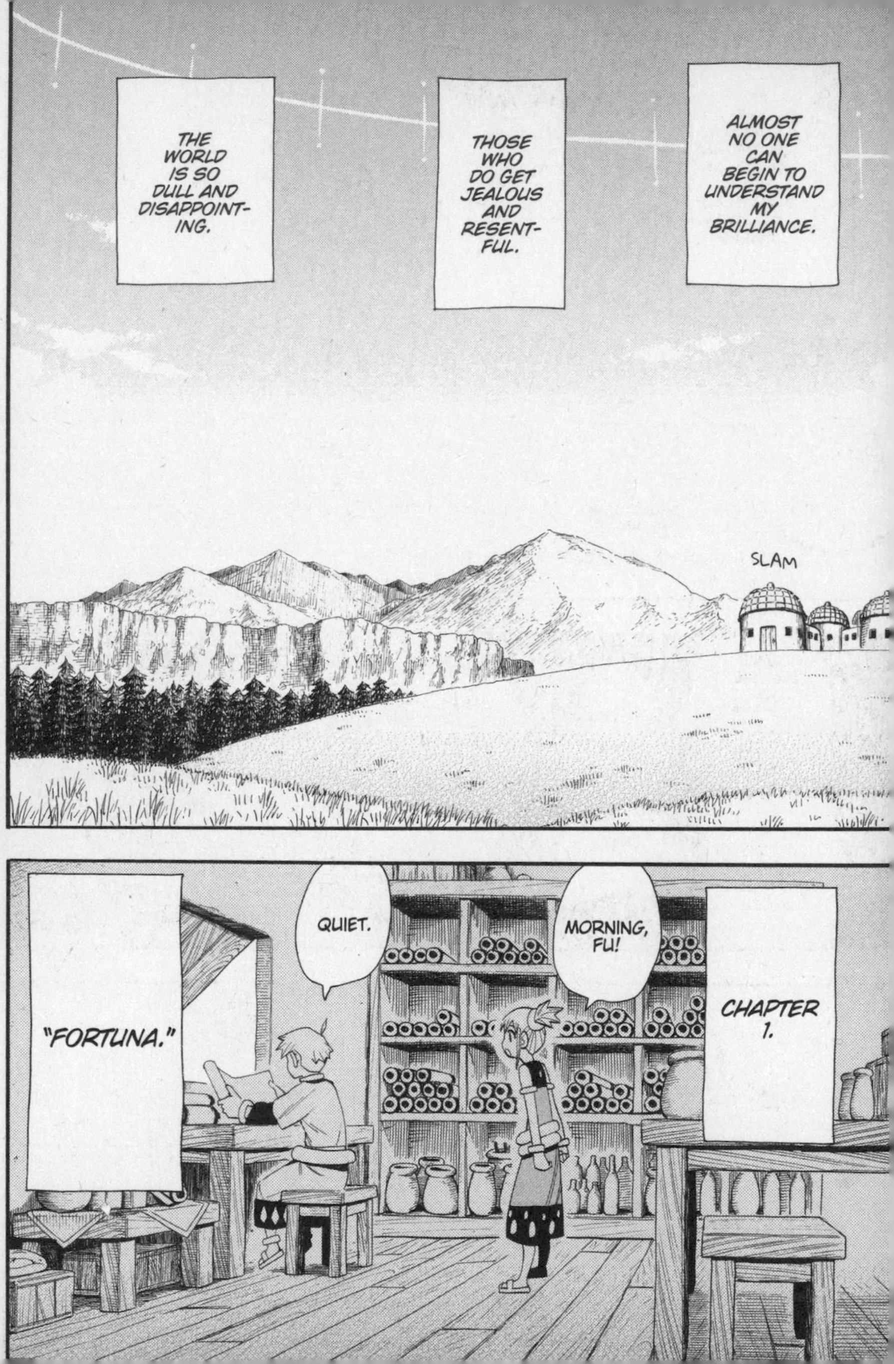
ALMOST NO ONE CAN BEGIN TO UNDERSTAND MY BRILLIANCE.
THOSE WHO DO GET JEALOUS AND RESENT-FUL.
THE WORLD IS SO DULL AND DISAPPOINT-ING.
SLAM
CHAPTER 1.
MORNING, FU!
QUIET.
"FORTUNA."

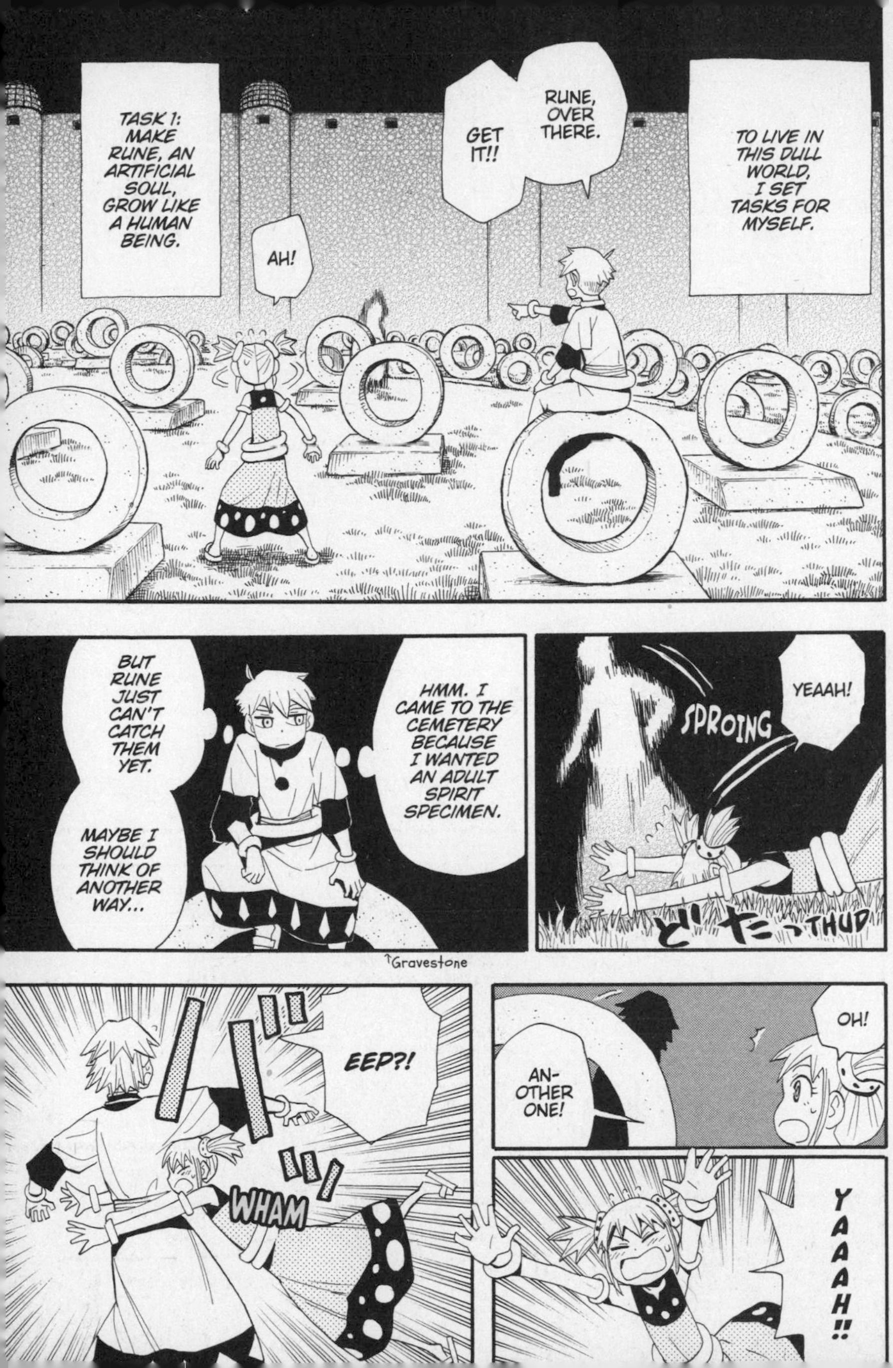
TO LIVE IN THIS DULL WORLD, I SET TASKS FOR MYSELF.
RUNE, OVER THERE.
GET IT!!
TASK 1: MAKE RUNE, AN ARTIFICIAL SOUL, GROW LIKE A HUMAN BEING.
AH!
YEAAH!
SPROING
THUD
HMM. I CAME TO THE CEMETERY BECAUSE I WANTED AN ADULT SPIRIT SPECIMEN.
BUT RUNE JUST CAN'T CATCH THEM YET.
MAYBE I SHOULD THINK OF ANOTHER WAY...
↑Gravestone
OH!
AN-OTHER ONE!
YAAAAH!!
EEP?!
WHAM

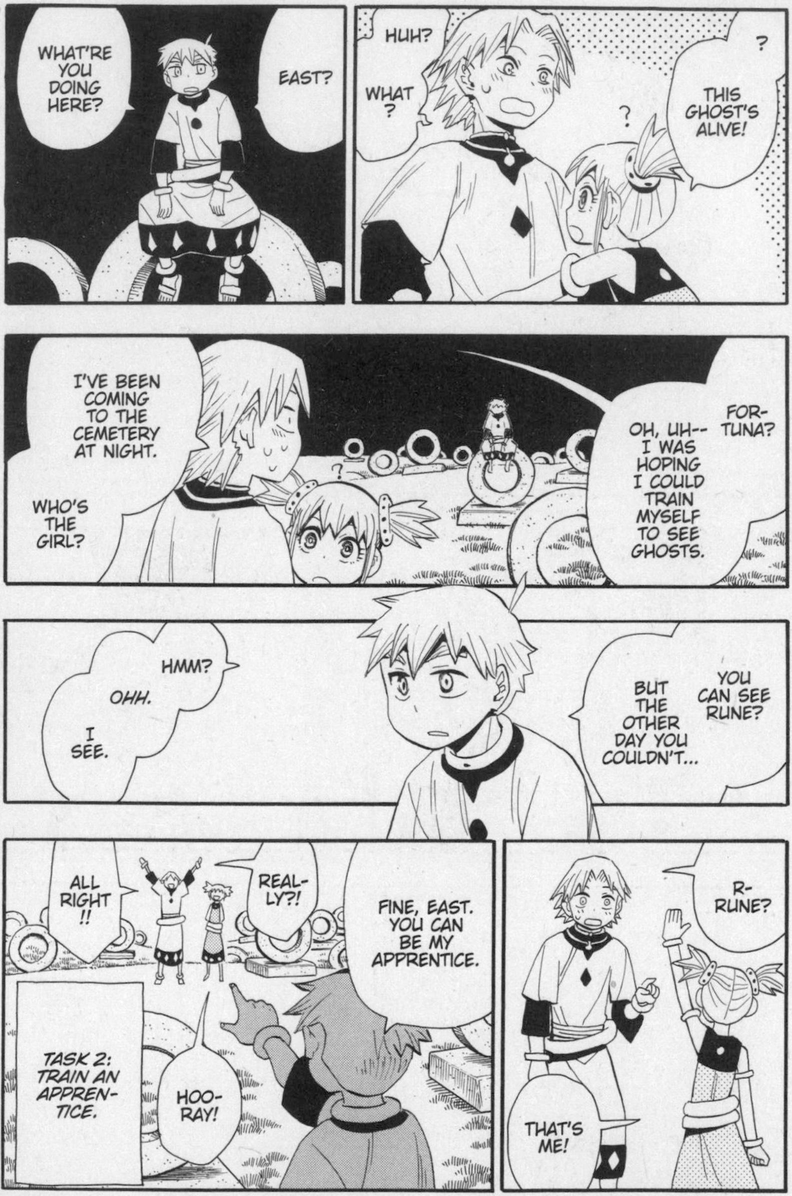
?
THIS GHOST'S ALIVE!
HUH?
WHAT?
?
EAST?
WHAT'RE YOU DOING HERE?
FOR-TUNA?
OH, UH-- I WAS HOPING I COULD TRAIN MYSELF TO SEE GHOSTS.
I'VE BEEN COMING TO THE CEMETERY AT NIGHT.
WHO'S THE GIRL?
YOU CAN SEE RUNE?
BUT THE OTHER DAY YOU COULDN'T...
HMM?
OHH.
I SEE.
R-RUNE?
THAT'S ME!
FINE, EAST. YOU CAN BE MY APPRENTICE.
REAL-LY?!
ALL RIGHT!!
HOO-RAY!
TASK 2: TRAIN AN APPREN-TICE.

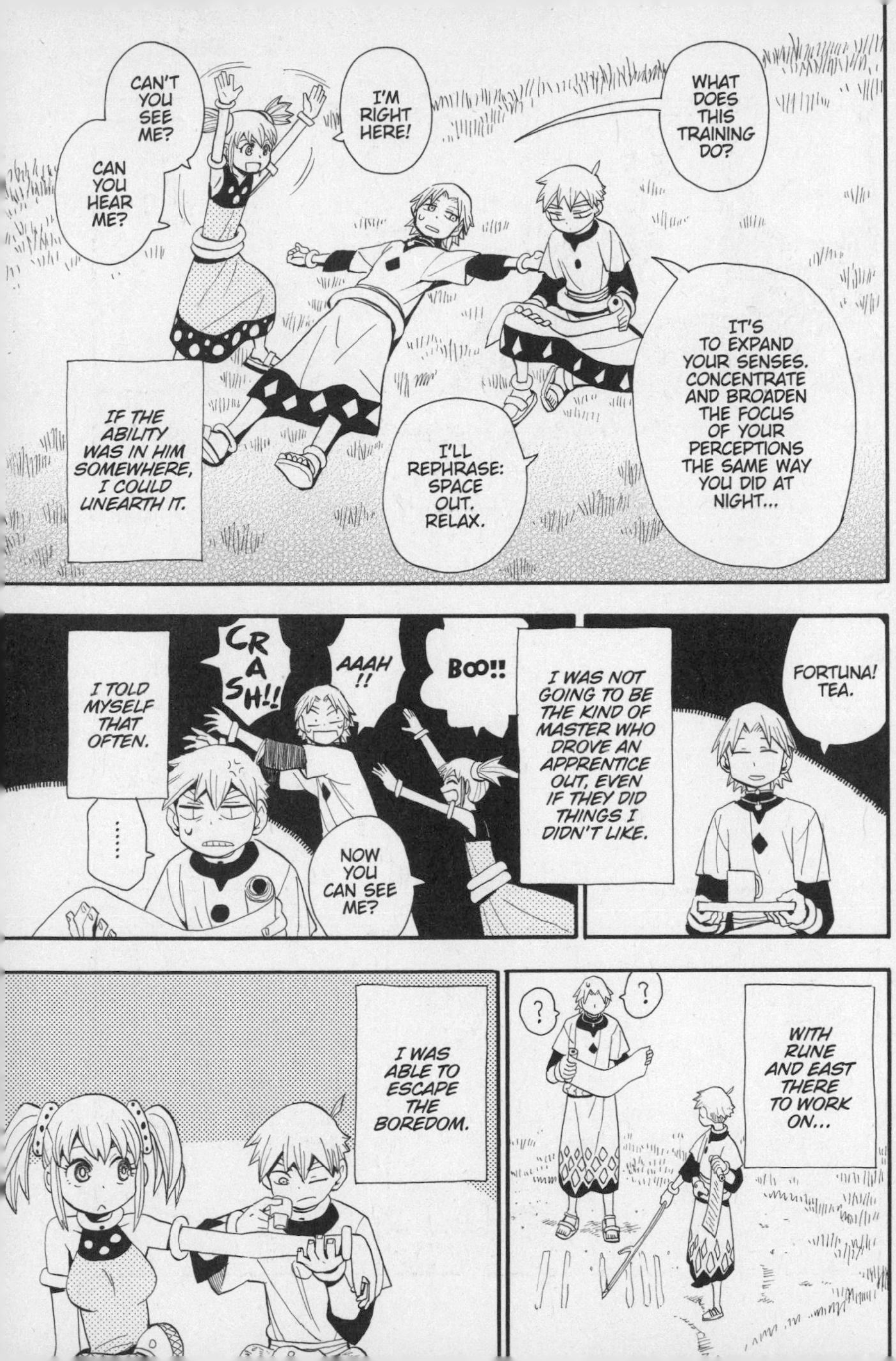
WHAT DOES THIS TRAINING DO?
IT'S TO EXPAND YOUR SENSES. CONCENTRATE AND BROADEN THE FOCUS OF YOUR PERCEPTIONS THE SAME WAY YOU DID AT NIGHT...
I'LL REPHRASE: SPACE OUT. RELAX.
I'M RIGHT HERE!
CAN'T YOU SEE ME?
CAN YOU HEAR ME?
IF THE ABILITY WAS IN HIM SOMEWHERE, I COULD UNEARTH IT.
FORTUNA! TEA.
I WAS NOT GOING TO BE THE KIND OF MASTER WHO DROVE AN APPRENTICE OUT, EVEN IF THEY DID THINGS I DIDN'T LIKE.
BOO!!
AAAH!!
CRASH!!
I TOLD MYSELF THAT OFTEN.
NOW YOU CAN SEE ME?
......
?
?
WITH RUNE AND EAST THERE TO WORK ON...
I WAS ABLE TO ESCAPE THE BOREDOM.

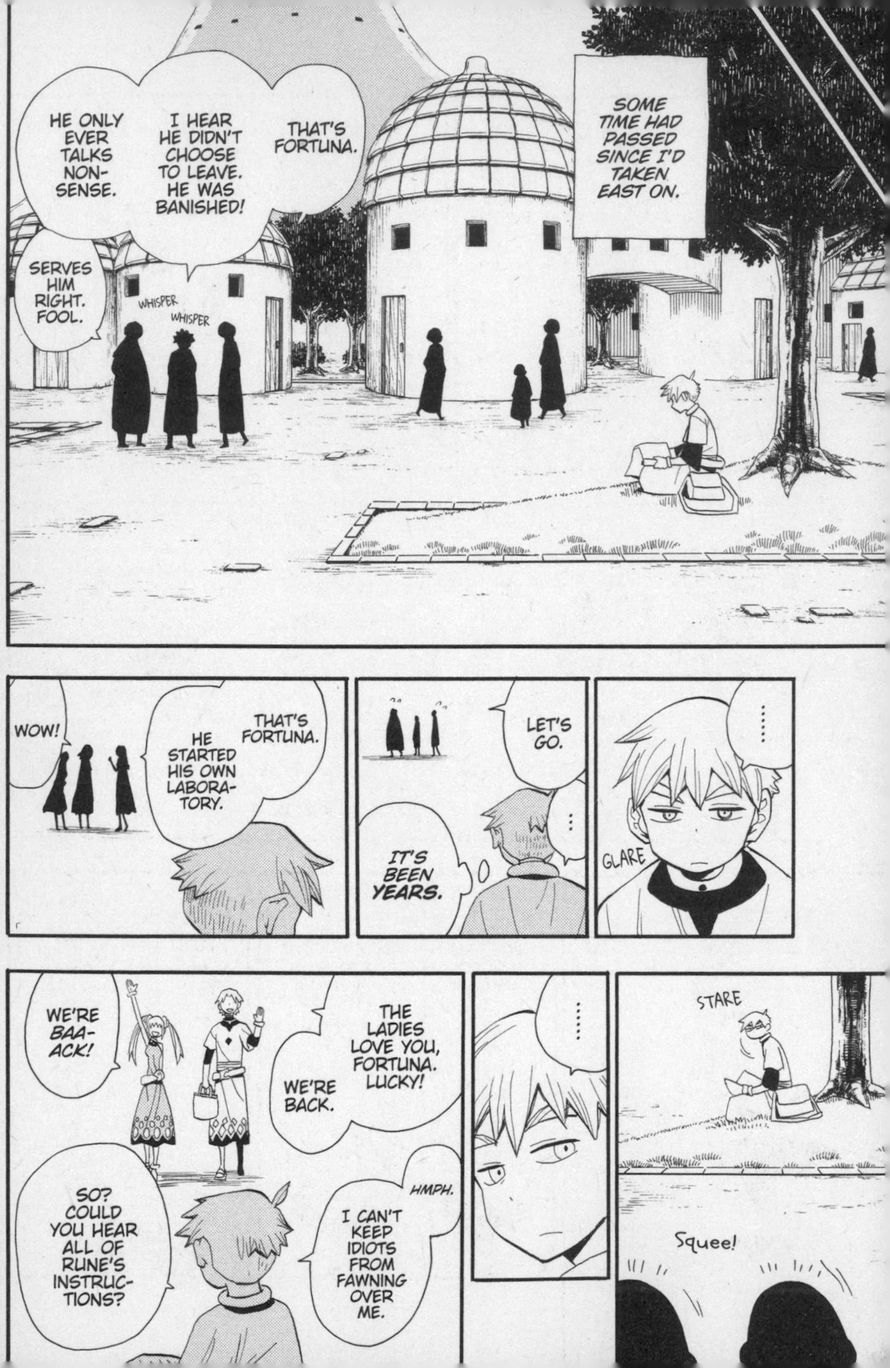
SOME TIME HAD PASSED SINCE I'D TAKEN EAST ON.
THAT'S FORTUNA.
I HEAR HE DIDN'T CHOOSE TO LEAVE. HE WAS BANISHED!
HE ONLY EVER TALKS NON-SENSE.
WHISPER
WHISPER
SERVES HIM RIGHT. FOOL.
......
GLARE
LET'S GO.
...
IT'S BEEN YEARS.
THAT'S FORTUNA.
HE STARTED HIS OWN LABORATORY.
WOW!
STARE
Squee!
......
THE LADIES LOVE YOU, FORTUNA. LUCKY!
WE'RE BACK.
WE'RE BAAACK!
HMPH.
I CAN'T KEEP IDIOTS FROM FAWNING OVER ME.
SO? COULD YOU HEAR ALL OF RUNE'S INSTRUCTIONS?

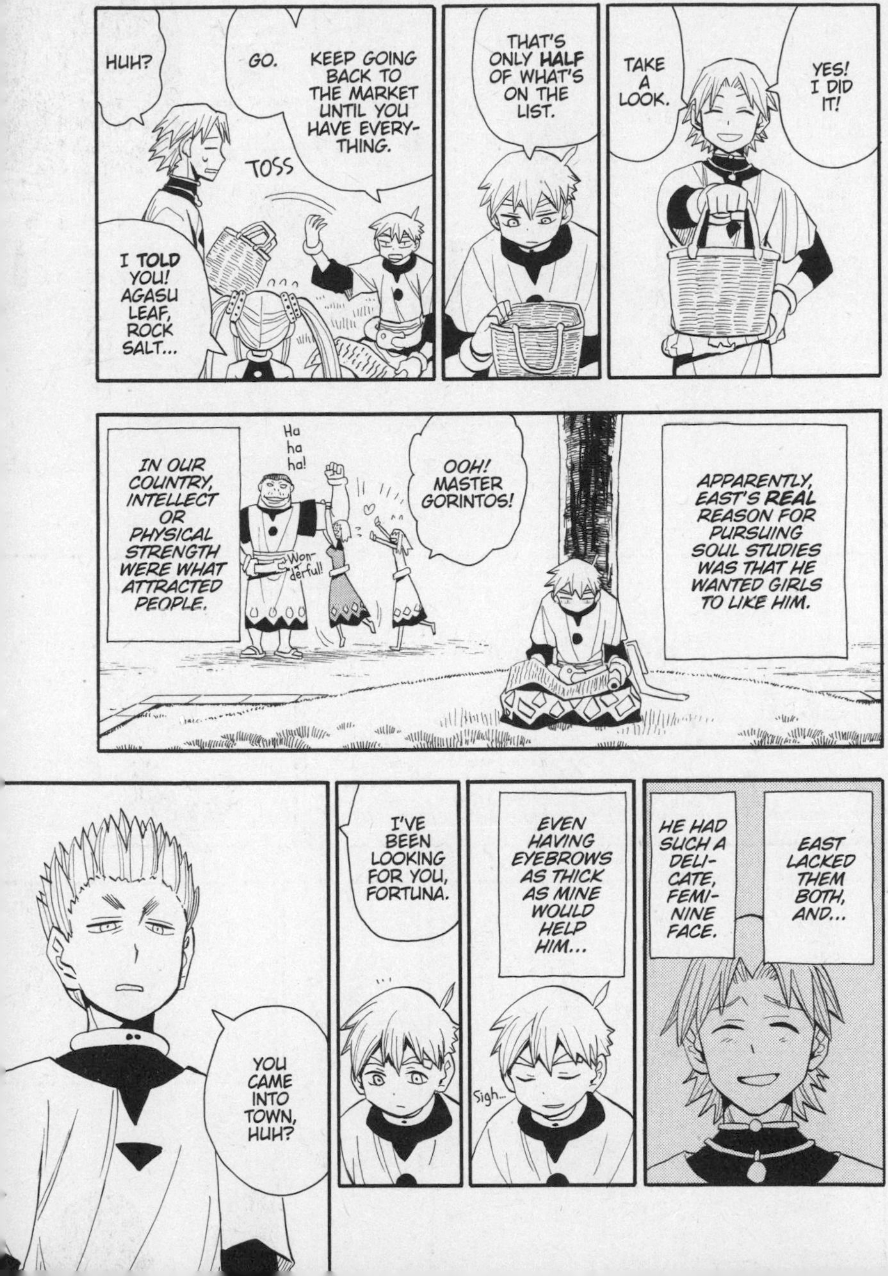
YES! I DID IT!
TAKE A LOOK.
THAT'S ONLY HALF OF WHAT'S ON THE LIST.
KEEP GOING BACK TO THE MARKET UNTIL YOU HAVE EVERYTHING.
GO.
HUH?
TOSS
I TOLD YOU! AGASU LEAF, ROCK SALT...
APPARENTLY, EAST'S REAL REASON FOR PURSUING SOUL STUDIES WAS THAT HE WANTED GIRLS TO LIKE HIM.
OOH! MASTER GORINTOS!
Ha ha ha!
Wonderful!
IN OUR COUNTRY, INTELLECT OR PHYSICAL STRENGTH WERE WHAT ATTRACTED PEOPLE.
EAST LACKED THEM BOTH, AND...
HE HAD SUCH A DELICATE, FEMININE FACE.
EVEN HAVING EYEBROWS AS THICK AS MINE WOULD HELP HIM...
Sigh...
I'VE BEEN LOOKING FOR YOU, FORTUNA.
YOU CAME INTO TOWN, HUH?

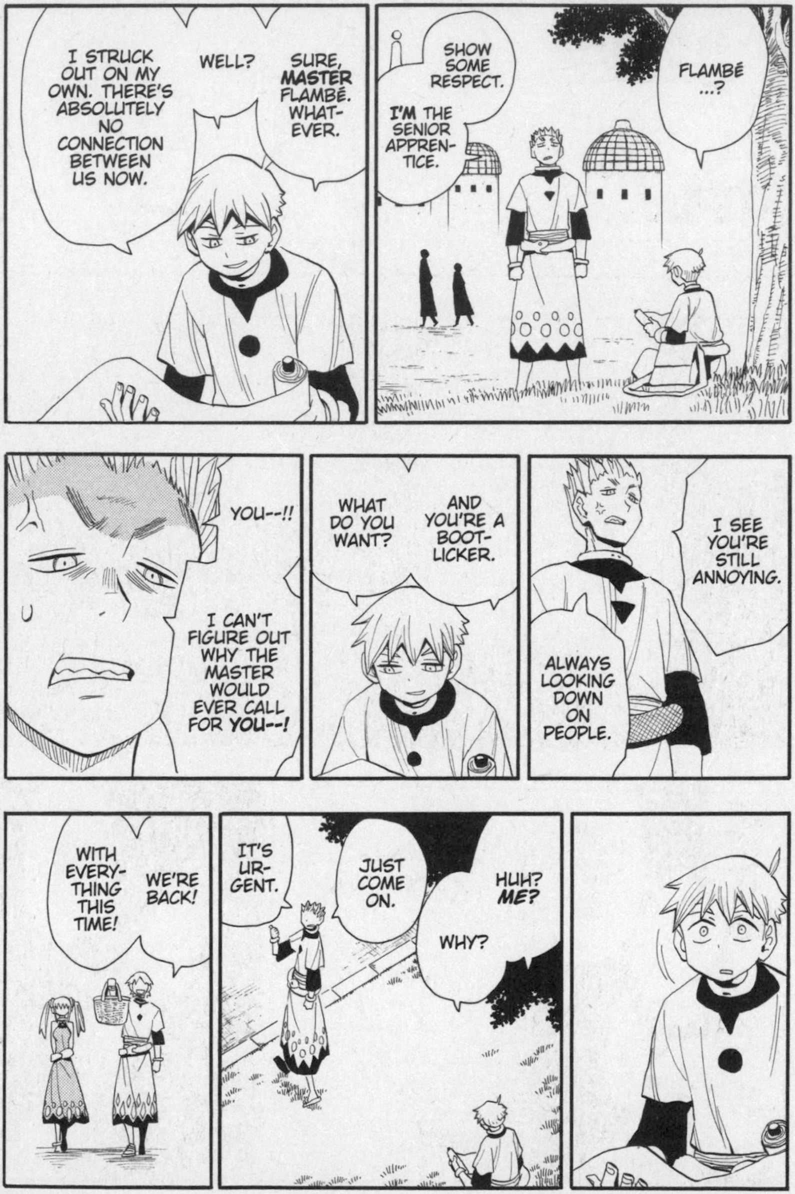
FLAMBÉ ...?
SHOW SOME RESPECT.
I'M THE SENIOR APPRENTICE.
SURE, MASTER FLAMBÉ. WHATEVER.
WELL?
I STRUCK OUT ON MY OWN. THERE'S ABSOLUTELY NO CONNECTION BETWEEN US NOW.
I SEE YOU'RE STILL ANNOYING.
ALWAYS LOOKING DOWN ON PEOPLE.
AND YOU'RE A BOOTLICKER.
WHAT DO YOU WANT?
YOU--!!
I CAN'T FIGURE OUT WHY THE MASTER WOULD EVER CALL FOR YOU--!
HUH? ME?
JUST COME ON.
WHY?
IT'S URGENT.
WE'RE BACK!
WITH EVERYTHING THIS TIME!

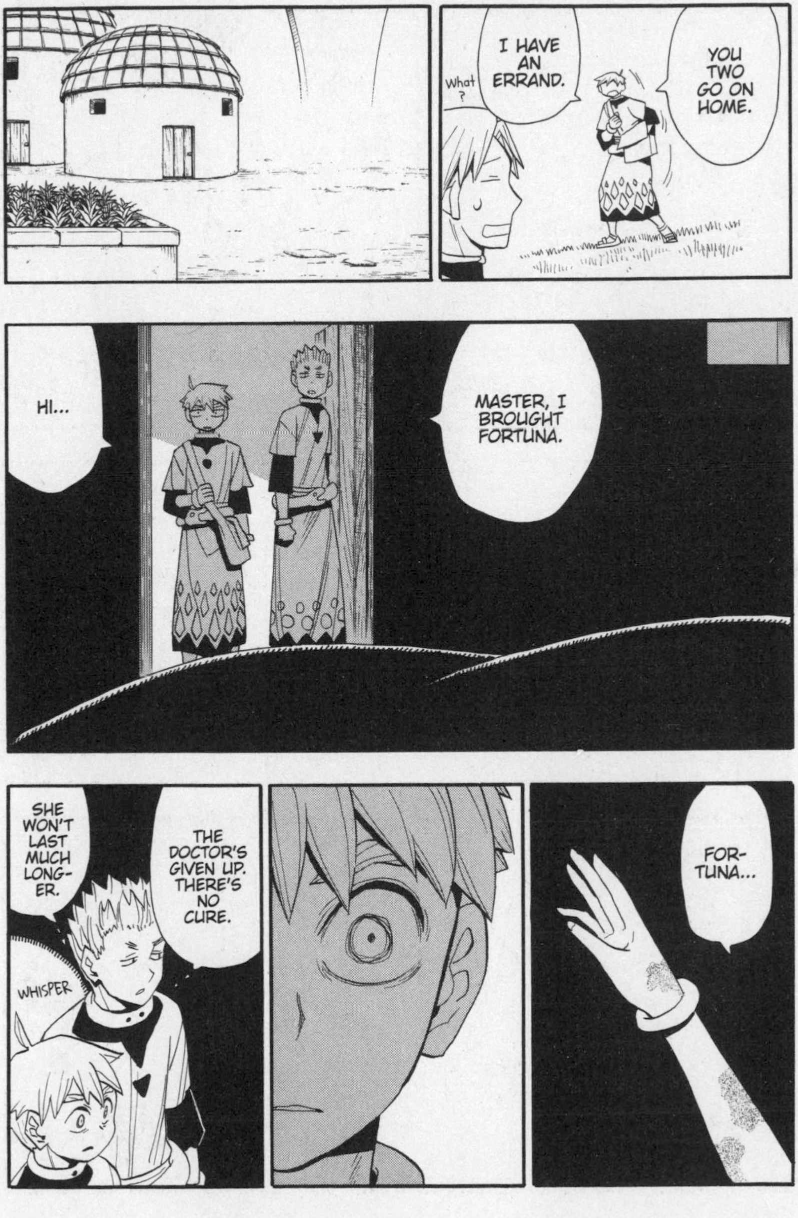
YOU TWO GO ON HOME.
I HAVE AN ERRAND.
What?
MASTER, I BROUGHT FORTUNA.
HI...
FOR-TUNA...
THE DOCTOR'S GIVEN UP. THERE'S NO CURE.
SHE WON'T LAST MUCH LONG-ER.
WHISPER

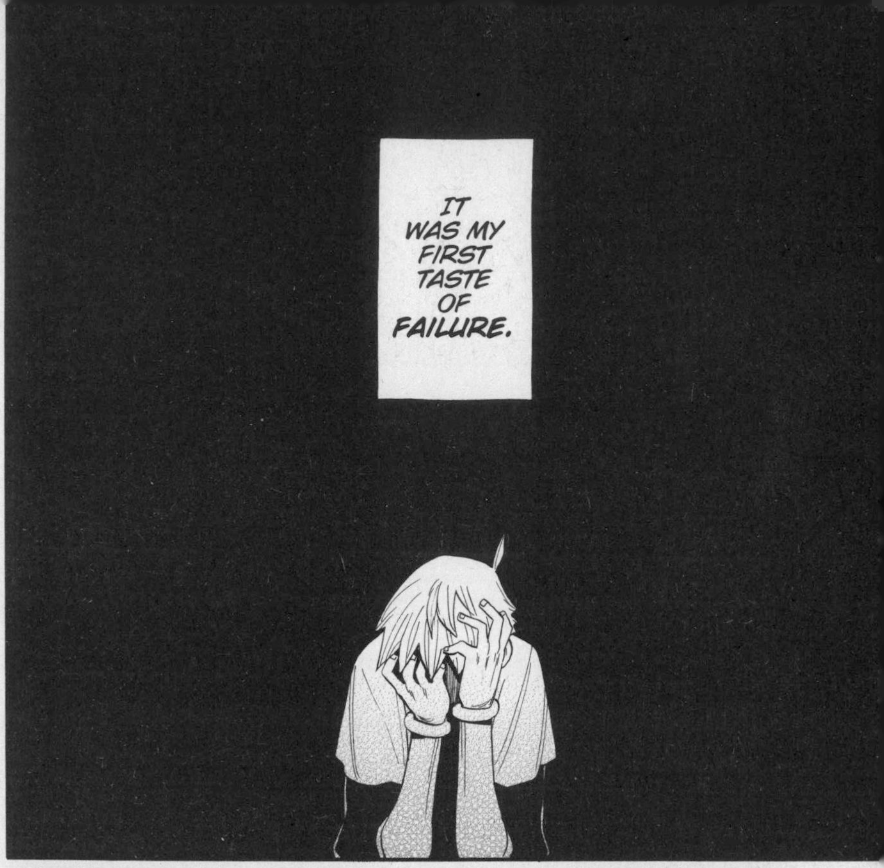
IT WAS MY FIRST TASTE OF FAILURE.

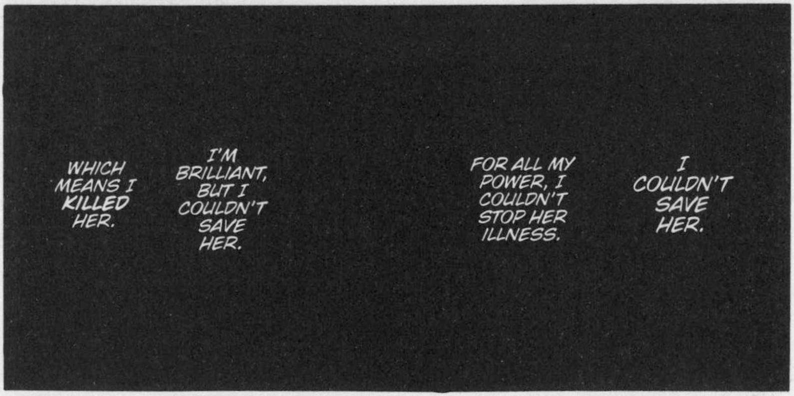
I COULDN'T SAVE HER.
FOR ALL MY POWER, I COULDN'T STOP HER ILLNESS.
I'M BRILLIANT, BUT I COULDN'T SAVE HER.
WHICH MEANS I KILLED HER.

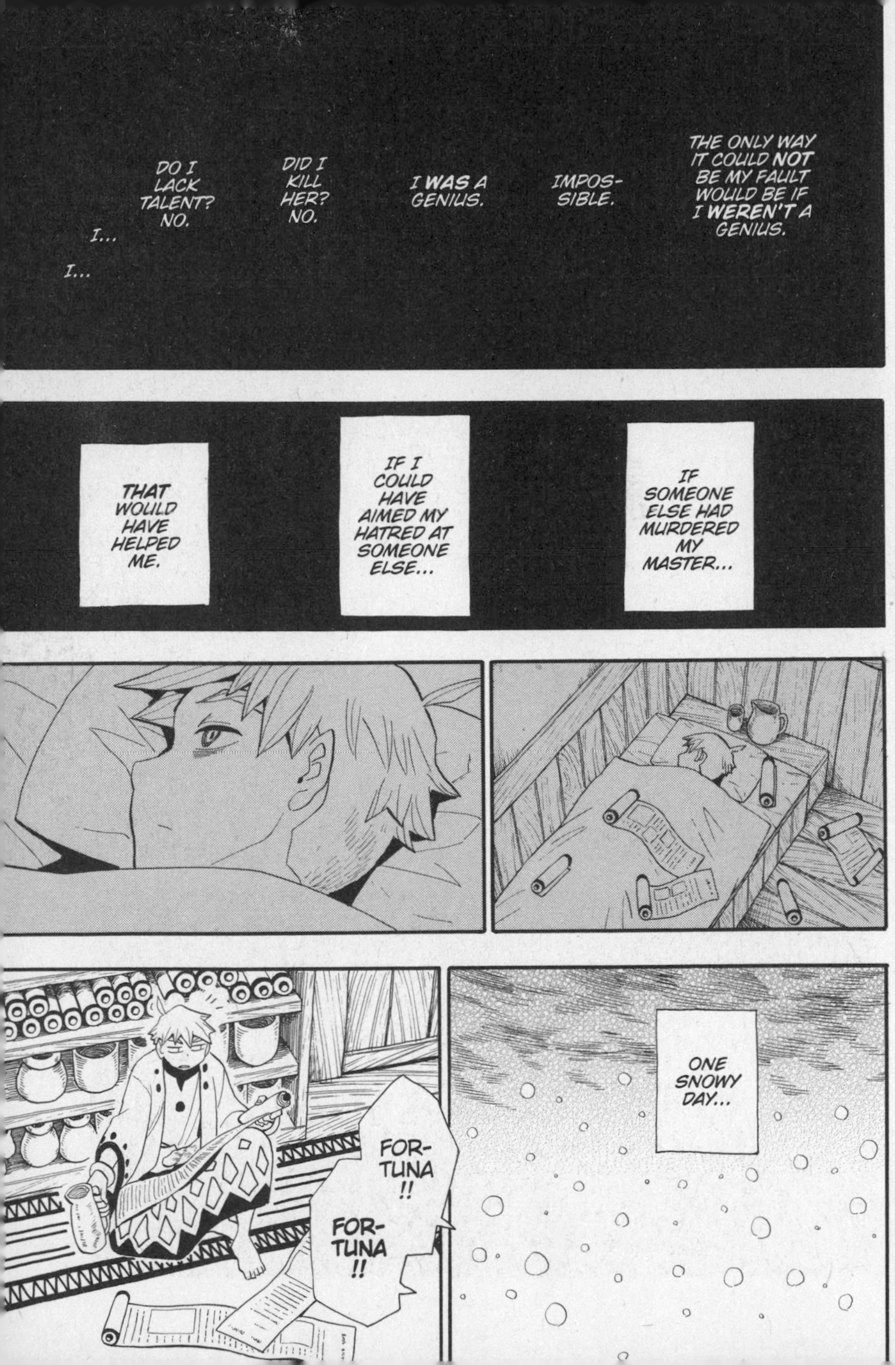

THE ONLY WAY IT COULD NOT BE MY FAULT WOULD BE IF I WEREN'T A GENIUS.
IMPOSSIBLE.
I WAS A GENIUS.
DID I KILL HER? NO.
DO I LACK TALENT? NO.
I...
I...
IF SOMEONE ELSE HAD MURDERED MY MASTER...
IF I COULD HAVE AIMED MY HATRED AT SOMEONE ELSE...
THAT WOULD HAVE HELPED ME.
ONE SNOWY DAY...
FORTUNA!!
FORTUNA!!

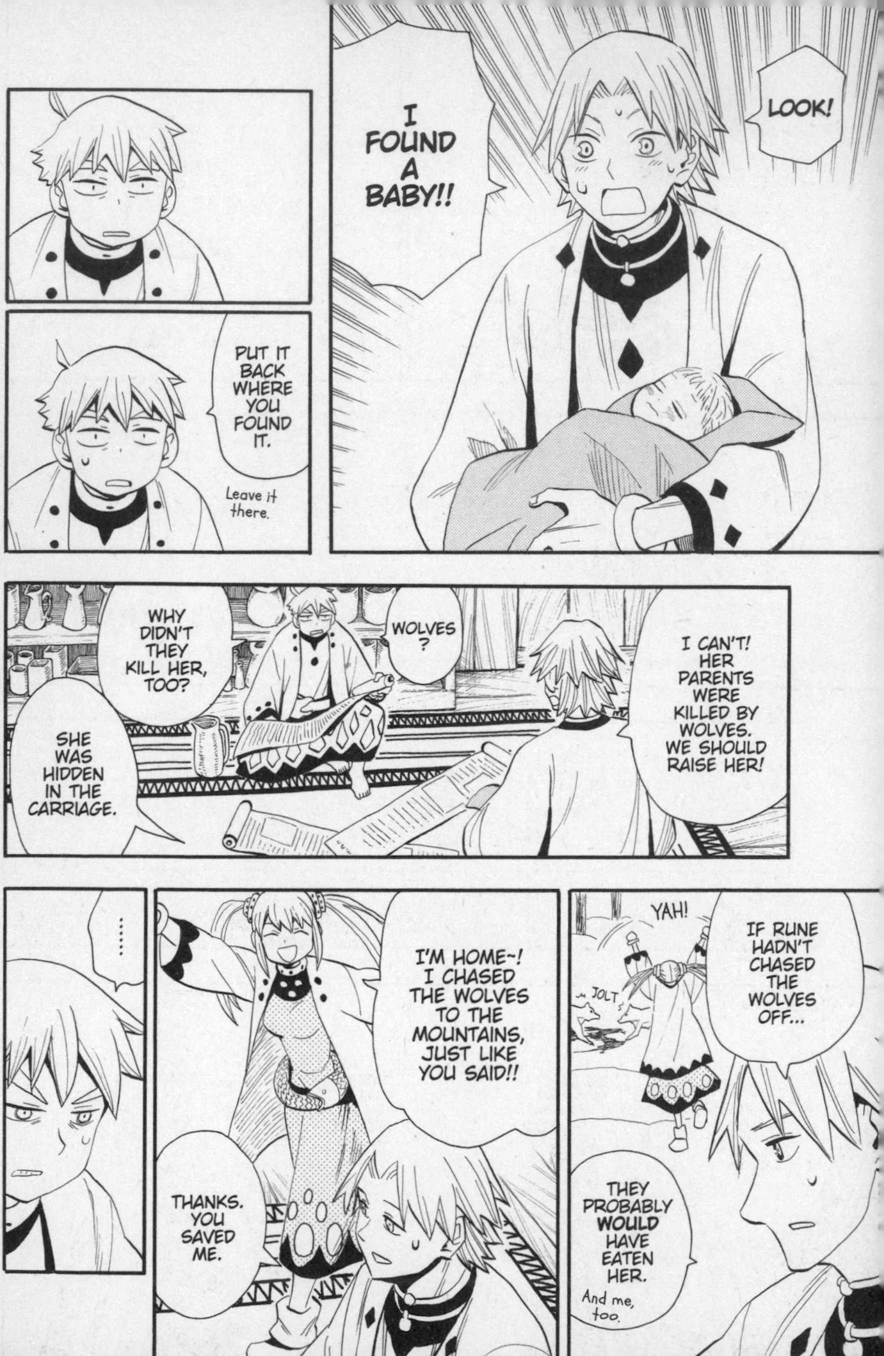
LOOK!
I FOUND A BABY!!
PUT IT BACK WHERE YOU FOUND IT.
Leave it there.
I CAN'T! HER PARENTS WERE KILLED BY WOLVES. WE SHOULD RAISE HER!
WOLVES?
WHY DIDN'T THEY KILL HER, TOO?
SHE WAS HIDDEN IN THE CARRIAGE.
YAH!
JOLT
IF RUNE HADN'T CHASED THE WOLVES OFF...
THEY PROBABLY WOULD HAVE EATEN HER.
And me, too.
I'M HOME~! I CHASED THE WOLVES TO THE MOUNTAINS, JUST LIKE YOU SAID!!
THANKS. YOU SAVED ME.
......

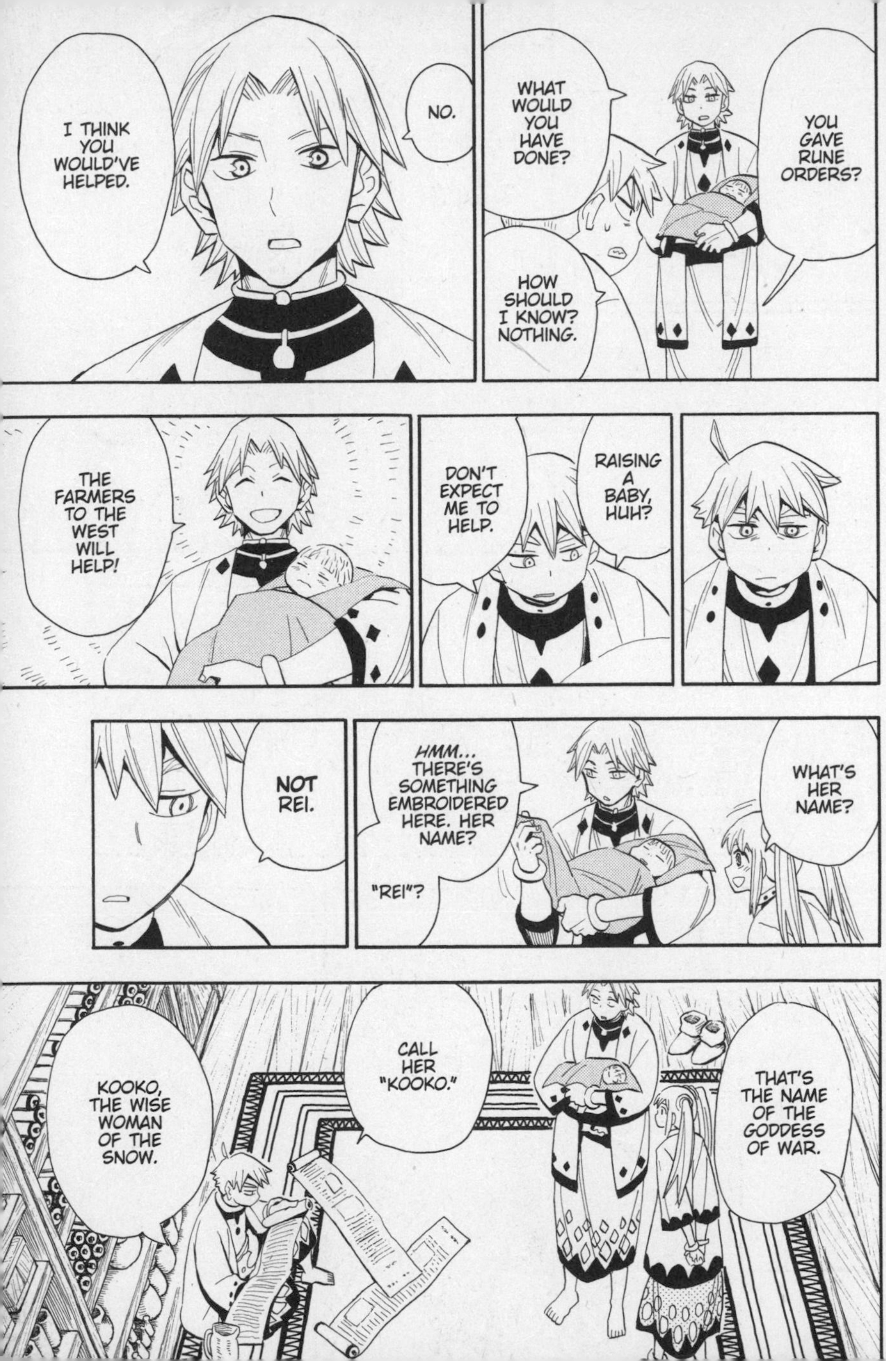
YOU GAVE RUNE ORDERS?
WHAT WOULD YOU HAVE DONE?
HOW SHOULD I KNOW? NOTHING.
NO.
I THINK YOU WOULD'VE HELPED.
RAISING A BABY, HUH?
DON'T EXPECT ME TO HELP.
THE FARMERS TO THE WEST WILL HELP!
WHAT'S HER NAME?
HMM... THERE'S SOMETHING EMBROIDERED HERE. HER NAME?
"REI"?
NOT REI.
CALL HER "KOOKO."
THAT'S THE NAME OF THE GODDESS OF WAR.
KOOKO, THE WISE WOMAN OF THE SNOW.

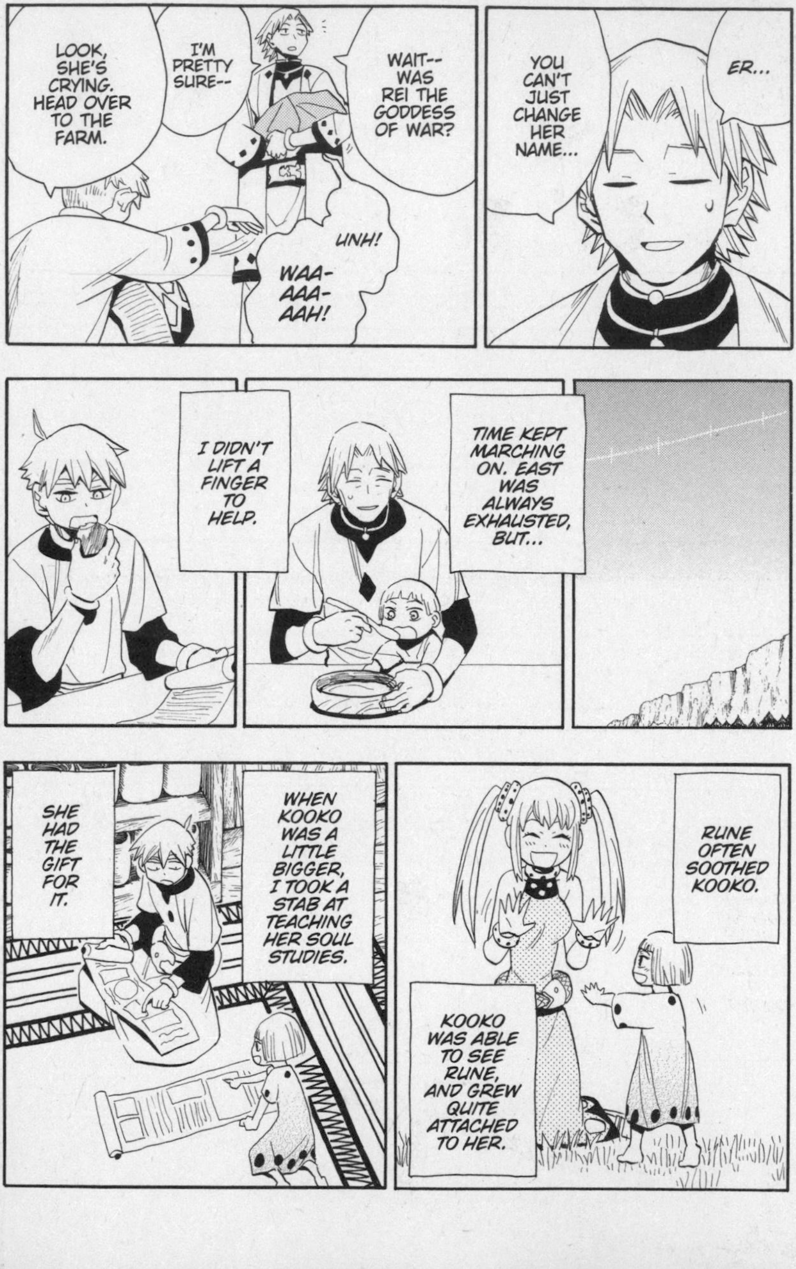
ER...
YOU CAN'T JUST CHANGE HER NAME...
WAIT-- WAS REI THE GODDESS OF WAR?
I'M PRETTY SURE--
LOOK, SHE'S CRYING. HEAD OVER TO THE FARM.
UNH!
WAA-AAA-AAH!
TIME KEPT MARCHING ON. EAST WAS ALWAYS EXHAUSTED, BUT...
I DIDN'T LIFT A FINGER TO HELP.
RUNE OFTEN SOOTHED KOOKO.
KOOKO WAS ABLE TO SEE RUNE, AND GREW QUITE ATTACHED TO HER.
WHEN KOOKO WAS A LITTLE BIGGER, I TOOK A STAB AT TEACHING HER SOUL STUDIES.
SHE HAD THE GIFT FOR IT.

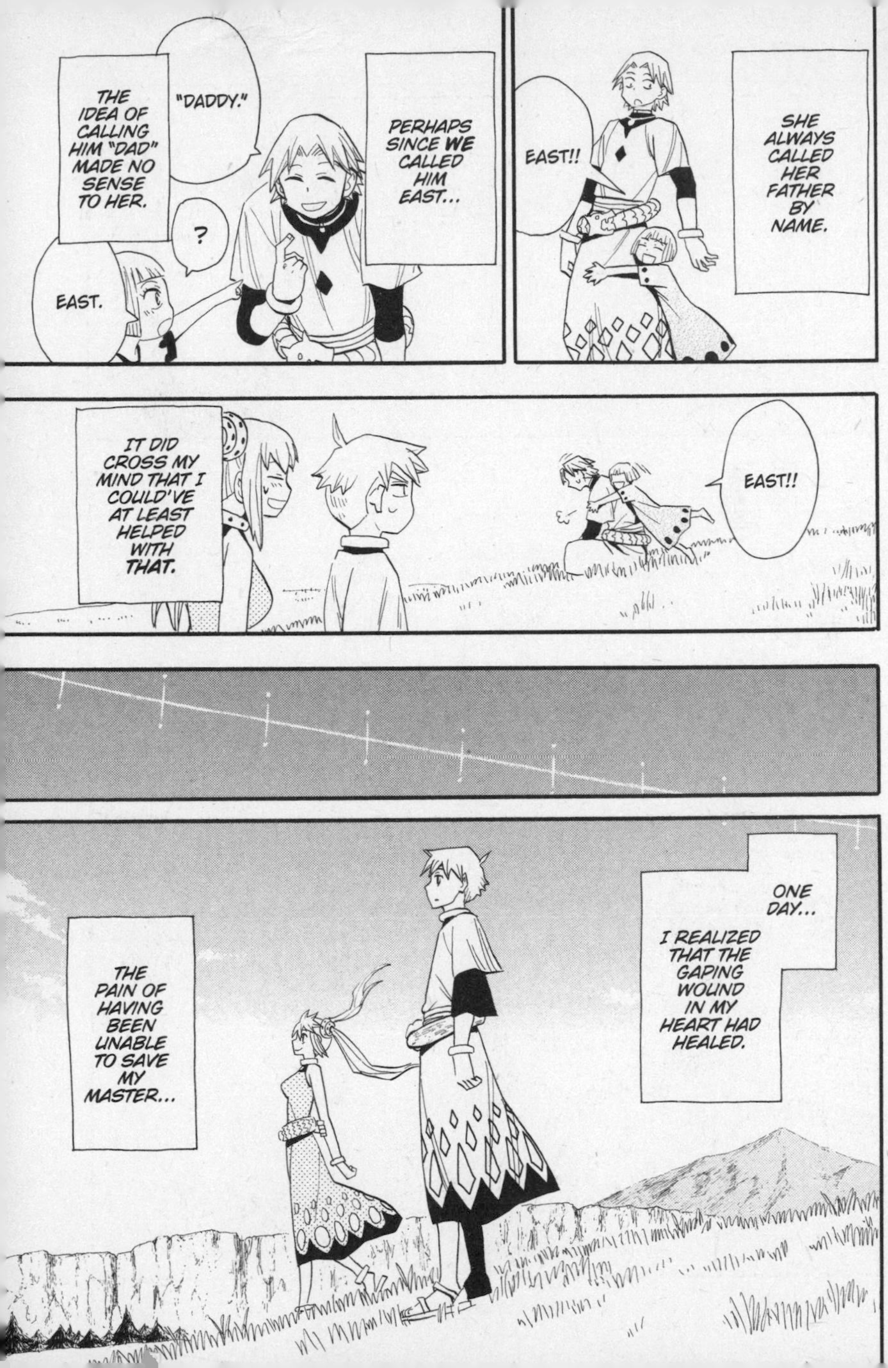
SHE ALWAYS CALLED HER FATHER BY NAME.
EAST!!
PERHAPS SINCE WE CALLED HIM EAST...
"DADDY."
THE IDEA OF CALLING HIM "DAD" MADE NO SENSE TO HER.
?
EAST.
EAST!!
IT DID CROSS MY MIND THAT I COULD'VE AT LEAST HELPED WITH THAT.
ONE DAY... I REALIZED THAT THE GAPING WOUND IN MY HEART HAD HEALED.
THE PAIN OF HAVING BEEN UNABLE TO SAVE MY MASTER...

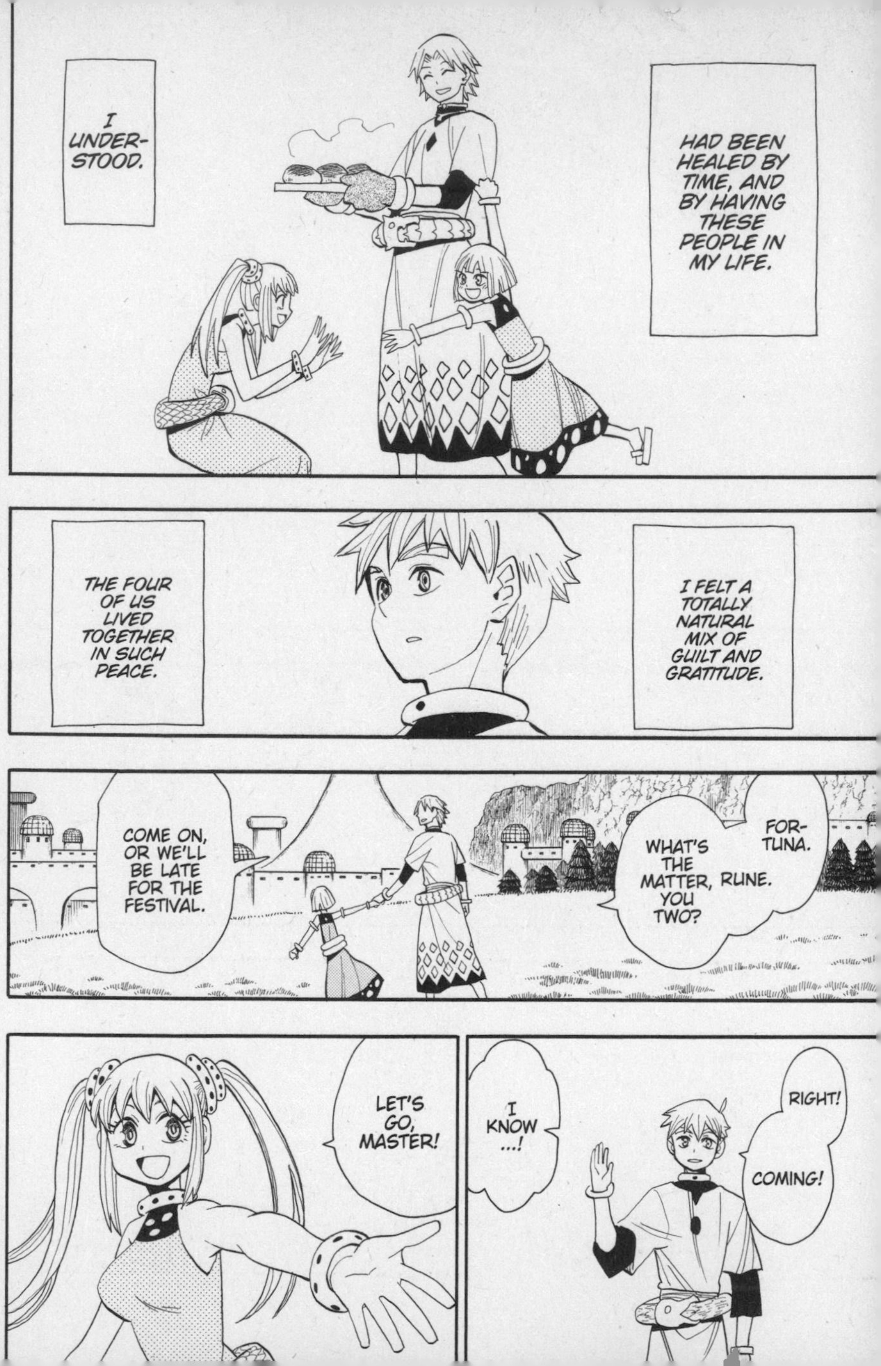
HAD BEEN HEALED BY TIME, AND BY HAVING THESE PEOPLE IN MY LIFE.
I UNDERSTOOD.
I FELT A TOTALLY NATURAL MIX OF GUILT AND GRATITUDE.
THE FOUR OF US LIVED TOGETHER IN SUCH PEACE.
FORTUNA. RUNE.
WHAT'S THE MATTER, YOU TWO?
COME ON, OR WE'LL BE LATE FOR THE FESTIVAL.
RIGHT!
COMING!
I KNOW...!
LET'S GO, MASTER!

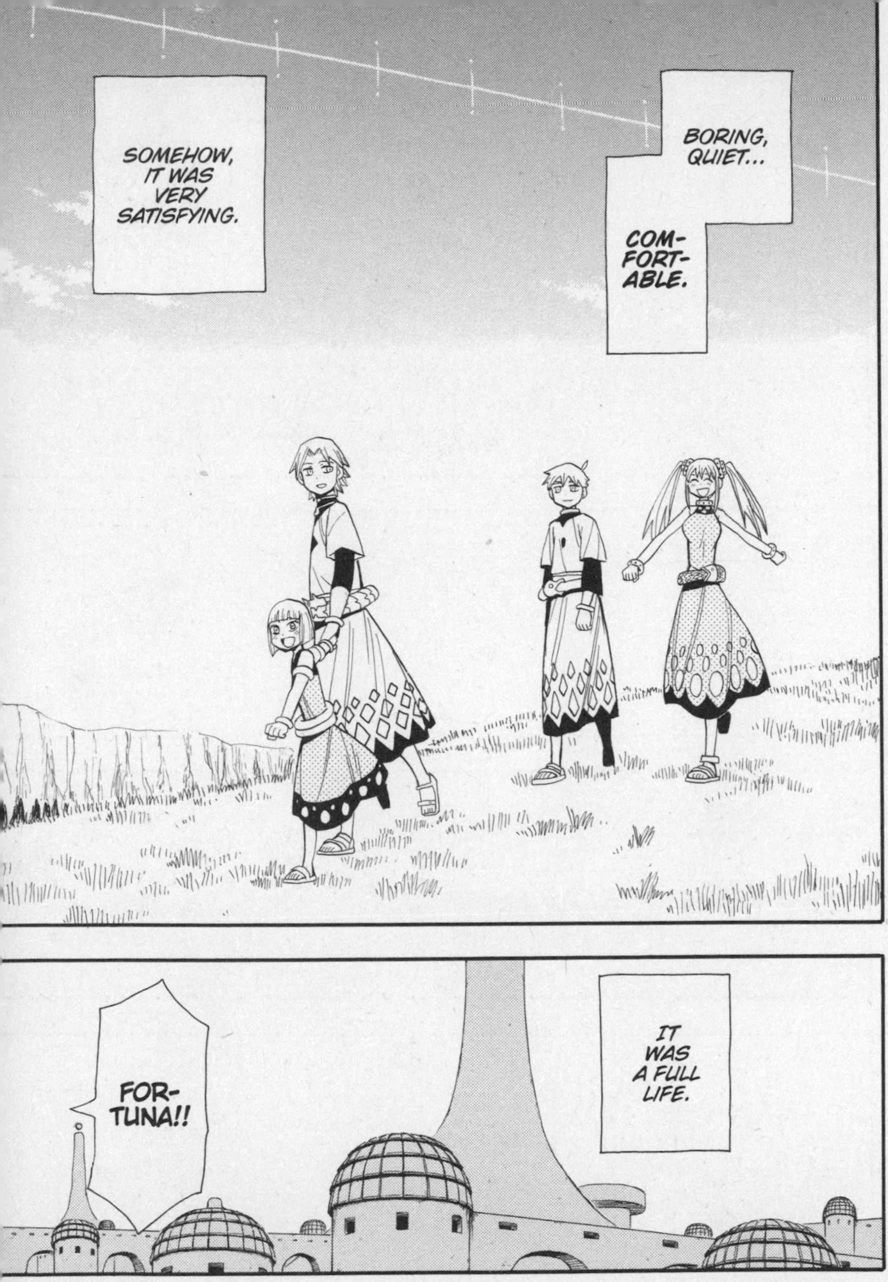
BORING, QUIET...
COM-FORT-ABLE.
SOMEHOW, IT WAS VERY SATISFYING.
IT WAS A FULL LIFE.
FOR-TUNA!!

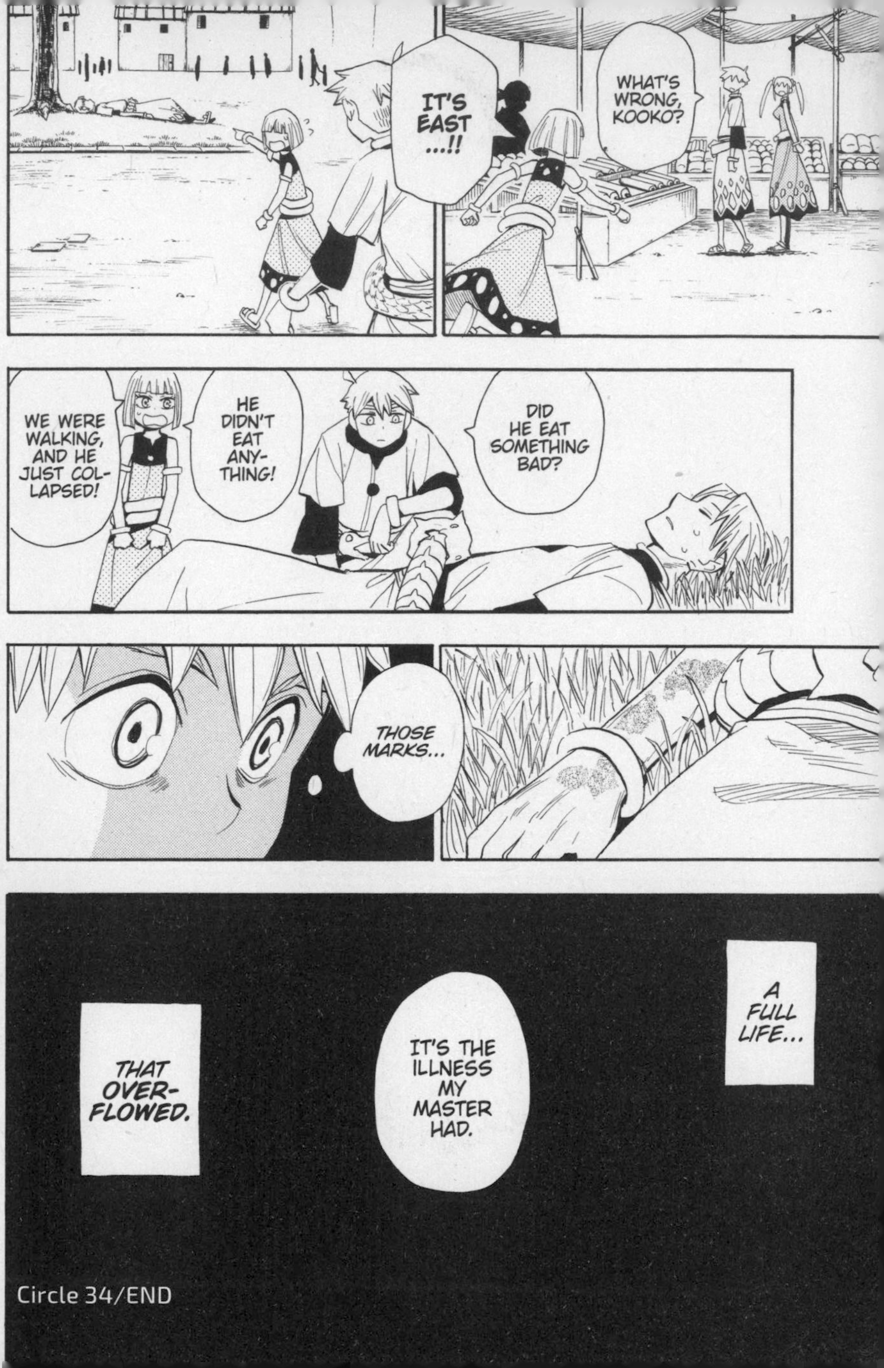
WHAT'S WRONG, KOOKO?
IT'S EAST ...!!
DID HE EAT SOMETHING BAD?
HE DIDN'T EAT ANY-THING!
WE WERE WALKING, AND HE JUST COL-LAPSED!
THOSE MARKS...
A FULL LIFE...
IT'S THE ILLNESS MY MASTER HAD.
THAT OVER-FLOWED.
Circle 34/END

Circle 35
Fortuna
2

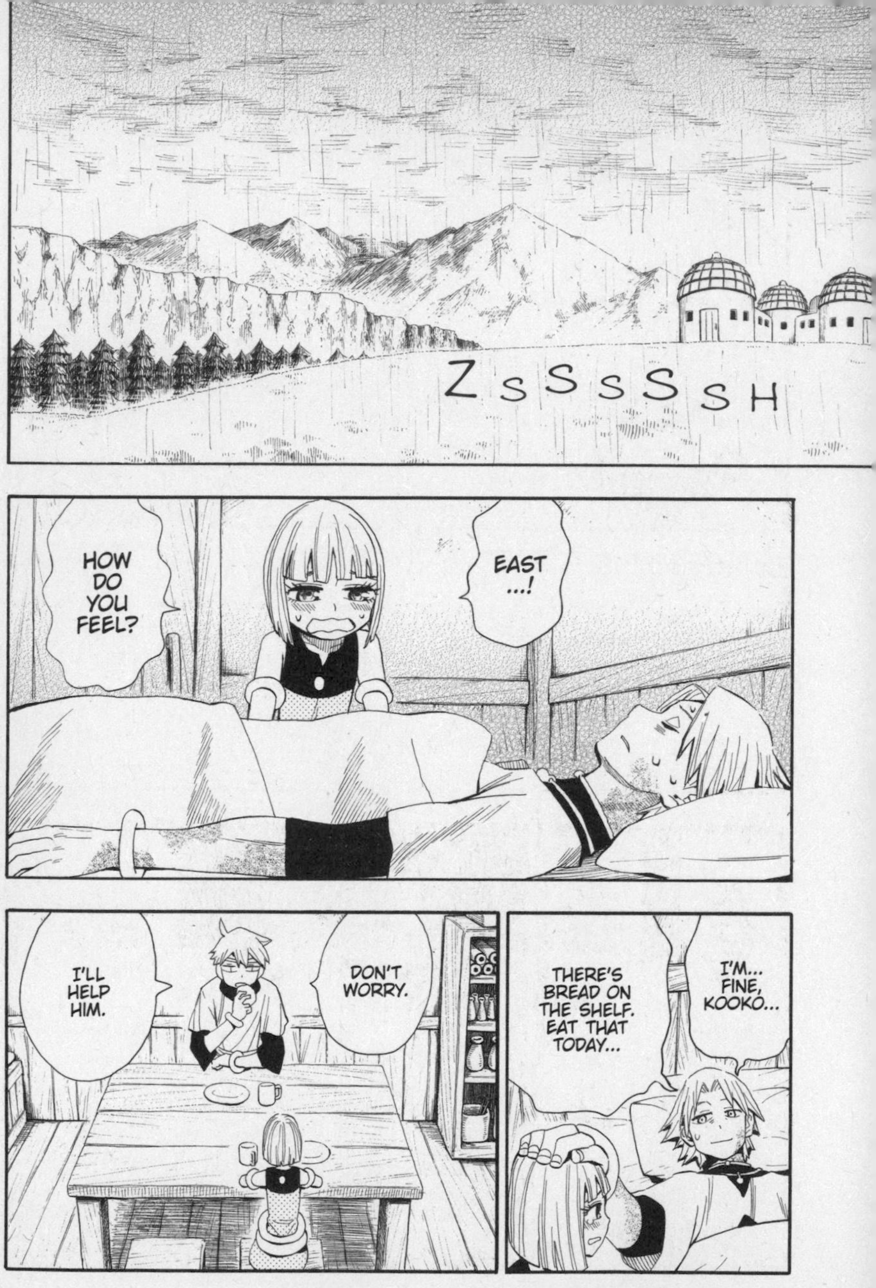
ZSSSSSH
EAST ...!
HOW DO YOU FEEL?
I'M... FINE, KOOKO...
THERE'S BREAD ON THE SHELF. EAT THAT TODAY...
DON'T WORRY.
I'LL HELP HIM.

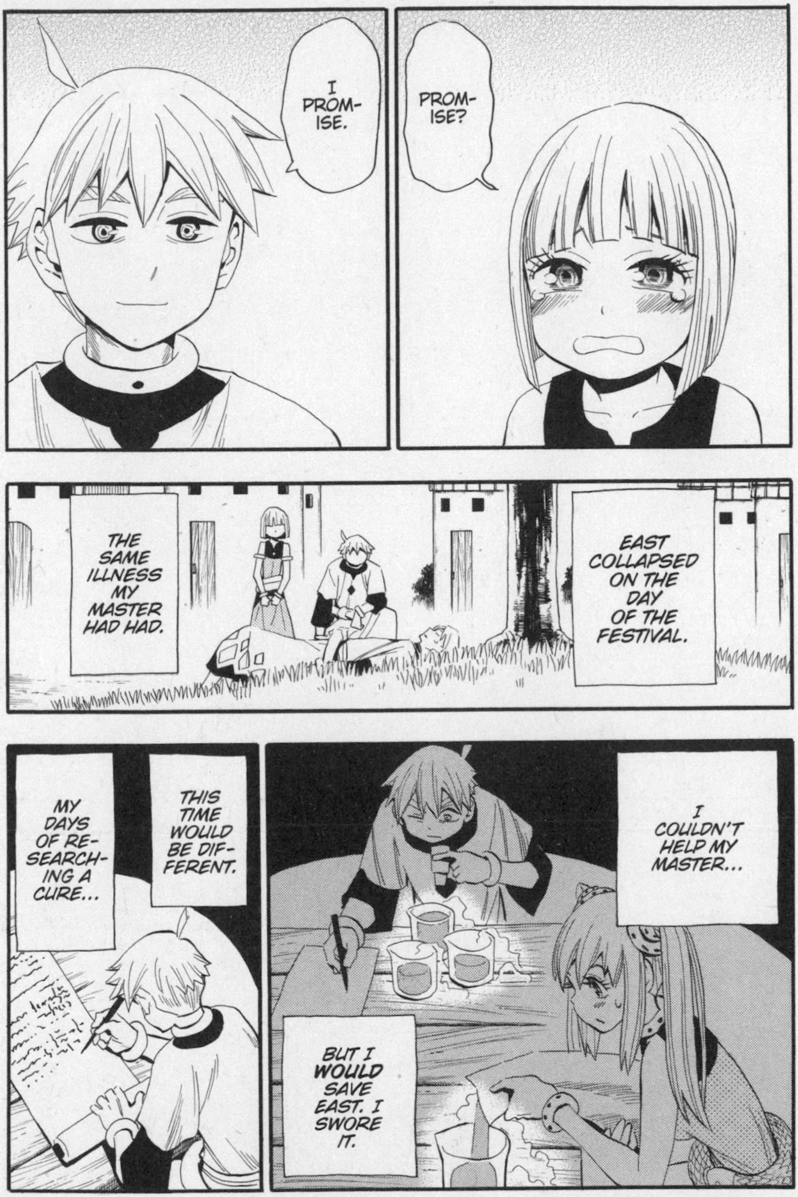
PROMISE?
I PROMISE.
EAST COLLAPSED ON THE DAY OF THE FESTIVAL.
THE SAME ILLNESS MY MASTER HAD HAD.
I COULDN'T HELP MY MASTER...
BUT I WOULD SAVE EAST. I SWORE IT.
THIS TIME WOULD BE DIFFERENT.
MY DAYS OF RESEARCHING A CURE...

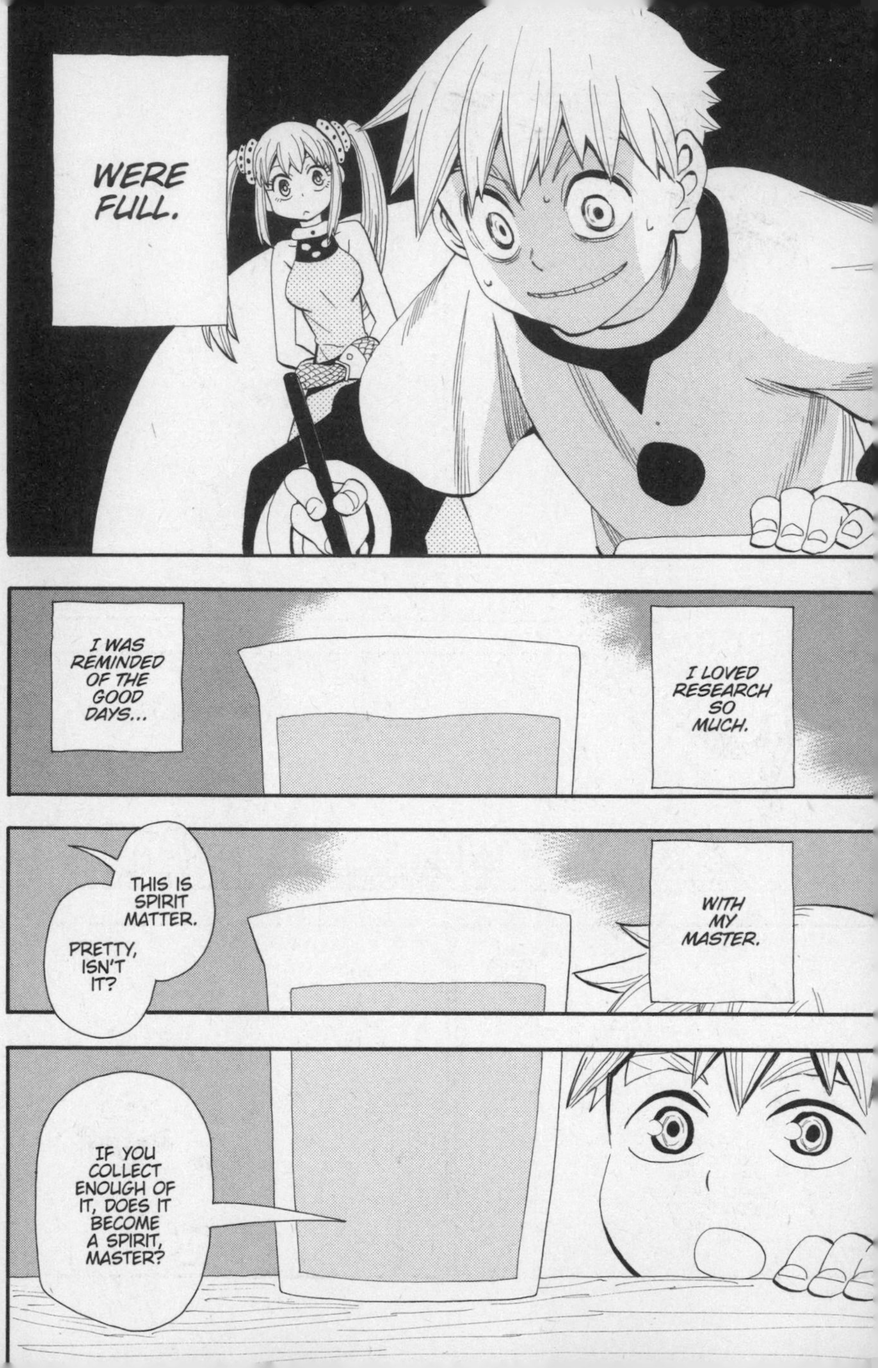
WERE FULL.
I LOVED RESEARCH SO MUCH.
I WAS REMINDED OF THE GOOD DAYS...
WITH MY MASTER.
THIS IS SPIRIT MATTER.
PRETTY, ISN'T IT?
IF YOU COLLECT ENOUGH OF IT, DOES IT BECOME A SPIRIT, MASTER?

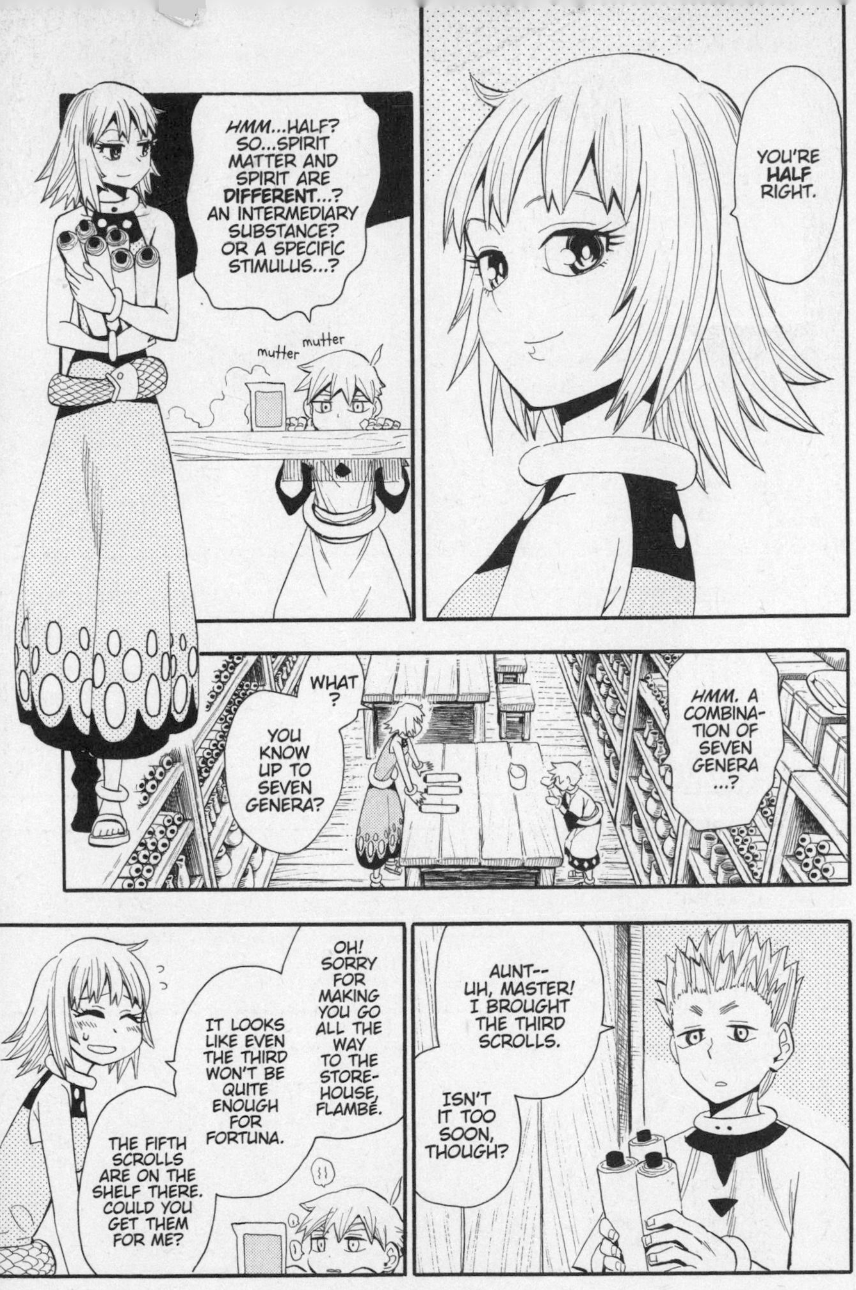
YOU'RE **HALF** RIGHT.
HMM...HALF? SO...SPIRIT MATTER AND SPIRIT ARE **DIFFERENT**...? AN INTERMEDIARY SUBSTANCE? OR A SPECIFIC STIMULUS...?
mutter mutter
HMM. A COMBINATION OF SEVEN GENERA ...?
WHAT?
YOU KNOW UP TO SEVEN GENERA?
AUNT-- UH, MASTER! I BROUGHT THE THIRD SCROLLS.
ISN'T IT TOO SOON, THOUGH?
OH! SORRY FOR MAKING YOU GO ALL THE WAY TO THE STOREHOUSE, FLAMBÉ.
IT LOOKS LIKE EVEN THE THIRD WON'T BE QUITE ENOUGH FOR FORTUNA.
THE FIFTH SCROLLS ARE ON THE SHELF THERE. COULD YOU GET THEM FOR ME?

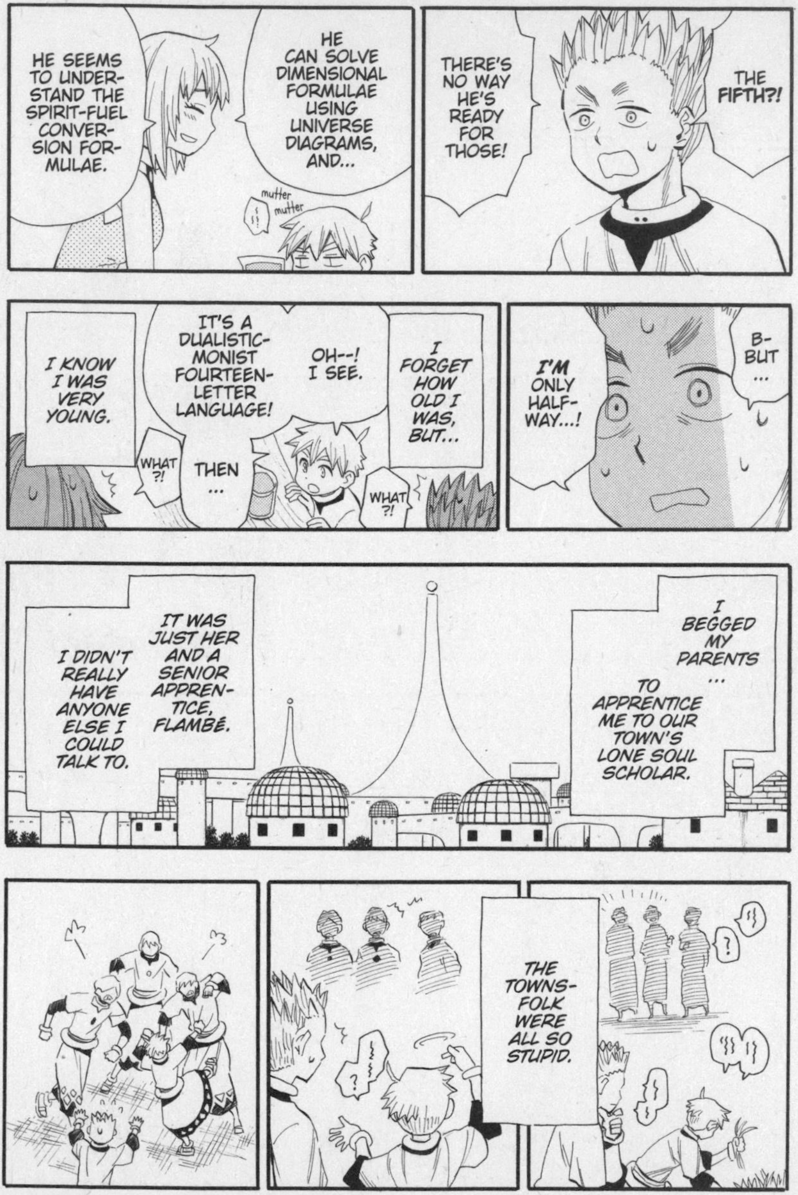
THE FIFTH?!
THERE'S NO WAY HE'S READY FOR THOSE!
HE CAN SOLVE DIMENSIONAL FORMULAE USING UNIVERSE DIAGRAMS, AND...
HE SEEMS TO UNDERSTAND THE SPIRIT-FUEL CONVERSION FORMULAE.
mutter mutter
B-BUT...
I'M ONLY HALFWAY...!
I FORGET HOW OLD I WAS, BUT...
OH--! I SEE.
IT'S A DUALISTIC-MONIST FOURTEEN-LETTER LANGUAGE!
WHAT?!
THEN...
WHAT?!
I KNOW I WAS VERY YOUNG.
I BEGGED MY PARENTS...
TO APPRENTICE ME TO OUR TOWN'S LONE SOUL SCHOLAR.
IT WAS JUST HER AND A SENIOR APPRENTICE, FLAMBÉ.
I DIDN'T REALLY HAVE ANYONE ELSE I COULD TALK TO.
THE TOWNSFOLK WERE ALL SO STUPID.
?
?

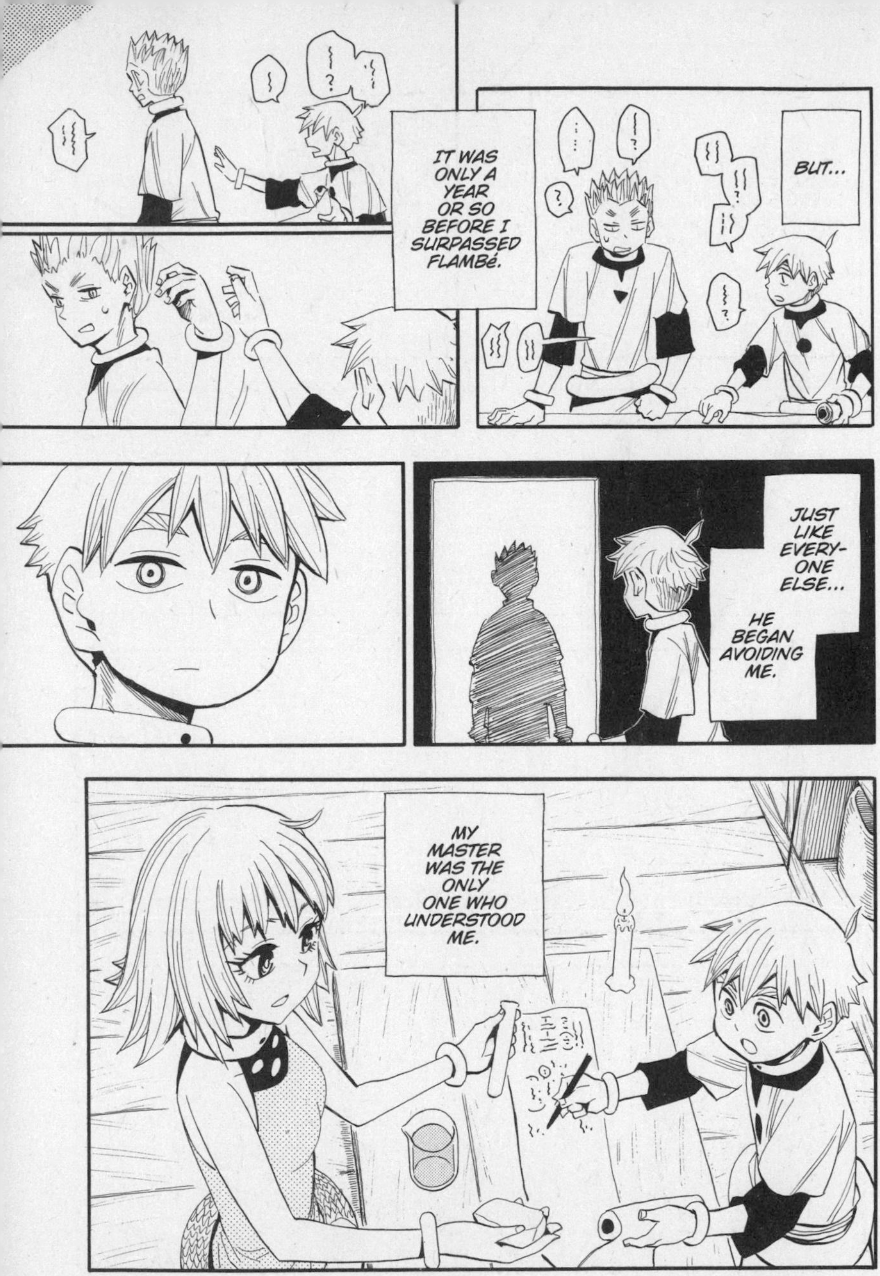
IT WAS ONLY A YEAR OR SO BEFORE I SURPASSED FLAMBé.
BUT...
JUST LIKE EVERY-ONE ELSE...
HE BEGAN AVOIDING ME.
MY MASTER WAS THE ONLY ONE WHO UNDERSTOOD ME.

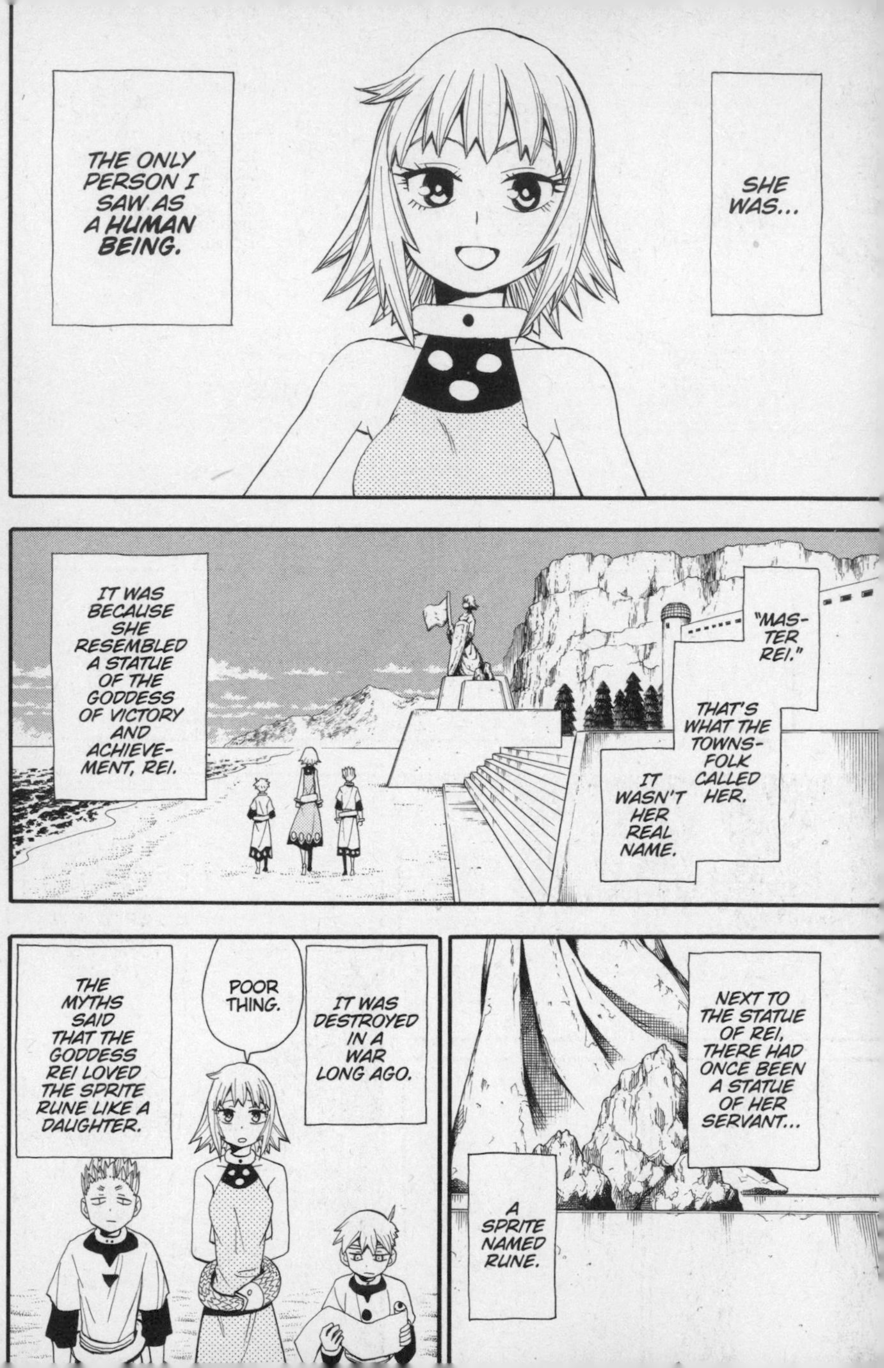
SHE WAS...
THE ONLY PERSON I SAW AS A HUMAN BEING.
"MASTER REI."
THAT'S WHAT THE TOWNSFOLK CALLED HER.
IT WASN'T HER REAL NAME.
IT WAS BECAUSE SHE RESEMBLED A STATUE OF THE GODDESS OF VICTORY AND ACHIEVEMENT, REI.
NEXT TO THE STATUE OF REI, THERE HAD ONCE BEEN A STATUE OF HER SERVANT...
A SPRITE NAMED RUNE.
IT WAS DESTROYED IN A WAR LONG AGO.
POOR THING.
THE MYTHS SAID THAT THE GODDESS REI LOVED THE SPRITE RUNE LIKE A DAUGHTER.

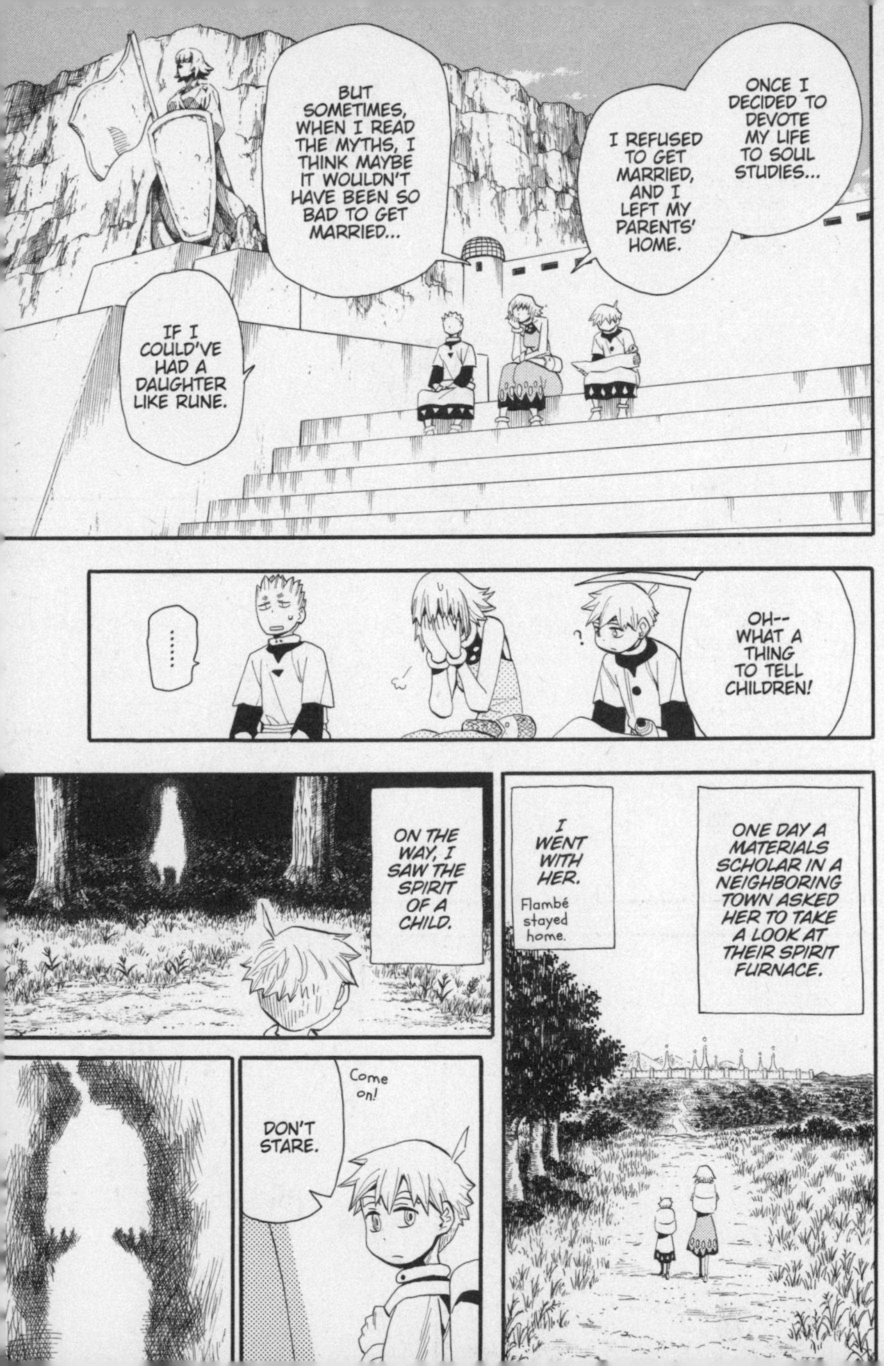
ONCE I DECIDED TO DEVOTE MY LIFE TO SOUL STUDIES...
I REFUSED TO GET MARRIED, AND I LEFT MY PARENTS' HOME.
BUT SOMETIMES, WHEN I READ THE MYTHS, I THINK MAYBE IT WOULDN'T HAVE BEEN SO BAD TO GET MARRIED...
IF I COULD'VE HAD A DAUGHTER LIKE RUNE.
OH-- WHAT A THING TO TELL CHILDREN!
?
......
ONE DAY A MATERIALS SCHOLAR IN A NEIGHBORING TOWN ASKED HER TO TAKE A LOOK AT THEIR SPIRIT FURNACE.
I WENT WITH HER.
Flambé stayed home.
ON THE WAY, I SAW THE SPIRIT OF A CHILD.
Come on!
DON'T STARE.

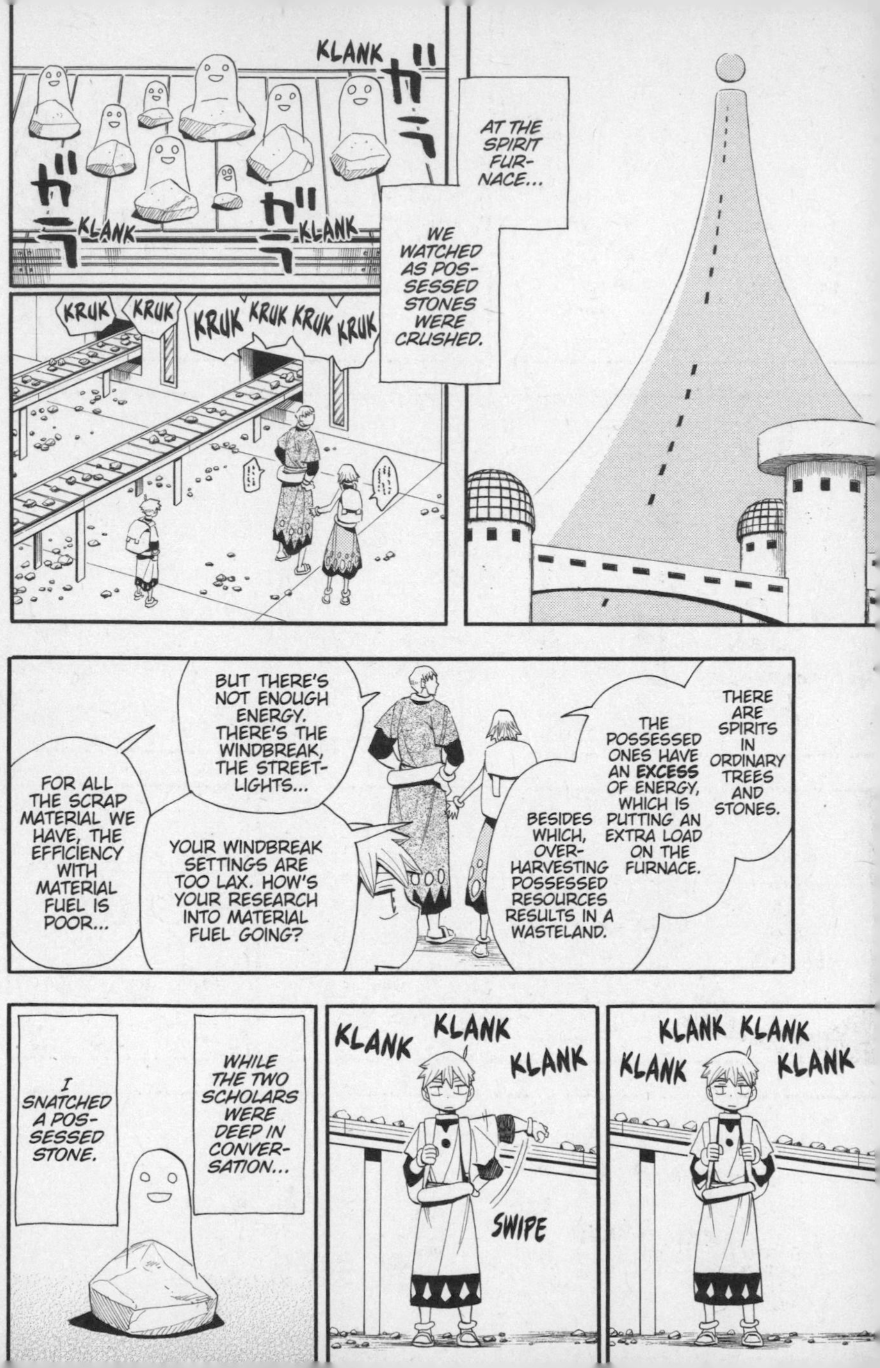
AT THE SPIRIT FURNACE...
WE WATCHED AS POSSESSED STONES WERE CRUSHED.
KLANK
KLANK
KLANK
KRUK KRUK KRUK KRUK
KRUK
KRUK
THERE ARE SPIRITS IN ORDINARY TREES AND STONES.
THE POSSESSED ONES HAVE AN **EXCESS** OF ENERGY, WHICH IS PUTTING AN EXTRA LOAD ON THE FURNACE.
BESIDES WHICH, OVER-HARVESTING POSSESSED RESOURCES RESULTS IN A WASTELAND.
BUT THERE'S NOT ENOUGH ENERGY. THERE'S THE WINDBREAK, THE STREET-LIGHTS...
YOUR WINDBREAK SETTINGS ARE TOO LAX. HOW'S YOUR RESEARCH INTO MATERIAL FUEL GOING?
FOR ALL THE SCRAP MATERIAL WE HAVE, THE EFFICIENCY WITH MATERIAL FUEL IS POOR...
KLANK KLANK
KLANK KLANK
KLANK KLANK
KLANK
SWIPE
WHILE THE TWO SCHOLARS WERE DEEP IN CONVERSATION...
I SNATCHED A POSSESSED STONE.

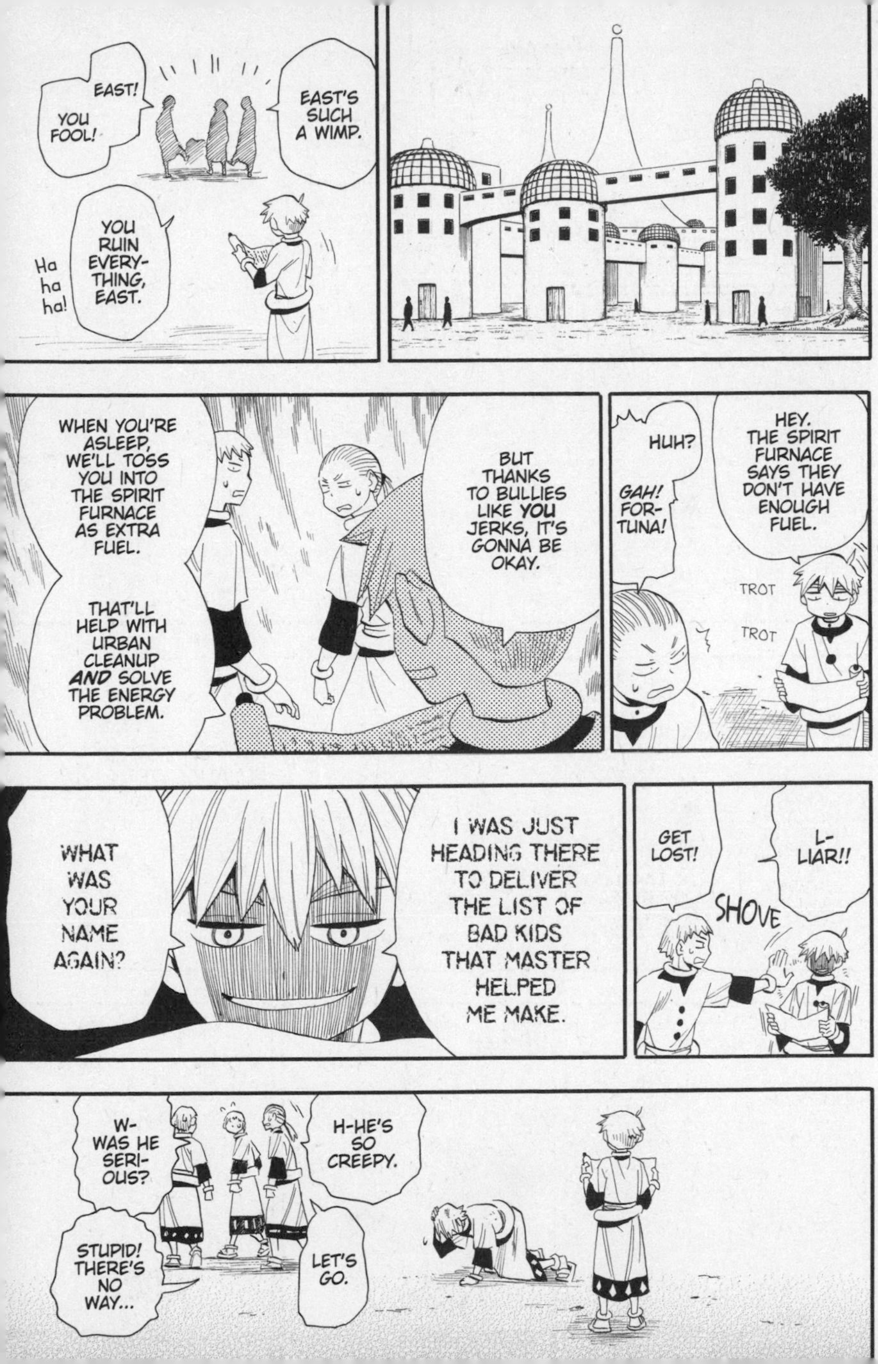

EAST'S SUCH A WIMP.
EAST! YOU FOOL!
YOU RUIN EVERYTHING, EAST.
Ha ha ha!
HEY. THE SPIRIT FURNACE SAYS THEY DON'T HAVE ENOUGH FUEL.
TROT
TROT
HUH?
GAH! FORTUNA!
BUT THANKS TO BULLIES LIKE YOU JERKS, IT'S GONNA BE OKAY.
WHEN YOU'RE ASLEEP, WE'LL TOSS YOU INTO THE SPIRIT FURNACE AS EXTRA FUEL.
THAT'LL HELP WITH URBAN CLEANUP AND SOLVE THE ENERGY PROBLEM.
L-LIAR!!
GET LOST!
SHOVE
I WAS JUST HEADING THERE TO DELIVER THE LIST OF BAD KIDS THAT MASTER HELPED ME MAKE.
WHAT WAS YOUR NAME AGAIN?
H-HE'S SO CREEPY.
W-WAS HE SERIOUS?
LET'S GO.
STUPID! THERE'S NO WAY...

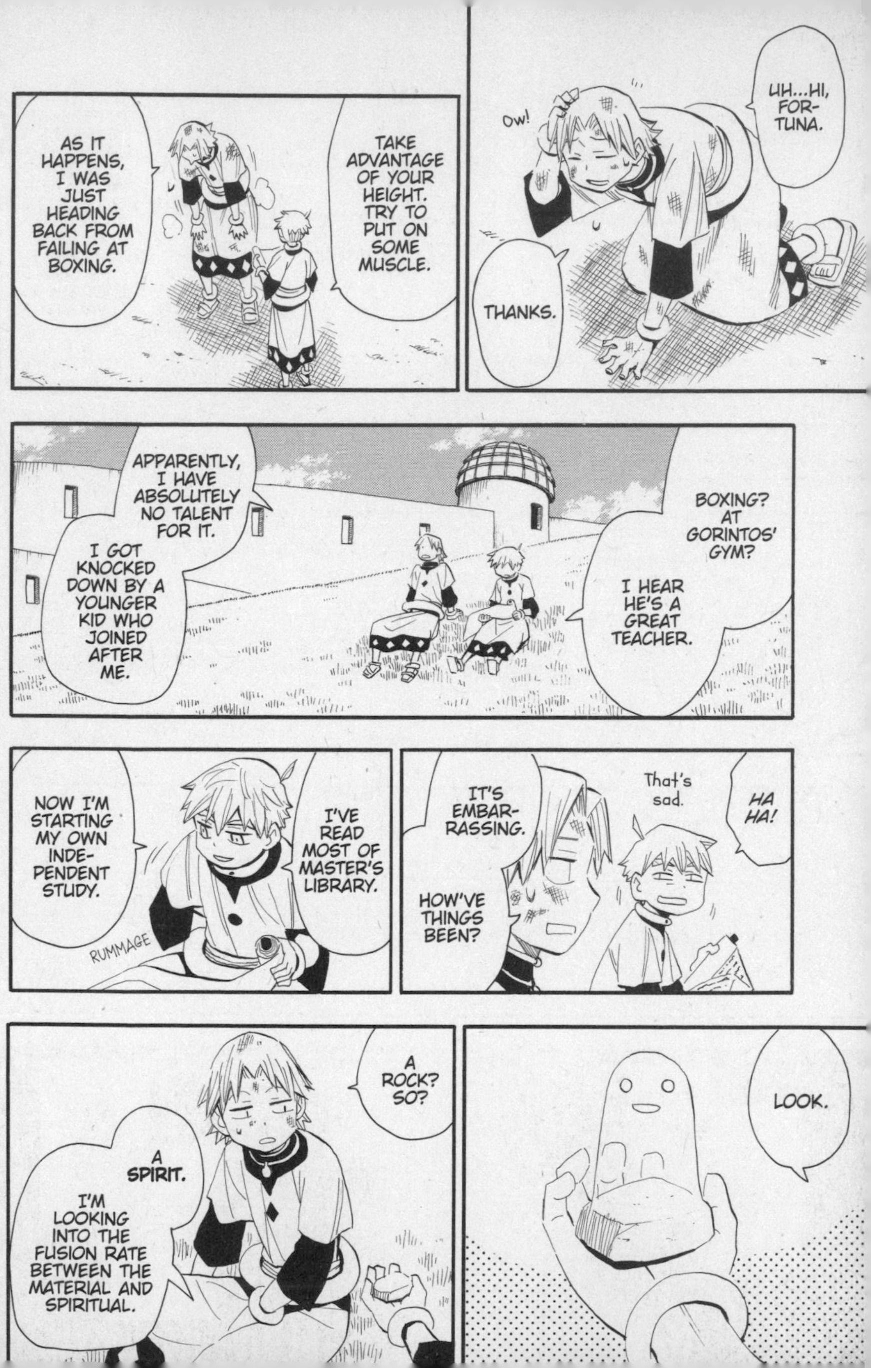
UH...HI, FOR-TUNA.
Ow!
THANKS.
TAKE ADVANTAGE OF YOUR HEIGHT. TRY TO PUT ON SOME MUSCLE.
AS IT HAPPENS, I WAS JUST HEADING BACK FROM FAILING AT BOXING.
BOXING? AT GORINTOS' GYM?
I HEAR HE'S A GREAT TEACHER.
APPARENTLY, I HAVE ABSOLUTELY NO TALENT FOR IT.
I GOT KNOCKED DOWN BY A YOUNGER KID WHO JOINED AFTER ME.
HA HA!
That's sad.
IT'S EMBAR-RASSING.
HOW'VE THINGS BEEN?
I'VE READ MOST OF MASTER'S LIBRARY.
NOW I'M STARTING MY OWN INDE-PENDENT STUDY.
RUMMAGE
LOOK.
A ROCK? SO?
A SPIRIT.
I'M LOOKING INTO THE FUSION RATE BETWEEN THE MATERIAL AND SPIRITUAL.

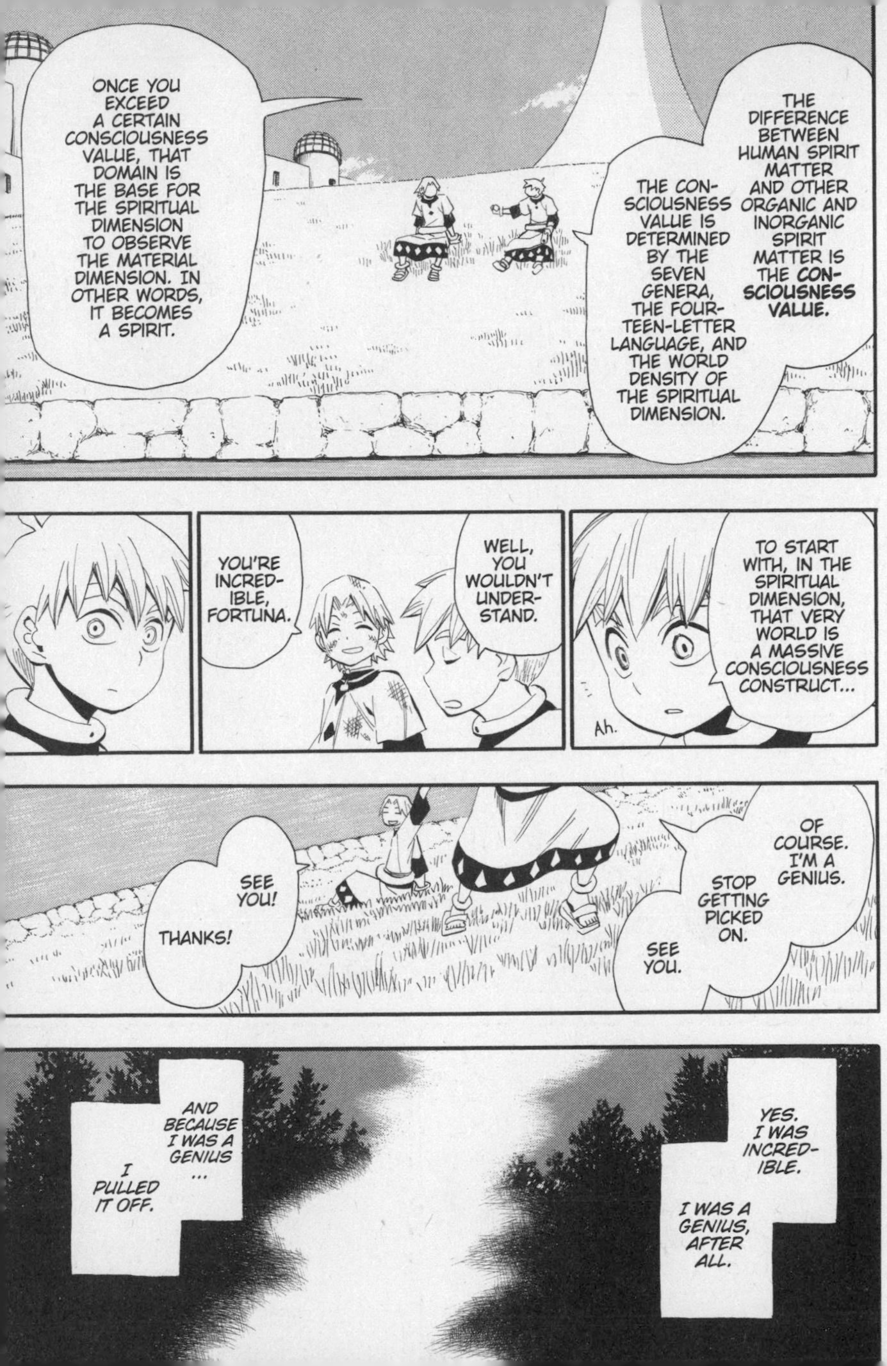
THE DIFFERENCE BETWEEN HUMAN SPIRIT MATTER AND OTHER ORGANIC AND INORGANIC SPIRIT MATTER IS THE **CONSCIOUSNESS VALUE.**
THE CONSCIOUSNESS VALUE IS DETERMINED BY THE SEVEN GENERA, THE FOURTEEN-LETTER LANGUAGE, AND THE WORLD DENSITY OF THE SPIRITUAL DIMENSION.
ONCE YOU EXCEED A CERTAIN CONSCIOUSNESS VALUE, THAT DOMAIN IS THE BASE FOR THE SPIRITUAL DIMENSION TO OBSERVE THE MATERIAL DIMENSION. IN OTHER WORDS, IT BECOMES A SPIRIT.
TO START WITH, IN THE SPIRITUAL DIMENSION, THAT VERY WORLD IS A MASSIVE CONSCIOUSNESS CONSTRUCT...
Ah.
WELL, YOU WOULDN'T UNDERSTAND.
YOU'RE INCREDIBLE, FORTUNA.
OF COURSE. I'M A GENIUS.
STOP GETTING PICKED ON.
SEE YOU.
SEE YOU!
THANKS!
YES. I WAS INCREDIBLE.
I WAS A GENIUS, AFTER ALL.
AND BECAUSE I WAS A GENIUS...
I PULLED IT OFF.

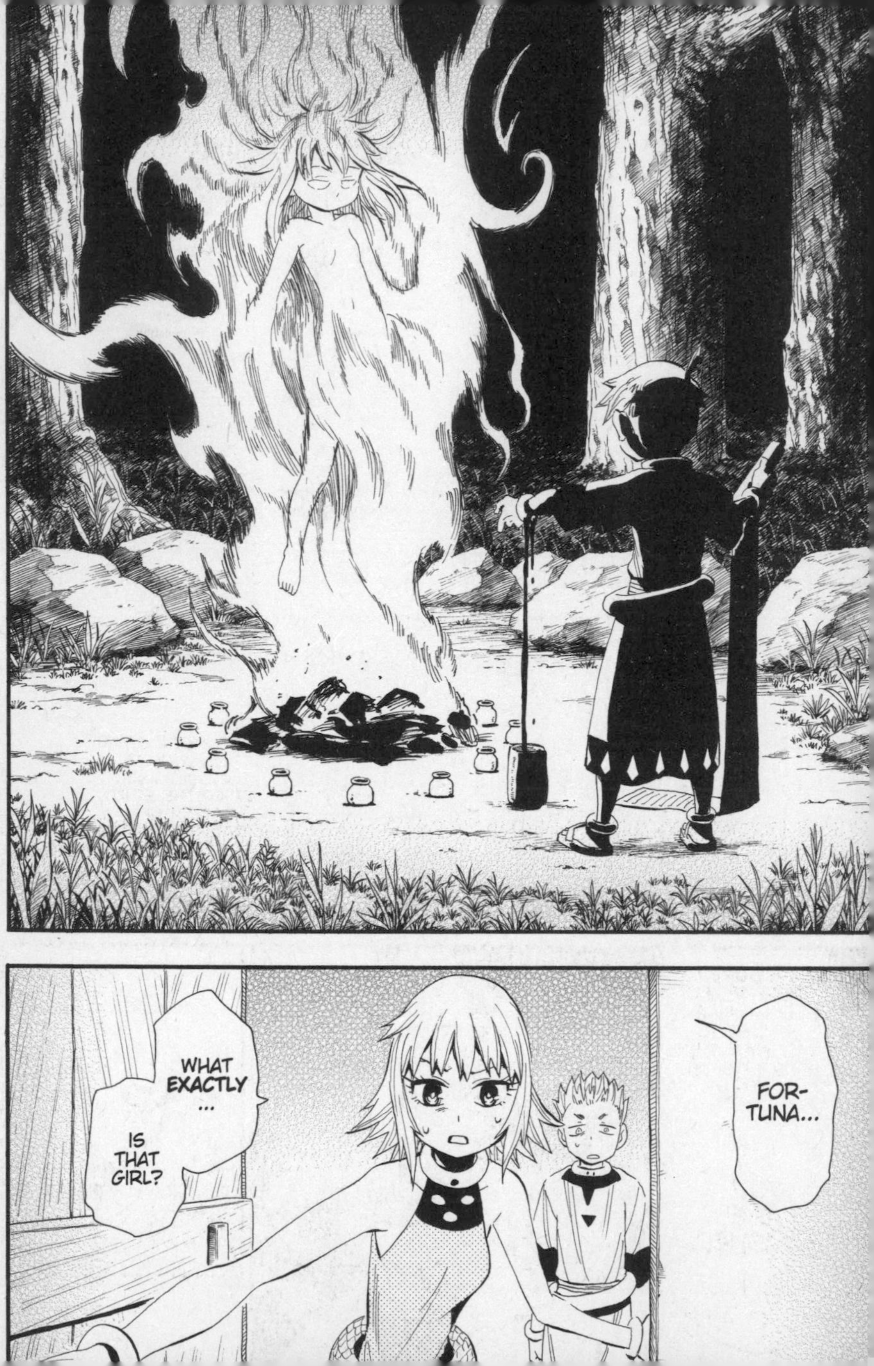
FOR-TUNA...
WHAT EXACTLY ...
IS THAT GIRL?

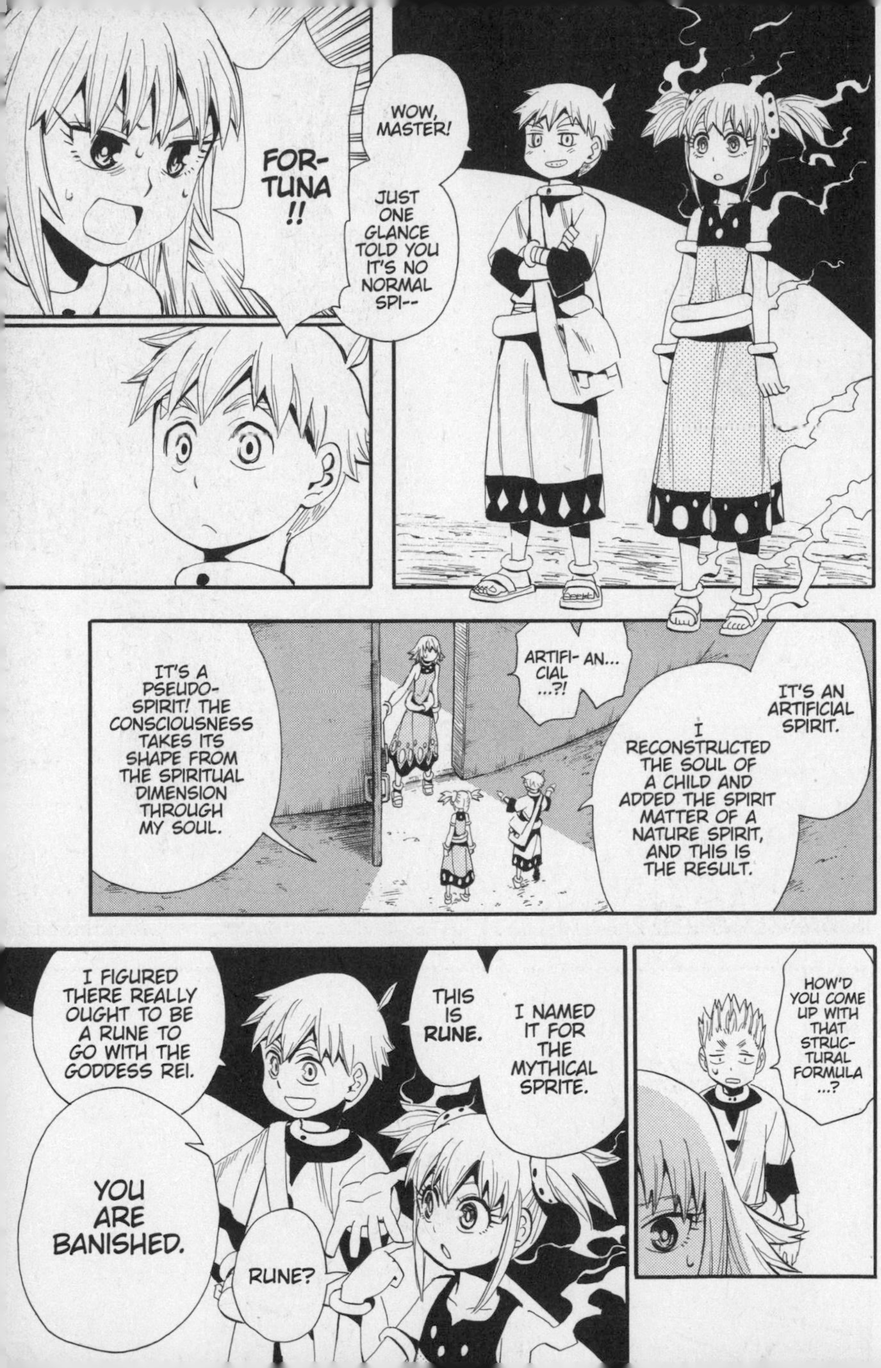
WOW, MASTER!
JUST ONE GLANCE TOLD YOU IT'S NO NORMAL SPI--
FOR-TUNA!!
AN... ARTIFI-CIAL ...?!
IT'S AN ARTIFICIAL SPIRIT.
I RECONSTRUCTED THE SOUL OF A CHILD AND ADDED THE SPIRIT MATTER OF A NATURE SPIRIT, AND THIS IS THE RESULT.
IT'S A PSEUDO-SPIRIT! THE CONSCIOUSNESS TAKES ITS SHAPE FROM THE SPIRITUAL DIMENSION THROUGH MY SOUL.
HOW'D YOU COME UP WITH THAT STRUC-TURAL FORMULA ...?
THIS IS RUNE.
I NAMED IT FOR THE MYTHICAL SPRITE.
RUNE?
I FIGURED THERE REALLY OUGHT TO BE A RUNE TO GO WITH THE GODDESS REI.
YOU ARE BANISHED.

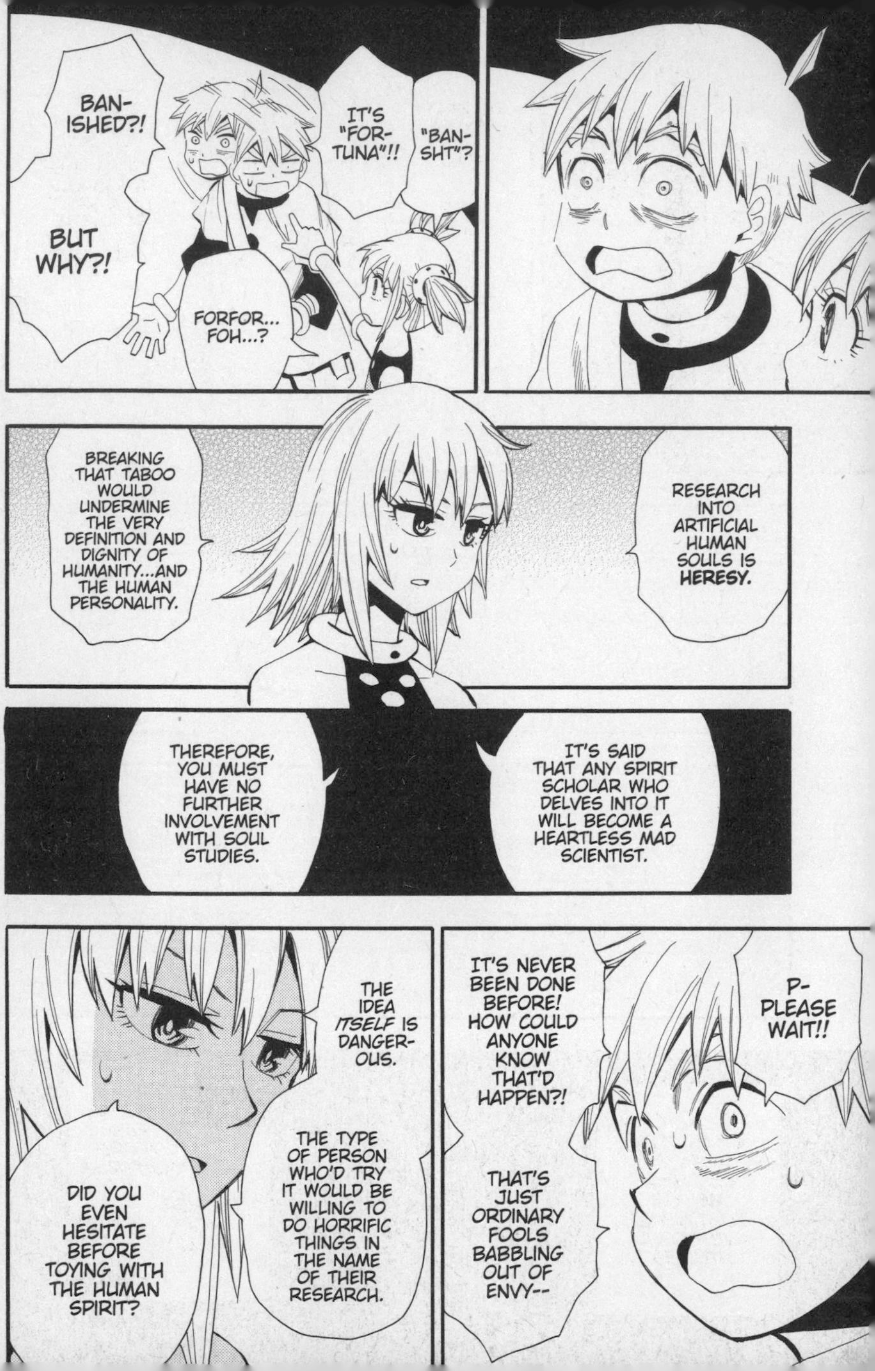
BAN-ISHED?!
BUT WHY?!
FORFOR... FOH...?
IT'S "FOR-TUNA"!!
"BAN-SHT"?
RESEARCH INTO ARTIFICIAL HUMAN SOULS IS HERESY.
BREAKING THAT TABOO WOULD UNDERMINE THE VERY DEFINITION AND DIGNITY OF HUMANITY...AND THE HUMAN PERSONALITY.
IT'S SAID THAT ANY SPIRIT SCHOLAR WHO DELVES INTO IT WILL BECOME A HEARTLESS MAD SCIENTIST.
THEREFORE, YOU MUST HAVE NO FURTHER INVOLVEMENT WITH SOUL STUDIES.
P-PLEASE WAIT!!
IT'S NEVER BEEN DONE BEFORE! HOW COULD ANYONE KNOW THAT'D HAPPEN?!
THAT'S JUST ORDINARY FOOLS BABBLING OUT OF ENVY--
THE IDEA *ITSELF* IS DANGER-OUS.
THE TYPE OF PERSON WHO'D TRY IT WOULD BE WILLING TO DO HORRIFIC THINGS IN THE NAME OF THEIR RESEARCH.
DID YOU EVEN HESITATE BEFORE TOYING WITH THE HUMAN SPIRIT?

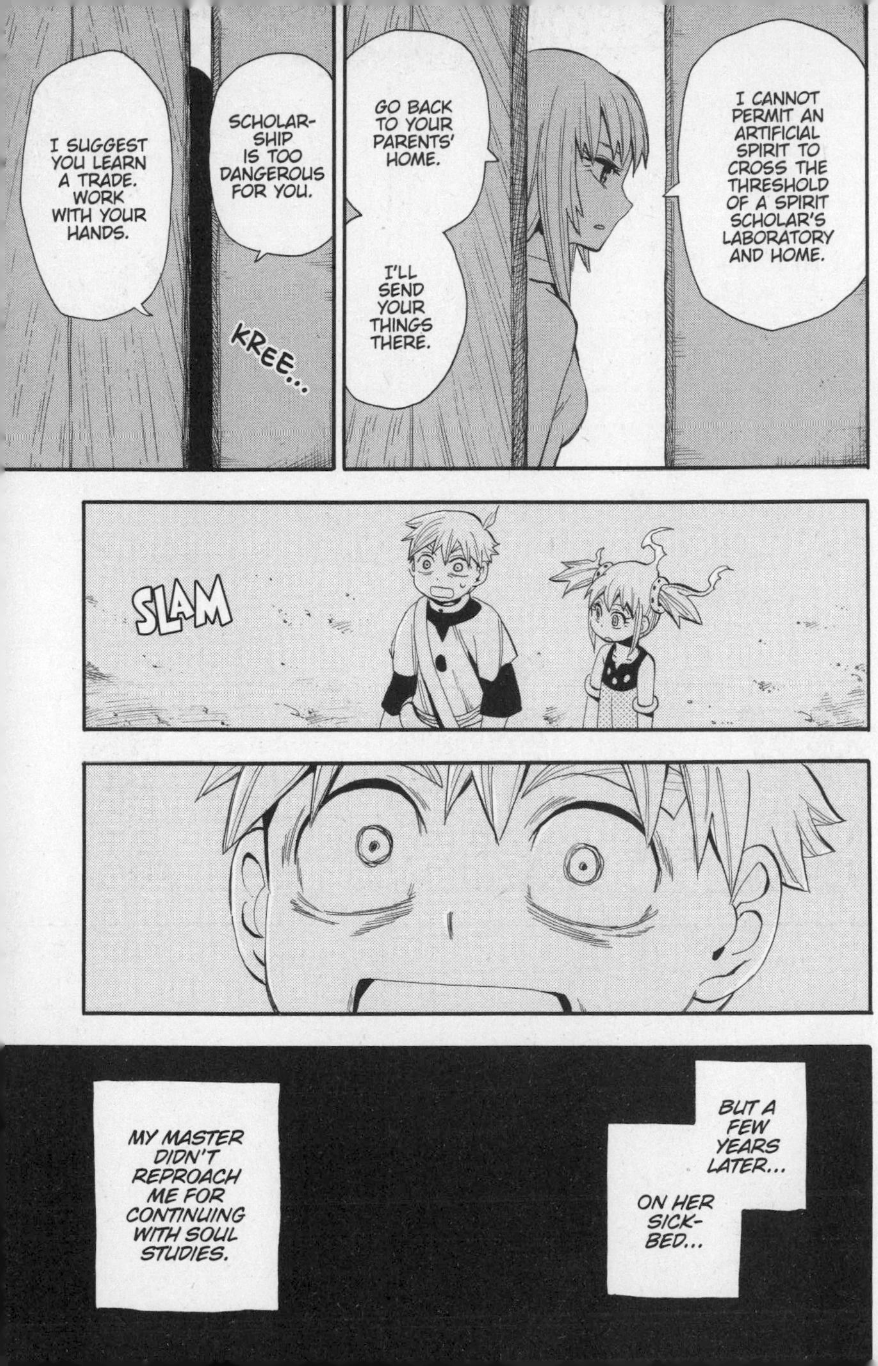

I CANNOT PERMIT AN ARTIFICIAL SPIRIT TO CROSS THE THRESHOLD OF A SPIRIT SCHOLAR'S LABORATORY AND HOME.
GO BACK TO YOUR PARENTS' HOME.
I'LL SEND YOUR THINGS THERE.
SCHOLAR-SHIP IS TOO DANGEROUS FOR YOU.
KREE...
I SUGGEST YOU LEARN A TRADE. WORK WITH YOUR HANDS.
SLAM
MY MASTER DIDN'T REPROACH ME FOR CONTINUING WITH SOUL STUDIES.
BUT A FEW YEARS LATER...
ON HER SICK-BED...

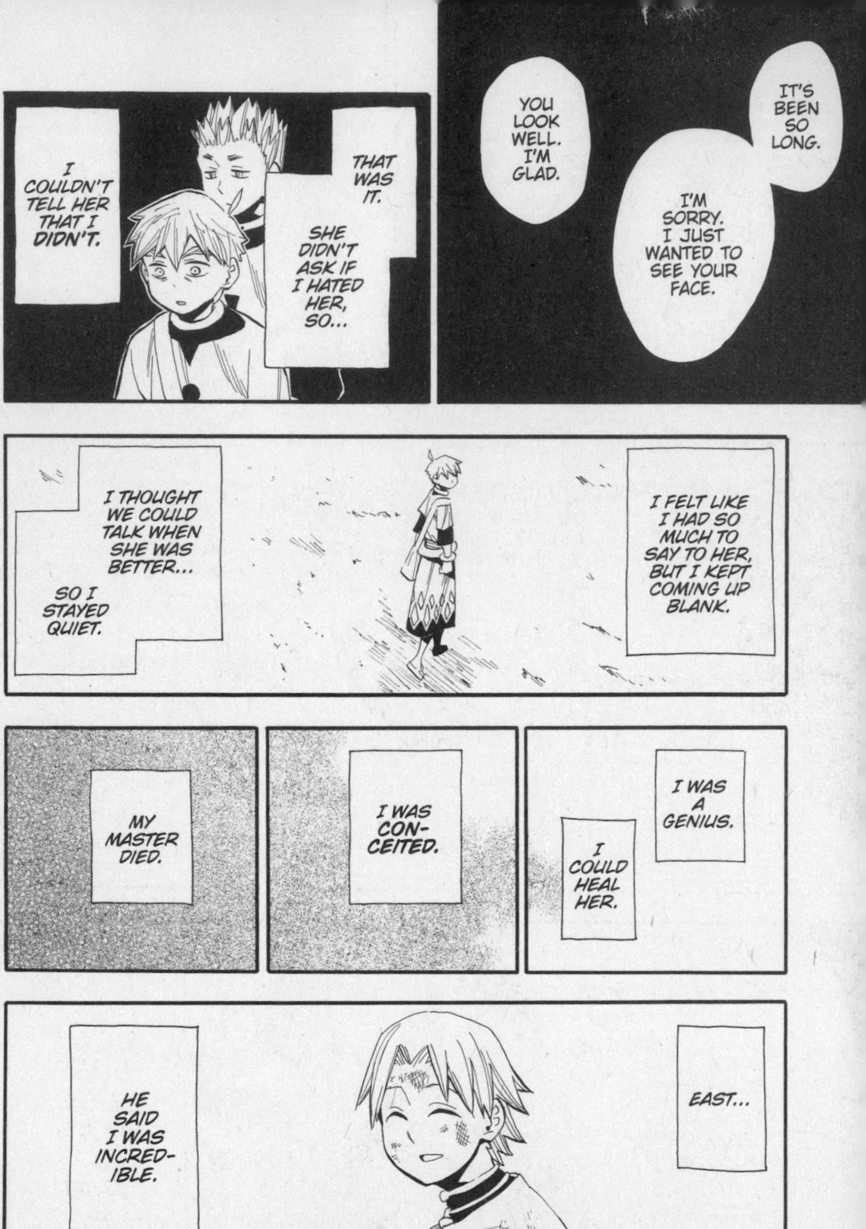
IT'S BEEN SO LONG.
I'M SORRY. I JUST WANTED TO SEE YOUR FACE.
YOU LOOK WELL. I'M GLAD.
THAT WAS IT.
SHE DIDN'T ASK IF I HATED HER, SO...
I COULDN'T TELL HER THAT I DIDN'T.
I FELT LIKE I HAD SO MUCH TO SAY TO HER, BUT I KEPT COMING UP BLANK.
I THOUGHT WE COULD TALK WHEN SHE WAS BETTER...
SO I STAYED QUIET.
I WAS A GENIUS.
I COULD HEAL HER.
I WAS CON-CEITED.
MY MASTER DIED.
EAST...
HE SAID I WAS INCRED-IBLE.

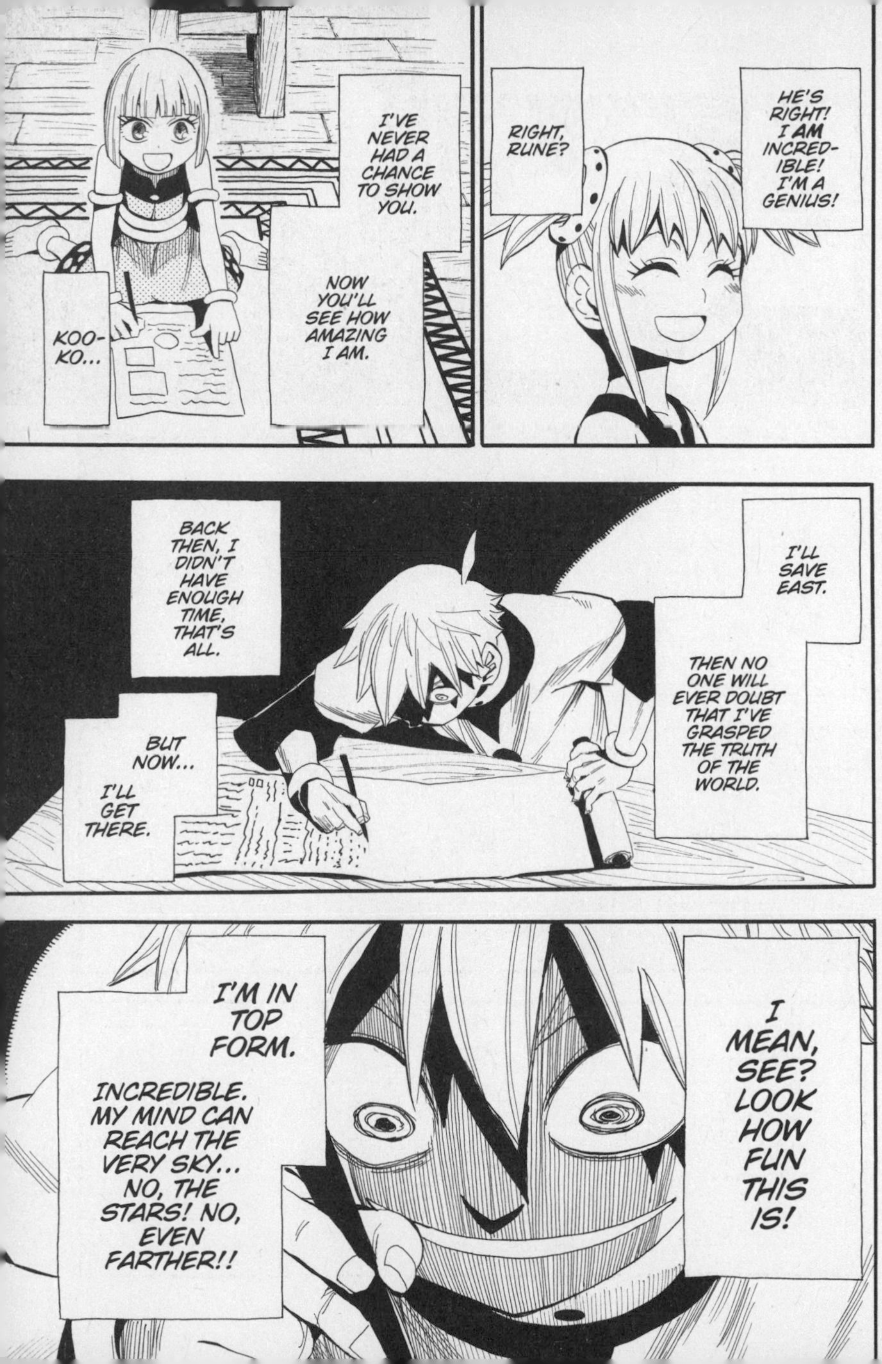
HE'S RIGHT! I AM INCREDIBLE! I'M A GENIUS!
RIGHT, RUNE?
I'VE NEVER HAD A CHANCE TO SHOW YOU.
NOW YOU'LL SEE HOW AMAZING I AM.
KOO-KO...
I'LL SAVE EAST.
THEN NO ONE WILL EVER DOUBT THAT I'VE GRASPED THE TRUTH OF THE WORLD.
BACK THEN, I DIDN'T HAVE ENOUGH TIME, THAT'S ALL.
BUT NOW...
I'LL GET THERE.
I MEAN, SEE? LOOK HOW FUN THIS IS!
I'M IN TOP FORM.
INCREDIBLE. MY MIND CAN REACH THE VERY SKY... NO, THE STARS! NO, EVEN FARTHER!!

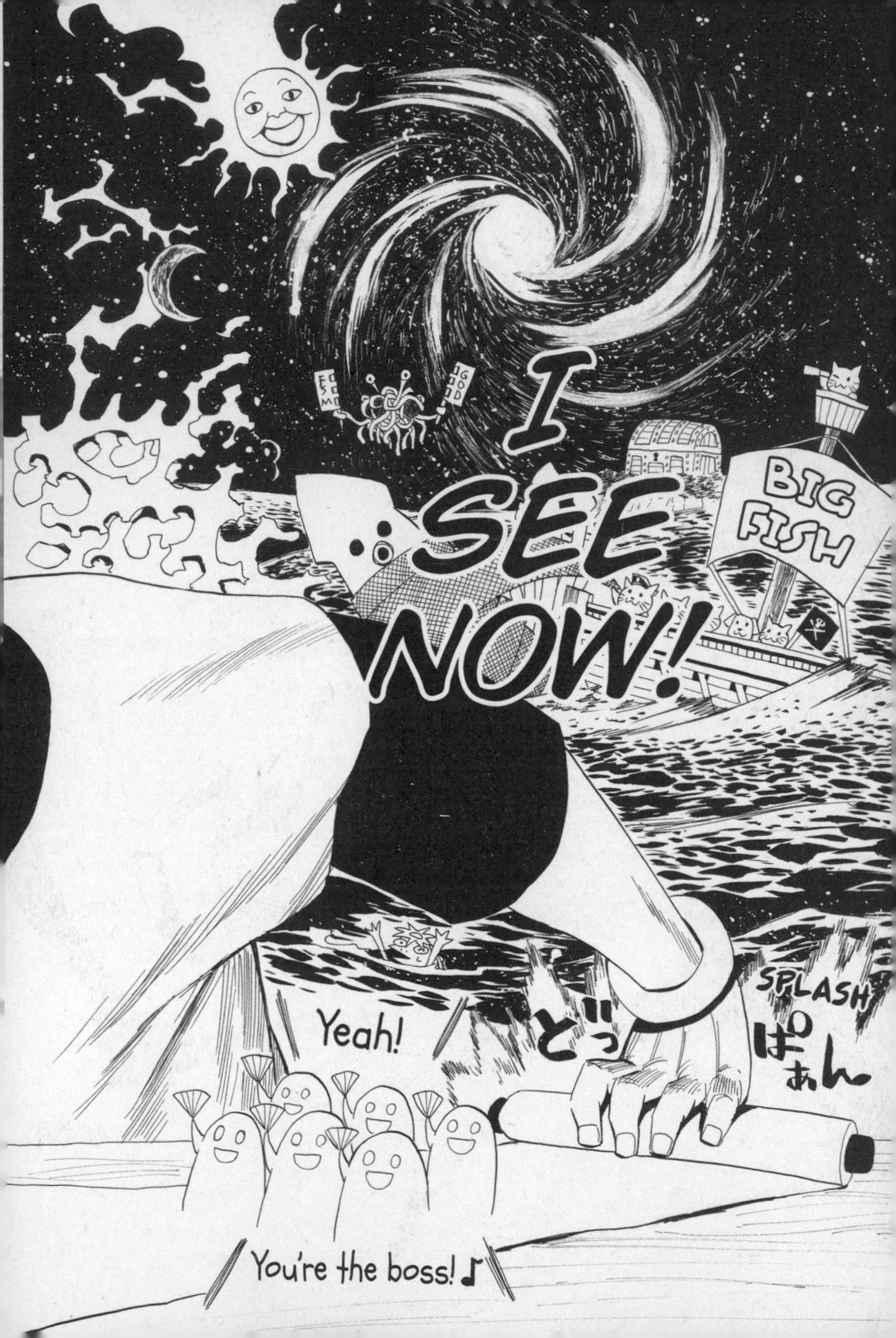
I SEE NOW!
BIG FISH
GOD
FSM
SPLASH
ぱぁん
どっ
Yeah!
You're the boss! ♪

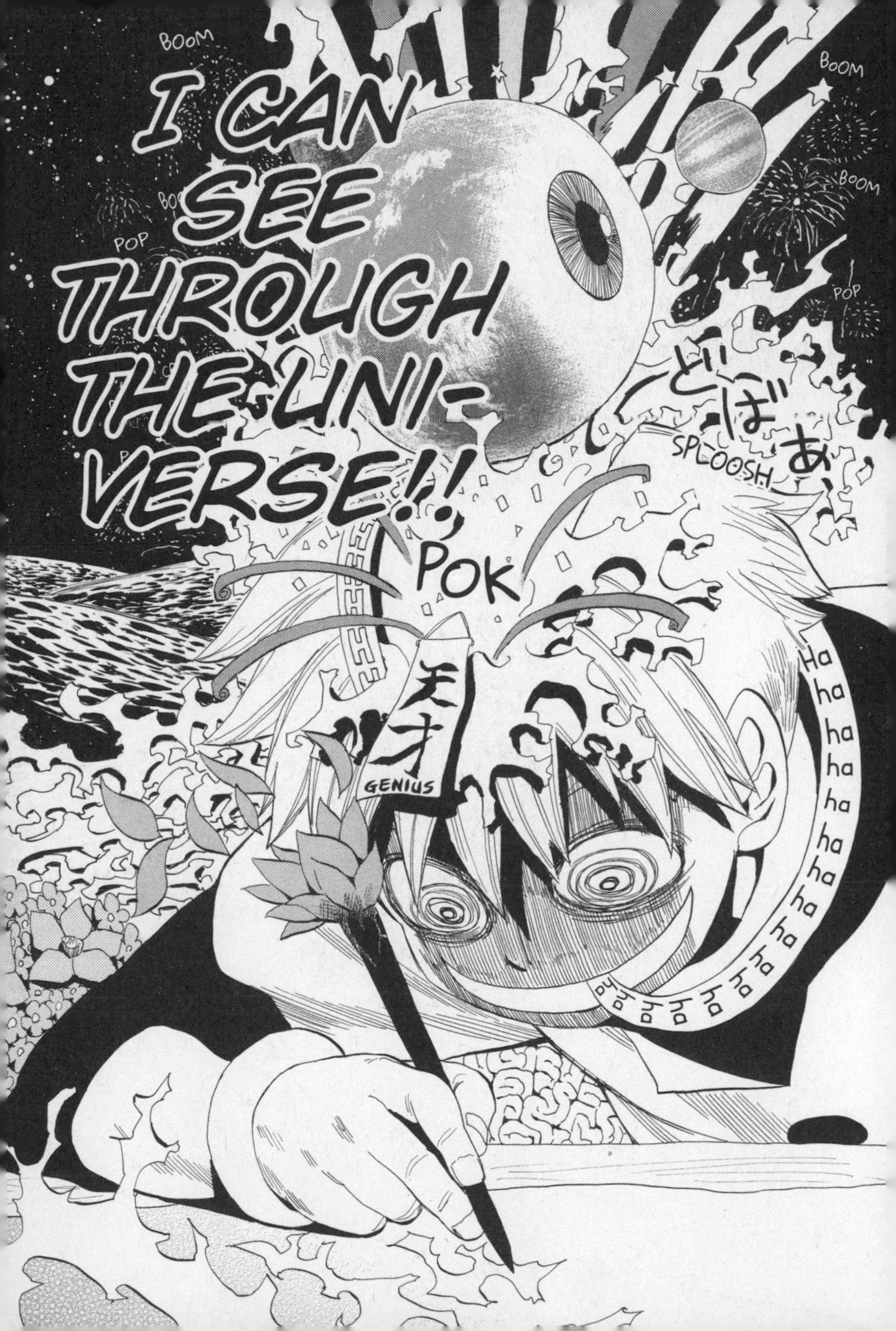
BOOM
BOOM
BOOM
POP
POP
I CAN SEE THROUGH THE UNI-VERSE!!
どばあ
SPLOOSH
POK
天才
GENIUS
Ha ha ha ha ha ha ha ha ha ha ha ha ha ha ha ha ha

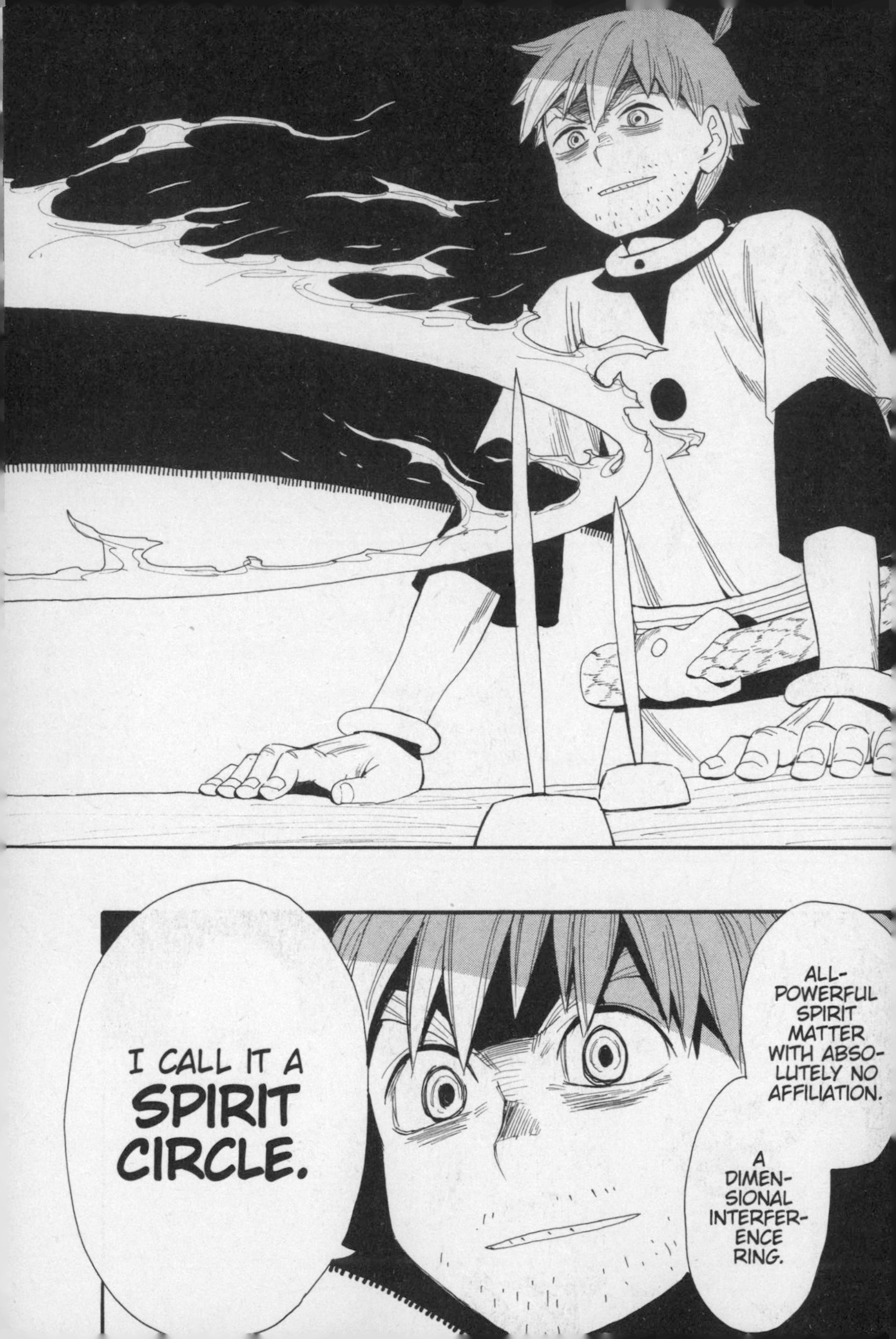
ALL-POWERFUL SPIRIT MATTER WITH ABSOLUTELY NO AFFILIATION.
A DIMENSIONAL INTERFERENCE RING.
I CALL IT A SPIRIT CIRCLE.

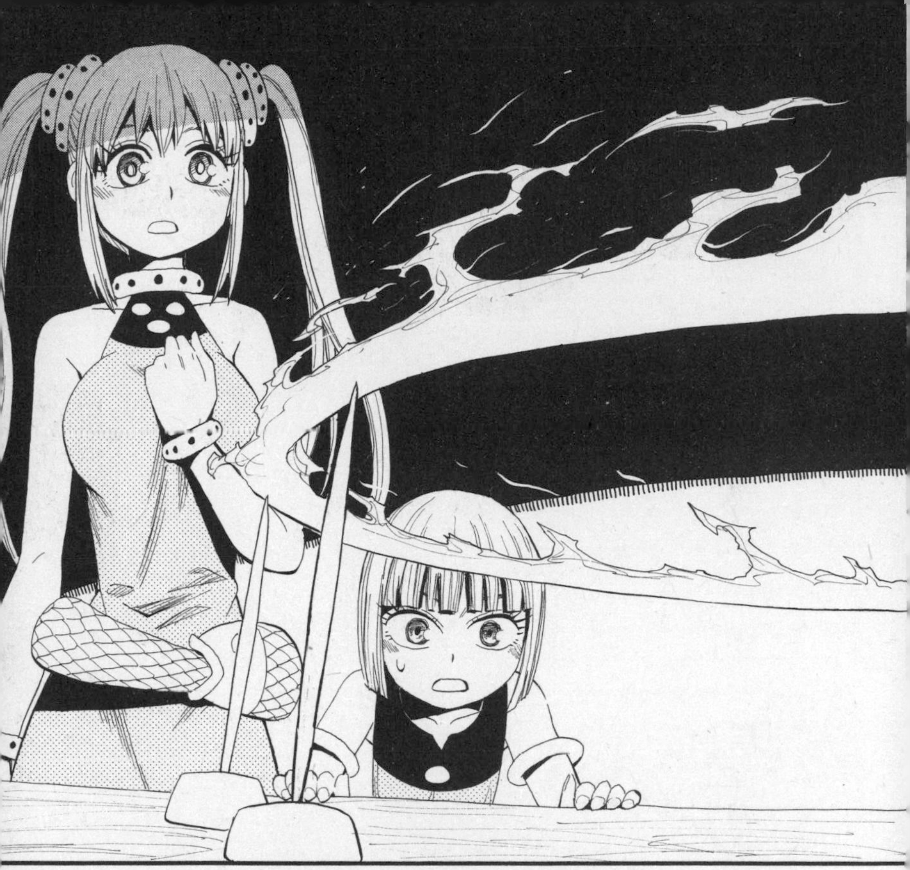

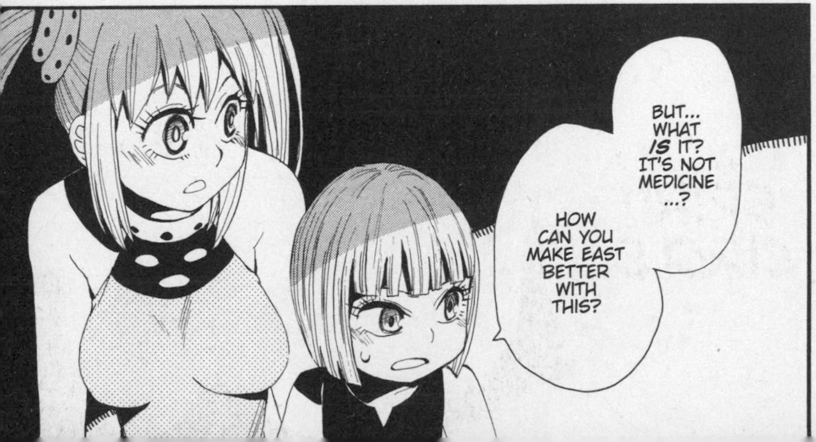
BUT... WHAT IS IT? IT'S NOT MEDICINE ...?
HOW CAN YOU MAKE EAST BETTER WITH THIS?

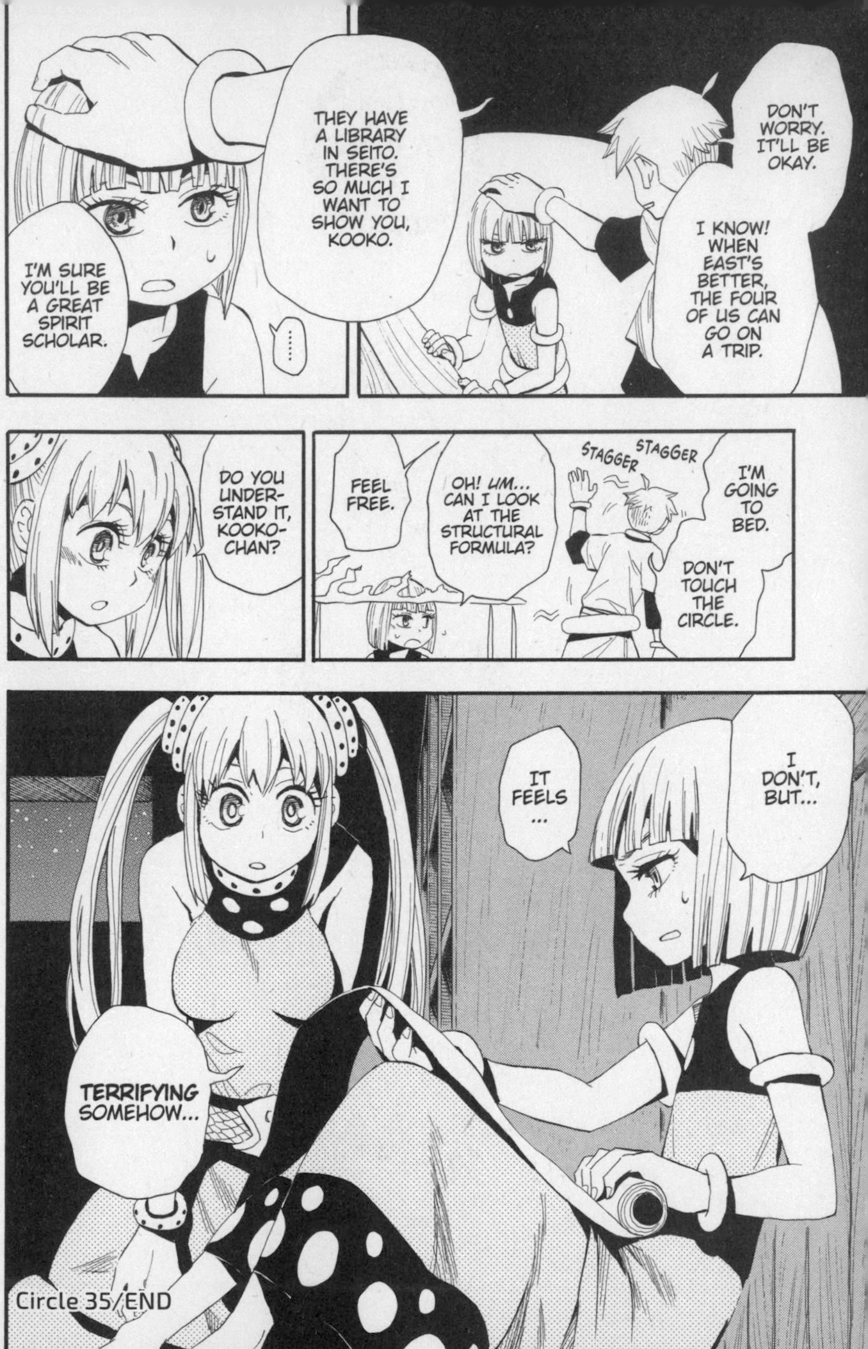
DON'T WORRY. IT'LL BE OKAY.
I KNOW! WHEN EAST'S BETTER, THE FOUR OF US CAN GO ON A TRIP.
THEY HAVE A LIBRARY IN SEITO. THERE'S SO MUCH I WANT TO SHOW YOU, KOOKO.
......
I'M SURE YOU'LL BE A GREAT SPIRIT SCHOLAR.
STAGGER STAGGER
I'M GOING TO BED.
DON'T TOUCH THE CIRCLE.
OH! UM... CAN I LOOK AT THE STRUCTURAL FORMULA?
FEEL FREE.
DO YOU UNDER-STAND IT, KOOKO-CHAN?
I DON'T, BUT...
IT FEELS ...
TERRIFYING SOMEHOW...
Circle 35/END

Circle 36
Fortuna
3

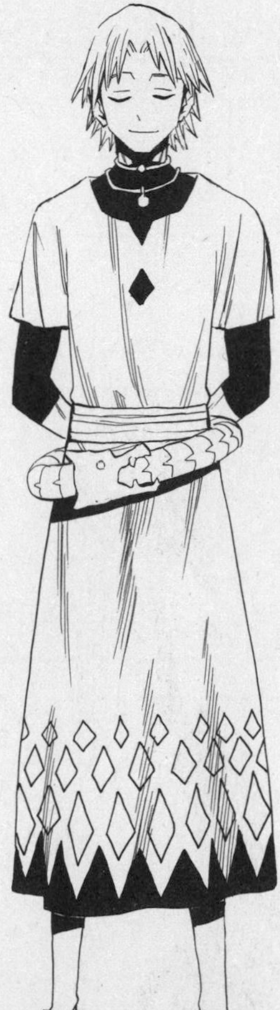

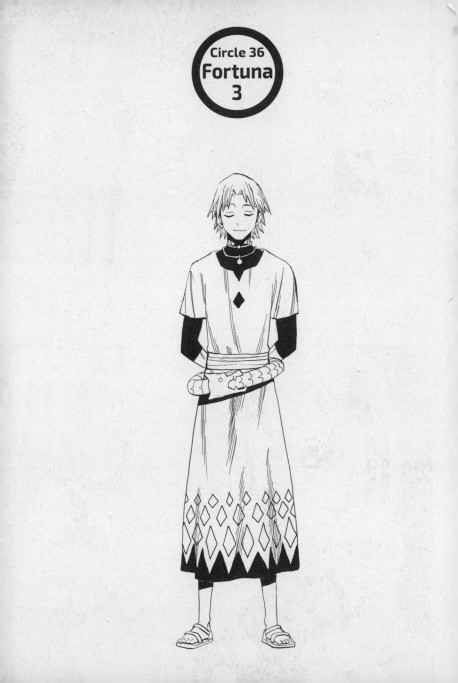

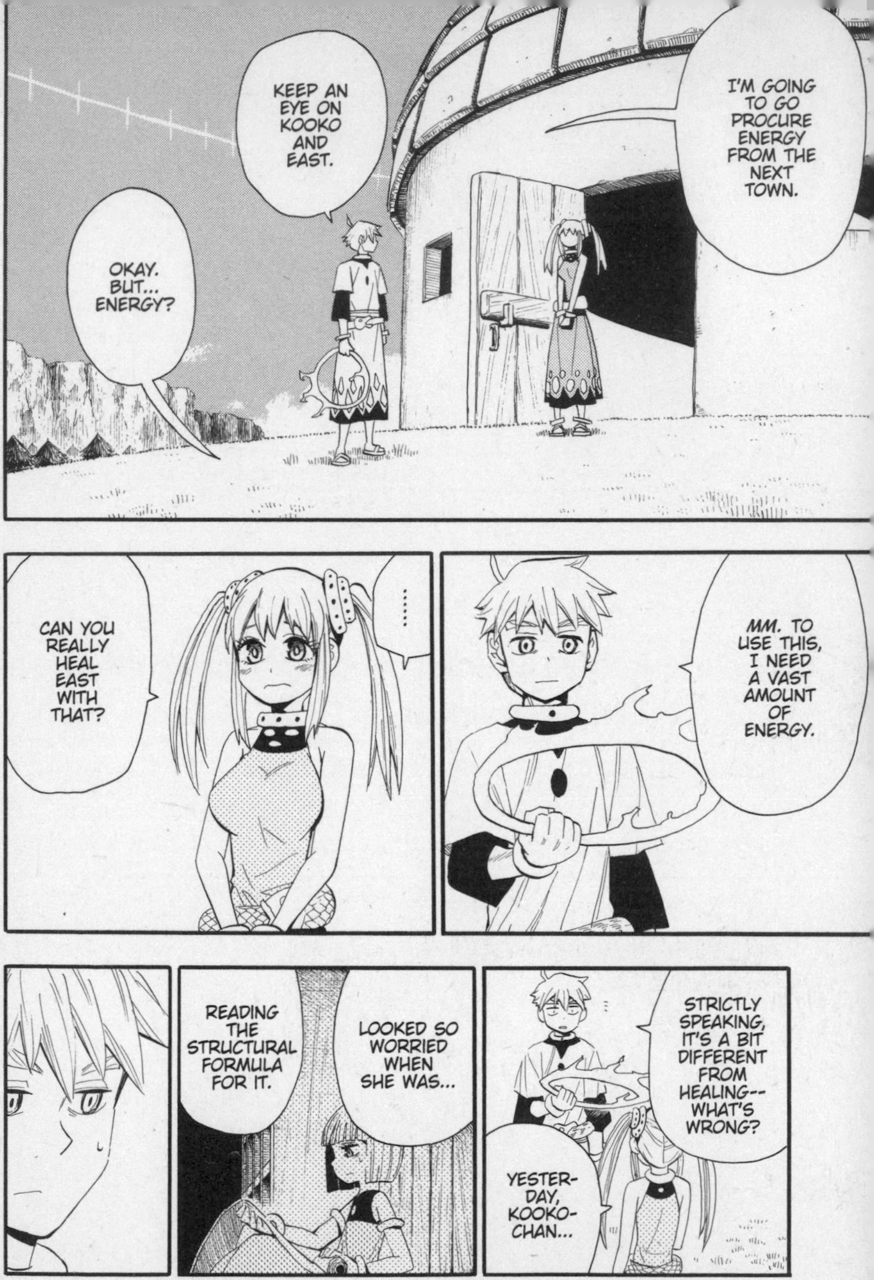
I'M GOING TO GO PROCURE ENERGY FROM THE NEXT TOWN.
KEEP AN EYE ON KOOKO AND EAST.
OKAY. BUT... ENERGY?
MM. TO USE THIS, I NEED A VAST AMOUNT OF ENERGY.
......
CAN YOU REALLY HEAL EAST WITH THAT?
STRICTLY SPEAKING, IT'S A BIT DIFFERENT FROM HEALING-- WHAT'S WRONG?
YESTER-DAY, KOOKO-CHAN...
LOOKED SO WORRIED WHEN SHE WAS...
READING THE STRUCTURAL FORMULA FOR IT.

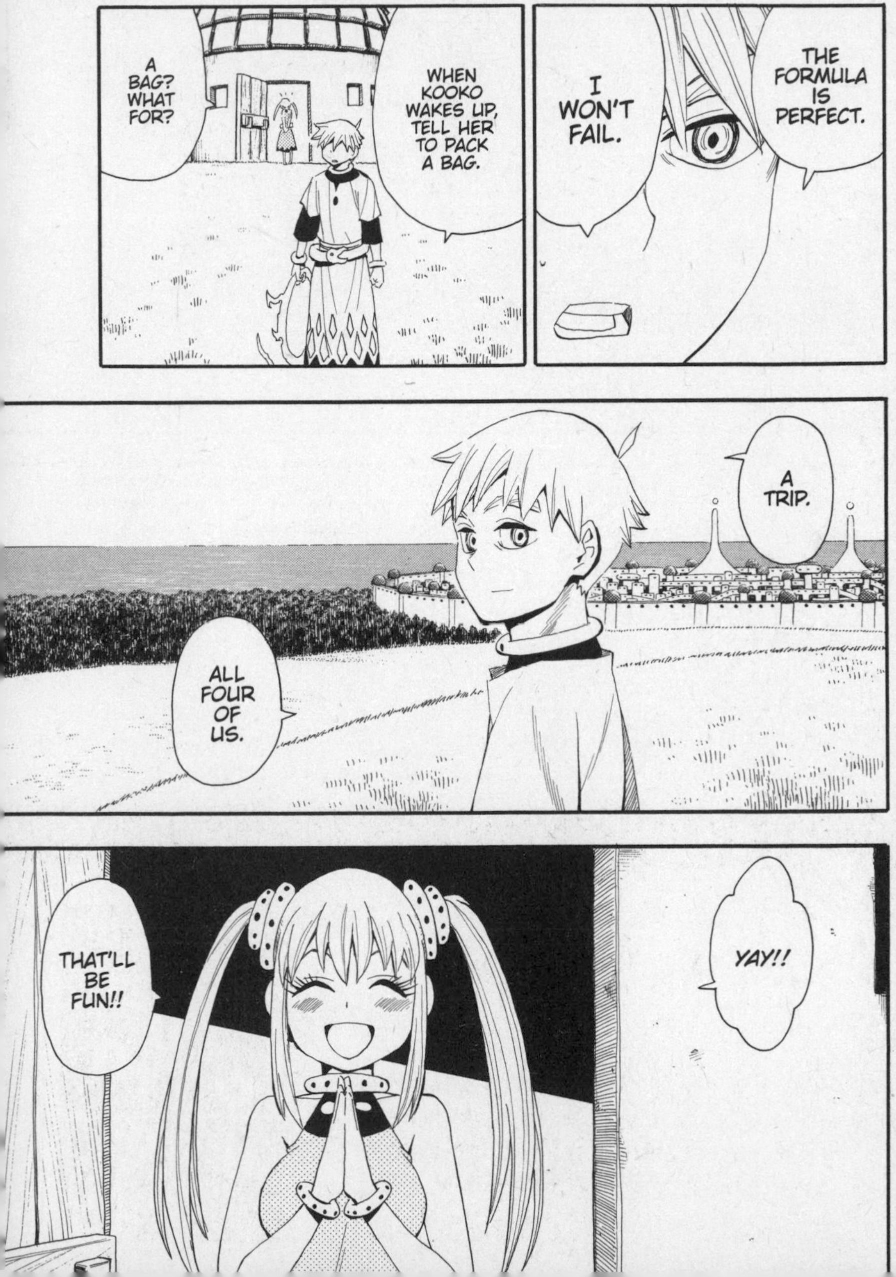
THE FORMULA IS PERFECT.
I WON'T FAIL.
WHEN KOOKO WAKES UP, TELL HER TO PACK A BAG.
A BAG? WHAT FOR?
A TRIP.
ALL FOUR OF US.
YAY!!
THAT'LL BE FUN!!

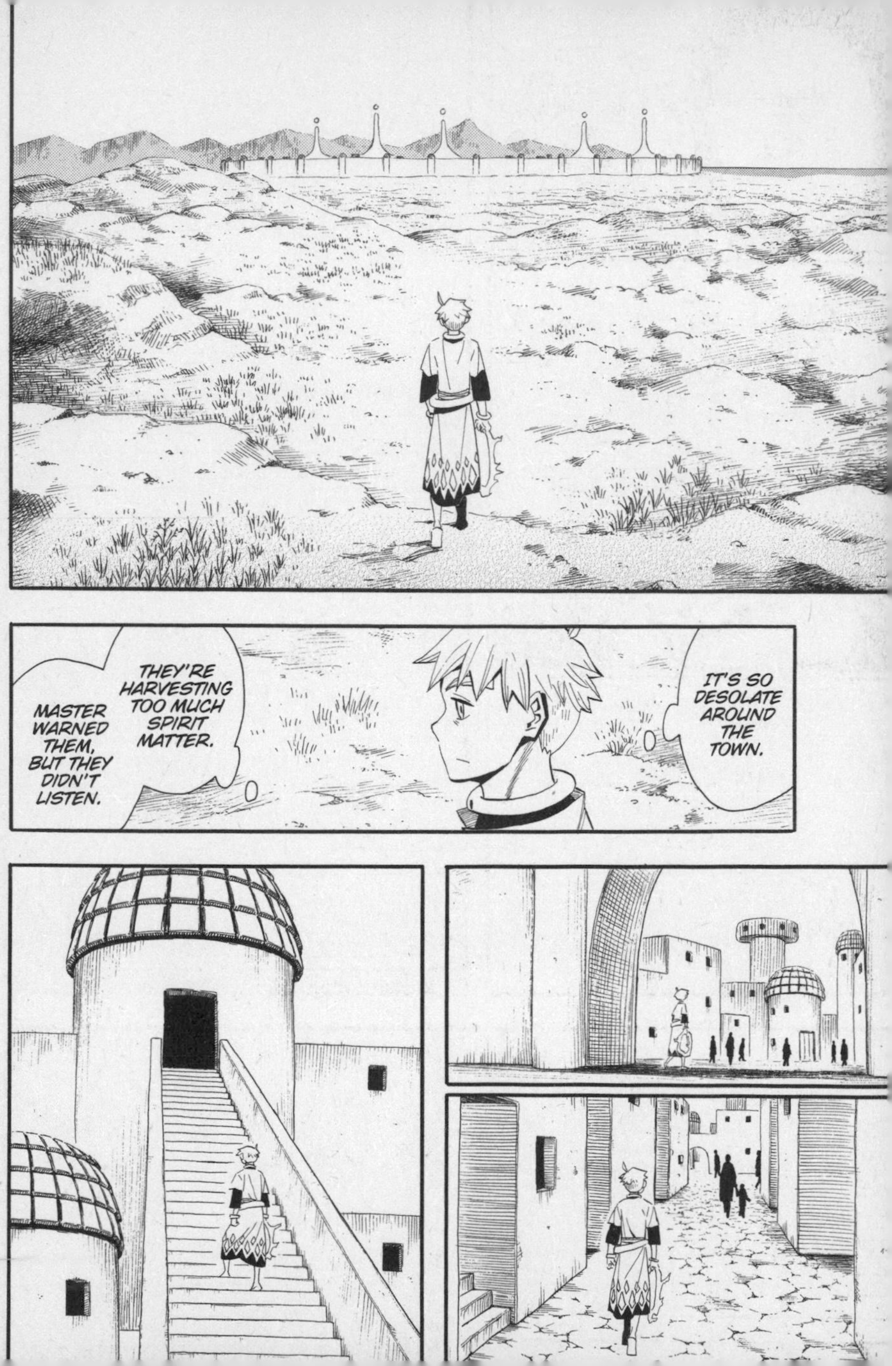
IT'S SO DESOLATE AROUND THE TOWN.
THEY'RE HARVESTING TOO MUCH SPIRIT MATTER.
MASTER WARNED THEM, BUT THEY DIDN'T LISTEN.

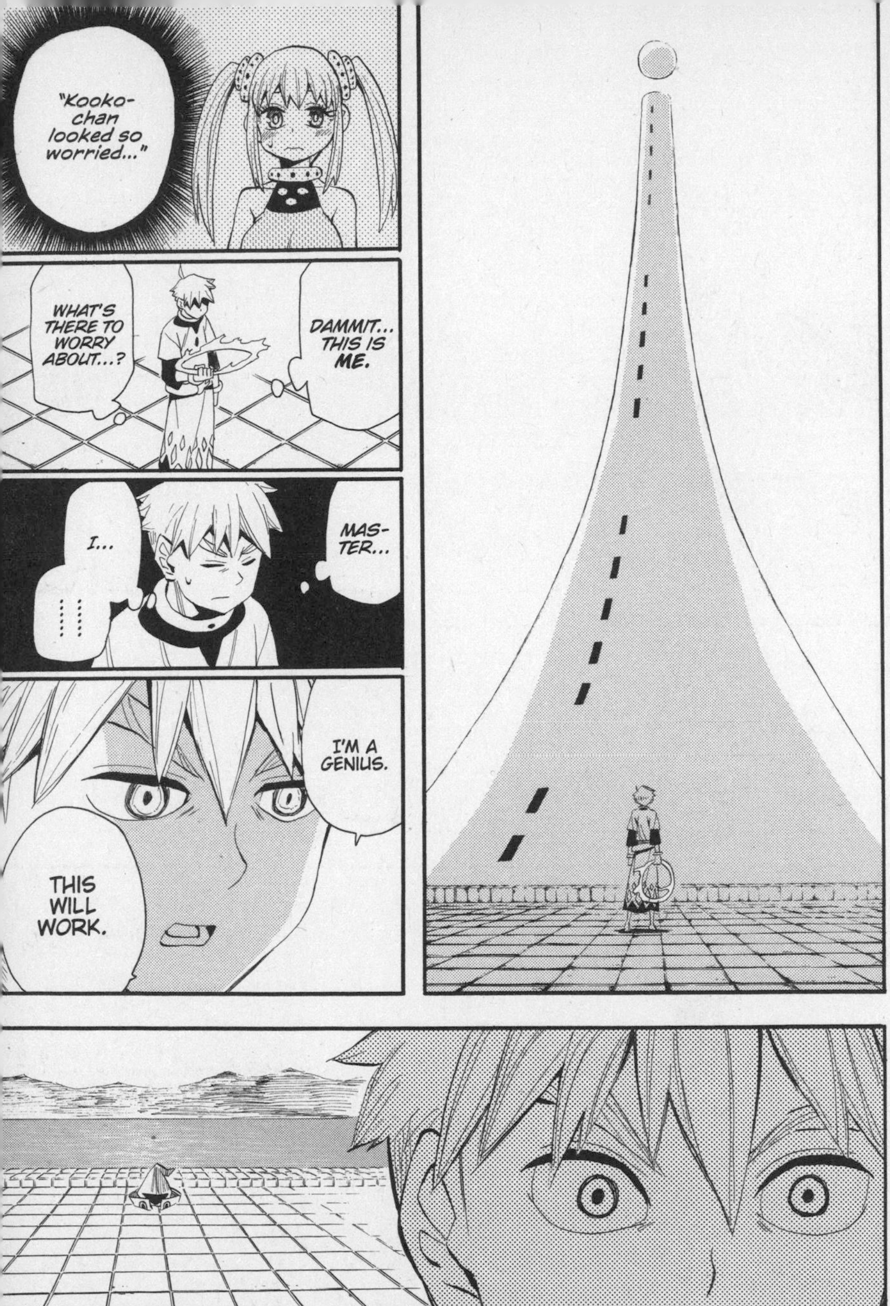
"Kooko-chan looked so worried..."
DAMMIT... THIS IS ME.
WHAT'S THERE TO WORRY ABOUT...?
MASTER...
I... ......
I'M A GENIUS.
THIS WILL WORK.

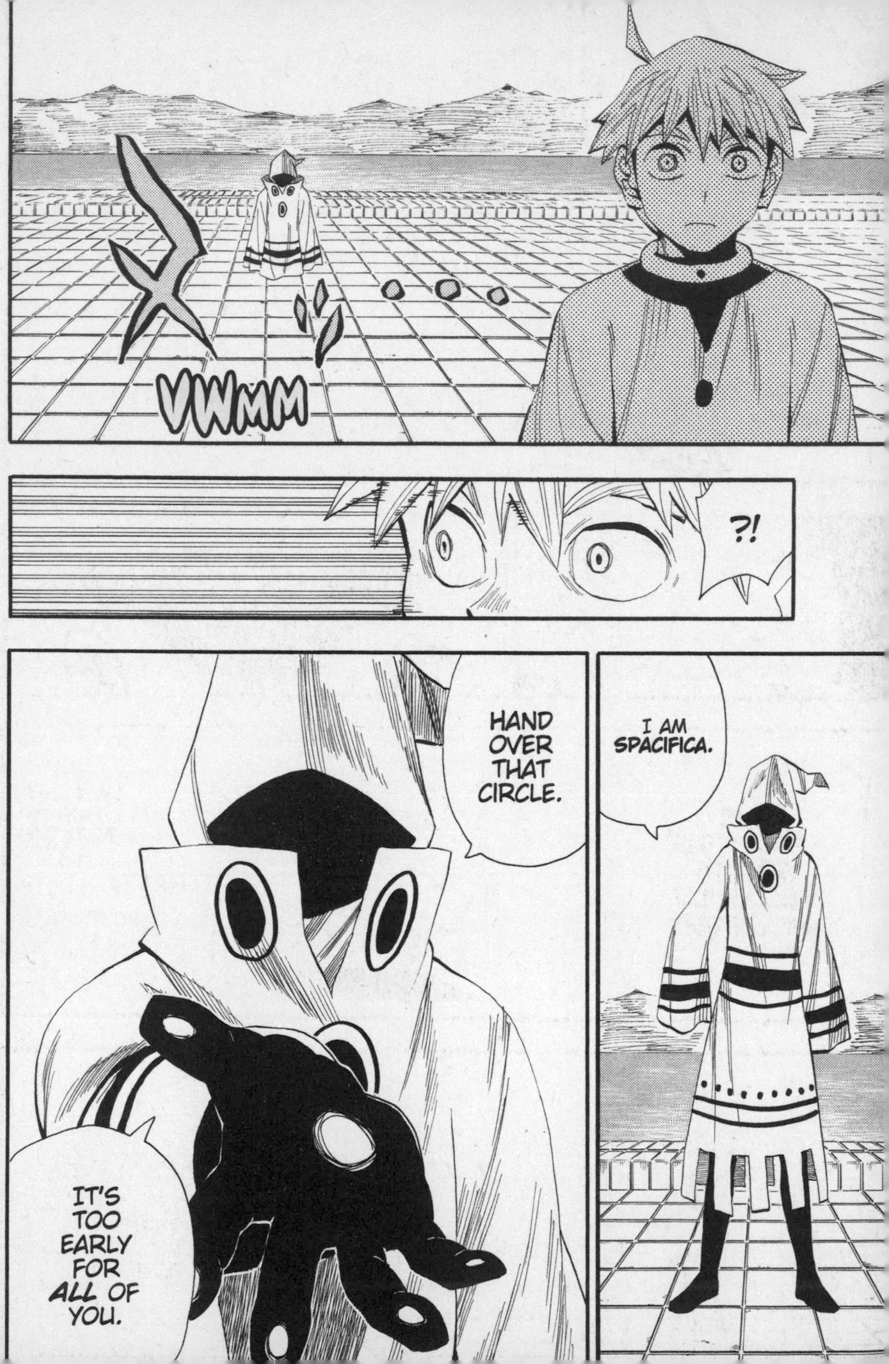
VWMM
?!
I AM SPACIFICA.
HAND OVER THAT CIRCLE.
IT'S TOO EARLY FOR ALL OF YOU.

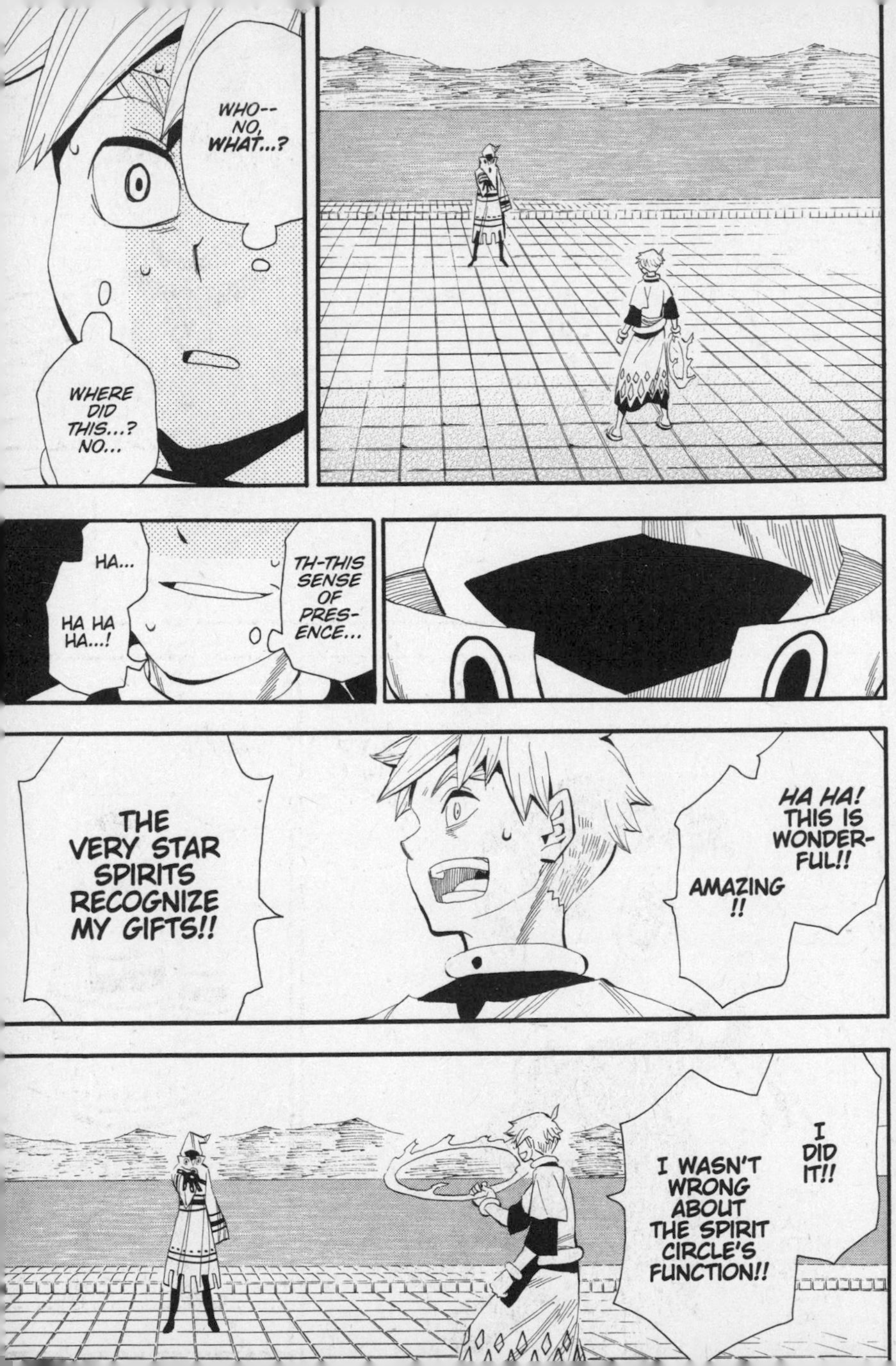
WHO-- NO, WHAT...?
WHERE DID THIS...? NO...
TH-THIS SENSE OF PRESENCE...
HA...
HA HA HA...!
HA HA! THIS IS WONDERFUL!!
AMAZING !!
THE VERY STAR SPIRITS RECOGNIZE MY GIFTS!!
I DID IT!!
I WASN'T WRONG ABOUT THE SPIRIT CIRCLE'S FUNCTION!!

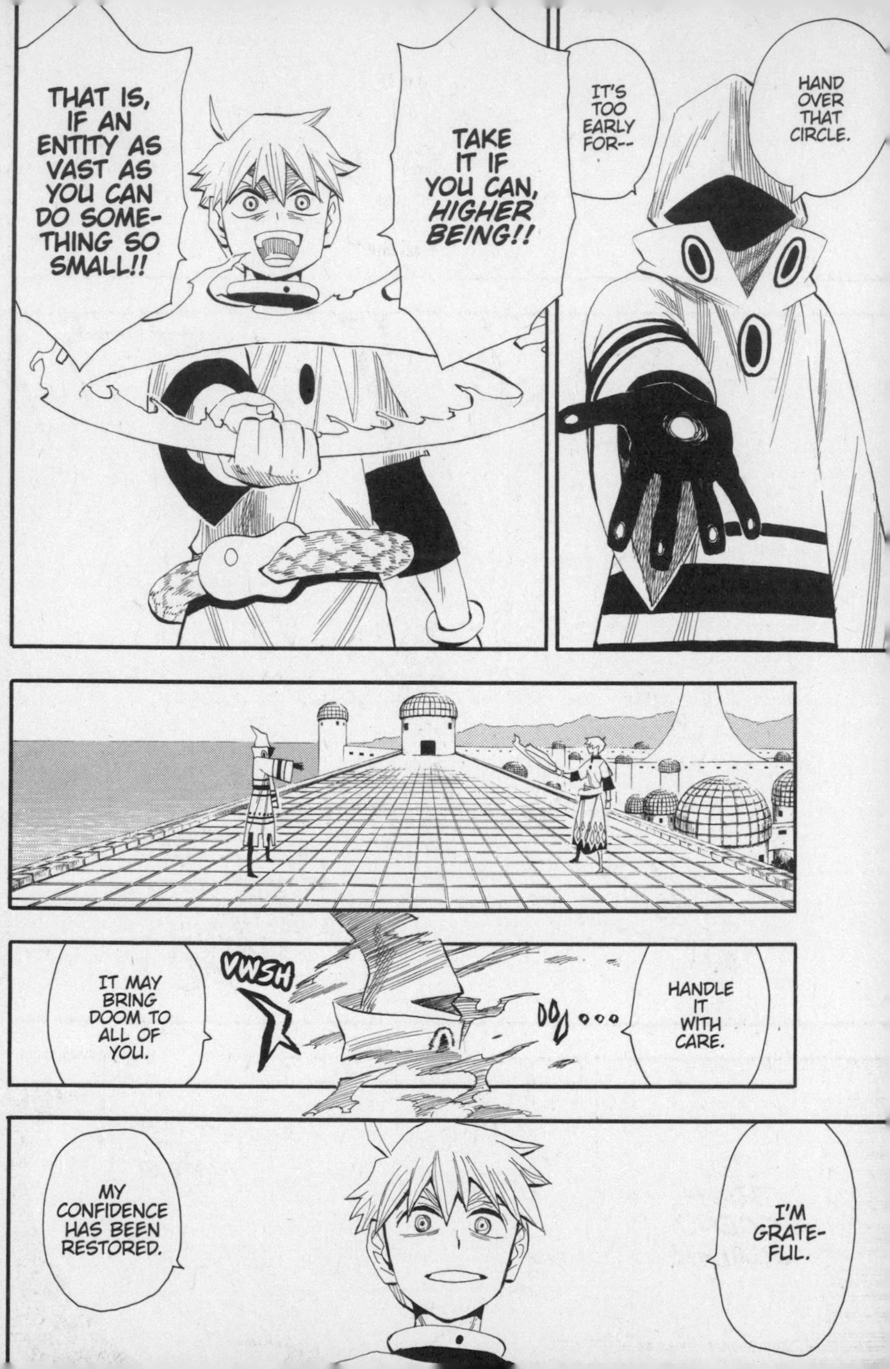
HAND OVER THAT CIRCLE.
IT'S TOO EARLY FOR--
TAKE IT IF YOU CAN, HIGHER BEING!!
THAT IS, IF AN ENTITY AS VAST AS YOU CAN DO SOMETHING SO SMALL!!
HANDLE IT WITH CARE.
VWSH
IT MAY BRING DOOM TO ALL OF YOU.
I'M GRATEFUL.
MY CONFIDENCE HAS BEEN RESTORED.

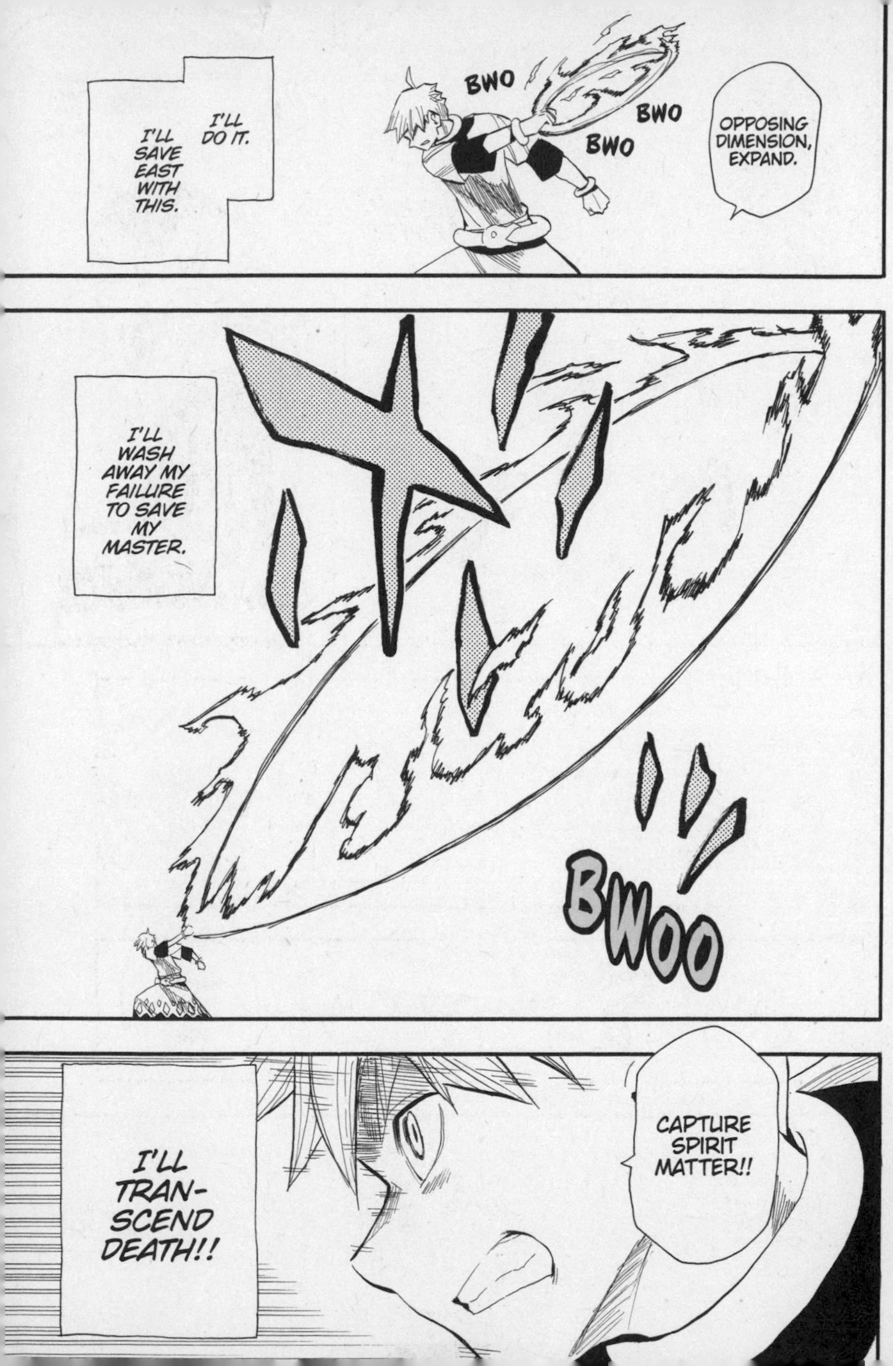
OPPOSING DIMENSION, EXPAND.
BWO
BWO
BWO
I'LL DO IT.
I'LL SAVE EAST WITH THIS.
I'LL WASH AWAY MY FAILURE TO SAVE MY MASTER.
BWOO
CAPTURE SPIRIT MATTER!!
I'LL TRAN-SCEND DEATH!!

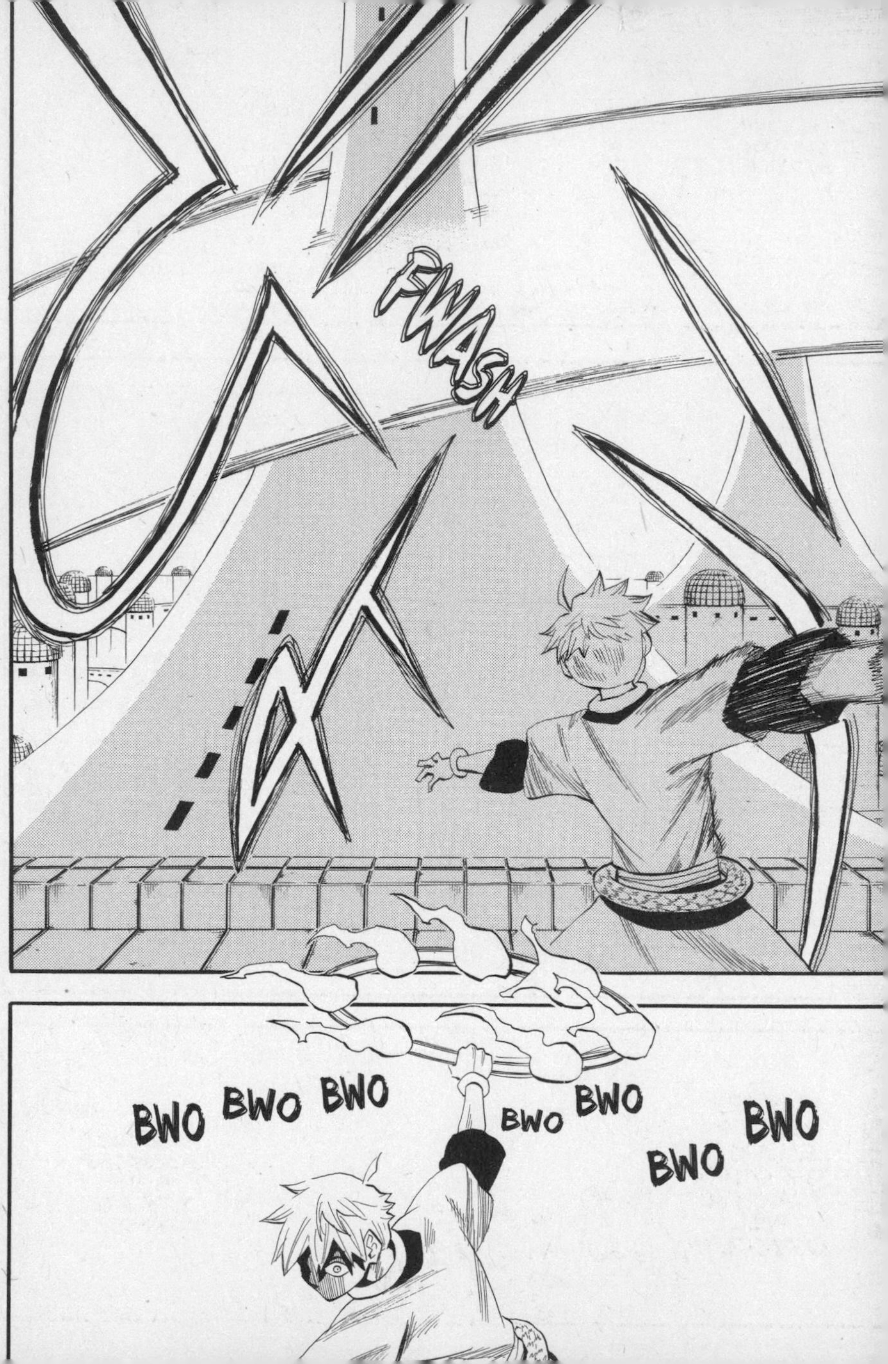
FWASH
BWO
BWO
BWO
BWO
BWO
BWO
BWO
BWO

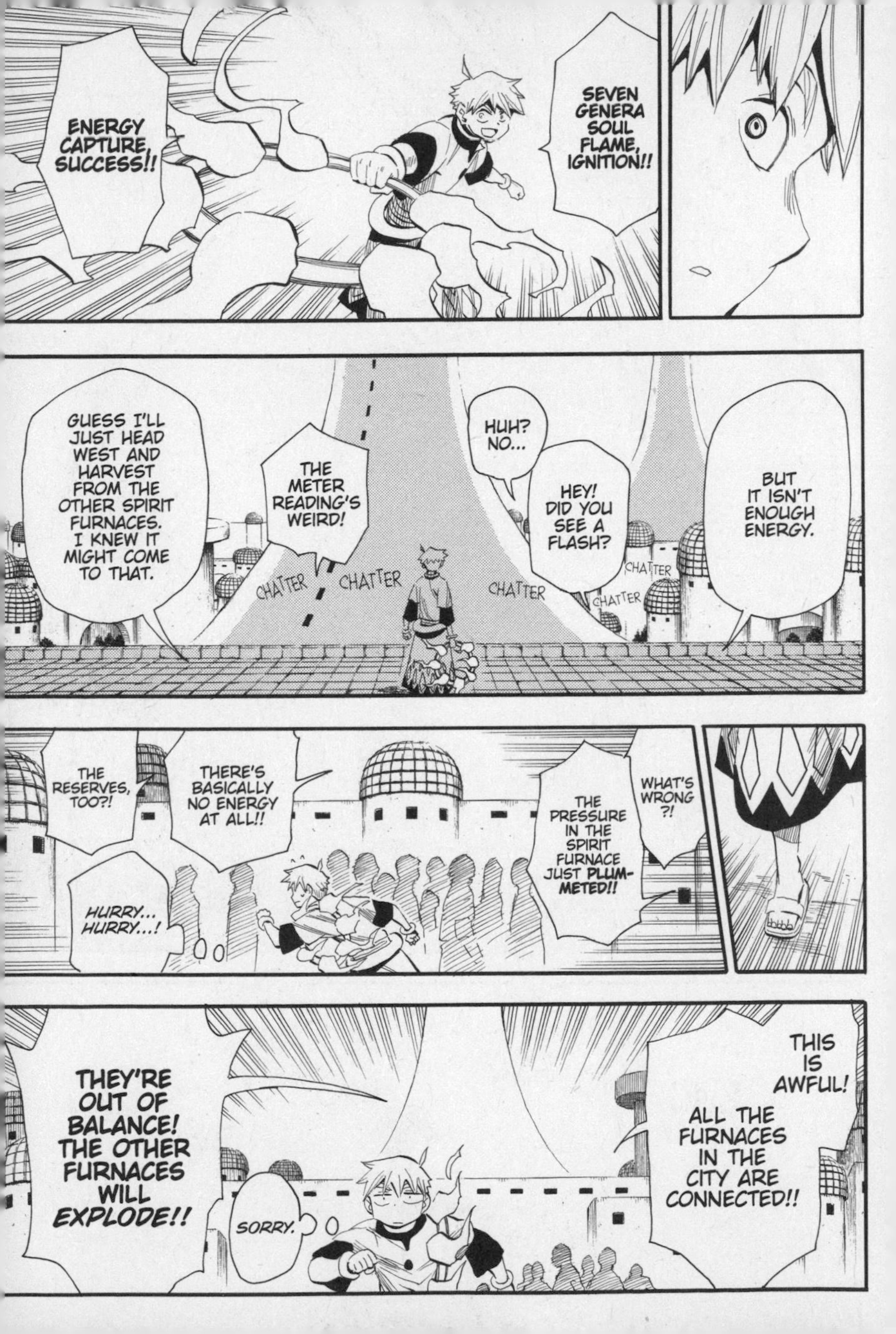
SEVEN GENERA SOUL FLAME, IGNITION!!
ENERGY CAPTURE, SUCCESS!!
BUT IT ISN'T ENOUGH ENERGY.
HEY! DID YOU SEE A FLASH?
HUH? NO...
CHATTER
CHATTER
CHATTER
CHATTER
THE METER READING'S WEIRD!
GUESS I'LL JUST HEAD WEST AND HARVEST FROM THE OTHER SPIRIT FURNACES. I KNEW IT MIGHT COME TO THAT.
WHAT'S WRONG?!
THE PRESSURE IN THE SPIRIT FURNACE JUST PLUMMETED!!
THERE'S BASICALLY NO ENERGY AT ALL!!
THE RESERVES, TOO?!
HURRY... HURRY...!
THIS IS AWFUL!
ALL THE FURNACES IN THE CITY ARE CONNECTED!!
THEY'RE OUT OF BALANCE! THE OTHER FURNACES WILL EXPLODE!!
SORRY.

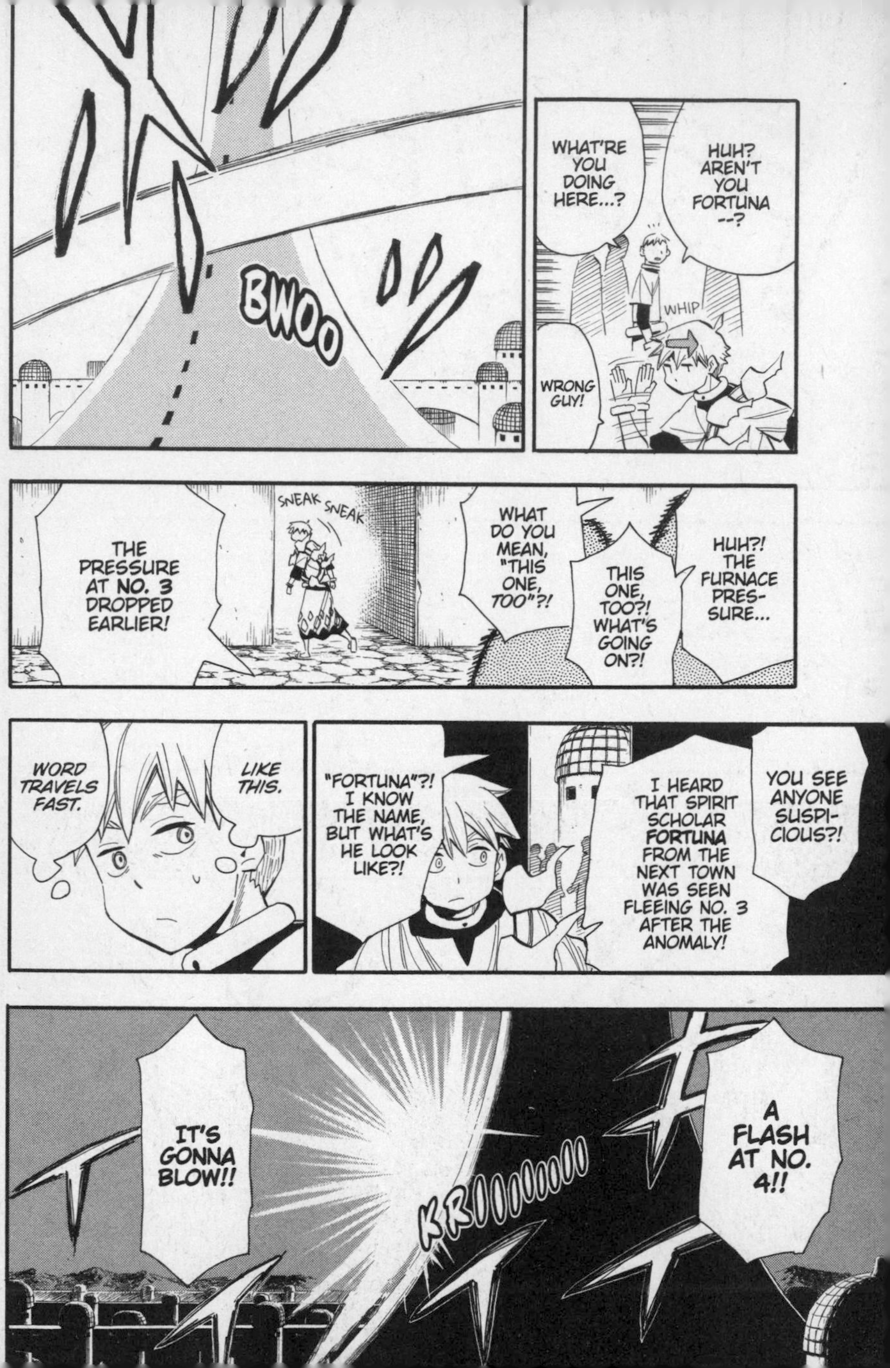
HUH? AREN'T YOU FORTUNA --?
WHAT'RE YOU DOING HERE...?
WHIP
WRONG GUY!
BWOO
HUH?! THE FURNACE PRES-SURE...
THIS ONE, TOO?! WHAT'S GOING ON?!
WHAT DO YOU MEAN, "THIS ONE, TOO"?!
SNEAK SNEAK
THE PRESSURE AT NO. 3 DROPPED EARLIER!
YOU SEE ANYONE SUSPI-CIOUS?!
I HEARD THAT SPIRIT SCHOLAR FORTUNA FROM THE NEXT TOWN WAS SEEN FLEEING NO. 3 AFTER THE ANOMALY!
"FORTUNA"?! I KNOW THE NAME, BUT WHAT'S HE LOOK LIKE?!
LIKE THIS.
WORD TRAVELS FAST.
A FLASH AT NO. 4!!
KRIOOOOOOOO
IT'S GONNA BLOW!!

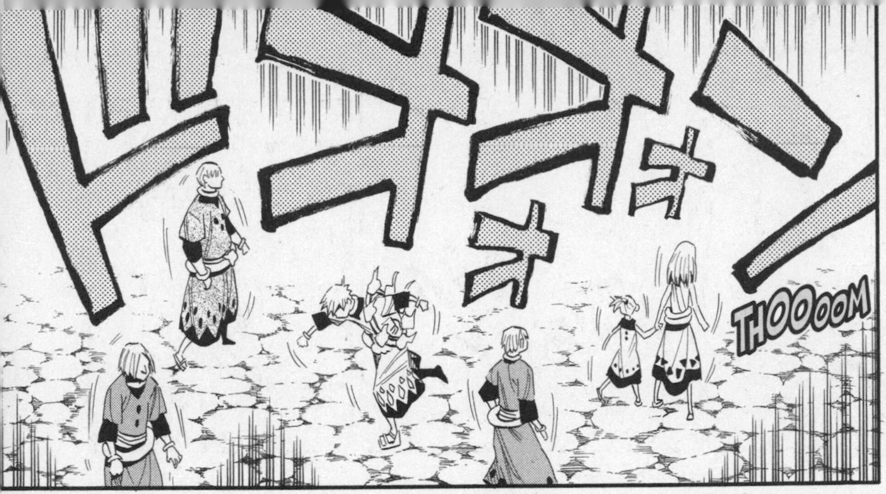
THOOoom
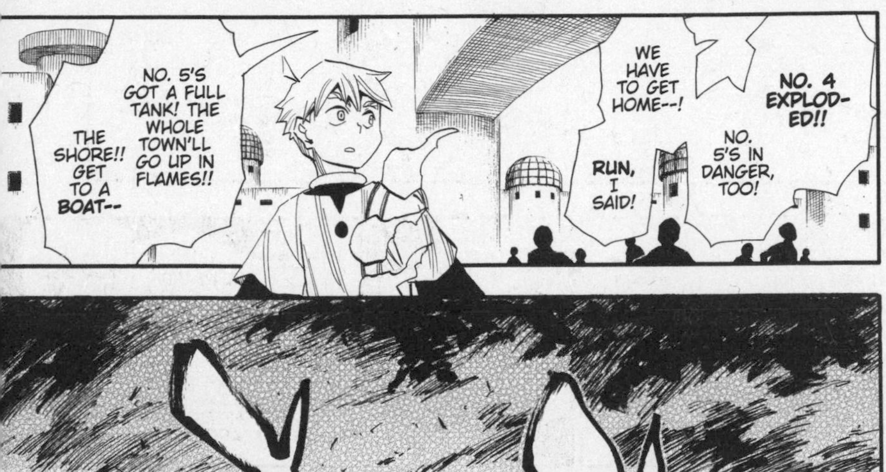
NO. 4 EXPLODED!!
NO. 5'S IN DANGER, TOO!
WE HAVE TO GET HOME--!
RUN, I SAID!
NO. 5'S GOT A FULL TANK! THE WHOLE TOWN'LL GO UP IN FLAMES!!
THE SHORE!! GET TO A BOAT--
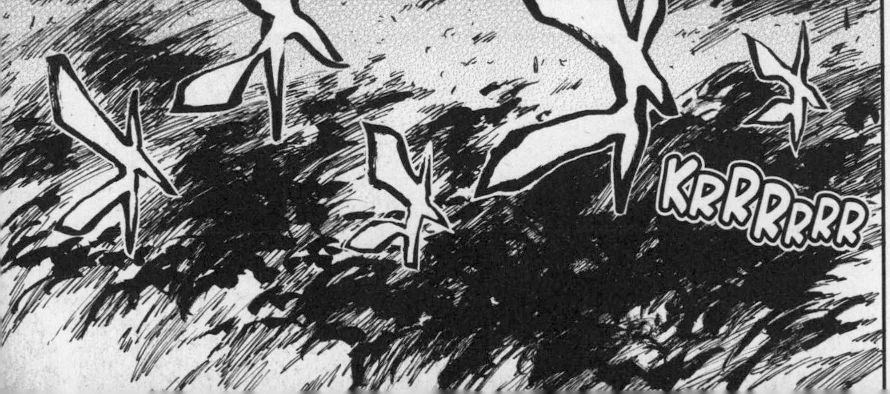
KRRRRRR

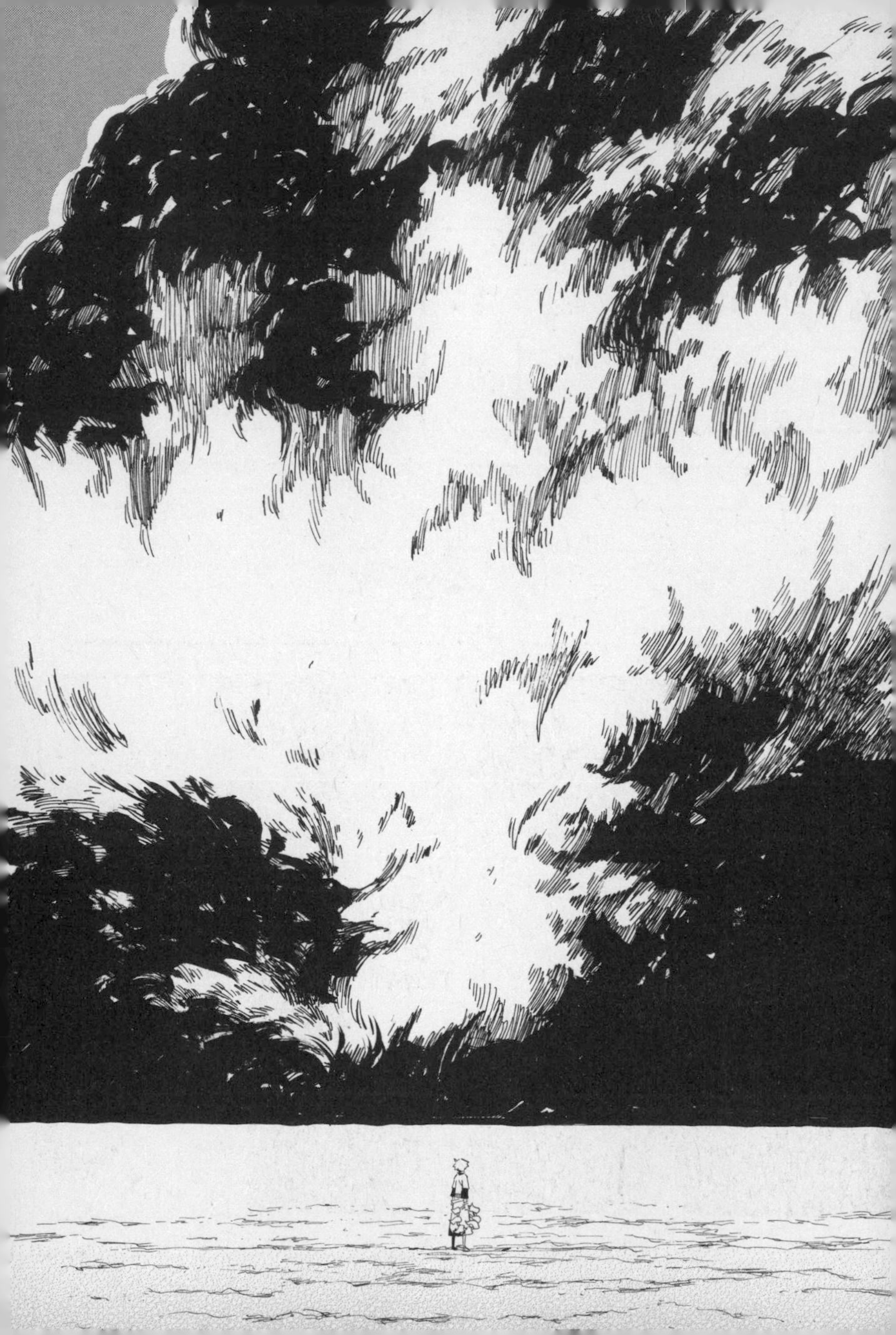

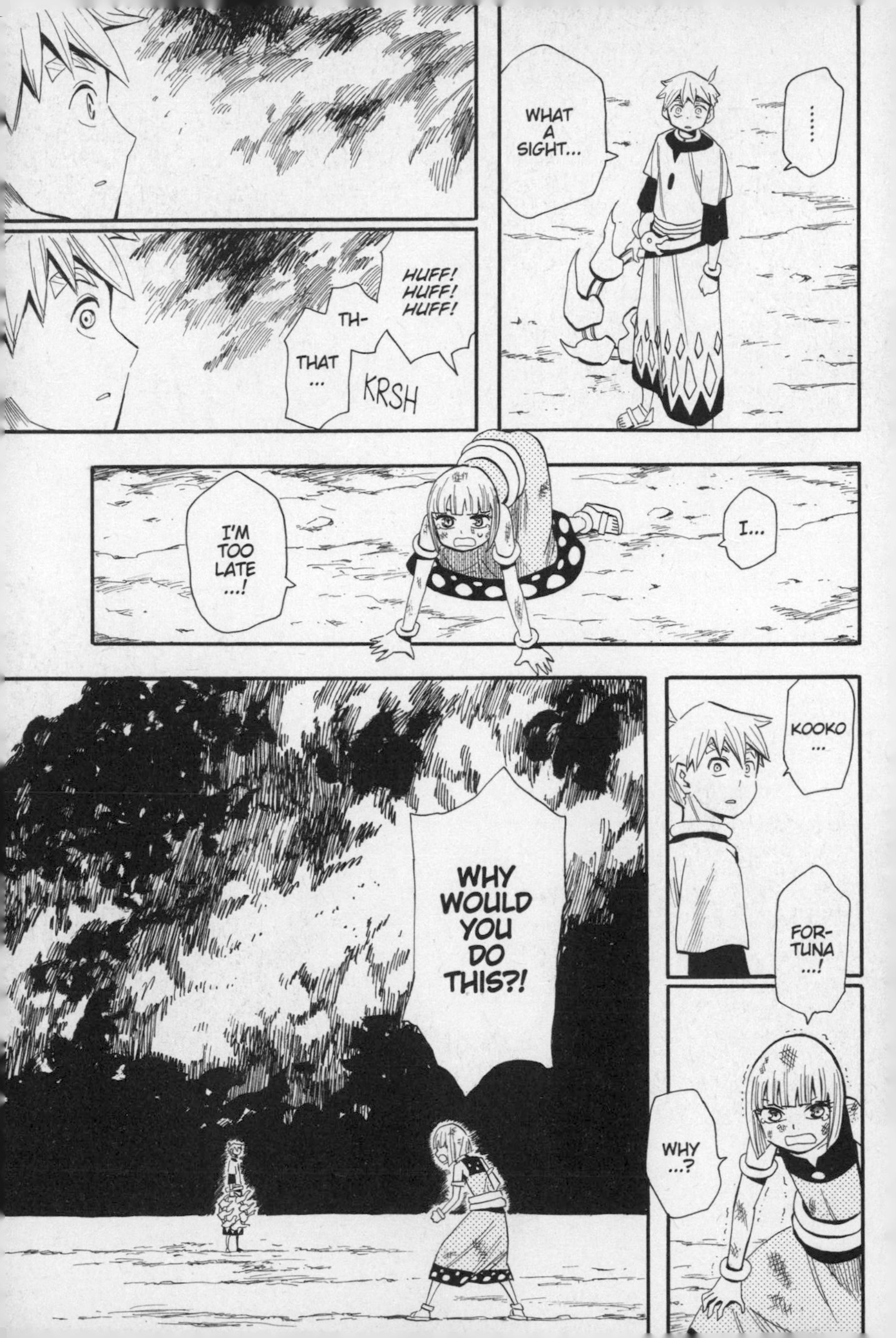
......
WHAT A SIGHT...
HUFF! HUFF! HUFF!
TH-
THAT ...
KRSH
I...
I'M TOO LATE ...!
KOOKO ...
FOR-TUNA ...!
WHY ...?
WHY WOULD YOU DO THIS?!

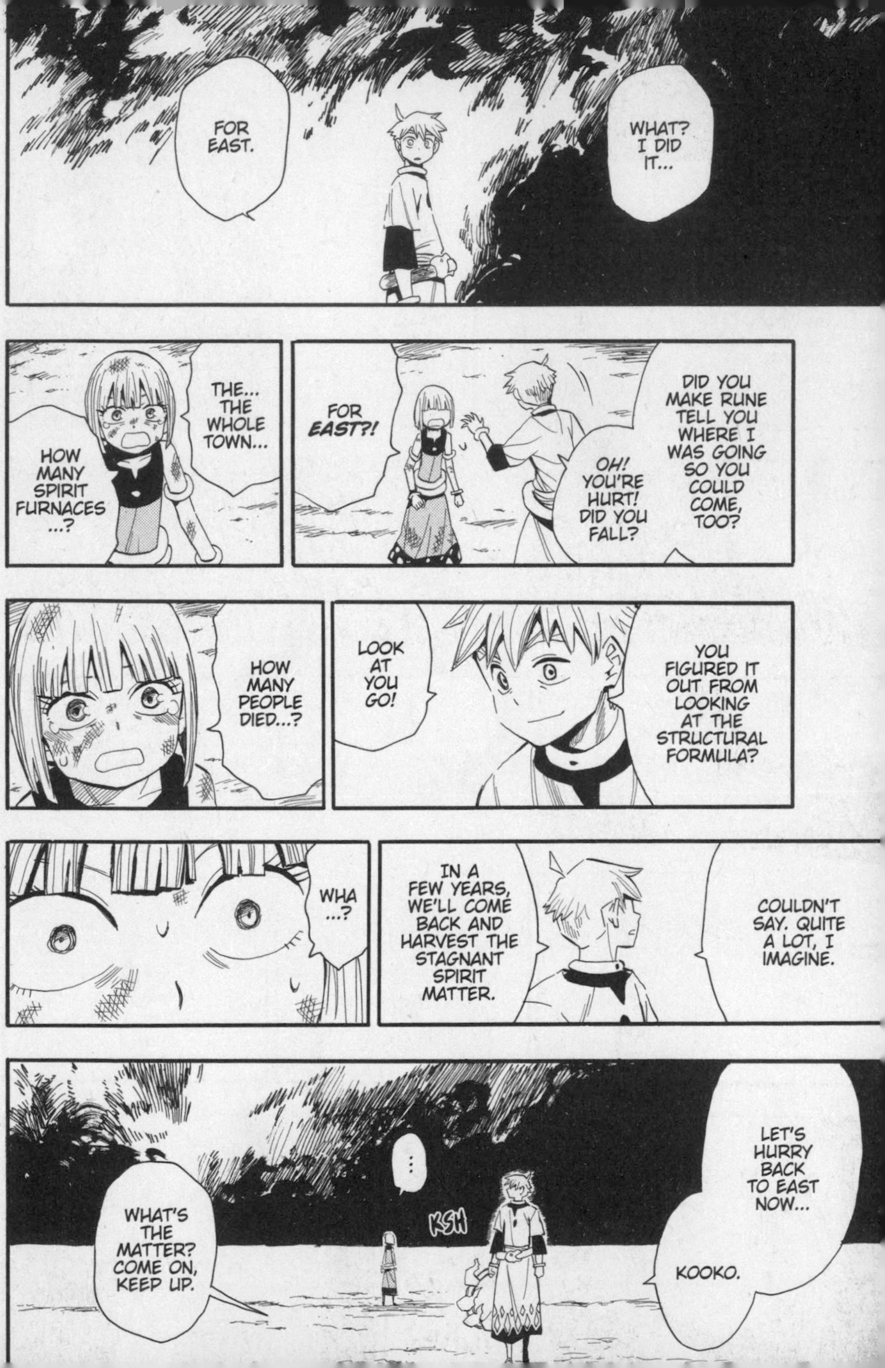
WHAT? I DID IT...
FOR EAST.
DID YOU MAKE RUNE TELL YOU WHERE I WAS GOING SO YOU COULD COME, TOO?
OH! YOU'RE HURT! DID YOU FALL?
FOR EAST?!
THE... THE WHOLE TOWN...
HOW MANY SPIRIT FURNACES ...?
YOU FIGURED IT OUT FROM LOOKING AT THE STRUCTURAL FORMULA?
LOOK AT YOU GO!
HOW MANY PEOPLE DIED...?
COULDN'T SAY. QUITE A LOT, I IMAGINE.
IN A FEW YEARS, WE'LL COME BACK AND HARVEST THE STAGNANT SPIRIT MATTER.
WHA ...?
LET'S HURRY BACK TO EAST NOW...
KOOKO.
KSH
...
WHAT'S THE MATTER? COME ON, KEEP UP.

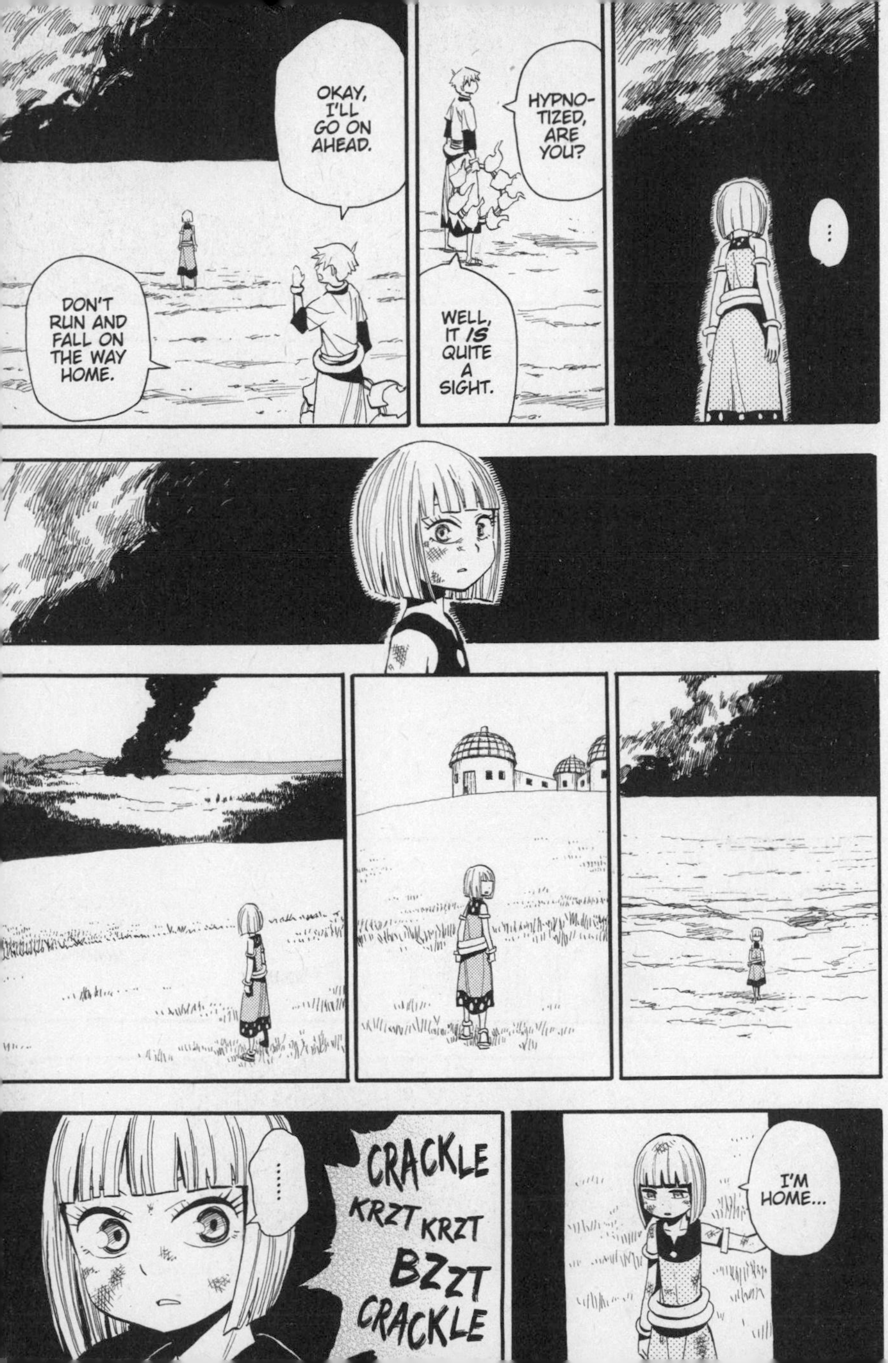
...
HYPNO-TIZED, ARE YOU?
WELL, IT *IS* QUITE A SIGHT.
OKAY, I'LL GO ON AHEAD.
DON'T RUN AND FALL ON THE WAY HOME.
I'M HOME...
......
CRACKLE
KRZT KRZT
BZZT
CRACKLE

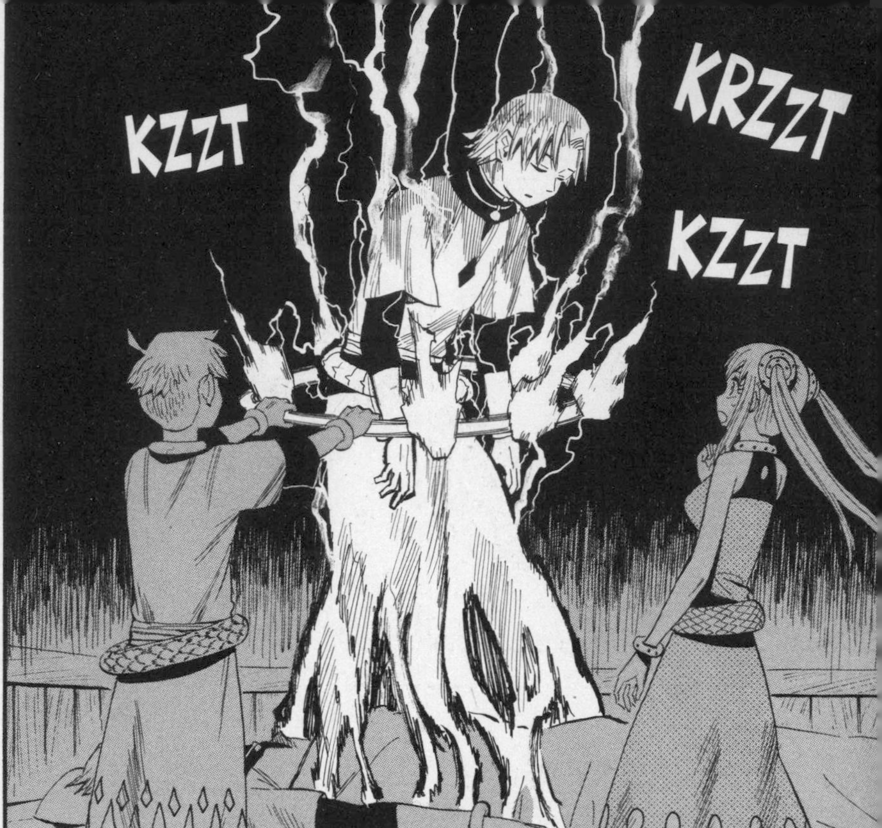
KRZZT
KZZT
KZZT
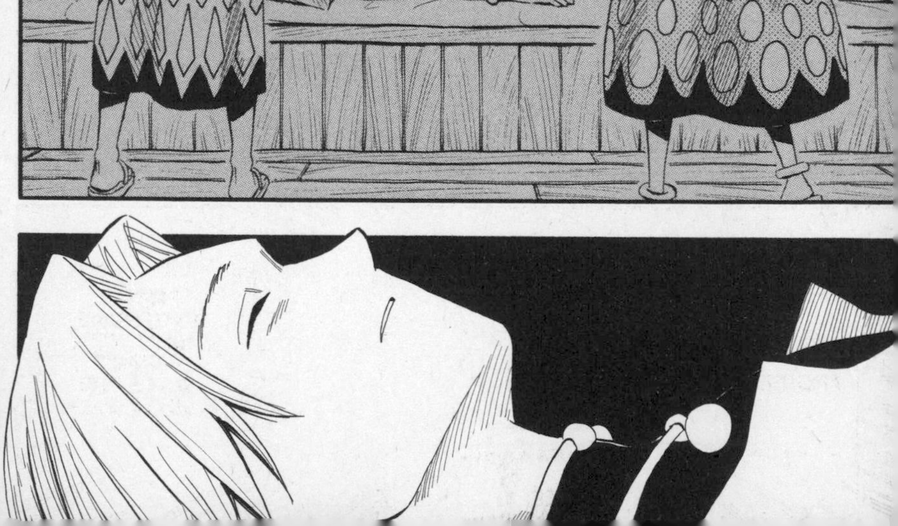

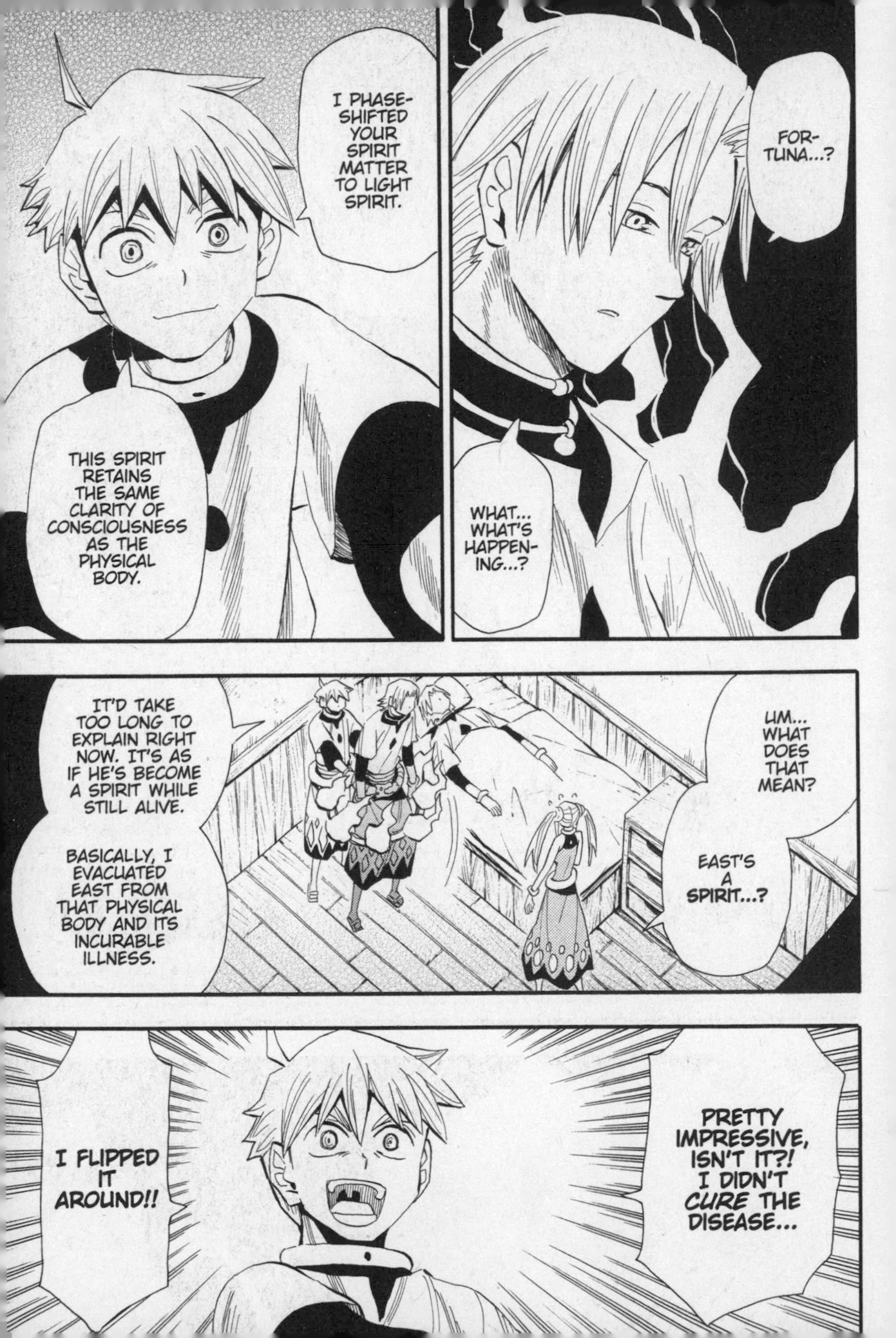
FOR-TUNA...?
WHAT... WHAT'S HAPPEN-ING...?
I PHASE-SHIFTED YOUR SPIRIT MATTER TO LIGHT SPIRIT.
THIS SPIRIT RETAINS THE SAME CLARITY OF CONSCIOUSNESS AS THE PHYSICAL BODY.
UM... WHAT DOES THAT MEAN?
EAST'S A SPIRIT...?
IT'D TAKE TOO LONG TO EXPLAIN RIGHT NOW. IT'S AS IF HE'S BECOME A SPIRIT WHILE STILL ALIVE.
BASICALLY, I EVACUATED EAST FROM THAT PHYSICAL BODY AND ITS INCURABLE ILLNESS.
PRETTY IMPRESSIVE, ISN'T IT?! I DIDN'T *CURE* THE DISEASE...
I FLIPPED IT AROUND!!

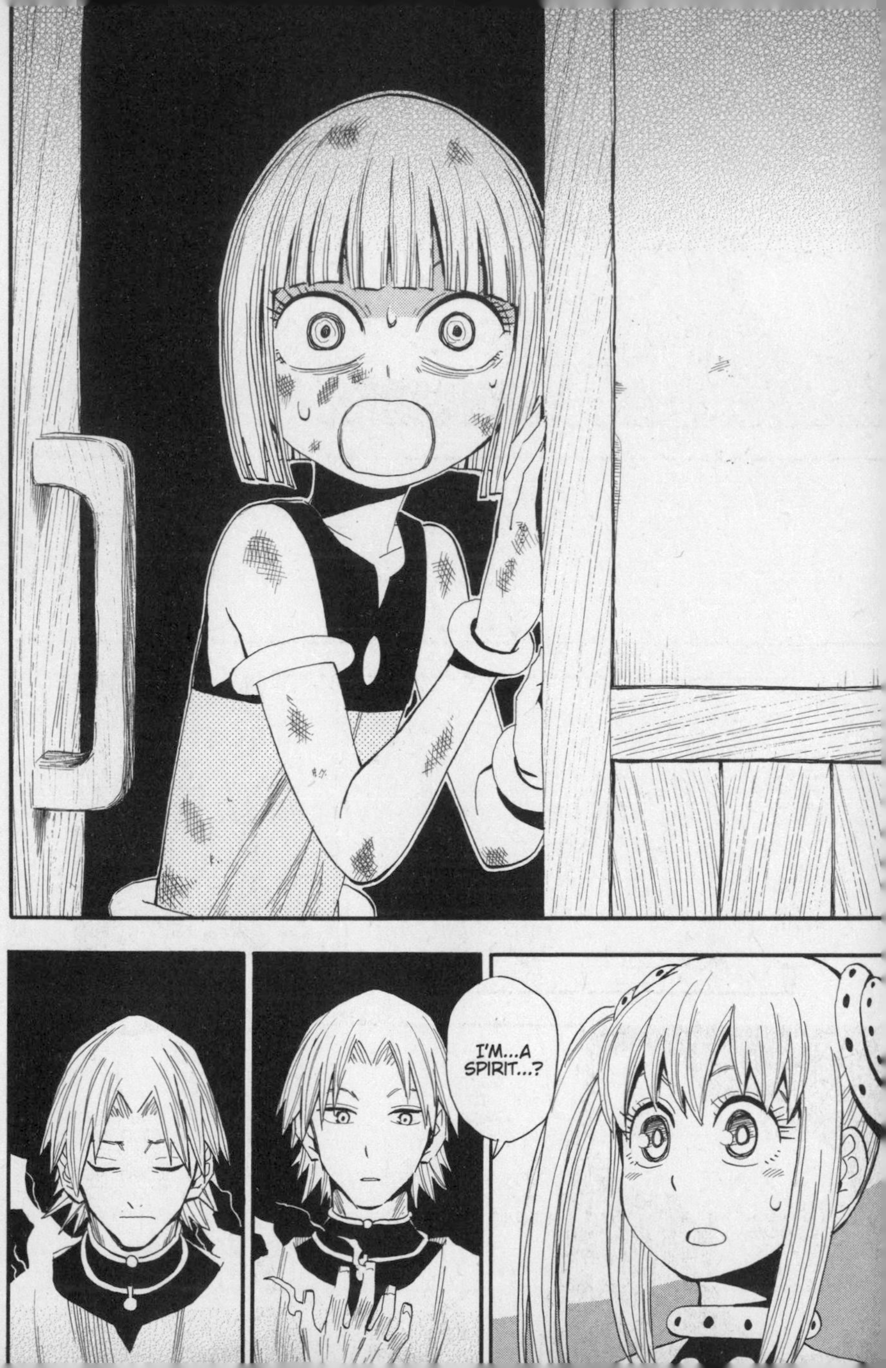
I'M...A SPIRIT...?

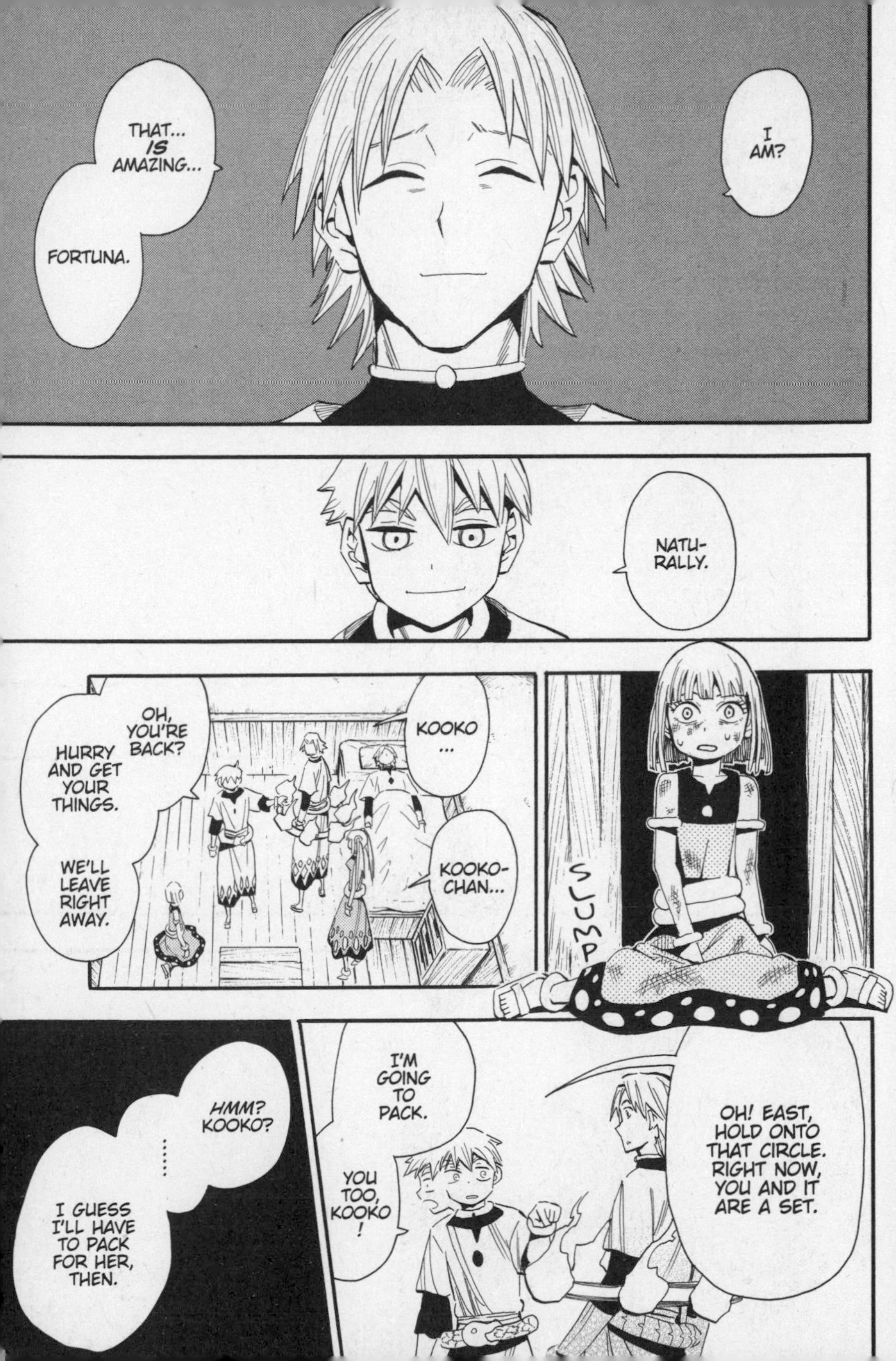
I AM?
THAT... *IS* AMAZING...
FORTUNA.
NATU-RALLY.
SLUMP
KOOKO...
KOOKO-CHAN...
OH, YOU'RE BACK?
HURRY AND GET YOUR THINGS.
WE'LL LEAVE RIGHT AWAY.
OH! EAST, HOLD ONTO THAT CIRCLE. RIGHT NOW, YOU AND IT ARE A SET.
I'M GOING TO PACK.
YOU TOO, KOOKO!
HMM? KOOKO?
......
I GUESS I'LL HAVE TO PACK FOR HER, THEN.

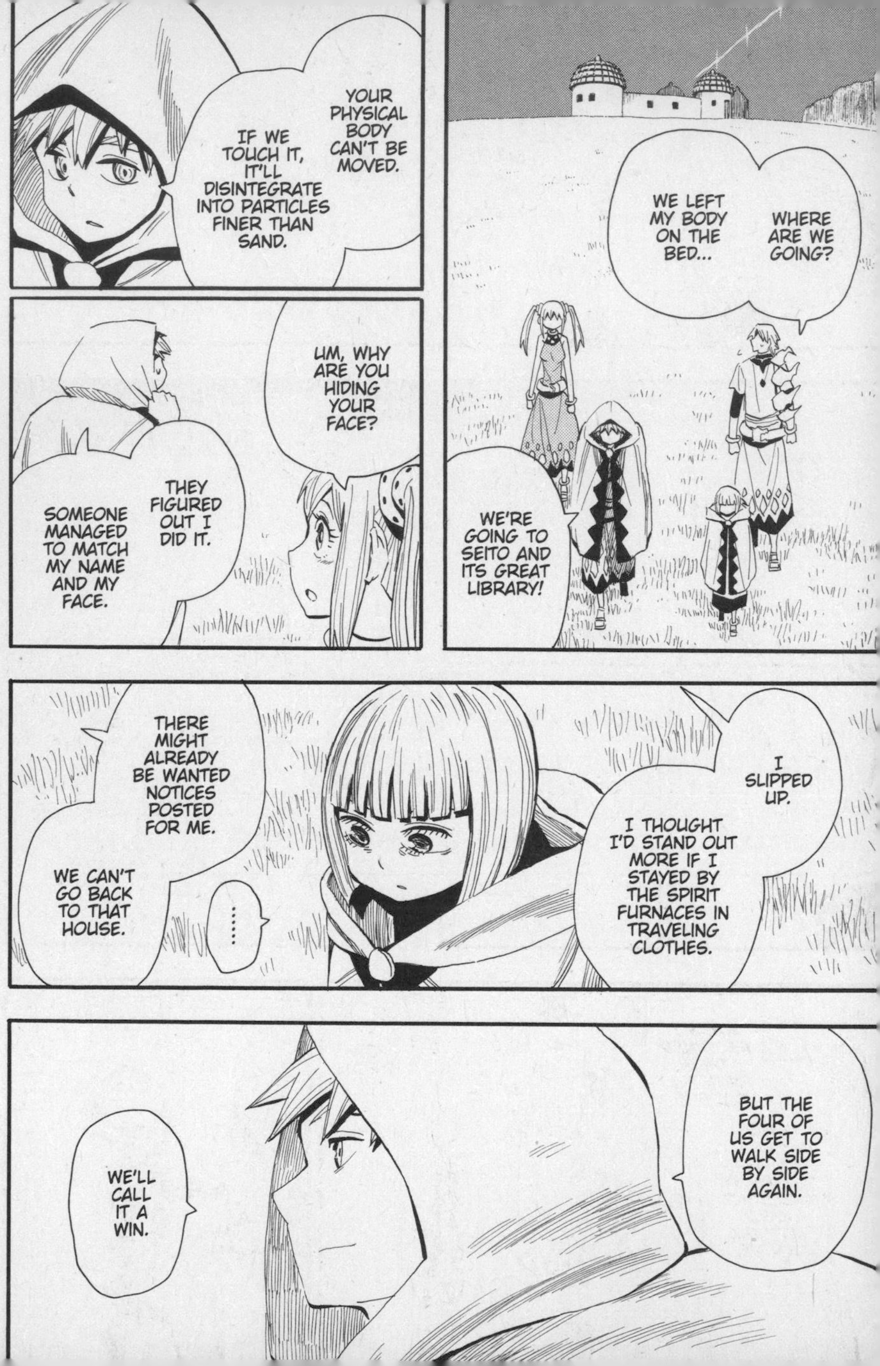
WHERE ARE WE GOING?
WE LEFT MY BODY ON THE BED...
WE'RE GOING TO SEITO AND ITS GREAT LIBRARY!
YOUR PHYSICAL BODY CAN'T BE MOVED.
IF WE TOUCH IT, IT'LL DISINTEGRATE INTO PARTICLES FINER THAN SAND.
UM, WHY ARE YOU HIDING YOUR FACE?
THEY FIGURED OUT I DID IT.
SOMEONE MANAGED TO MATCH MY NAME AND MY FACE.
I SLIPPED UP.
I THOUGHT I'D STAND OUT MORE IF I STAYED BY THE SPIRIT FURNACES IN TRAVELING CLOTHES.
THERE MIGHT ALREADY BE WANTED NOTICES POSTED FOR ME.
......
WE CAN'T GO BACK TO THAT HOUSE.
BUT THE FOUR OF US GET TO WALK SIDE BY SIDE AGAIN.
WE'LL CALL IT A WIN.

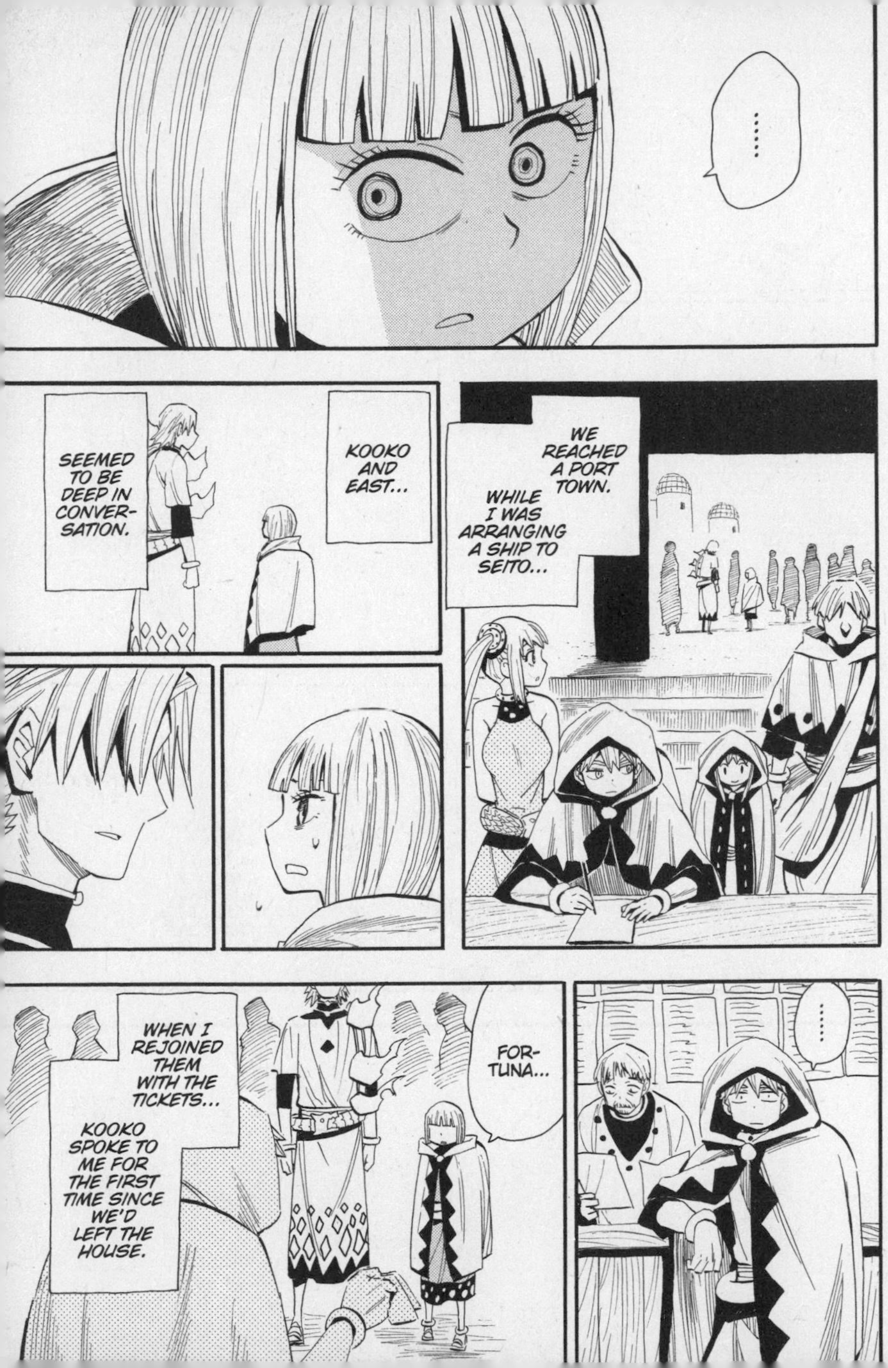
......
WE REACHED A PORT TOWN.
WHILE I WAS ARRANGING A SHIP TO SEITO...
KOOKO AND EAST...
SEEMED TO BE DEEP IN CONVERSATION.
......
WHEN I REJOINED THEM WITH THE TICKETS...
KOOKO SPOKE TO ME FOR THE FIRST TIME SINCE WE'D LEFT THE HOUSE.
FOR-TUNA...

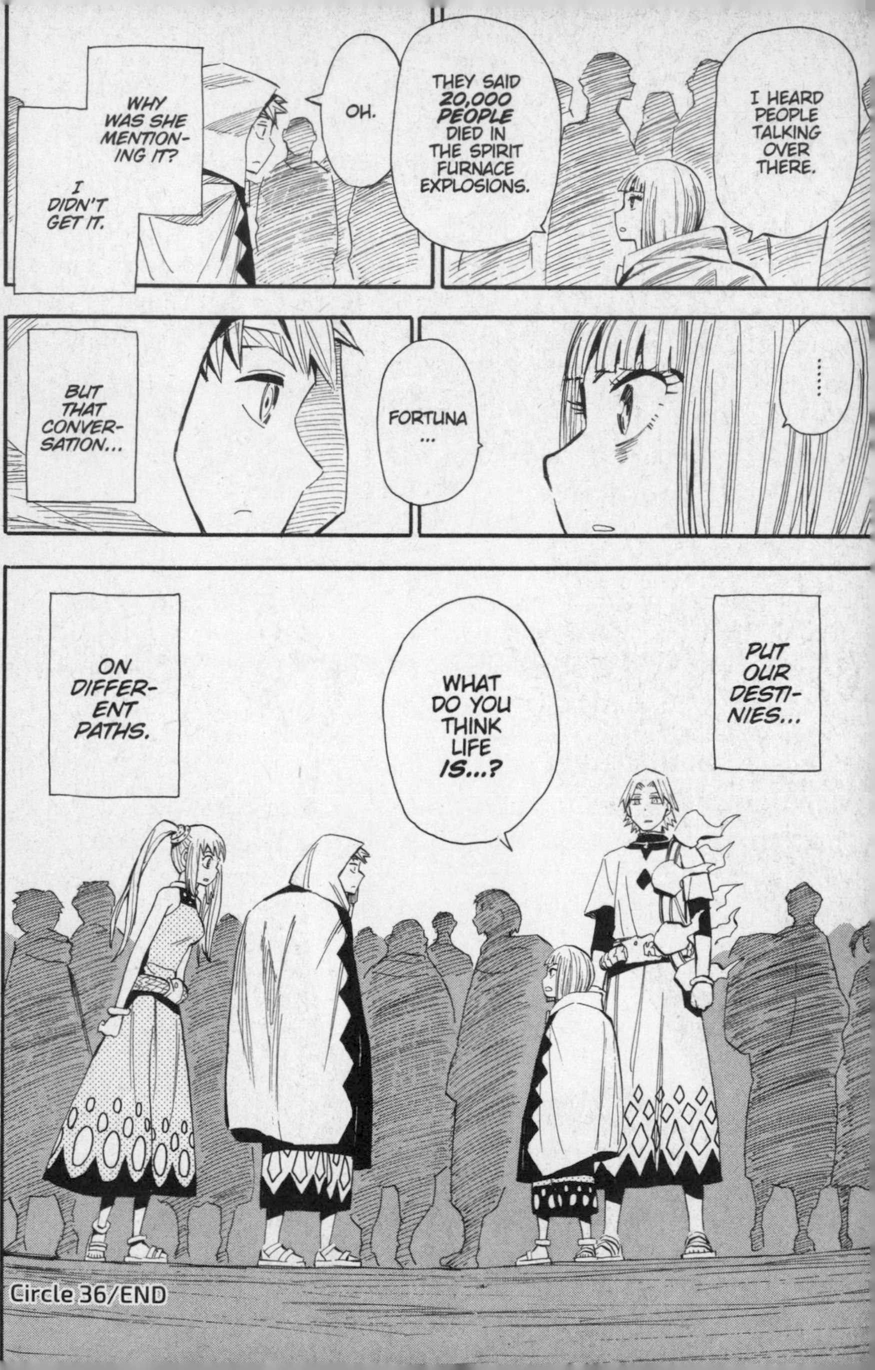
I HEARD PEOPLE TALKING OVER THERE.
THEY SAID 20,000 PEOPLE DIED IN THE SPIRIT FURNACE EXPLOSIONS.
OH.
WHY WAS SHE MENTIONING IT?
I DIDN'T GET IT.
......
FORTUNA...
BUT THAT CONVERSATION...
PUT OUR DESTINIES...
WHAT DO YOU THINK LIFE IS...?
ON DIFFERENT PATHS.
Circle 36/END

Circle 37
Fortuna 4

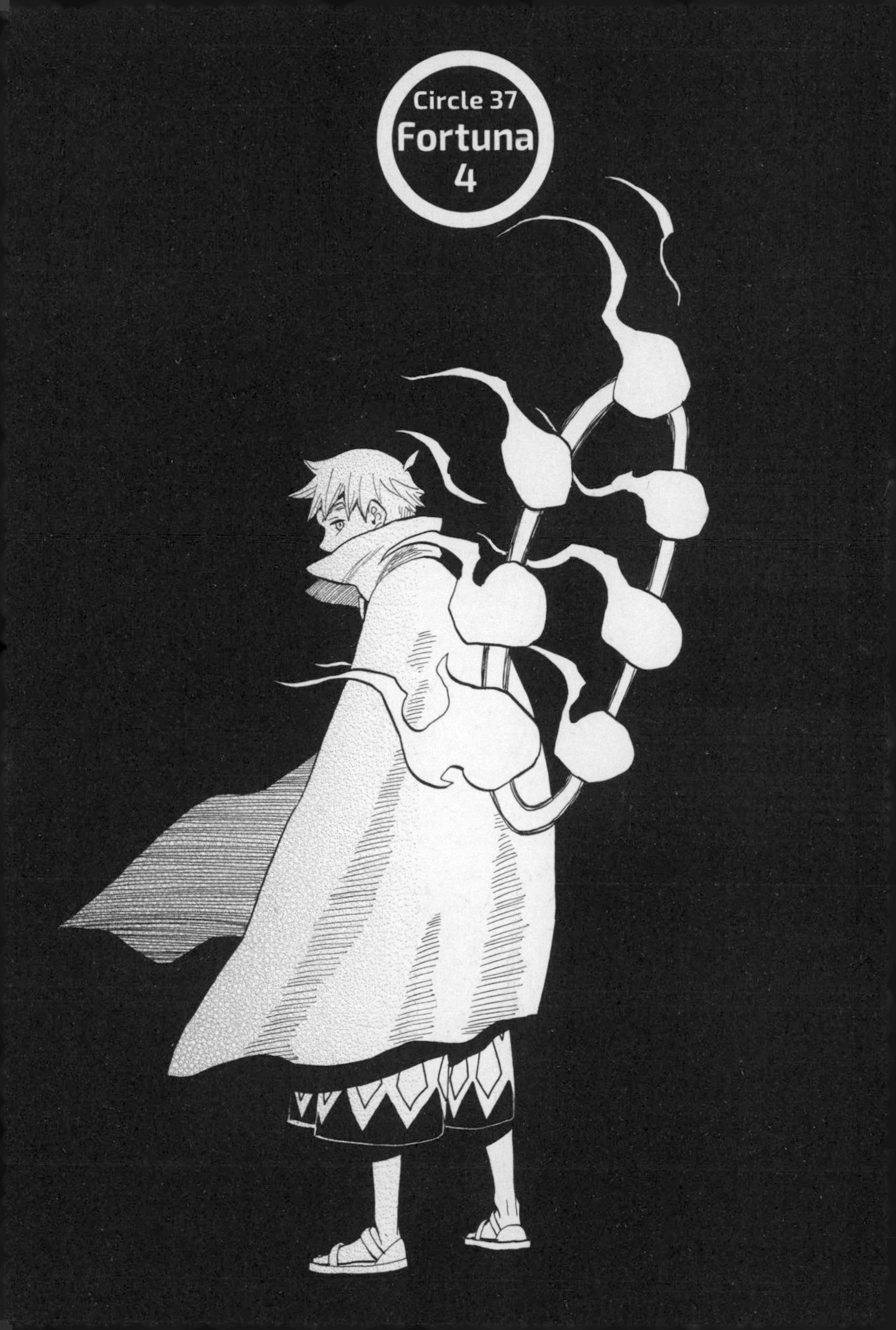

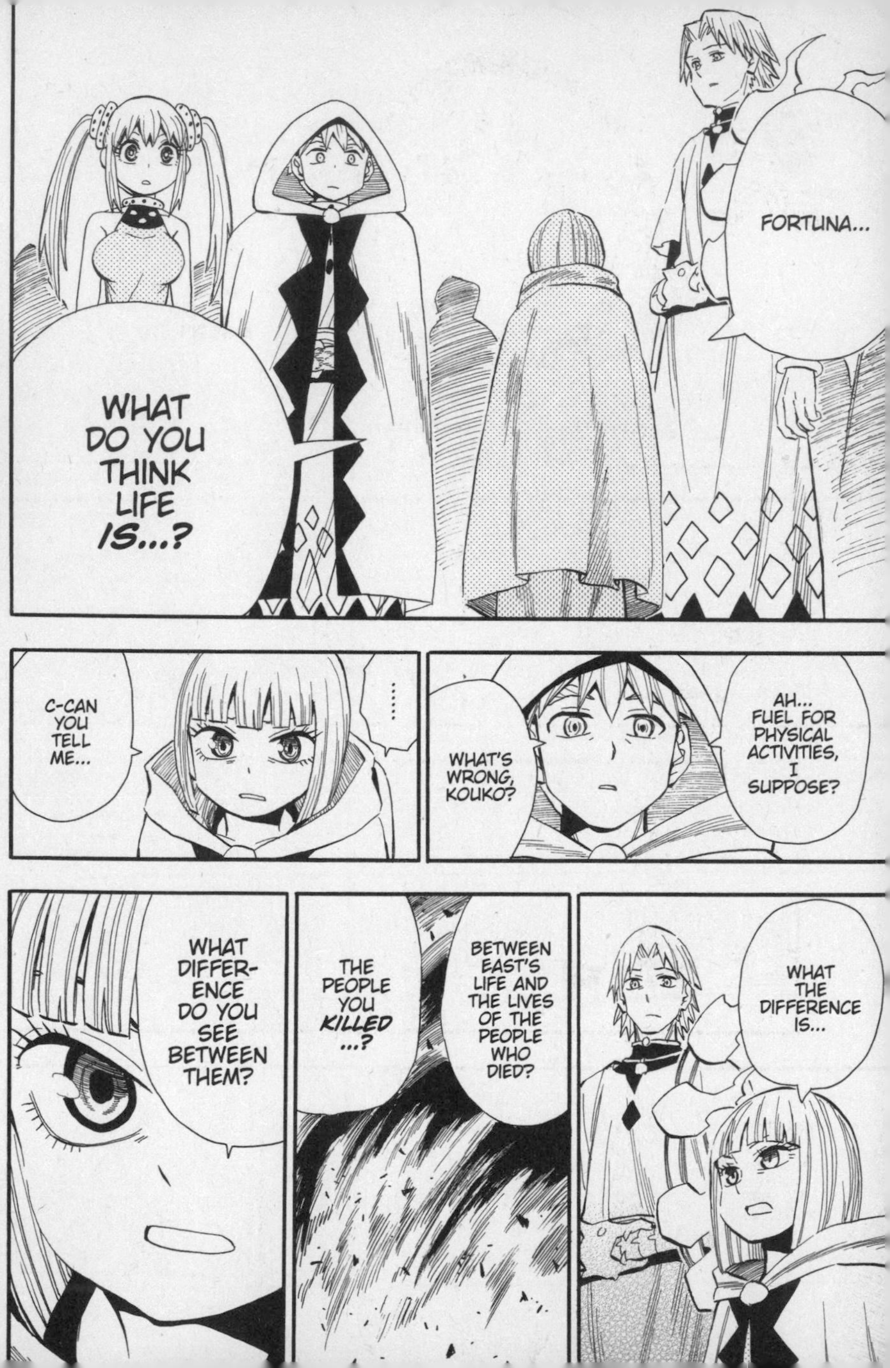
FORTUNA...
WHAT DO YOU THINK LIFE IS...?
AH... FUEL FOR PHYSICAL ACTIVITIES, I SUPPOSE?
WHAT'S WRONG, KOUKO?
......
C-CAN YOU TELL ME...
WHAT THE DIFFERENCE IS...
BETWEEN EAST'S LIFE AND THE LIVES OF THE PEOPLE WHO DIED?
THE PEOPLE YOU KILLED...?
WHAT DIFFERENCE DO YOU SEE BETWEEN THEM?

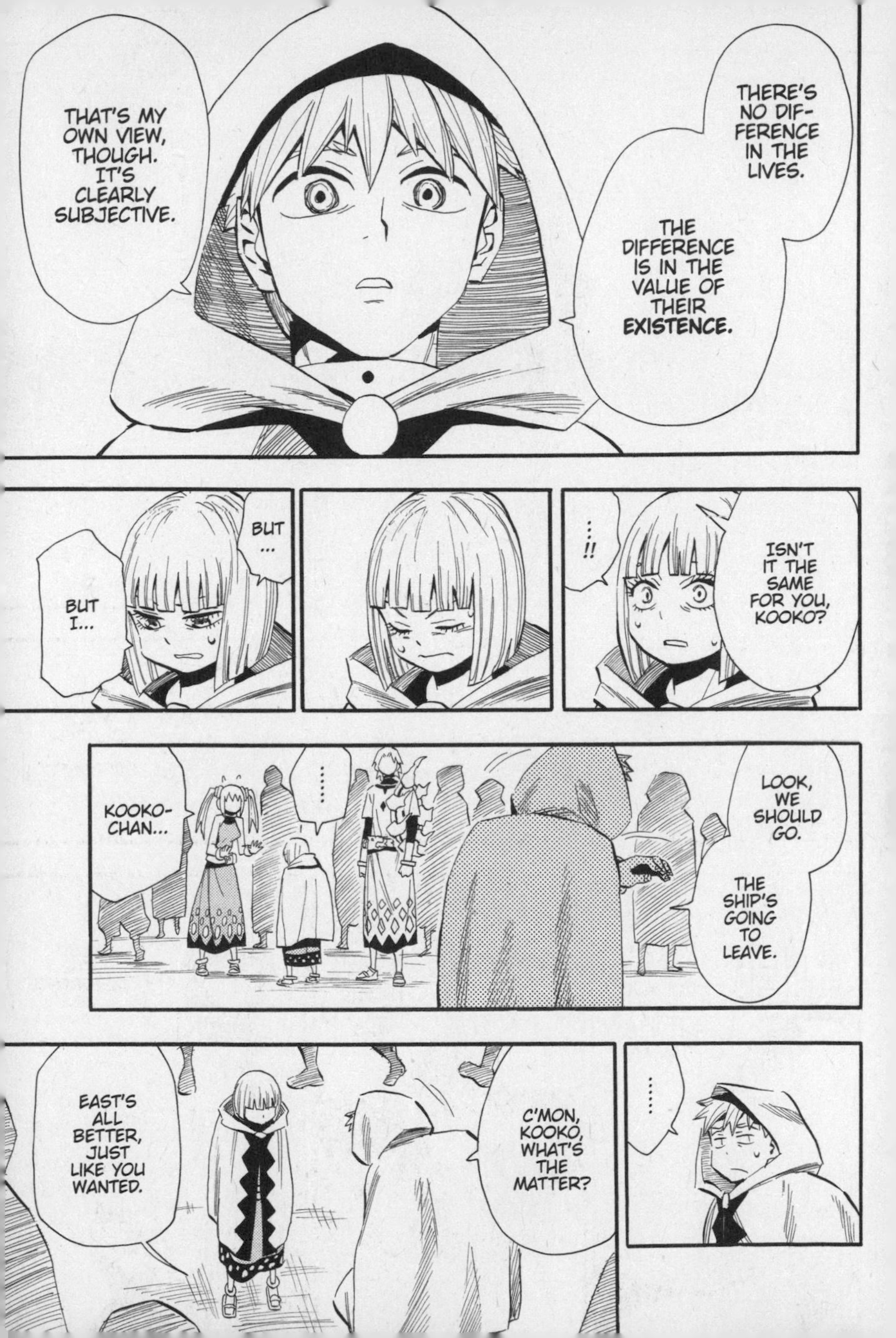
THERE'S NO DIFFERENCE IN THE LIVES.
THE DIFFERENCE IS IN THE VALUE OF THEIR EXISTENCE.
THAT'S MY OWN VIEW, THOUGH. IT'S CLEARLY SUBJECTIVE.
ISN'T IT THE SAME FOR YOU, KOOKO?
...!!
BUT ...
BUT I...
LOOK, WE SHOULD GO.
THE SHIP'S GOING TO LEAVE.
......
KOOKO-CHAN...
......
C'MON, KOOKO, WHAT'S THE MATTER?
EAST'S ALL BETTER, JUST LIKE YOU WANTED.

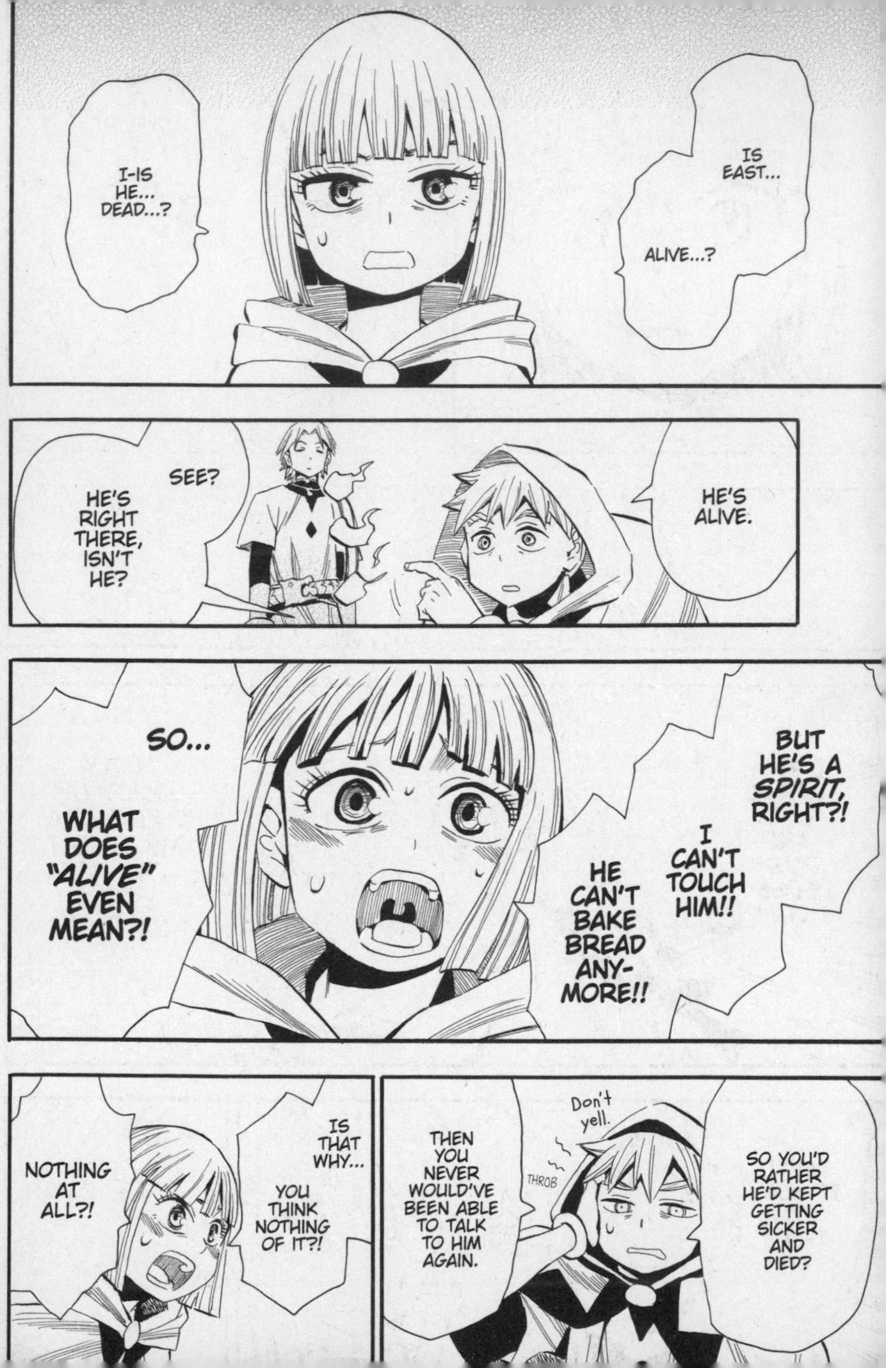
IS EAST...
ALIVE...?
I-IS HE... DEAD...?
HE'S ALIVE.
SEE?
HE'S RIGHT THERE, ISN'T HE?
BUT HE'S A *SPIRIT*, RIGHT?!
I CAN'T TOUCH HIM!!
HE CAN'T BAKE BREAD ANY-MORE!!
SO...
WHAT DOES "*ALIVE*" EVEN MEAN?!
SO YOU'D RATHER HE'D KEPT GETTING SICKER AND DIED?
Don't yell.
THROB
THEN YOU NEVER WOULD'VE BEEN ABLE TO TALK TO HIM AGAIN.
IS THAT WHY...
YOU THINK NOTHING OF IT?!
NOTHING AT ALL?!

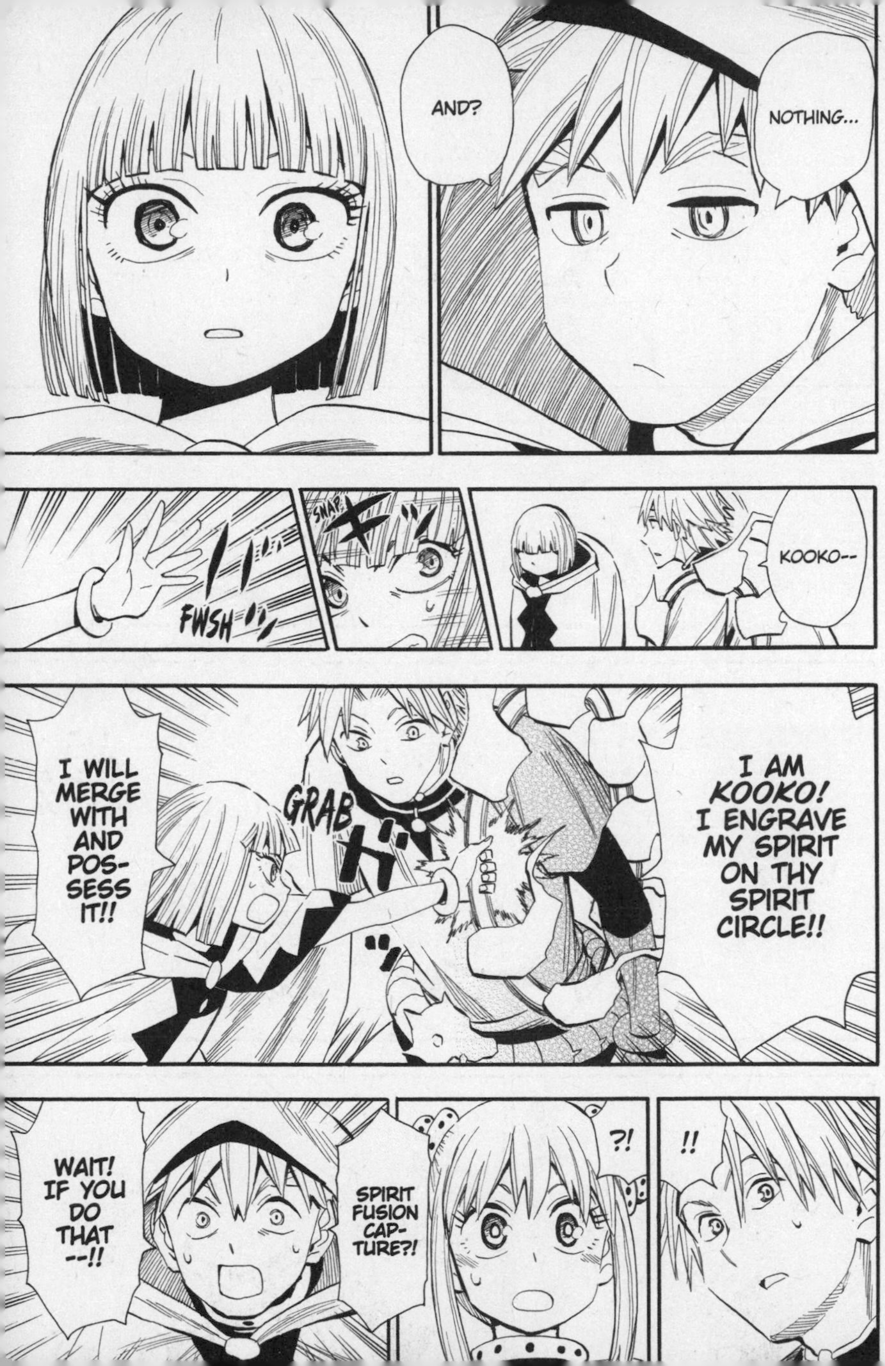
NOTHING...
AND?
KOOKO--
SNAP
FWSH
I AM KOOKO! I ENGRAVE MY SPIRIT ON THY SPIRIT CIRCLE!!
GRAB
I WILL MERGE WITH AND POSSESS IT!!
!!
?!
SPIRIT FUSION CAPTURE?!
WAIT! IF YOU DO THAT--!!

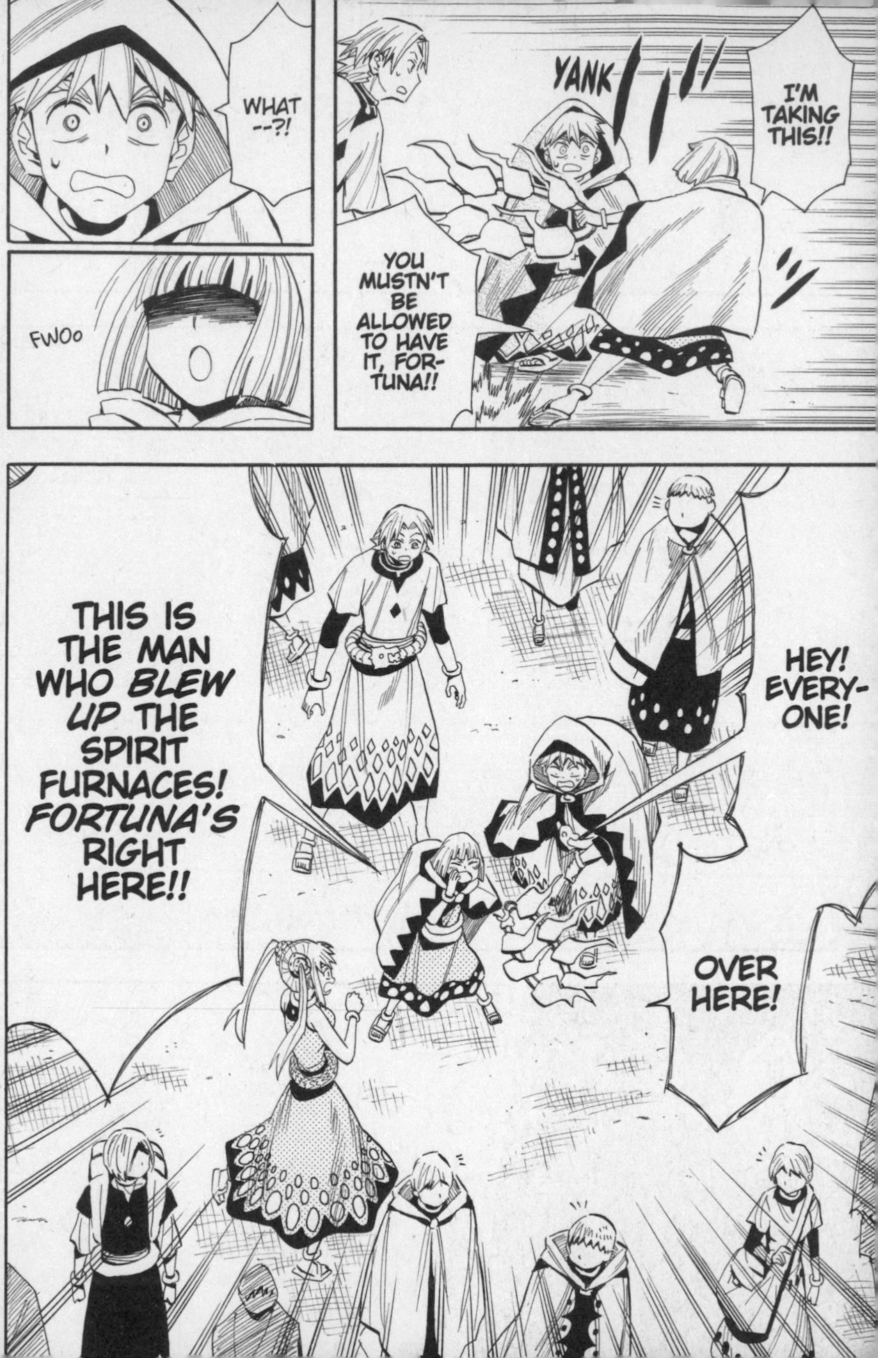
I'M TAKING THIS!!
YANK
YOU MUSTN'T BE ALLOWED TO HAVE IT, FOR-TUNA!!
WHAT --?!
FWOo
HEY! EVERY-ONE!
OVER HERE!
THIS IS THE MAN WHO *BLEW UP* THE SPIRIT FURNACES! *FORTUNA'S* RIGHT HERE!!

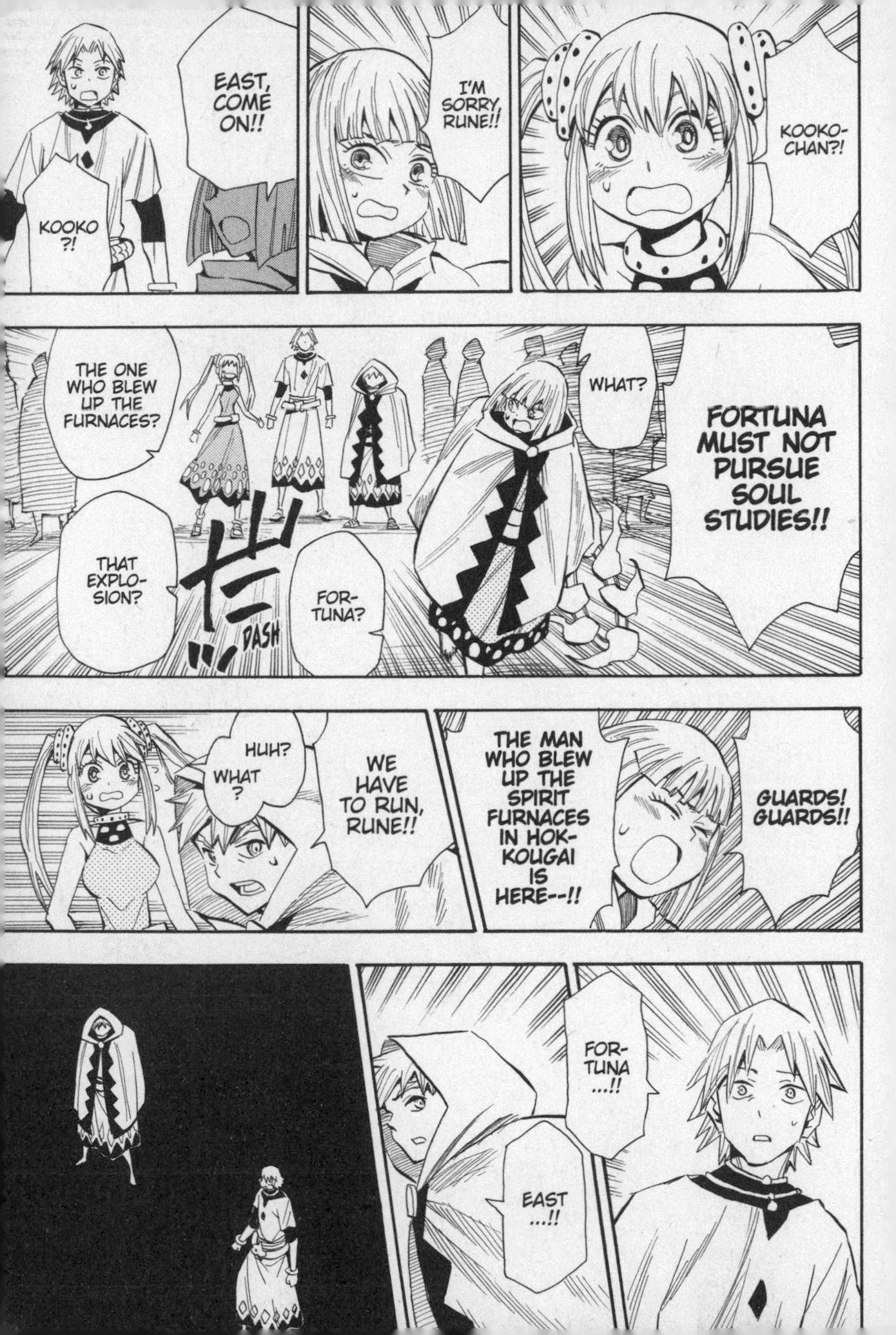
KOOKO-CHAN?!
I'M SORRY, RUNE!!
EAST, COME ON!!
KOOKO?!
FORTUNA MUST NOT PURSUE SOUL STUDIES!!
WHAT?
THE ONE WHO BLEW UP THE FURNACES?
FOR-TUNA?
DASH
THAT EXPLO-SION?
GUARDS! GUARDS!!
THE MAN WHO BLEW UP THE SPIRIT FURNACES IN HOK-KOUGAI IS HERE--!!
WE HAVE TO RUN, RUNE!!
HUH?
WHAT?
FOR-TUNA ...!!
EAST ...!!

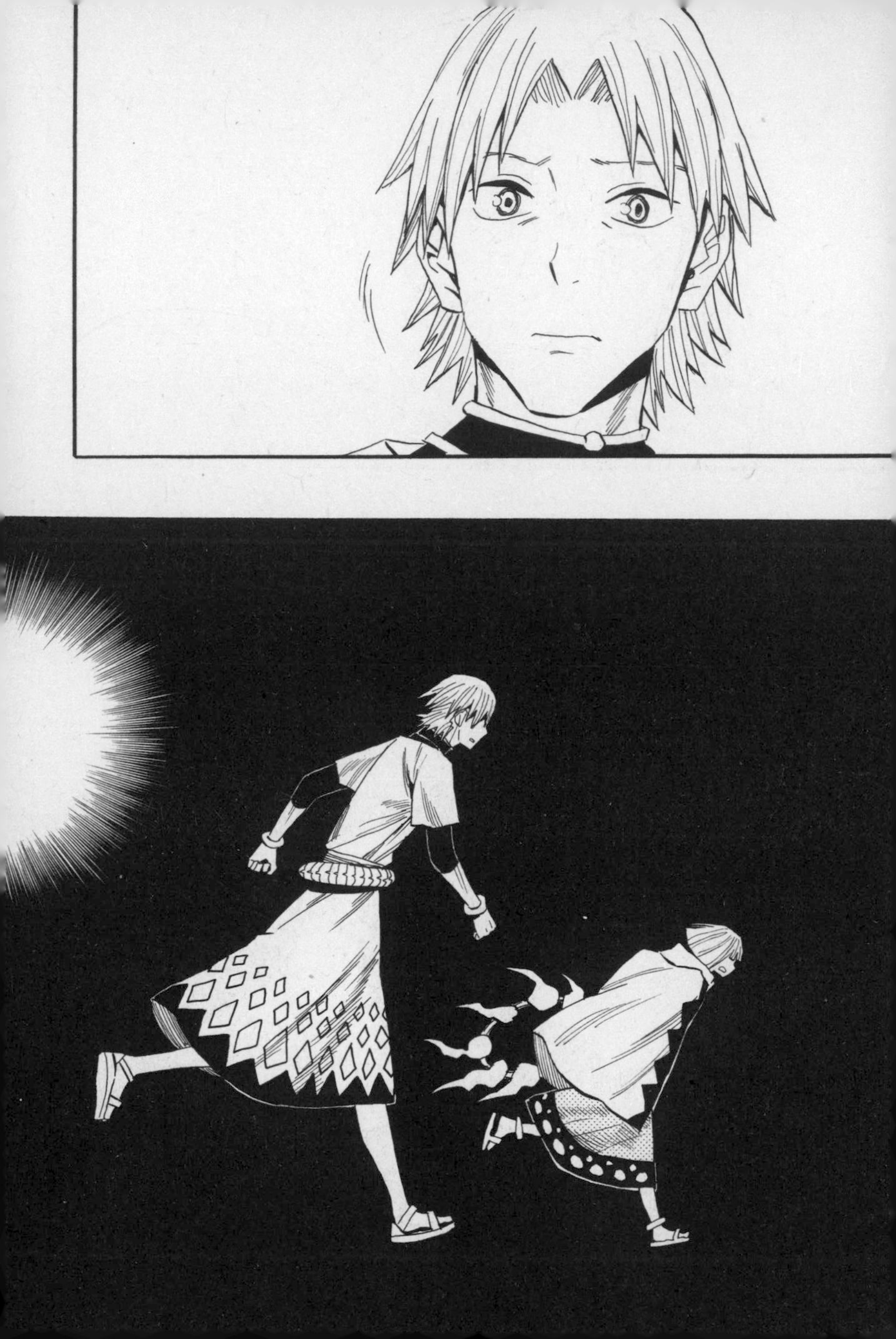

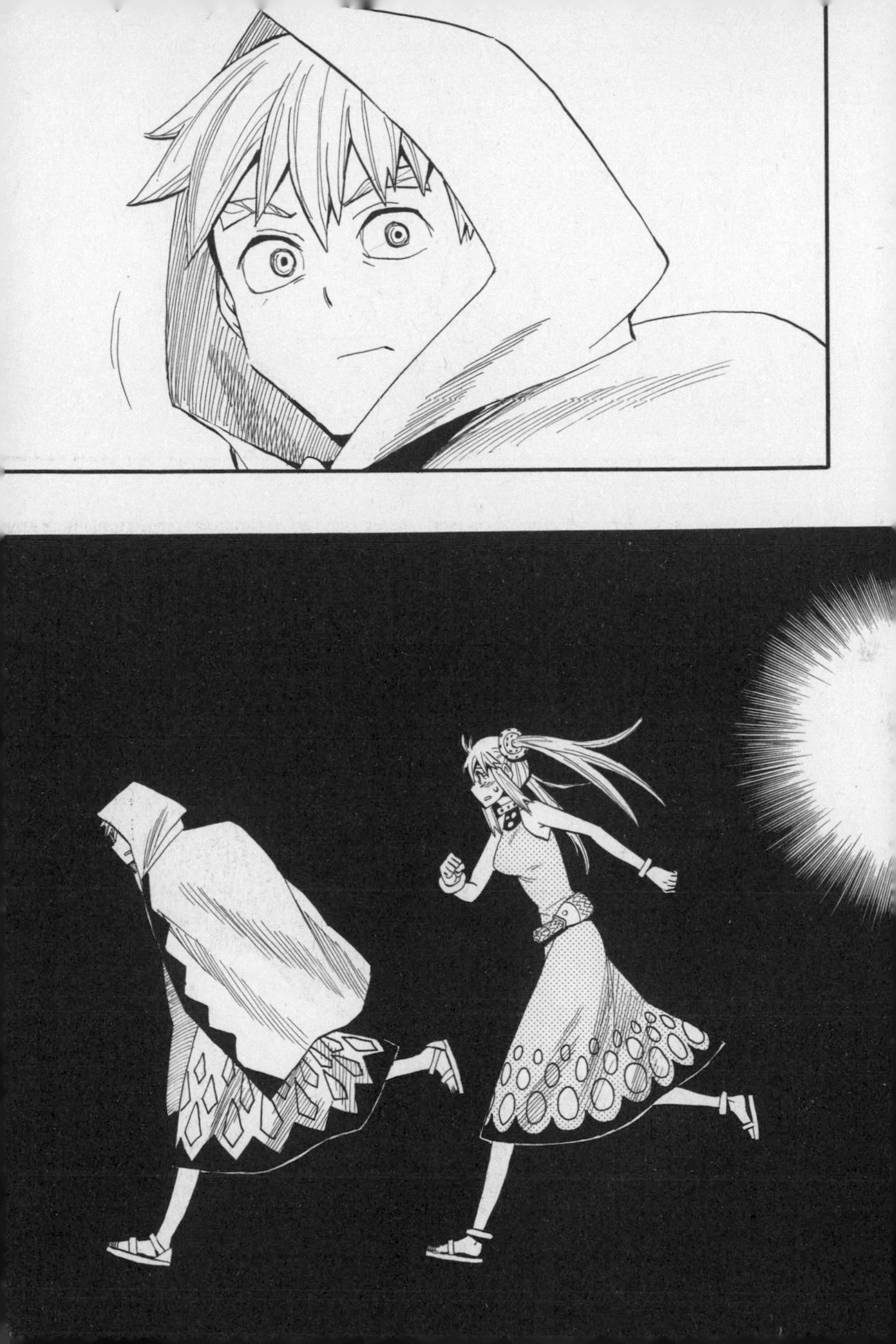

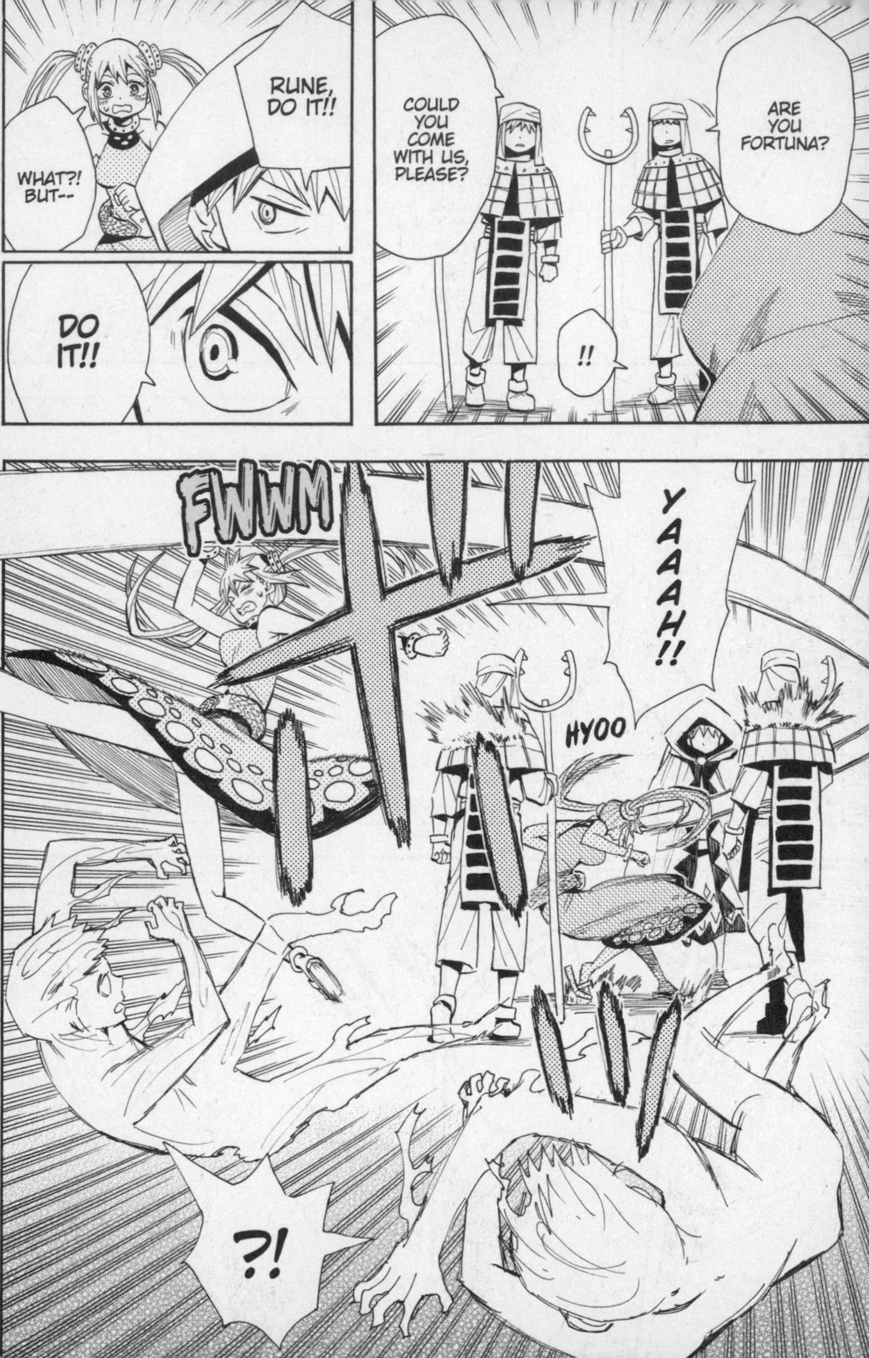
ARE YOU FORTUNA?
COULD YOU COME WITH US, PLEASE?
!!
RUNE, DO IT!!
WHAT?! BUT--
DO IT!!
YAAAAH!!
FWWM
HYOO
?!

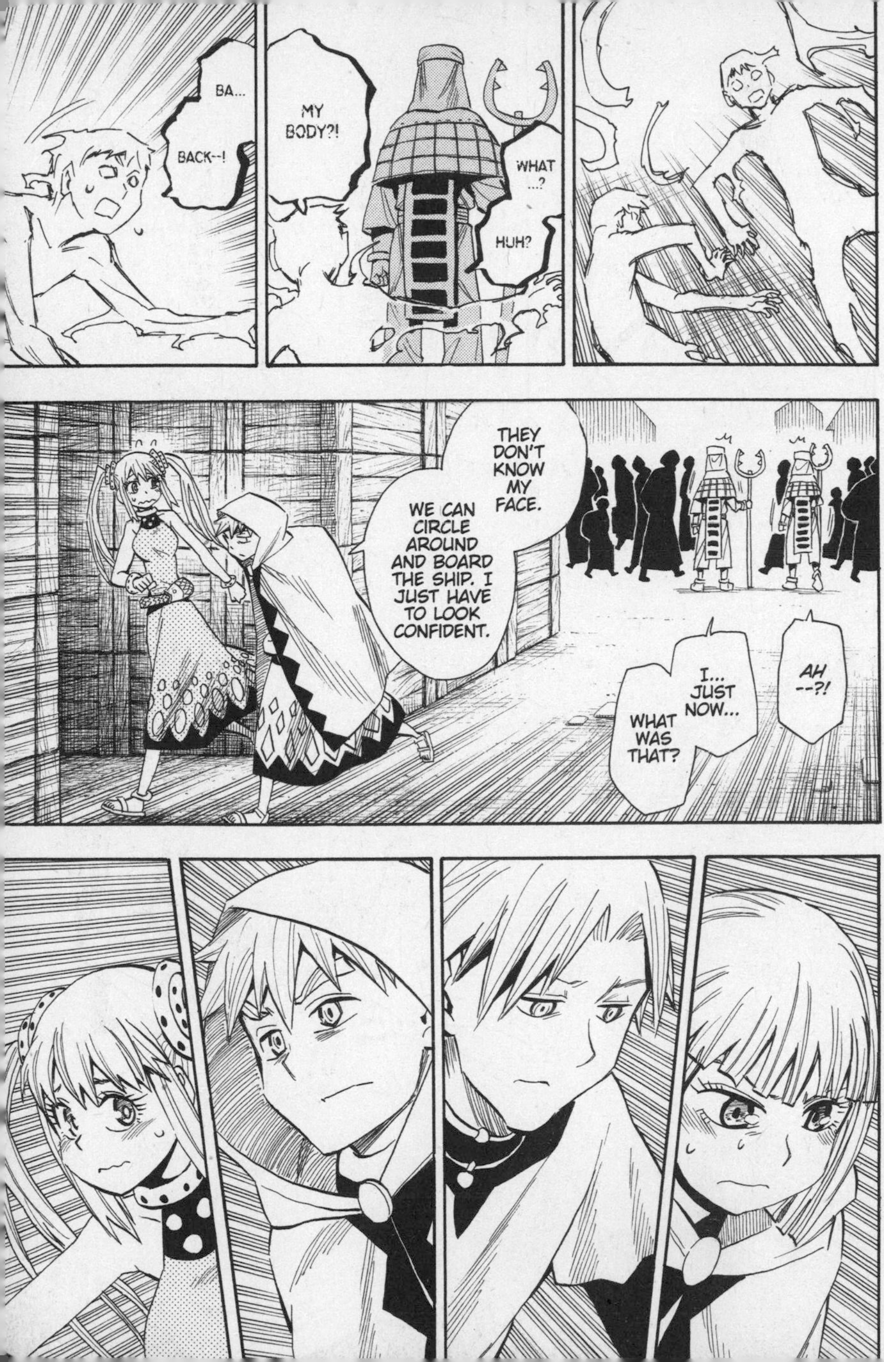
WHAT ...?
HUH?
MY BODY?!
BA...
BACK--!
AH --?!
I... JUST NOW...
WHAT WAS THAT?
THEY DON'T KNOW MY FACE.
WE CAN CIRCLE AROUND AND BOARD THE SHIP. I JUST HAVE TO LOOK CONFIDENT.

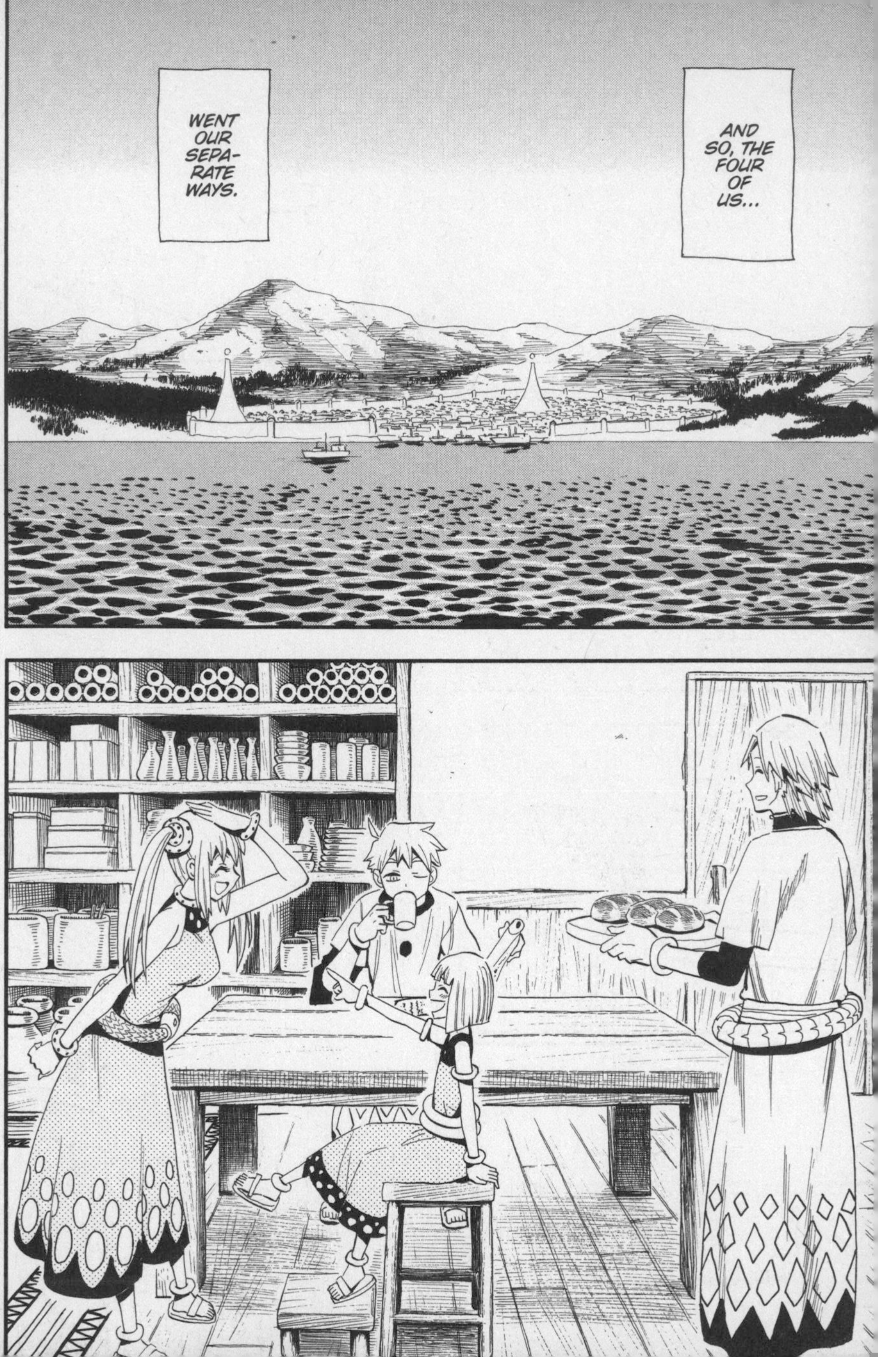
AND SO, THE FOUR OF US...
WENT OUR SEPARATE WAYS.

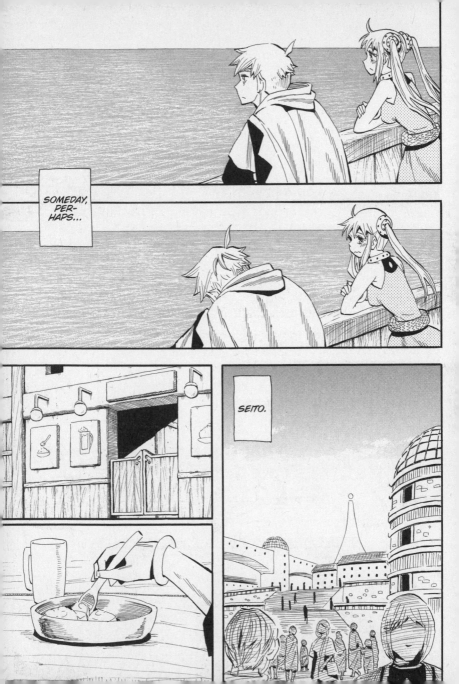

SOMEDAY, PER- HAPS...

SEITO.

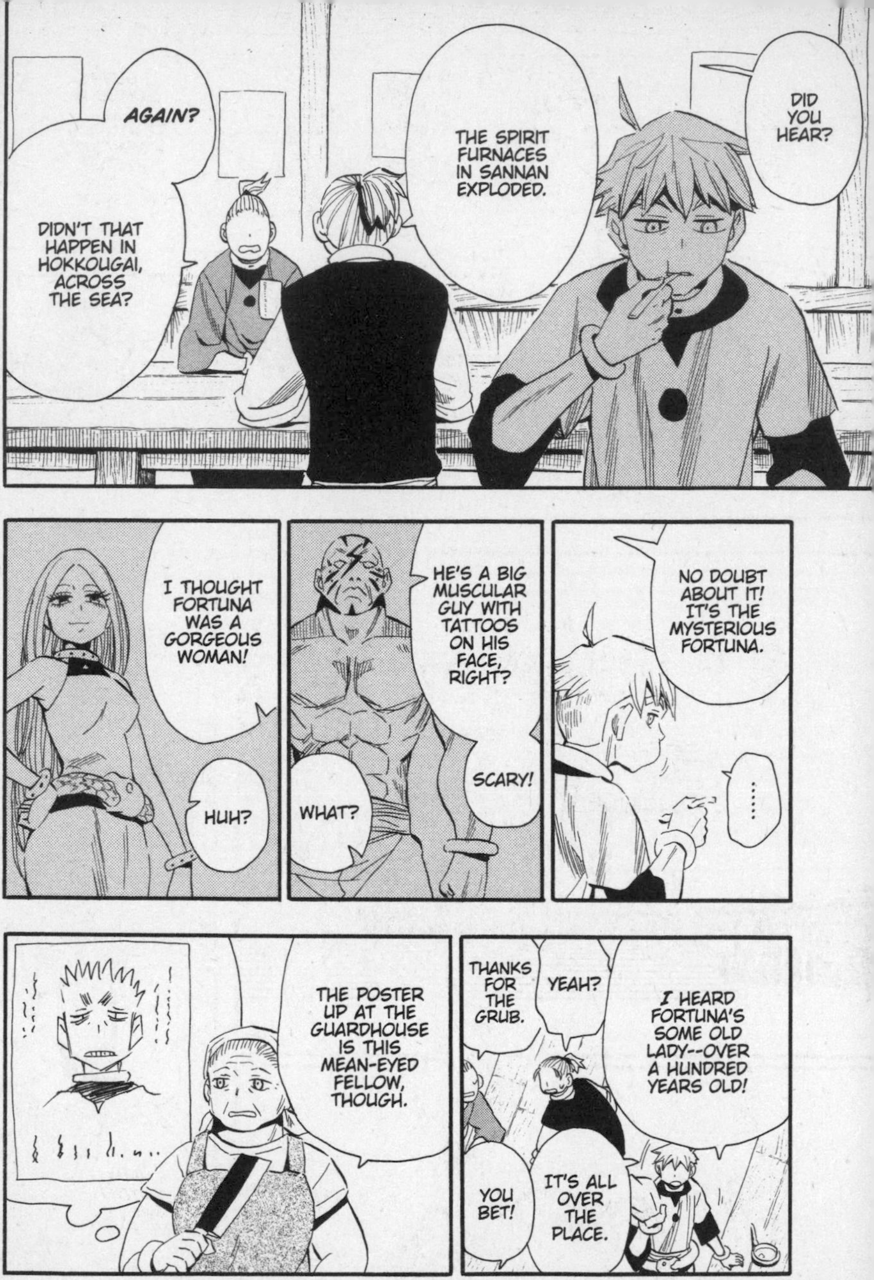
DID YOU HEAR?
THE SPIRIT FURNACES IN SANNAN EXPLODED.
AGAIN?
DIDN'T THAT HAPPEN IN HOKKOUGAI, ACROSS THE SEA?
NO DOUBT ABOUT IT! IT'S THE MYSTERIOUS FORTUNA.
......
HE'S A BIG MUSCULAR GUY WITH TATTOOS ON HIS FACE, RIGHT?
SCARY!
WHAT?
I THOUGHT FORTUNA WAS A GORGEOUS WOMAN!
HUH?
I HEARD FORTUNA'S SOME OLD LADY--OVER A HUNDRED YEARS OLD!
YEAH?
THANKS FOR THE GRUB.
IT'S ALL OVER THE PLACE.
YOU BET!
THE POSTER UP AT THE GUARDHOUSE IS THIS MEAN-EYED FELLOW, THOUGH.

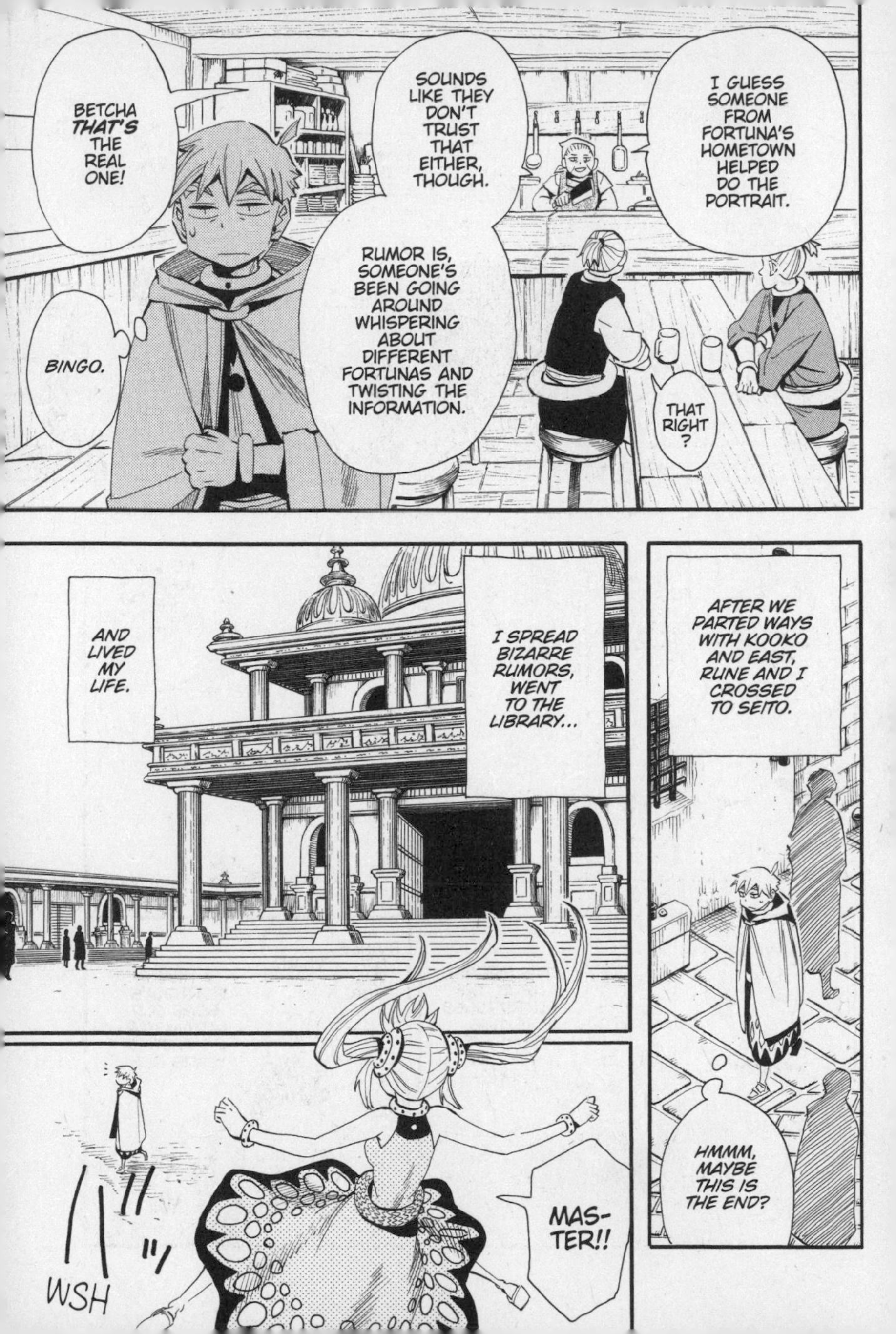
I GUESS SOMEONE FROM FORTUNA'S HOMETOWN HELPED DO THE PORTRAIT.
THAT RIGHT?
SOUNDS LIKE THEY DON'T TRUST THAT EITHER, THOUGH.
RUMOR IS, SOMEONE'S BEEN GOING AROUND WHISPERING ABOUT DIFFERENT FORTUNAS AND TWISTING THE INFORMATION.
BETCHA *THAT'S* THE REAL ONE!
BINGO.
AFTER WE PARTED WAYS WITH KOOKO AND EAST, RUNE AND I CROSSED TO SEITO.
HMMM, MAYBE THIS IS THE END?
I SPREAD BIZARRE RUMORS, WENT TO THE LIBRARY...
AND LIVED MY LIFE.
MAS-TER!!
WSH

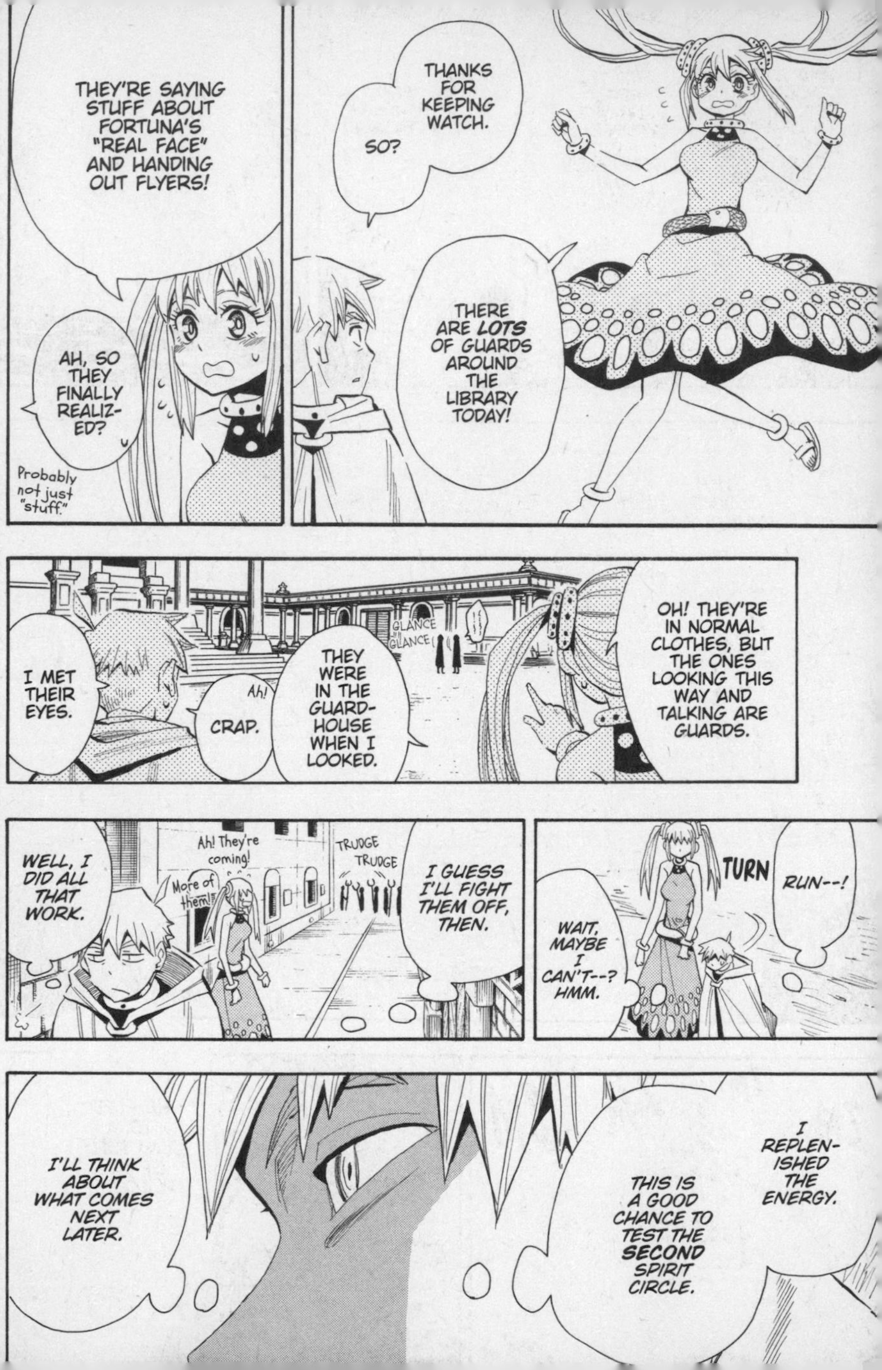
THANKS FOR KEEPING WATCH.
SO?
THERE ARE *LOTS* OF GUARDS AROUND THE LIBRARY TODAY!
THEY'RE SAYING STUFF ABOUT FORTUNA'S "REAL FACE" AND HANDING OUT FLYERS!
AH, SO THEY FINALLY REALIZ-ED?
Probably not just "stuff."
OH! THEY'RE IN NORMAL CLOTHES, BUT THE ONES LOOKING THIS WAY AND TALKING ARE GUARDS.
GLANCE GLANCE
THEY WERE IN THE GUARD-HOUSE WHEN I LOOKED.
Ah!
CRAP.
I MET THEIR EYES.
RUN--!
TURN
WAIT, MAYBE I CAN'T--? HMM.
I GUESS I'LL FIGHT THEM OFF, THEN.
TRUDGE TRUDGE
Ah! They're coming!
More of them!
WELL, I DID ALL THAT WORK.
I REPLEN-ISHED THE ENERGY.
THIS IS A GOOD CHANCE TO TEST THE **SECOND** SPIRIT CIRCLE.
I'LL THINK ABOUT WHAT COMES NEXT LATER.

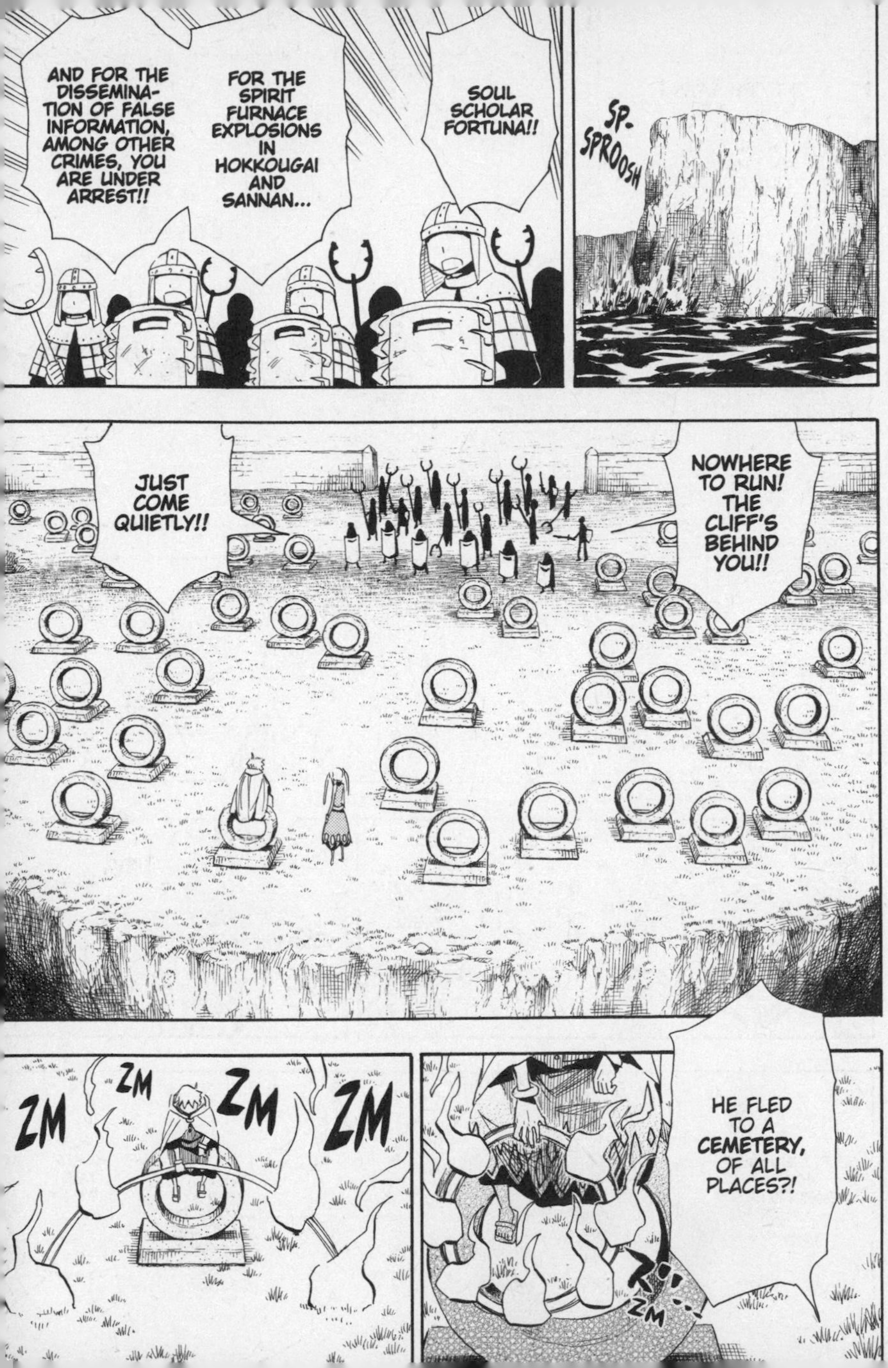
SP-SPROOSH
SOUL SCHOLAR FORTUNA!!
FOR THE SPIRIT FURNACE EXPLOSIONS IN HOKKOUGAI AND SANNAN...
AND FOR THE DISSEMINATION OF FALSE INFORMATION, AMONG OTHER CRIMES, YOU ARE UNDER ARREST!!
NOWHERE TO RUN! THE CLIFF'S BEHIND YOU!!
JUST COME QUIETLY!!
HE FLED TO A CEMETERY, OF ALL PLACES?!
ZM
ZM
ZM
ZM
ZM

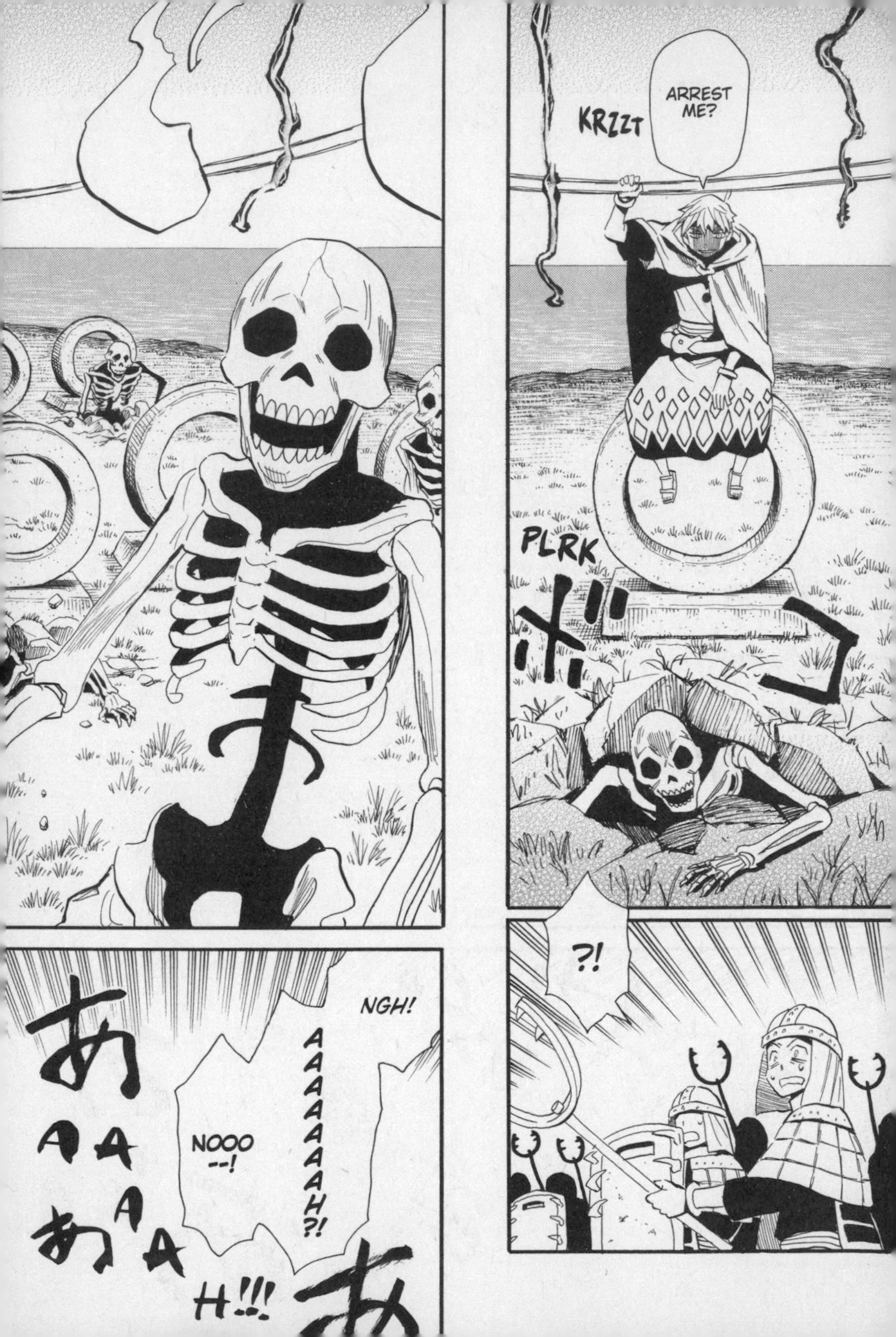
ARREST ME?
KRZZT
PLRK
ボコ
?!
NGH!
AAAAAAAAAH?!
NOOO --!
あAAAあAA H!!!
あ

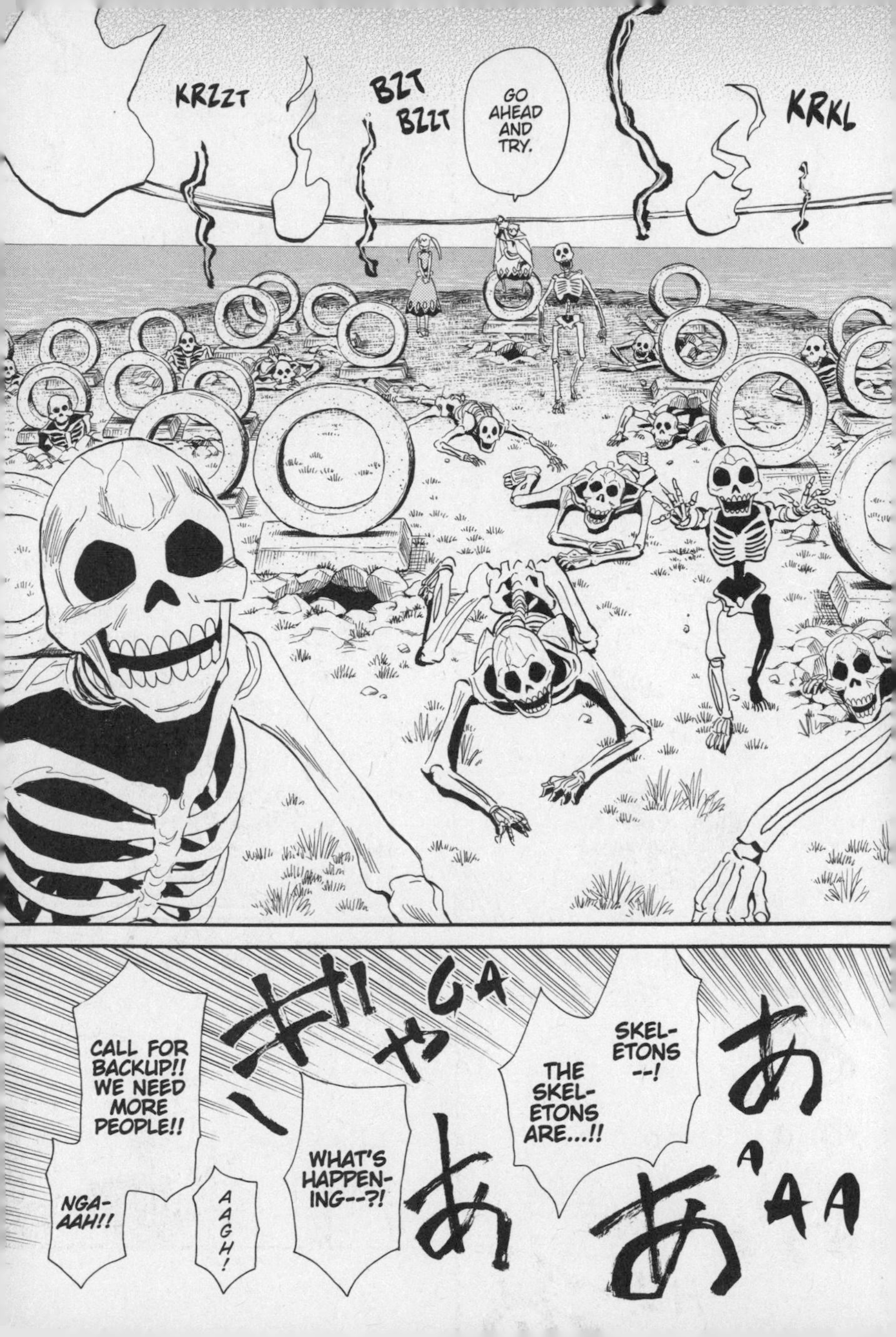
KRKL
GO AHEAD AND TRY.
BZT BZZT
KRZZT
あ A AA A
SKEL-ETONS--!
THE SKEL-ETONS ARE...!!
ぎゃ GA
あ
WHAT'S HAPPEN-ING--?!
CALL FOR BACKUP!! WE NEED MORE PEOPLE!!
AAGH!
NGA-AAH!!

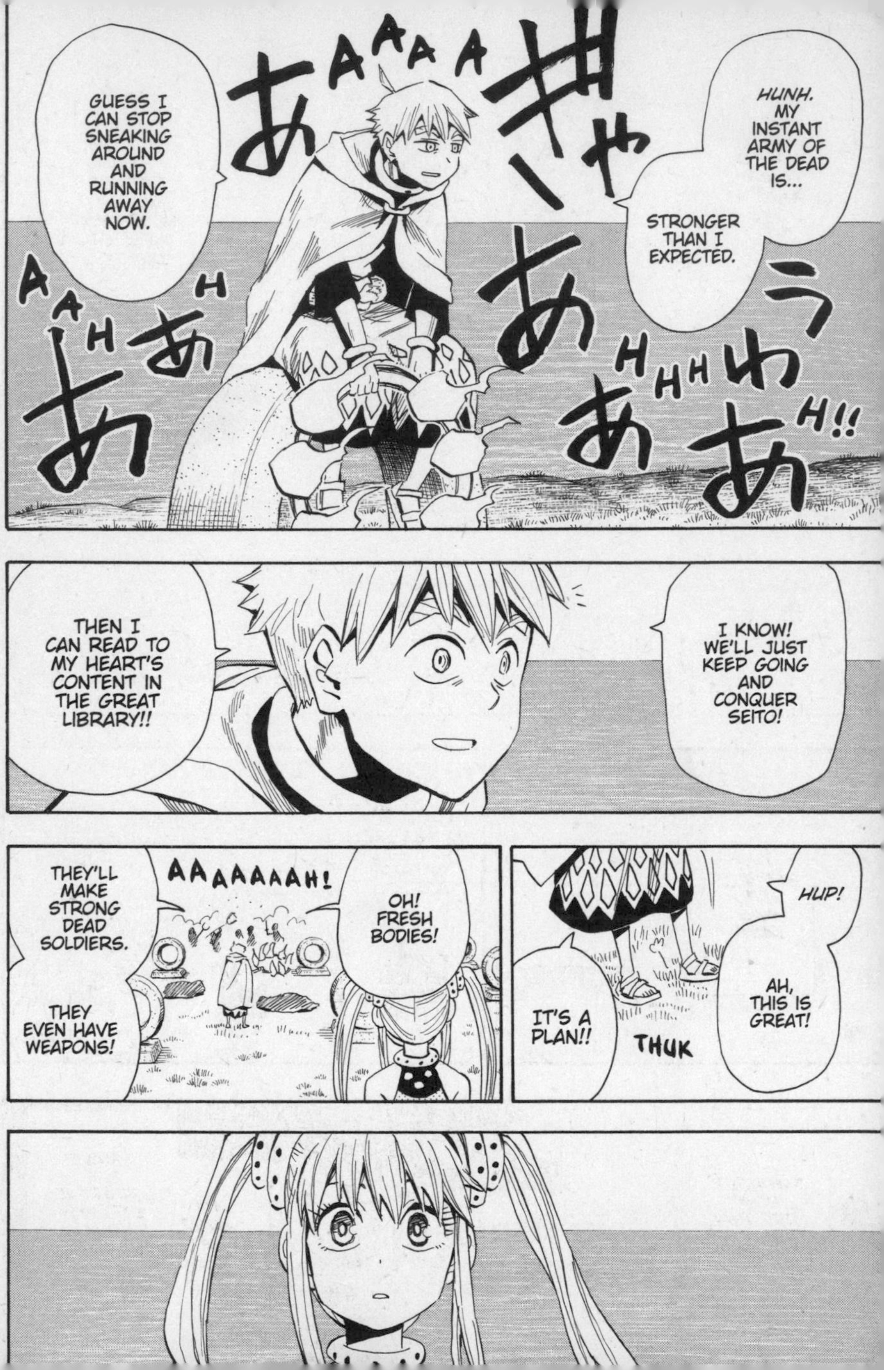
HUNH. MY INSTANT ARMY OF THE DEAD IS...
STRONGER THAN I EXPECTED.
GUESS I CAN STOP SNEAKING AROUND AND RUNNING AWAY NOW.
I KNOW! WE'LL JUST KEEP GOING AND CONQUER SEITO!
THEN I CAN READ TO MY HEART'S CONTENT IN THE GREAT LIBRARY!!
HUP!
AH, THIS IS GREAT!
THUK
IT'S A PLAN!!
OH! FRESH BODIES!
AAAAAAAH!
THEY'LL MAKE STRONG DEAD SOLDIERS.
THEY EVEN HAVE WEAPONS!

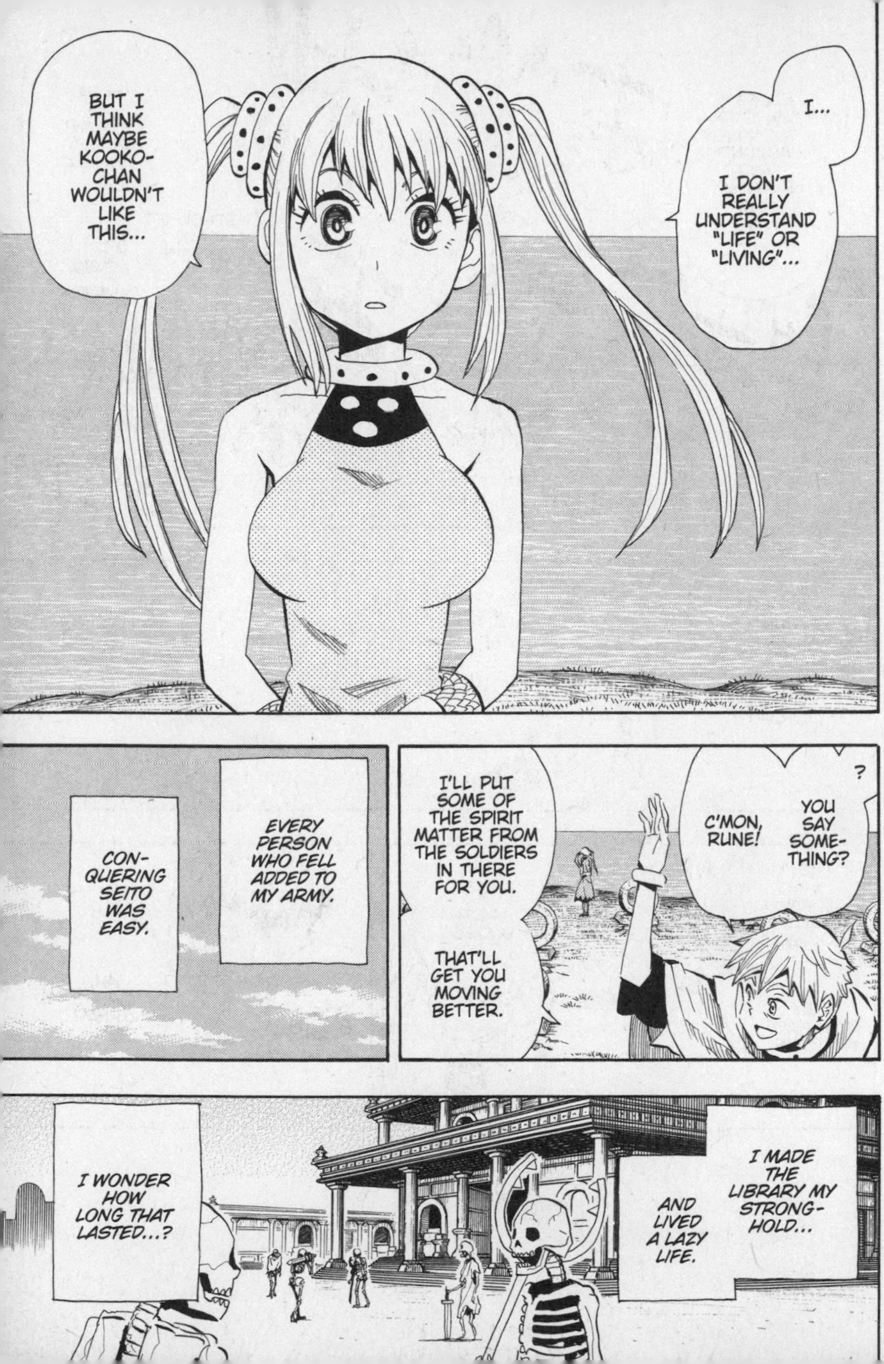
I...
I DON'T REALLY UNDERSTAND "LIFE" OR "LIVING"...
BUT I THINK MAYBE KOOKO-CHAN WOULDN'T LIKE THIS...
?
YOU SAY SOME-THING?
C'MON, RUNE!
I'LL PUT SOME OF THE SPIRIT MATTER FROM THE SOLDIERS IN THERE FOR YOU.
THAT'LL GET YOU MOVING BETTER.
EVERY PERSON WHO FELL ADDED TO MY ARMY.
CON-QUERING SEITO WAS EASY.
I MADE THE LIBRARY MY STRONG-HOLD...
AND LIVED A LAZY LIFE.
I WONDER HOW LONG THAT LASTED...?

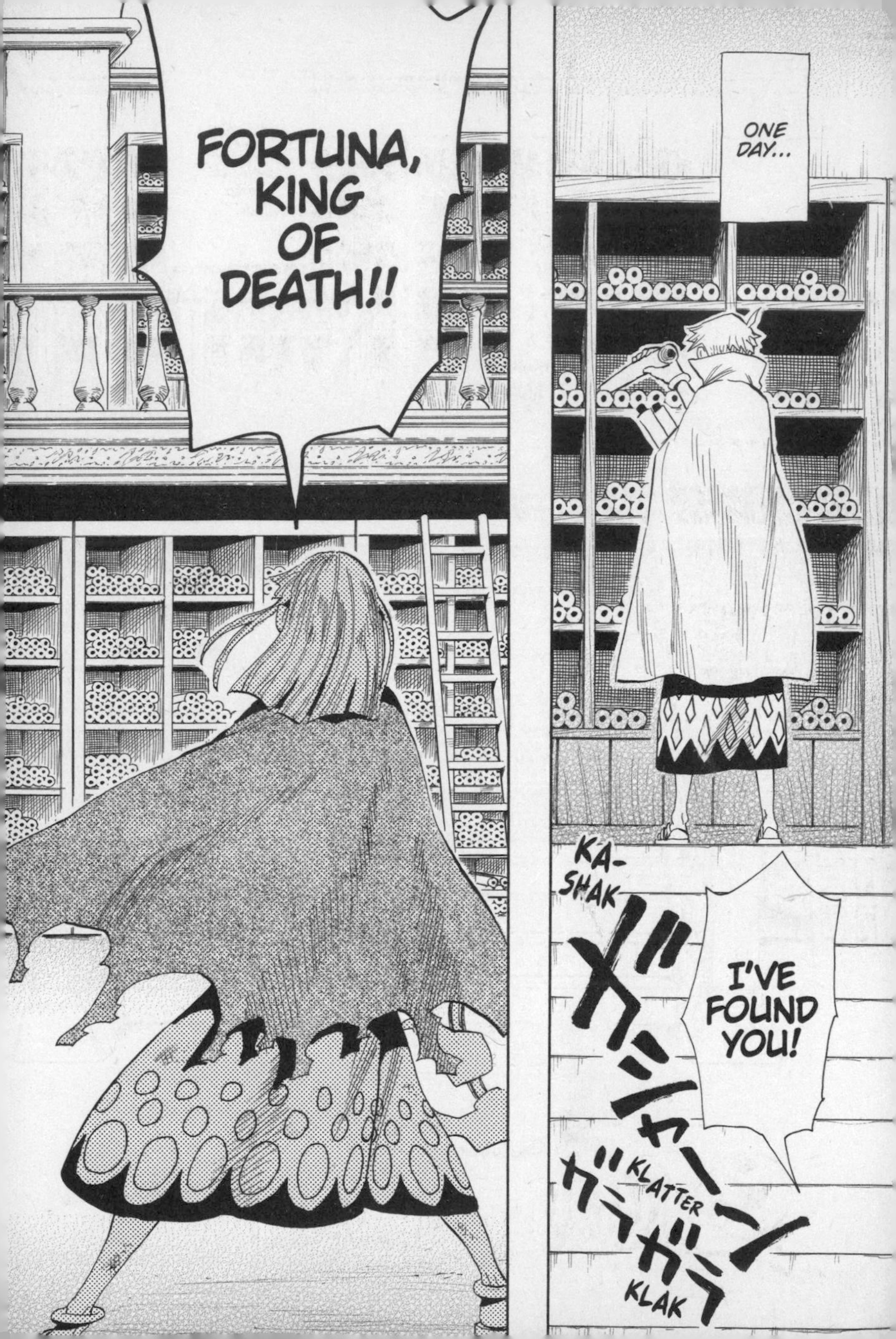
ONE DAY...
I'VE FOUND YOU!
KA-SHAK
KLATTER
KLAK
FORTUNA, KING OF DEATH!!

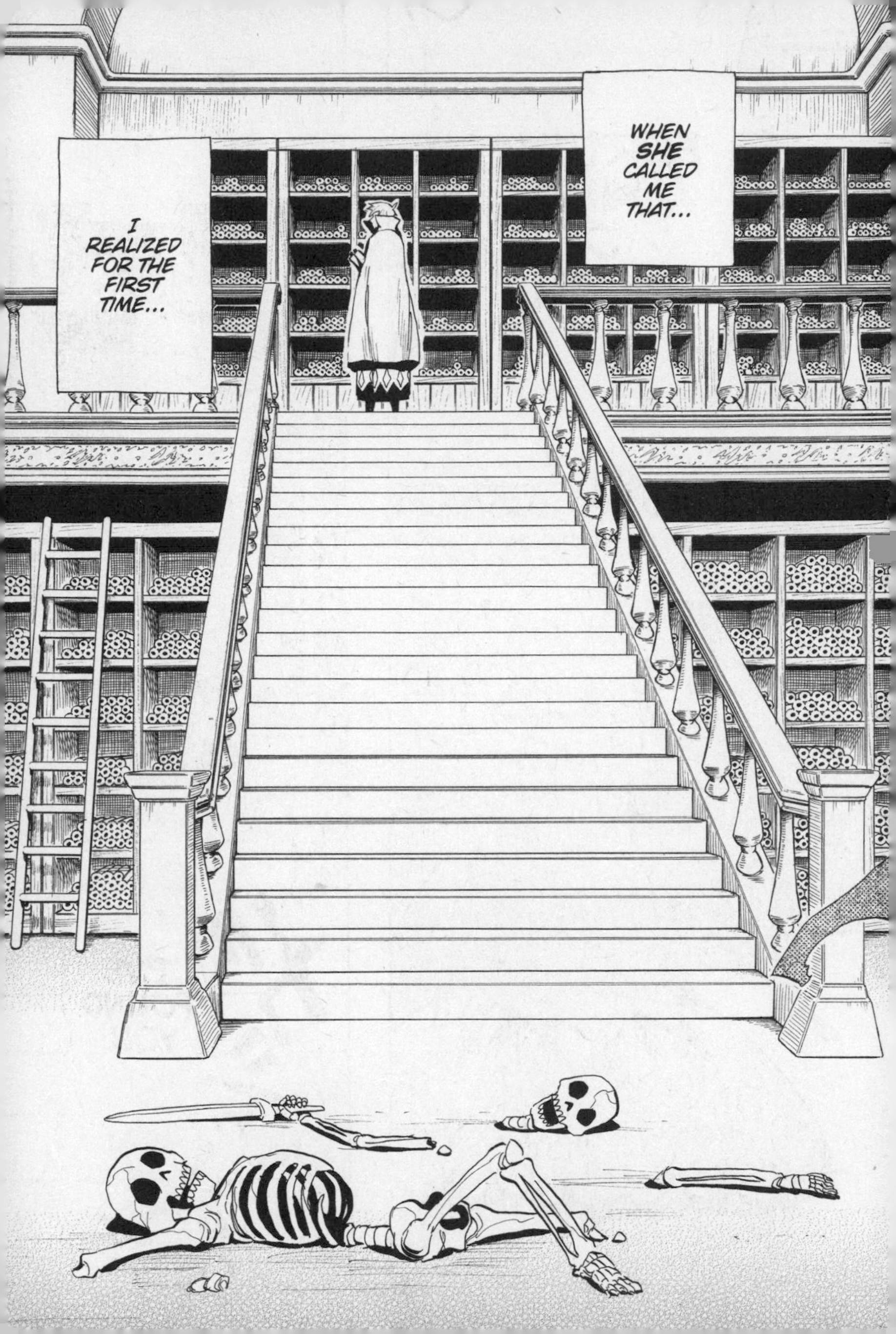
WHEN SHE CALLED ME THAT...
I REALIZED FOR THE FIRST TIME...

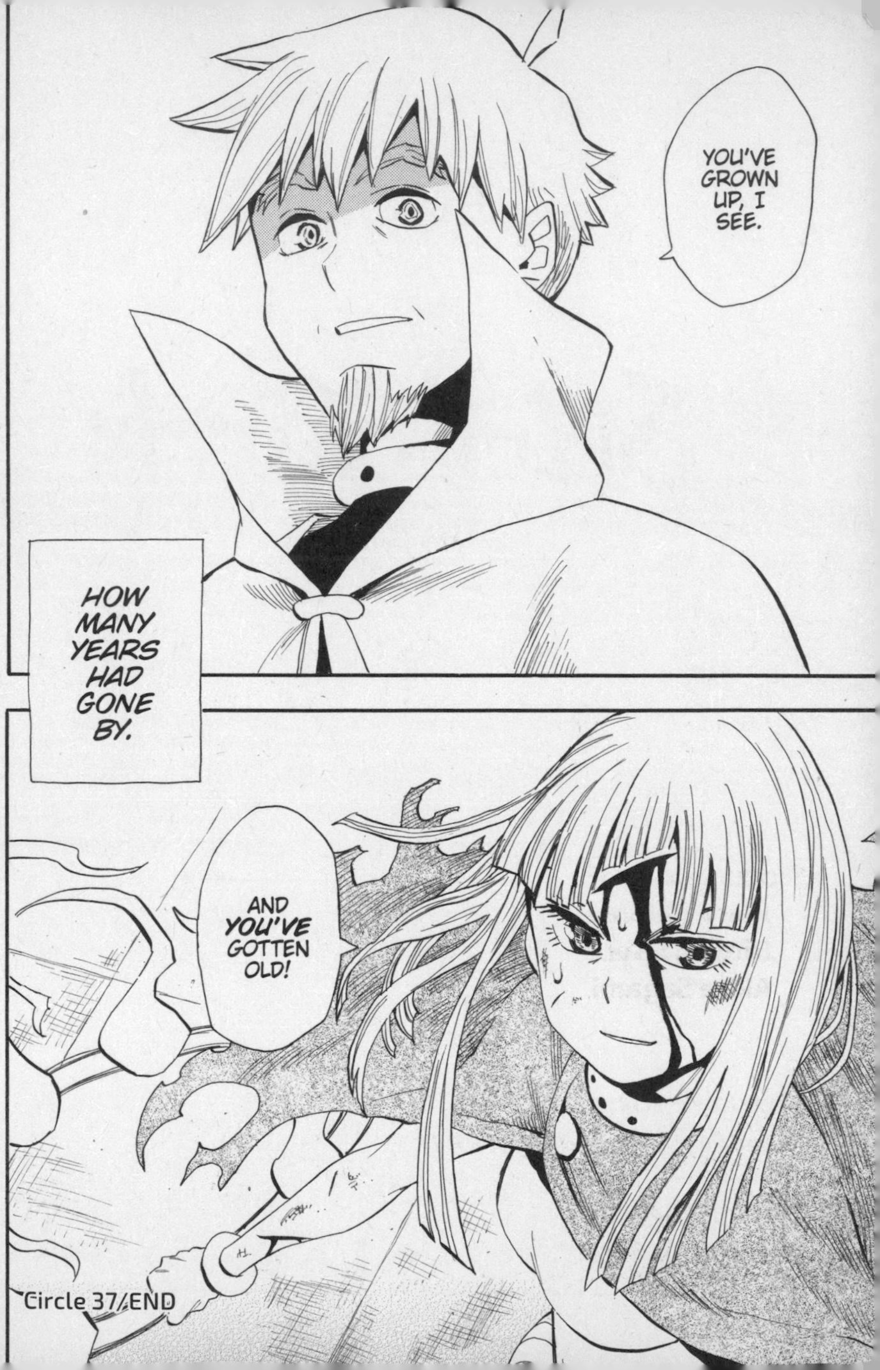
YOU'VE GROWN UP, I SEE.
HOW MANY YEARS HAD GONE BY.
AND YOU'VE GOTTEN OLD!
Circle 37/END

Spirit Circle

Volume 5

Production staff
Jueru Choden
Hitoshi Usui
Akira Sagami

Title logo/Cover design
Eiichi Hagiwara (bigbody)

Supervising editor
Takehiro Sumi

SEVEN SEAS ENTERTAINMENT PRESENTS

Spirit Circle VOL.5

story and art by **SATOSHI MIZUKAMI**

TRANSLATION
Jocelyne Allen

ADAPTATION
Ysabet Reinhardt MacFarlane

LETTERING AND LAYOUT
Lys Blakeslee

COVER DESIGN
Nicky Lim

PROOFREADER
Shanti Whitesides
Danielle King

ASSISTANT EDITOR
J.P. Sullivan

PRODUCTION ASSISTANT
CK Russell

PRODUCTION MANAGER
Lissa Pattillo

EDITOR-IN-CHIEF
Adam Arnold

PUBLISHER
Jason DeAngelis

SPIRIT CIRCLE VOL. 5

Originally published in Japan in 2015 by SHONENGAHOSHA Co., Ltd., Tokyo.
English translation rights arranged through TOHAN CORPORATION, Tokyo.

ISBN: 978-1-626929-24-1

Printed in Canada

First Printing: October 2018

FOLLOW US ONLINE: www.

READING DIRECTIONS

This book reads from ***right to left***, Japanese style. If this is your first time reading manga, you start reading from the top right panel on each page and take it from there. If you get lost, just follow the numbered diagram here. It may seem backwards at first, but you'll get the hang of it! Have fun!!

1
2
3
4
5
6
7
8
9

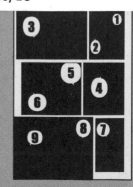